Global Burnout:
A Worldwide Pandemic Explored
by the Phase Model

MONOGRAPHS IN ORGANIZATIONAL BEHAVIOR AND INDUSTRIAL RELATIONS, Volume 21

Editor: Samuel B. Bacharach, *Department of Organizational Behavior, New York State School of Industrial and Labor Relations, Cornell University*

Monographs in Organizational Behavior and Industrial Relations

Edited by **Samuel B. Bacharach**, *Department of Organizational Behavior, New York State School of Industrial and Labor Relations, Cornell University*

To our children

> *Alice, Hope, Geoffrey;*
> *Rylan Jules, Evyn James, Wyatt Ferguson;*
> *Zachary, Joseph;*
> *Yiran.*

Global Burnout:
A Worldwide Pandemic Explored
by the Phase Model

by **ROBERT T. GOLEMBIEWSKI**
Department of Political Science
The University of Georgia

ROBERT A. BOUDREAU
Faculty of Management
The University of Lethbridge

ROBERT F. MUNZENRIDER
Division of Public Affairs
Pennsylvania State University, at Harrisburg

HUAPING LUO
Department of Political Science
The University of Georgia

 JAI PRESS INC.

Greenwich, Connecticut

London, England

Library of Congress Cataloging-in-Publication Data

Global burnout : a worldwide pandemic explored by the phase model / by
Robert T. Golembiewski ... [et al.].
    p.   cm. — (Monographs in organizational behavior and
industrial relations ; v. 21)
    Includes bibliographical references and index.
    ISBN 0-7623-0116-3
    1. Job stress.   2. Burn out (Psychology)   I. Golembiewski, Robert
T.   II. Series.
    HF5548.85.G56   1996
    158.7—dc20   96-27574
                                                                        CIP

Copyright © 1996 JAI Press Inc.
55 Old Post Road, No. 2
Greenwich, Connecticut 06836

JAI PRESS LTD.
38 Tavistock Street
Covent Garden
London, WC2E 7PB
England

ISBN: 0-7623-0116-3

Library of Congress Catalog Number: 96-27574

Manufactured in the United States of America

Contents

List of Tables

Chapter VII

Chapter VIII

List of Figures

List of Exhibits

Preface

No human work is ever complete, and so it is with *Global Burnout*. Nonetheless, some projects are far enough along to justify a comprehensive accounting; and so it is with *Global Burnout*.

A conviction and a hope urge us to let go, and now. We authors offer this book as the product of work extending over the period of a decade or so, and we see it as a substantial addition to available theory and practice. We await the reactions of others, and hope to motivate the further research required to fill-in the gaps left by us and the other contributors to *Global Burnout*.

Here, we focus on several undeniables. Paramountly, all time-extended projects are ineffably connected and relational and, if anything, *Global Burnout* seems moreso than most. This obviously holds for the volume's research base. As one indicator, index cards identifying the names of references overflowed a conventional shoebox. In a less-obvious sense, perhaps, the book rests on another class of connections and relations: those with the numerous organizational hosts of research on the phase model; and those with the tens of thousands of respondents who contributed their time and reactions when they could have finessed requests for information, easily and without fanfare.

In sum, this volume walks on many intellectual feet, and rests on numerous shoulders. We authors acknowledge this book as a truly-shared product. Specific indebtednesses are identified at numerous points.

xix

Moreover, in terms of intellectual lineage, *Global Burnout* directly builds on two earlier books: *Stress in Organizations* (Golembiewski, Munzenrider, & Stevenson, 1986) and *Phases of Burnout* (Golembiewski and Munzenrider, 1988). This building-upon perforce involves much of the substance of these predecessor publications, and on occasions even relies on snippets of the earlier prose.

How does *Global Burnout* extend and transcend these ideational predecessors, as it builds upon them? Each reader no doubt will generate an individualized list, but nine points should be consensus entries on anyone's list. In no particular order, *Global Burnout* is the capstone expression of the decade-long testing of the phase model in the significant senses detailed below.

• Basically, the book provides far stronger evidence that the phase model measures burnout, validly and reliably. That we can tolerably measure "it" has profound meanings for theory as well as practice, and rests on a consistent effort to move toward this level of confidence by multiple replications that keep many factors relatively constant. Relatively-consistent findings, then, imply a tolerably-useful instrument for measuring burnout. *Global Burnout* reports just such findings. Indeed, at times, those findings appear almost-eerily consistent.

No other comprehensive measure of burnout permits similar confidence, for one or the other of two reasons. In almost all studies, researchers have focused on each of several components of burnout, and provide no tested procedures for combining those individualities in a holistic estimate of burnout. In a few cases, operational definitions *in principle* permit estimates of who has which degree of burnout, but the validity and reliability of these holistic measures are only-gently established.

The end is not yet, of course, when it comes to a valid and reliable operational definition of burnout. But the beginning of the middle parts of burnout research do seem behind us, as it were. The valid and reliable phase model of burnout constitutes the vehicle for moving beyond these middle stages, which already provide a solid base for seeking to extend theory and practice.

In substantial contrast, most behavioral research seeks to leap from early indications of usefulness to comprehensive theory, while basic operational definitions typically vary widely. This has been true in the earlier days of behavioral research (e.g., Golembiewski, 1962), and it unfortunately continues to be so in recent days (e.g., Miller & Friesen, 1984), on definite balance. Indeed, it is almost as if *the* goal were innovation concerning operational definitions, rather than findings that build on one another.

In any case, the approach here fixates on one consistent operational definition of the phases. This began as a deliberate limitation to see how far it would take us. Now, it is clear to us that this restriction not only carried us a long way and simplifies the interpretation of results, but also can carry us further.

- Our confidence rests on a collection of studies far larger than that available in earlier years. The panel of research on the phase model now amounts to over 80 entries, for some purposes. This approaches a 150 percent increase over 1988-90. Then, also, almost all of the entries referred to North American settings—the United States and Canada.

- Of special relevance to our confidence are recently-available studies from global work settings, which now surpass 20 for some purposes. As late as 1990, only a handful of phase model studies were available from global settings.

This was a risky reliance on the consistent operational definition of the phases, for much advice proposed this was a fool's errand. Not so, as it turns out. Indeed, it will come as a surprise to those readers who favor culturally-specific approaches that the effects isolated by the phase model have a strong generic component. That is, this book's title was not casually chosen.

- In addition, *Global Burnout* includes a review of over 100 published pieces of strain-related research conducted in over 30 countries outside of North America. This research deals with stress as well as burnout, and supports a covey of generalizations that provide context as well as motivation for the effort to extend research on the phase model of burnout.

Consider an elemental time-line. Until 1990 or thereabouts, phase research focused largely on North American work contexts—that is, in the United States and Canada. Since then, phase model research has been extended to global settings. The review of well over 100 non-North American studies not only justifies this extension of research on the phase model, but also highlights several practical and conceptual problems that the phase model can help resolve.

- *Global Burnout* provides comprehensive and otherwise unavailable estimates of how many people suffer from which degrees of burnout, with data now coming from over 80 settings in over a dozen countries. Not all data-sets serve equally-comprehensive purposes, but they all help in drawing a worldwide picture.

Two singularities stand out here. Only the phase model presently permits such estimates. In addition, the magnitudes of the estimates are attention-getting, even frightening. Alone among operational measures of burnout, then, the phase model directs—even demands— attention to the critical practical and political issues implied by the formidable incidences of advanced burnout.

- Although less satisfying than the estimates of incidence, substantial post-1990 research provides useful perspective on the persistence of burnout phases. The available evidence is not comforting. Directly, one's phase of burnout does not seem the psychological equivalent of a fly of a summer. *The* bottom-line: many people, worldwide, are experiencing advanced burnout; and that status has a strong tendency to persist over extended periods of time.

    This newly-available evidence powerfully adds to the significance of *Global Burnout*. Even if far from ideal, that is to say, the new evidence about persistence of phases is almost-completely unavailable for other operational definitions of burnout. This is no mere oversight. Simply, these alternative measures are so designed as to complicate estimates of persistence, if not to preclude them. A few clinically-oriented studies do exist, but these permit only gentle estimates of persistence in small populations (e.g., Cherniss, 1989).

- Both in North American and global populations, the phases of burnout are directly associated with a progressive worsening of virtually all variables assessed. For those who like numbers, "virtually all" means about 95 percent of all variables tested. The percentage may even be higher. But why quibble? The record is substantial, even amazing. The phases reflect a strong pattern of progressive virulence.

    Directly, as the phases progress I ———> VIII, things seem to get worse for individuals, groups, and the systems employing them. Thus, those with the lowest burnout—that is, those classified as Phase I— have (for example) the highest satisfaction with work, the lowest physical and mental symptoms, the lowest costs of medical insurance, and so on. Those classified in Phase II are worse off than Is, and IIIs compare unfavorably to both Is and IIs. And these paired-comparisons are very consistent, as subsequent reviews of evidence will establish.

    This research record implies the progressive virulence of the phases of burnout, in North American and global worksettings alike. Prior to 1990, research on the phase model was largely confined to North American work settings, where the progressive virulence was first observed and replicated. Today, a growing inventory of global studies isolates *much the same pattern* of covariants of the phases, using the same operational definition of burnout to measure "it," *wherever*. This is a powerful combination supporting the validity and reliability of the phase model.

- As the previous generalization implies, research on the phase model of burnout has a major generic component. Arguments about the cultural-relativity or the cultural-specificity of behavioral research are common, of course, but the phase model seems to deny the more facile interpretations of this position.

  Specifically, two major points seem to characterize the phase model of burnout. Thus, the phases seem generic to many cultures in several ways: that is, the same psychological components of burnout seem to be useful, more or less worldwide; and the covariants of the phases also are much the same from one work setting to all others.

  What of cultural specificity? It is there in a basic way. Variations in the distributions of phases exist, and sometimes those variations are very large. These variations may reflect micro-differences between organizations or their sub-units; these may be macro-differences between the social or national settings of different worksites; or both micro- and macro-differences may be relevant.

  However, generic features of the phase model seem to dominate. Whatever the distribution of phases, the pattern of covariants is much the same in different worksettings in almost all of the available studies of the phase model. Thus, country A or worksetting B may have proportionately more (or less) employees in Phase VIII than country C or worksetting D. Commonly, however, VIIIs will be worse-off than VIIs, and so on, in each of the contexts.

- Finally, the 1995 panel of studies not only encompasses a broader range of "marker variables" or possible covariants of the phases, but analysis now includes more "hard" or "objective" measures. "Soft" or self-report data all-but-monopolized pre-1990 studies of the phase model.

  The encompassing of multiple measures from both "hard" and "soft" domains is far from complete, but the progress reported here requires no basic modifications of interpretations of the phase model. The "hard" variables considered now include: turnover; performance appraisals; estimates of productivity; aspects of blood chemistry and other health-related measures; and costs of medical insurance. In this significant aspect, as well as in others, the phase model extends beyond the high-water marks of studies using other operational measures of burnout, although many issues remain open.

These nine bullets provide a template within which readers can make their individualized judgments about the value-added they attribute to *Global Burnout*. Basically, this book joins those expanding ranks which give attention to the cross-cultural aspects of the behavioral sciences (e.g., Triandis & Berry, 1980). Historically, the focus has been on cultural universals or variations. In the former mode, the focus has tended to be on the creation of general theory, in which case "culture furnishes the proving ground for the universality" of some theoretical variants (Gergen, Gulerce, Lock, & Misra, 1996, p. 496). In cross-cultural research in the variation mode, cultural aspects serve as moderators or intervening variables. More recently, scholars have been concerned that a kind of intellectual imperialism has dominated both historic traditions, with North American or European Traditions having been the independent variables, as it were (e.g., Sinha, 1984).

Global Burnout stands a limited but useful distance outside of such intellectual cross-currents. Determinedly, *the* focus is on the cross-contextual applicability of a specific operational definition of burnout, as estimated by the concurrent validity of the phase model in isolating a consistent pattern of covariation within a large panel of variables. Relative success in testing such an operational definition will permit later grounded judgments about the salience of specific cross-cultural effects. Much behavioral research as an opposed character. It luxuriates in generating different operational definitions which, in the present view, will tend to obfuscate relationships in nature if it does not result in a slough of despond that only highly-contingent relationships will be shown to exist, if any at all.

Similar effects to roll the dice—to hold operational definitions constant in extended programs of research—do exist, but they are rare (e.g., Altemeyer, 1981). Hence, *Global Burnout* proposes, the poverty of much behavioral and organizational research. Absent substantial confidence in key operational definitions, the best bet is that replications will generate an unseemly gaggle of results—positive and negative findings as well as no associations. This is the fuel for indecisiveness, and probably pessimism.

Global Burnout proposes a stout claim in this significant regard. The phase model of burnout can make a substantial claim to validity and reliability. As such it provides a solid basis for successful research forays— with expanding panels of variables into different cultural contexts. Indeed, the phase model seems to identify a centroid in nature, with the term referring to core variable with stout associations to many dimensions of reality.

ACKNOWLEDGMENT

As this manuscript is in its final stages being sent off to the printer, the contributions of our pre-production team loom large. Special thanks go to Sandra B. Daniel, in overall charge of preparing copy, as well as to Tammy L. Rivera and Mark D. Bradbury, two graduate students who helped with much tedious (but crucial) proof-reading.

Chapter I

Phase Model and Burnout As Global: Motivations and Challenges Concerning Measurement

This book describes one way of circumscribing complex realities, and the detailed effort is usefully placed in the developmental context that gives it life. Here, "developmental context" refers to three sets of considerations. In turn, attention gets directed at several motivators urging the measurement of burnout, which also carry with them challenges to that measurement. These motivations/challenges relate to:

- the apparently-growing incidence of people who "go around the bend," or "just snap"
- four reasons to focus on burnout that gradually displaced a skepticism about that concept
- early studies of burnout as global, which reinforced the flood of publications describing burnout as *a* key North American phenomenon, or perhaps even *the* quintessential phenomenon

"GOING AROUND THE BEND": SOME TRAGIC MINI-HISTORIES

Personal experiences in consulting, as well as reports from others, played a major role in investigating the build-up of negative forces implied by burnout. The overall sense of it suggests a rubberband being stretched by powerful forces: the rubberband first is distorted, and then can snap. Increasing evidence suggests that growing numbers of people are under heightening stress, and unmistakable signs also indicate that more people than ever are surpassing their safety zones. They "snap," or "go around the bend." At times, the work environment is an especially demanding one (e.g., Golembiewski & Kiepper, 1983), but everyday jobs provide no sure refuge (e.g., Cherniss, 1989).

Readers of the media all have learned of cases-in-point at work. Recent news stories tell us that person-to-person violence is the second largest cause of death at work, surpassed only by transportation (Rosato, 1995). Even this shocking news far underrepresents the violence at the worksite, however, which properly should take into account the violence directed at self and at others as well. Sometimes the weapon is a fist, knife, or gun; but more typically we use words and negative emotions. These verbal attacks also can hurt. They can provide the "straw that broke the camel's back," thereby inducing a major "snap" or "going around the bend."

Cases will help clarify our meaning, and we provide three exemplars in Exhibit I.1. These three descriptions introduce type-cases of those who "snapped," or "went around the bend." All describe things that really happened, although many details are omitted. In the context of today's times, they are not exceptional exemplars: many others could be cited; and we are all-too-familiar with similar build-ups that lead to comparable explosions—at workplaces and elsewhere. In common, the major actors in the exemplars found themselves in situations beyond their comfort zones of coping skills, attitudes, and experiences.

Questions crowd into our attention. How many Marys, Maurices, and Kellys exist in our world of work? Can they be identified early enough to avoid major reactions? Can their emotional systems be relieved sufficiently to reduce the build-up of strain before it reaches critical levels? Or do we need to help people develop less-pregnable emotional armoring?

Such questions triggered the successful search which this book reports. Beyond these early searches, signally, the original research has been extended into worldwide contexts. So *Global Burnout* presents developments in both greater depth as well as wider breadth than any other available source.

The reader will have to wait until the last chapter has been read and digested to assess whether this effort provides substantial value-added, or represents just another version of what some label psychobabble. For the authors, no doubt exists. We signal our reactions in the book's title.

GLOBAL BURNOUT: A WORLDWIDE PANDEMIC EXPLORED BY THE PHASE MODEL

Several introductory comments may help readers make their individualized judgments about value-added. To begin, this book can be distinguished from others on burnout in several major senses. Thus, it adds further substance about the validity and reliability of *an instrument for measurement* introduced in two earlier books (Golembiewski, Munzenrider, & Stevenson, 1986; Golembiewski & Munzenrider, 1988). This instrument is the phase model of burnout. It is perhaps awkwardly labelled, but that is water long since over the dam.

Exhibit I.1.   Three People Who "Went Around the Bend."

Exemplar I:

- Mary was a loving single-parent, who one morning kissed her children at the bus stop as they went off to school. Soon afterward, she purchased a large caliber handgun, with which she subsequently shot her supervisor.

    There was little warning. Mary had what seemed a manageable dispute with her supervisor about a performance appraisal, but that seemed of moderate intensity and was being worked on.

    There were other surprises. Mary had no experience with revolvers, and had never even held one; nonetheless, Mary shot six times, with five hitting their target.

    Two days after the shooting, she returned to her office to pick-up a salary check and to resign. Exit interviews led to her eventual arrest.

Exemplar II:

- Maurice had moved from a good job near his family, to take on major responsibilities where he experienced strong cross-pressures about his race, his job, and especially about leaving an ailing father. There were early physical signs of a stress-reaction, which prompted medical attention.

    Things seemed under reasonable control until Maurice received an emergency call that his father's death was imminent. He rushed to the airport, bought a ticket, and rushed to the departure gate.

    His job responsibilities came to dominate while he waited. He suddenly remembered an important business meeting downtown—indeed, a critical meeting, as Maurice saw it. He left for the meeting, without checking with others about rescheduling, whether somebody could sit-in for him, or whatever.

    Later that day, Maurice's father died. Remorse quickly set in, and he grew suddenly-ineffective at work. He was soon on full-time disability.

Exemplar III:

- Kelly was a street-level lawyer, serving clients who had little money and experienced frequent brushes with the law. Kelly was dedicated to social justice and forfeited substantial income to perform this job.

    Around Christmas one year, Kelly had too much. Several clients came by to lament that they, and especially their children, would have a sorry holiday. Finances were tight, the clients all complained, and presents would be few and humble.

    > There was one such visit too many. Kelly exploded:
    > "What do you want me to do?
    > "Go out and rob a bank, and buy your kids some presents with the money."
    > "After you're arrested, I can help you.
    > "What do you want me to do now? Things aren't too great for me, either, you know."

Kelly emptied his desk, and never returned, even with nearly a month's pay to his credit.

In addition, this instrument now has been *applied widely in North America as well as at a growing number of global locations.* The results of this worldwide research are reported here, often in detail. And this puts *Global Burnout* in a sparsely-populated class, along with a few other useful titles that also have comprehensive targets (e.g., Schaufeli, Maslach, & Marek, 1993).

This point verges on being self-serving, but we emphasize it nonetheless. "Going global" means great value-added gained at substantial cost. This volume reflects extended periods of delicate negotiations for respondents from many overseas sites, weeks of work to get the relevant survey items translated into about 10 languages, and some modest adventures in transporting data beyond the boundaries of some nations with very weak commitments to behavioral research. We trust that the results of this complex effort between ourselves and colleagues shows through the pages of this book in its value-added.

If research in global worksettings constituted a giant step, major value-added also inheres in a substantial number of incremental North American additions to research with the phase model. *Global Burnout* summarizes many useful replications, in short. Directly, this volume joins a large and growing literature in further documenting that burnout induces costs and deficiencies for both individuals and organizations, in direct proportion to the degree of burnout. These costs and deficiencies are so regular and robust, in the United States as well as everywhere else we have been privileged to look, that it takes great restraint to avoid this linkage: the greater the burnout, on definite average, the worse the health of organizations as well as of the individuals in them.

We will resist such convenient simplifications, but the preponderance of evidence seems quite clear to us, even though we can understand that some observers will emphasize doubts and inconclusivities. Burnout is definitely bad news. High degrees of burnout are associated with conditions that imply *major trouble for individuals and their employing organizations,* as judged by several hundred variables in numerous studies. In sum, advanced phases have been linked to many conditions we all prefer to avoid. Put another way, research almost never fails to associate the phases with dour (if not dire) consequences.

Moreover, this volume estimates the specific *incidences of burnout* in numerous worksettings, worldwide, as well as provides rare data about the *persistence of burnout.* These estimates are not written-in-stone, but they come from enough worksettings to raise real concerns, if not fear. These estimates put this volume in a class by itself. No other wide-ranging efforts provide even remotely-comparable estimates.

Of course, we do not advocate a straight-vanilla interpretation of the results below. Indeed, we later highlight several factors that may moderate our findings, as in connection with the basic norms used to make phase assignments. But more of that, later. Here note only that these qualifications tend to influence interpretations in narrow bands and—whether qualified or not—the estimates of both persistence and incidence are so marked that our analysis has major theoretical and practical implications even if the findings need substantial fine-tuning.

Indeed, *Global Burnout* suggests incidences and persistences that are so great as to strain our available vocabularies. "Epidemic" is too mild for what this volume reports. We settle on the term "pandemic," which Webster's 1974 New Collegiate Dictionary defines as "occurring over a wide geographic area and affecting an exceptionally high proportion of the population." Even "pandemic" may be too mild a label, however.

FOUR MOTIVATORS THAT REPLACED INITIAL SKEPTICISM

The processes of these developments toward the phase model of burnout were uneven, and even casual at the outset. Burnout was an early target-of-opportunity for research, and we authors viewed it as a kind of basic training for more serious things to come. The research effort has now encompassed many contributors, but it began with a compatible trio: in alphabetical order, Robert T. Golembiewski, Robert F. Munzenrider, and Jerry G. Stevenson.

We were all initially biased toward debunking the notion of burnout. To be sure, the concept had made a splashy entrance into the public consciousness a decade or so earlier, but it then had less substance than star quality. Its spectacular appearance on the social scene had its serious downsides, amidst all the attendant hoopla. Indeed, researchers often had to devote time to establishing that burnout is more than just a darling of pop psychology, more than an equivalent of the fashionable fly of a summer's social commentary. Hence our fundamental suspicion, at the beginning. Since the term "burnout" was being applied to everything, we reasoned, the probability was strong that nothing much could be explained by it in rigorous terms.

Our opinions changed as our knowledge increased, and four motivators have now replaced debunking. We catalog these motivators briefly. First, burnout is consistent with much that is old, even as it explores new territory. In this aspect, the concept does double-duty, permitting us to link newly-observed phenomena with established pathways of commentary and research.

Second, burnout seems phenomenally significant. Although the evidence is not all in, and never will be, burnout now seems far from a catch-all category. In sharp contrast, we now insist that a long list of advantages are associated with burnout as a theme, both when approached as research as well as application. Conceptually, it seems to be a real "something" that helps describe our world; operationally, it can be measured with substantial reliability and validity; and burnout also seems of practical as well as theoretical significance, as judged by its associations with a broad range of variables relating to health, well-being, and productivity.

Let us put our present and still-evolving sense in a few words. Rather than being ephemeral, we now see burnout as a *centroid* in nature—as related to virtually everything of any concern in understanding people at their work. The tables and text below will leave little doubt in this critical regard. Just wait and see.

Third, burnout also can lay a strong claim to being something new, at least in the sense that it reflects a novel or highly-augmented contribution to our understanding of important social phenomena.

At the very least, fourth, "burnout" is a useful metaphor for guiding thought and action, as a key to understanding our age. Have we really moved beyond the self-referential excesses of the 1960s that credibly led to the heightened acquisitiveness, if not greed, that grew so prominent in later decades? And how profound the implications of the observation that the new metaphor is "burnout," which implies a depletion of resources and plummeting levels of energy! Earlier metaphors had an optimistic sense of power and of expansive change. These four motivators came to dominate our initial skepticism about burnout, and deserve greater attention. In turn, discussion elaborates on the brief catalog above, relying on the structure as well as a bit of the wording of an earlier formulation (Golembiewski & Munzenrider, 1988, pp. 7-12).

Burnout as Something Old

Knowledge comes as a building-upon, and in that sense it is useful to consider three ways that establish a long time-line for burnout as a focus of investigation. First, a growing body of data suggests that, while we may be newly-aware of the multiple expressions of burnout, it has been long with us. Our mind's eye scans caring or obsessed people, attempting to cope with complex situations that burgeon more rapidly than do the skills and attitudes that permit successful coping (e.g., Schwartz & Will, 1953).

This first perspective on burnout as something old deserves some tethering. Although occupational stress and burnout are viewed by many researchers as recently-created subareas, the study of the strain experience in the workplace has a history with deep roots. A liberal paraphrasing of Boudreau (1985, pp. 139-140) helps establish the general point. Let us go back only to Sir William Osler, who died in 1919 at age 70. As early as the later 1800s, Osler wrote about problems facing physicians and "equated 'stress and strain' with 'hard work and worry'" (Spielberger, 1979, p. 7). Breay, in a 1913 article, discussed the "overstrain" of nurses of that period which—according to her—could be moderated by "sufficient time for sleep and recreation, comfortable quarters...better conditions of labor, [and] more adequate remuneration" (pp. 156-157).

Over the first century or so in the study of the strain experience, then, it was: the more things change, the more they remain the same. Thus, "overstrain" was replaced by terms like shellshock, combat or battle fatigue, job stress, and burnout, depending on the era and the worksetting. Nonetheless, the critical center held firm. Reasonably-rigorous research remained sparse until about the time Kahn and his co-workers (Kahn, Wolfe, Quinn, Snoeck, & Rosenthal, 1964) published the results of their national survey on role conflict and role ambiguity.

Let us do a fast-forward on this history, in effect, to suggest why "overstrain" or similar labels cannot be avoided: they came relatively early, stayed late, and even now have an escalating prominence. Our public schools provide a convenient illustration. They have taken on, or been forced to accept, an escalating range of social and familial as well as narrowly-educational responsibilities. Why? People with a growing range of abilities and disabilities have become more insistent about having their needs met in schools, and the national consciousness increasingly accords legitimacy to these aspirations. Illustratively, even the medium-sized town of Athens, Georgia, has students in its schools who have over 50 first-languages, with all that entails for achieving positive educational outcomes. Add to this elemental a huge range of differences in early-life experiences, the conditioning effects of sometimes-great differences in family income, often-divergent aspirations, and the inevitable diversity of natural endowments. No wonder, then, about the stressor-filled school year.

Overall, these educational challenges have proved a game that has not been won for losing. For example, systems of rewards in educational settings have not kept pace with, and in many cases have fallen further behind, accumulating technical, interpersonal, and ethical demands. No wonder, then, that the "burnout" or "flameout" of teachers and school administrators has received great attention—both in the popular press and, more recently, in the research literature. Several work sites considered below—Sites KK, NN, and OO, among others—indicate the substantial incidence of harmful burnout effects in educational settings. Indeed, that incidence can be seen as frightening.

In sum, burnout is like venereal herpes. Both are now identified and partially understood; they have serious consequences for people as well as their systems; both have been with us a long time; and, as aggravated by today's cultural mores and practices, both now clearly stand in growing need of greater knowledge and caring.

Second, viewing burnout as an old phenomenon, we have numerous conceptual jumping-off points for circumscribing our realities. This vocabulary includes alienation, the several depressions, free-floating anxiety, stress, or whatever. It requires only a direct if bold extension—*some* stress becomes *too much*: accumulating stressors lead to strain, and sufficient strain can induce the coping deficits implied by burnout. In sum, burnout can be seen as a direct extension of the vocabulary we have long used to describe our lives and our reactions to them. This possibility encourages, even requires, a building-upon.

Third, some observers propose a more radical sense in which burnout is something old. From this perspective, the concept is a vague verbal tent that covers several phenomenal areas, carelessly aggregating what would be better left to stand alone rather than being firmly but carelessly thrust under the conceptual tent of "burnout."

Right or wrong, burnout as old in this final sense especially merits attention. Parsimony and economy will be served, that is to say, if this conceptual lumping together is correct. On the other hand, we will only camouflage or distort necessary targets for research and application, if we fail to test aggressively the view that the conceptual tenting merely covers our embarrassment at knowing too little and assuming too much. Either way, critical research has a high priority.

Burnout as Something Substantial

Even if some are not convinced that burnout is something old, it requires a very special kind of denial to doubt its virulence. Thus, Kahn (1978, p. 61) sees burnout as "a syndrome of inappropriate attitudes toward clients and toward self, often associated with uncomfortable physical and emotional symptoms." Relatedly, the range of these symptoms seems very broad. Maslach and Jackson observe (1981, p. 2) that, along with reductions in the quality of care or service, burnout "appears to be a factor in job turnover, absenteeism, and low morale [and] various self-reported indices of personal distress, including physical exhaustion, insomnia, increased use of alcohol and drugs, and marital and family problems." Others present even longer lists of significant signs and symptoms that also imply a substantial "something" (Cherniss, 1980b, esp. p. 17).

The substantial research reported on later adds many details concerning how and why the phase model of burnout taps substantial phenomena, both in North American as well as global settings. Whether the concept is old or not, we authors see burnout as substantial in its effects.

Burnout as Something New or Newly-Heightened

Burnout is also clearly something new, at least in the sense of a heightened incidence and severity of some "old" things (Cherniss, 1980; Freudenberger, 1980). Five points illustrate the arguments that convince the authors of this volume.

First, burnout may reasonably be associated with our escalating pace of life. Not so long ago, to illustrate, youngsters could rely on a long line of elders to provide help—grandparents and even great-grandparents could pass on reliable knowledge about basic job skills and values. Today, even mothers or fathers often cannot be relied on for that. Illustratively, the majority of job titles in the federal list of occupations did not even exist two or three decades ago. And, even where job titles have remained constant, job content often has changed radically. In effect, effective marksmanship concerning life's choices is more difficult because the targets keep moving, as it were.

Such descriptions suggest growing potentials for both greater freedom and greater insecurity. Each of these possibilities, in turn, suggests omnipresent stressors that could reasonably crescendo into the state implied by burnout—a level of strain beyond the individual's normal coping capabilities, a strain absorbing so much energy as to deplete an individual's reserves as well as to pollute the quality of life, which risks the depletion of personal and financial resources necessary to enjoy the full fruits of life.

The Mandarin pictogram for "change" economically captures the full sense of the matter. That pictogram simply and profoundly combines two other pictograms: one for "opportunity," and the second for "danger." No one has said it more briefly, or more powerfully.

Second, we are literally living in the first few generations of dramatically-extended individual life spans. This implies multiple tensions not only on a personal level, but also in abrasions with the social, economic, and political institutions built in response to the cadence of less-demanding times. Consider that, not many decades ago, few people over 80 entered hospitals, except to die. Today, the scheduling of major operations for octogenarians has become common, and everyone expects almost all of them to walk out of the hospital afterwards. This silver lining has its accompanying dark cloud, of course, whose full meaning will become manifest only in the years 2010 and beyond, when the legions of the post-World War II baby boomers approach the age now considered normal for retirement.

Third, our expectations continue to escalate—relative to ourselves, our intimates, and to our colleagues at work (Maslach, 1982). These expectations have multiple roots: they come in part from within ourselves; these expectations derive from the demands of work made upon us; and they often involve combined personal and vocational aspirations demanding long-term educational preparation which, in turn, generates some form of extended dependence on the part of professionals-to-be extending into their late twenties or early thirties. Commonly, such heightened expectations have sharply raised the ante we must pay just to begin to live the productive parts of our lives.

Fourth, fewer areas of life will easily tolerate half-baked commitment. Not so long ago, intense commitment was required only of the elites, if of them. Various forms of physical and economic coercion sufficed to elicit whatever degree of mass effort was required. Consider war. Whatever carnage may have occurred at the front lines in earlier wars, ordinarily the involvement of the civilian population was sharply limited. World War II changed that, decisively, and the thermonuclear age has so accentuated the shift that today elite warriors are the most safe. Brush-fire wars and terrorism similarly expand the legions who can be involved, up-front and personal.

Half-baked commitment at work also suffices far less frequently, nowadays (Freudenberger, 1980). Today's jobs often require higher levels of skill and greater self-starting abilities, particularly from knowledge workers. And upgrading has become an increasingly-common feature of worklives—as work is reengineered, or as knowledge and experience advance. Moreover, new trends like *coproduction* also add to the burdens of what used to be the consumer's role—we now often pump our own gas, and carry ourselves long distances to airport gates so that the airlines can lower their costs while still providing long-distance mass transport. We now also provide much "self-help" or "voluntary aid" in myriad public and private contexts, and will probably come to engage in far more of it in the future (Brudney, 1990).

Fifth, both the sheer number of stakeholders and their shopping lists have been growing exponentially of late, and probably will continue to do so. Social justice obviously has been extended unevenly to many in both the recent-past as well as today, and this exacerbates the problems of transition and adaptation (Mason, 1982). As more and more people have higher expectations about their lives and about how they should be treated, so also does the pressure on all grow.

These and similar factors often will contribute to an increasing incidence of burnout, and such a state of affairs powerfully motivates research. Why? Patently, it makes a *big* difference how many people have reached what level of burnout. Fineman demonstrates that early opinions provide unsure footing for generalizations. He notes (1985, p. 153): "The pervasiveness of burnout is unclear. The reader of the mainstream literature could be forgiven for assuming, from its tone, that all social workers and the like are on the path to chronic stress and inevitable burnout....But few studies provide a sense of perspective on the incidence of burnout...."

We shall see what guidance the phase model provides. The challenge is obvious: to do better in this basic regard of estimating how may people suffer from which degrees of burnout and soon. Only in this way can we make informed judgments about assigning a realistic priority to learning how to ameliorate burnout.

Burnout as Replacement for Failed Metaphors for Social Life

Burnout appears to be a central topic in today's behavioral sciences, perhaps even *the* topic. This may seem overstated, but social life seems to have become so complex that even the metaphors of recent decades provide unsure guidance. Our very words fail to describe our own conditions.

To paint with a very broad brush, the past four decades or so may be seen as reflecting preoccupation with forms of doing—doing different, good, well, and globally, respectively. Recall that the 1950s are considered the anxious years in which we first learned "to do different"—to live with the bomb and perhaps with permanent and pervasive "free-floating anxiety." The 1960s liberated the "me and mine generation," often characterized by an ardent openness and need to "do good"—to expand human potential by challenging conventional limits on people and their development, especially mentally and emotionally. These expansionist tendencies were reflected in various kinds of social awarenesses, such as that relating to civil rights, but they also led to narcissistic excesses. "Let people be free" typified the former; drug-induced "mind-blowing" came to represent the latter. Most observers see social consciousness as having retreated in the late 1970s and beyond, with the emphasis in today's society being on determined professionalism, if not just sheer acquisitiveness. Here the focus shifts to concerns about "doing well." Beginning with the 1990s, the arena for doing—whatever the modes—was expanded in ways only now becoming reasonably clear. The lives of many more of us would be acted on the global stage, at worldwide rhythms.

These characterizations are rough approximations, of course, but all have some sense of hope about them. They focus on *doing*—whether it be doing different, doing good, doing well, or doing in the global arena. Divergent and even contradictory as they may be, these modes share a sense of energy, and they even suggest *direction* for that energy. In turn, doing, energy, and direction encourage hope.

In contrast, burnout should cause pause, if not social alarm. Our world is full of stressors—stimuli that can induce fight or flight responses, and hence can either agitate or energize. Some of these stressors—often called *eu-stressors*—can be powerful motivators. They enhance and enrich; they quicken and enlarge our lives. Thus, simply avoiding stressors will not do: stressors often open the door to opportunity, so to speak, and can motivate the inventiveness required to capitalize on opportunity. However, stressors also can create strain, and sufficient strain can challenge and even outstrip our coping capabilities. Great energies may then be directed into mere maintenance or subsistence, leading to physical and emotional deficits and burnout. As usual in life, balance remains crucial but becomes increasingly elusive. We cannot live well without stressors, but it remains to live effectively with them.

If burnout is a suitable metaphor for the life experiences of a growing number of people, this implies that balance is frequently not achieved. Oppositely, indeed, burnout implies a state of exhaustion rather than one of hopeful becoming. And this metaphor consequently should cause concern in a world where, patently, so much needs doing, and soon.

EARLY STUDIES OF BURNOUT, NORTH AMERICAN AND GLOBAL

The motivation to come to analytic grips with burnout also comes from a second major source. In addition to the burgeoning literature on North American burnout, early evidence indicates that burnout has gone global. We can be brief here in summarizing these early materials, but usefully so because what follows augments an effort published not long ago which was unique in its comparative overview (Golembiewski, Scherb, & Boudreau, 1993), but even now badly needs extension and testing. *Global Burnout* provides just such extension and testing, while it builds upon the North American literature.

Anyone who titles a book "global..." has a lot of proving to do, and so it is with *Global Burnout*. Indeed, the need for explanation and evidence may be especially formidable in the present case. Let us put the point directly. Even if the conclusion must be clearly provisional, mounting evidence implies that burnout is a cross-national and perhaps a cross-cultural disease. However, this conclusion will grate on today's academic nerve-endings. Witness this contrary conclusion (Adler, Doktor, & Redding, 1986, p. 295), which is clearly the dominant one nowadays: "Research in developmental psychology, sociology, and anthropology shows that there are major differences among the cognitive processes of people from different cultures. In the era of the global corporation, cultural diversity has to be recognized, understood, and appropriately used in organizations."

So the basic conclusions drawn from early studies of burnout must swim against a substantial tide, as it were. But, so be it. The conceptual water of the phase model is fine, as much detail will establish.

The required explanation and evidence here come from two basic sources around which the following chapters will be organized. That is, attention to burnout began as a North American fixation, and even more narrowly as a major theme in U.S. behavioral science dealing with people-helping jobs or professions (e.g., Freudenberger, 1977, 1980). More directly, this volume is a direct lineal descendant of two books on the phase model which are preoccupied with that North American literature—summarizing it, evaluating it, and synthesizing as well as the testing the ability of the phase model to estimate burnout (Golembiewski, Munzenrider, & Stevenson, 1986; Golembiewski & Munzenrider, 1988). More recent research on burnout as a global or worldwide phenomenon has progressed sufficiently to support this test of the comprehensiveness of North American concepts, operations, and findings.

Hence, the warp and woof of this book is straightforward, even if the details of moving forward often will be daunting or only semi-conclusive. Typically, several sets of working answers to twin central questions constitute the basic structure of this book. What does research from North American worksettings have to tell us about burnout? And what does research from global settings have to tell us about the degrees to which North American initiatives are generic or nation- or culture-specific?

Two major caveats serve to tether this effort, but they are not sufficient to hobble a comprehensive review of what the available literature reveals about the cross-national character of burnout. Directly, the objective is an expansive one, even though the products of analysis cannot rise above the available literature, which has only fairly begun to exploit cross-cultural perspectives. Moreover, the focus is on cross-national samples. Arguably, these neither clearly nor necessarily constitute "cross-cultural" comparisons. For present purposes, however, the distinction gets no further attention despite its patent significance.

North American Research on Burnout

In effect, the North American approach to burnout plays the leading role in the present approach. Most developmental work on the "phase model of burnout" has been accomplished in the United States and Canada. Moreover, that work has been reviewed comprehensively through the late 1980s (Golembiewski & Munzenrider, 1988), and narrower syntheses have appeared even more recently (e.g., Golembiewski & Boss, 1992). The purpose here is to build on this earlier work, as well as to extend it comprehensively through 1995. Several later citations also are included.

What legitimates this building on largely-North American results and the detailed testing of their extension to global settings? For now, two considerations must suffice. Paramountly, early research indicates that the phase model of burnout estimates validly and reliably who has which degrees of burnout. These estimates are beyond other available burnout measures, and provide motivation enough to assess the global applicability of the phase model.

The early North American literature also provides a second and related major motivation for detailed attention to global burnout, as well as a search for new information drawn from North American settings. Basically, as the phases progress from least ——> most burnout, so also do changes occur in a large inventory of covariants from best ——> worst. Illustratively, as the burnout phases advance, so also increase the physical symptoms reported by individuals. And this pattern holds for virtually all of several hundred variables so far analyzed. Not insignificantly, the phases of burnout seem persistent as well as regularly and robustly associated with variables of organizational as well as personal concern.

Global Research on Burnout, Viewed Broadly

The subsequent detailed analysis of the phase model also gets general support from worldwide research on burnout, as variously defined. The immediate vehicle is a conventional survey of the literature on global burnout. In effect, it provides general counterpoint to the targeted analysis in later chapters of the phase model of burnout.

A few details frame the search process which generated this chapter's panel of worldwide burnout studies, as broadly conceived. The starting-point is a benchmark bibliography of over 700 items compiled by Kilpatrick (1986), whose cross-national entries were augmented in two waves—by a search of English language sources extending her coverage from 1985 through the end of 1990, and then later through 1995. This augmentation relies on a multi-dimensional search: two separate computer-assisted sweeps of the periodic literature using a range of key words and concepts; visual searches of *Psychological Abstracts* and *Sociological Abstracts* as well as of numerous journals; and personal contacts with a network of burnout researchers. This multipronged search isolated a 1996 panel of 110 citations that can be reasonably labeled "empirical and cross-national."

The cross-national panel encourages ten generalizations about the available literature on burnout-related phenomena dealing with non-North American settings. Several of these generalizations seem robust, but most require qualification because many operational definitions of "burnout" or stress-related phenomena are represented in the 1995 panel. In all cases, the general pattern seems clear enough. The following discussion builds on and also extends an earlier and similar effort.[1]

Cross-National Research's Growth, by Number and Nation. A first generalization can be stated boldly: burnout research is a growth industry. Only rare cross-national efforts with even a conceptual kinship to burnout appear in the worldwide literature before the early 1980s. Beyond that, two regularities seem clear. Thus, the incidence of burnout-related research in cross-national settings has increased markedly, and so has the specific focus on burnout rather than on stress or stressors.

Growth in Numbers. Some numbers provide a specific sense of this growth curve. While the exact totals can be quibbled about, the relative orders-of-magnitude leave us with a solid sense that a lot has been going on in recent years when it comes to burnout research in non-North American settings. Through 1990, more or less, an assiduous search of a very large number of English-language journals plus a selective review of periodicals in other languages generated a panel of 35 research studies, reasonably self-conscious about design and methods. Social commentary or general how-to pieces are excluded. In the ensuing 5 years, that panel has ballooned. In sum, the generalizations below are based on the 1996 panel of 110 studies, which approximates a tripling of the number found through 1990 as the result of a similar search process.[2] The References contain all citations, with * indicating items in the 1990 sub-panel and ** identifying pieces of research added in the 1990-1995 sub-panel.

Growth in Nations Represented. The 1996 panel of studies also permits a second way of estimating how burnout research has spread around the world. Table I.1 does the job of indicating the locus of studies, as well as the frequency with which populations from specific nation states or geographic territories have hosted research on burnout. That array is impressive: 33 countries are represented in the 1996 panel, excluding the U.S. and Canada.

No doubt exists, then. Burnout clearly is a global disease of such a magnitude as to motivate serious study. Indeed, a recently developed instrument for assessing burnout was both developed and validated cross-nationally (Schaufeli, Leiter, & Kalimo, 1995). This signals that burnout is no longer a North American phenomenon, if indeed it ever was.

A final note adds another dimension to Table I.1. By far, the most frequent hosts of burnout research have been North American—the United States and Canada. The References contain many citations establishing that burnout research there is definitely in vogue, and has been so for about two decades

Table I.1. Distribution of Burnout Research in 1996
Panel, by Nation State and Frequency

	Frequency[a]		Frequency[a]
Australia	5	Italy	4
Belarus	5	Japan	14
Brazil	3	Korea	2
Britain	14	Macaw	2
Chile	1	Mexico	1
China	3	Netherlands	16
Commonwealth of		New Zealand	6
Independent States	5		
(old USSR)		Nigeria	3
Egypt	2	Norway	3
Finland	2	Poland	3
France	2	Saudi Arabia	1
Germany	5	Singapore	2
Ghana	1	South Africa	3
Hong Kong	2	Sweden	8
India	2	Taiwan	4
Ireland	2	Yugoslavia	1
Israel	17	Zimbabwe	1

Note: [a] Several studies report on data from 2 or more nation states.

now. No one knows the exact size of this North American literature, but it is huge. Kilpatrick's (1986) survey is the last comprehensive one, and it contains about 700 pieces of serious research and commentary. *The* deluge came later.

Cross-National Research and Self-Reports. The 1996 vs. 1990 collections reflect both stability and significant change in a second set of related particulars. As was the case earlier, virtually all studies in the later panel rely on self-reports to estimate all variables—levels of burnout, their covariants, and so on. See also the section below on "Cross-National Research and Operational Measures."

However, the 1995 sub-panel reflects an explicit shift in advertised focus from "stress" or "stressors" to "burnout." This implies a changing research fashion. Earlier, only a small minority of studies advertised their interest in burnout, which can be broadly defined as "strain" or levels of stressors that surpass an individual's comfortable coping capacities—as determined by attitudes, expectations, and coping skills.

Multiple "hard" and "soft" measures in every study no doubt constitute the ideal, and hence concern is reasonable about the reliability and validity of most available cross-national research. Some observers would insist that only hard measures are capable of generating reliable and valid results, but "objective" measures are almost completely absent from both the 1990 and 1996 panels.

A recent major study (Schaufeli, Keijsers, & Miranda, 1995) represents the handful of available global studies that place a strong emphasis on objective or "hard" variables. Specifically, the research deals with Intensive Care Units, and attempts to estimate objective outcomes related to both effectiveness and efficiency, using as indicators mortality rates for the former and days in ICU for the latter. This piece of research tests for associations with burnout, and is all-but-singular in the 1995 panel (see also Randall & Scott, 1988).

Cross-National Research and Face Validity

Especially prior to 1985, burnout-related research seemed preoccupied with establishing its *raison d'etre*, typically reflected in efforts to associate the kind and intensity of stressors with health outcomes. This reasonable strategy suggests a desire for a kind of legitimacy-by-association.

Overall, these efforts succeeded even as they had limitations of design and findings. That is, studies report credible clusters of effects that seem common cross-nationally, as well as others that seem setting-specific. For example, Orth-Gomer (1979) focused on ischemic heart disease (IHD) among matched Swedish and American white men, with each sample having three subgroups: men registered with the medical departments of their companies for IHD (myocardial infarction or angina pectoris); men with one or more indicators of strong IHD risk; and a control group. A questionnaire administered to all subjects in both samples inquired about job satisfaction, conflicts, psychological strain, and stressful features of work. The findings suggest both generic and culturally-specific effects. That is, some significant differences exist between the three samples: for example, Swedish men in all subgroups are less satisfied with their careers than their American counterparts. Noteworthy similarities also appear. Paramountly, both Swedish and American samples report that very stressful periods preceded IHD onset. In both samples, moreover, men with IHD have less education and report significantly less satisfaction with family life.

This illustration typifies the full panel of studies: the results carry us forward, but in a clearly-limited way. In sum, our brief illustrative review focuses on "face validity" or "gross validity." In addition, the focus is on "stress" or "stressors," as variously defined, as contrasted with "burnout." Hence, the similarities/differences in results variously mirror nature as well as differences in designs, methods, and variables. So the results of our mini-analyses may be suggestive but they can never be definitive. As with virtually all studies in the panel, they whet our appetite but do not satisfy it.

Cross-National Research and Work. The claim to validity of burnout-related constructs is extended in the 1996 panel in two basic ways, and far beyond early efforts to associate stressors and strain with health. Illustratively, Karasek (1979) uses data from national surveys in the United States and Sweden to test a model of job strain viewed as deriving from the interaction of job demands and job decision latitude. For both countries, essentially, workers with jobs simultaneously low in job decision latitude and high in job demands report exhaustion after work, depression, nervousness, anxiety, insomnia, and trouble awakening in the morning.

The availability of other intriguing data also permits exploration of crucial paths of effects. For example, jobs with low decision latitude and high demand are strongly associated with pill consumption and use of sick days in the Swedish sample. Signally, the combination of low decision latitude and high demand is also associated with job dissatisfaction. Moreover, the satisfaction measures as well as the depression indicators tend to vary with the activity level of the job. Active jobs with high demands and high decision latitude are more satisfying than passive jobs. Hence, job strain might be reducible by increasing decision latitude, independent of changes in workload. This suggests an alternative to a troubling forecast: that job-related health can be improved only by decreasing productivity.

The centrality of burnout-related constructs also gets support from the pathways of effects commonly reported in the literature. Table I.2 attempts one such summary of the dominant associations reported in the 1996 panel of advanced burnout or strain. Clearly, the pattern is consistent with that attributed to North American studies: if only generally, increases in burnout or strain are associated with worsening conditions on a broad array of variables.

To be sure, Table I.2 reflects only a prevailing consensus in available studies, rather than near-certainties or inevitabilities, but even that hedged capability is attention-getting. For example, numerous moderating or intervening variables no doubt are relevant, and they could obscure even consistent relationships in nature. Thus, studies report different gender effects (e.g., Izraeli, 1988), class influences (e.g., Pines & Guendelman, 1994), or differences attributed to the shift that one works (e.g., Kandolin, 1993). Nonetheless, Table I.2 is neither a caricature nor a portrait of self-cancelling features.

Cross-National Research and Stages of Development

Viewed in terms of the relative maturation of specific work contexts, the 1995 cross-national panel also reflects several interesting contrasts within broad consistencies. Seven summary points illustrate clusters of these similarities/differences, and they amplify the motivation for studying burnout-related phenomena in worldwide settings.

Table I.2. Selected Major Covariants of Burnout in 1995 Cross-National Panel

I. Higher burnout or strain tend to be associated with *higher* levels of:

- physical and emotional symptomologies (e.g., Cox, Kuk, & Leiter, 1993, especially pp. 182-184; Golembiewski, Boudreau, Goto, & Murai, 1993; Lin, Sun, & Golembiewski, 1996; Kelloway & Barling, 1991)

- spurning the assistance of people helpers (e.g., Cheku, Wong, & Rosen, 1994; Cheku & Rosen, 1994)

- uncertainty about social realities and evaluations (e.g., Buunk & Schaufeli, 1993)

- helplessness (e.g., Golembiewski, Sun, Lin, & Boudreau, 1995)

- role ambiguity (e.g., Capel, 1987)

- escape-avoidance coping (e.g., Chan & Hui, 1995; Rees, Chan & Hui, 1995; Rees & Francis, 1991)

- intent to leave employing organization (Firth, McIntee, McKeown, & Britton, 1986b)

- absenteeism and turnover (Firth & Britton, 1989)

- negative emotional arousal (Kelman & Melamed, 1989; Naisberg, Fenning, & Elizur, 1995)

- environmental turbulence such as a war (Kushir & Melamed, 1992)

- cardiovascular risk factors (Appels

II. Higher burnout or strain tend to be associated with *lower* levels of:

- social support (e.g., Cheku, Wong, & Rosen, 1994; Winnubst, Marcelissen, & Klieber, 1988)

- autonomy (e.g., Pines, 1993)

- organizational "healthiness," as in less adequate problem-solving and task environments (e.g., Cox, Kuk, & Leiter, 1993, pp. 190-192; Pines, 1993; Dell'Erba, Rizzo, & Pancheri, 1994; McCulloch & O'Brien, 1986; Price & Spence, 1994; Van Der Ploeg & Leewen, 1990)

- job satisfaction (e.g., Golembiewski & Luo, 1996; Dolan, 1987; Gibson, McGrath, & Reid, 1989; Iverson, Olekans & Erwin, 1994)

- job involvement (e.g., Golembiewski, Sun, Lin, & Boudreau, 1995)

- self-rated productivity (e.g., Golembiewski, Boudreau, Goto, Murai, 1993; Boudreau, 1996)

- job challenge (Friesen & Sarros, 1994)

- creativity (Noworol, Zarczynski, Fafrowicz, & Marek, 1993)

- marital satisfaction (Greenglass & Burke, 1988; Greenglass, Fiksenbaum, & Burke, 1994)

- supervisory support (e.g., Greenglass & Burke, 1994)

(continued)

Table I.2.   *(Continued)*

& Schouten, 1991; Melamed, Kushir,
& Shirom, 1992)

- externalization (Wilson & Chiwakata,
  1989)

- trust (e.g., O'Driscoll &
  Schubert, 1988)

- sense of psychological
  community (Pretty, McCarthy,
  & Catano, 1992)
- hardiness (Boudreau &
  Golembiewski, 1995)

First, at the broadest level, research suggests that strain-related—and, hence, burnout-related—effects are of international interest, and nowhere moreso than in the "developing" or rapidly industrializing countries. For example, Cooper and Arbose (1984) report that, among 1,065 executives, those with the poorest mental health and lowest job satisfaction come from the "developing countries"—Singapore, Nigeria, Brazil, Egypt—as well as from one advanced country: Japan. For executives from these countries, significant stressors include work overload, time pressures and deadlines, long work hours, taking work home, and poor interpersonal relationships. See also Cooper and Hensman (1985).

Several differences also capture one's attention. In the economically-advanced or mature nations—Britain, United States, South Africa, Sweden, and Germany—threat of job loss and lack of autonomy are strong predictors of poor mental health and job dissatisfaction. Idiosyncratic predictors of stressors also characterize specific countries. Witness the competition for promotion and keeping up with new technology cited by the Japanese respondents.

The tempting implications in such data have to be hedged, however, and decisively. Paramountly, the estimates of both "development" and of "strain" remain only-loosely established.

Second, later studies in the 1995 panel promise a way out of such loosenesses. That is, the phase model permits specific estimates of the distribution of 8 degrees of burnout, and this specificity in turn permits the testing of discrete linkages. All succeeding chapters relate to this attractive possibility, but none more than Chapter VI on the incidence of the phases. Moreover, although the instrument gets no further attention here, the General Burnout Questionnaire is introduced by work in the 1995 panel (Schaufeli, Leiter, & Kalimo, 1995). The GBQ also suggests that cross-national research on burnout is coming-of-age, and no longer will be a simple importer of North American developments.

Third, replications tend to find high levels of stressors and poorer mental well-being among similar clusters of countries. For example, consider comparisons between American, Japanese, and Indian managers (DeFrank, Ivancevich, & Schweiger, 1988). To provide some limited but useful details, a principal components analysis of the mental health scores from each country produces a three-factor solution, with the factors designated as Tension, Dissatisfaction, and Ill Health. Overall, the Japanese report poorer health status and significantly more tension than the American and Indian managers. Japanese and Americans do not differ on Dissatisfaction, but both groups are significantly higher than the Indian sample. See also Chapter IV for partial tests of such speculations generated by early strain-related research in the worldwide panel.

Fourth, consistently, replications also tend to isolate more favorable burnout-related profiles in respondents from countries with a reputation for relaxed lifestyles. Illustratively, McCormick and Cooper (1988) report that levels of mental health, job satisfaction, and job stressors among senior executives in New Zealand differ favorably from those found in the 10 countries in Cooper and Hensman's (1985) study, excepting only Sweden. As the researchers expected, for example, New Zealand executives report the lowest rates of job dissatisfaction.

Fifth, the points above suggest that cross-national comparisons often isolate consistent cultural/behavioral differences, but this conclusion can easily outdistance our abilities to describe and estimate. Thus, the general ways in which these differences are identified leaves open many issues. "Nation" is easy to identify, that is to say, but assessing "cultures" poses unresolved conceptual and measurement issues, despite the common misinterpretations of such efforts as Hofstede's (1980) taxonomic *tour de force*. Basically, "culture" seems a mosaic rather than a monolith, which raises profound questions about isolating and interpreting differences between "cultures" viewed as homogeneous if not as unitary (e.g., Golembiewski, 1991).

What are some of the more obvious pitfalls in cross-national comparisons? Elementally, the specific features of *some* roles or tasks may distort or wash out even pronounced cultural/behavioral differences. For example, Shouksmith and Burrough (1988) compare self-reports from New Zealand air traffic controllers with responses to a set of items previously rated as stress-producing by Canadian air traffic controllers. The overall levels of stress perceived by the two national collections of controllers are approximately equal, and four of the top five stressors identified by both groups are similar—equipment limitations, workload in peak traffic situations, fear of causing accidents, and poor quality of the general working environment. This suggests that much strain in air traffic controllership inheres in common roles and tasks, as distinct from—and more powerful than—differences in both national cultural settings.

A similar conclusion about role similarities in different national settings holds for organizational consultants from European countries, Israel, and the United States (Pines & Caspi, 1992). *No* cross-national differences in burnout are observed. Although only a small number of consultants are involved (*N* = 40), the study also reports familiar burnout covariants, which adds to the study's credibility. Apparently, the demands of the consultant role are powerful enough to dilute or disguise any national or cultural differences.

The impacts of tasks/roles in cross-national comparisons need not always be direct, in addition, as research with university faculty suggests. Keinan and Perlberg (1987) administered a questionnaire using the Faculty Stress Index (FSI) to members from all Israeli universities and compared the results to an earlier survey of American faculty (Gmelch, Lovrich, & Wilke, 1983). Factor analysis of the FSI items isolates five distinct factors that seem similar to those identified in the Gmelch study: conflicts with the academic system, overload of administrative and public duties, academic overload and time constraints, teaching functions, and working conditions. Seven of the top 10 stressors identified by the Americans and Israelis are common to both samples, but no rigorous estimate is made of the congruency of the two factorial structures.

So far, this seems like the same story told in the case of air traffic controllers and consultants, but reason for caution exist. For example, Kenian and Perlberg (1987) also show that lower percentages of Israeli faculty perceive each source of stress as "serious" or "severe" than American faculty. Research, teaching, and service are all perceived as more stressful by Americans than by Israelis (see also the research discussed later by Etzion and her associates). In short, the *conceptual domains* may be cross-nationally similar while their *levels* may vary markedly. This distinction also seems to apply to global applications of the phase model of burnout, as Chapters II and VI especially demonstrate.

Sixth, demographic breakouts on occasion can inform cross-national research. Perhaps most confidence can be placed in gender, with virtually all studies implying higher levels of burnout-related effects among females. Deviant or mixed findings do exist (e.g., Pedrabissi, Rolland, & Santinello, 1993), but they seem in the definite minority. To illustrate the dominant tendencies concerning gender effects, Cohen (1976) reports that females— American retail clerks and German retail clerks as well as factory workers— experienced higher rates of felt discomfort than their male counterparts. Similarly, in Keinan and Perlberg's (1987) survey of university faculties, female respondents report higher levels of stressors. Consistently, Etzion and Pines (1986) find that the women in a sample of Israeli and American human service professionals report significantly more burnout than do men.

Such apparent similarities concerning gender effects can be accounted for in terms of similar patterns of cross-national socialization and acculturation. Thus, Etzion and Pines (1986) suggest the centrality of sex role stereotypes for masculine and feminine behavior, in addition to cultural values.

Seventh, later studies in the 1996 panel usefully extend the theoretic reach of burnout. Thus Pines (1993) uses burnout concepts and methods to add insight about political behavior and attitudes in Israel. Such extensions of both grasp as well as reach, of course, add to the motivation to analyze burnout in global contexts.

Cross-National Research and Personal Features

Both early and late, little consistent comparative research exists concerning the relationship of personal or personality features with burnout, strain, or stressors. For example, several studies look at measures of Type A, but the results can best be considered provisional and perhaps highly-contingent (e.g., Evans, Palsane, & Carrere, 1987; Xie & Jamal, 1989). Early reviews of the interactions of burnout and Type A (e.g., Golembiewski & Munzenrider, 1988) also trend in the same direction, overall.

At the same time, this lacuna in research should not be taken to imply a non-lawful state of nature. For example, Table I.2 contains entries relating to consistent covariation of the phases and a few personal features—for example, internalization and externalization. Several studies similarly suggest consistency in associations between burnout and hardiness (e.g., Boudreau & Levin, 1996), but such research is more characterized by promise rather than by demonstrated superiorities over formulations that have received greater attention in a burnout context (Boudreau & Golembiewski, 1995). See also, for example, the discussion of the active/passive condition in Chapters VII and VIII.

Cross-National Research and Cultural Profiles

Several of the generalizations above—indeed, perhaps all of them—encourage the search for distinct "cultural profiles," to use a convenient term to denote a very complex set of realities. Such profiles will permit explicit characterizations of the contexts underlaying broad similarities/differences in research populations, and the search for these profiles also may eventually generate broadly-useful typologies.

At an instrumental level, even developmental forms of such cultural profiles can help understand the results of burnout-related research. For example, one of the few studies providing data from eastern Europe examines stress predictors and mediators among American and Polish college students (Harari, Jones, & Sek, 1988). The American students score higher on internal locus of control and social support, with the Poles scoring higher on external locus of control, anxiety, and depression. For the Americans, internal locus of control buffers anxiety and depression, consistent with the researchers' assumption that an individualistic-privatistic orientation dominates among Americans. However, in the Polish sample—to which the researchers attribute a collectivistic-institutional orientation—social support does *not* buffer stressors. In sum, the notion of two contrasting national templates seems more suggestive than complete.

Directly, the issue in the specific case is no more settled than the broader case of a comprehensive set of cultural templates or profiles. For example, contemporary Polish conditions may explain the apparent anomaly of social support's puniness in an ostensibly collectivist context. To explain, low levels of self-confidence among highly-educated Poles, as well as intense competition for resources in Polish society, may exist. If this is the case, unfolding Polish developments will provide rich opportunities to test the validity and stability of findings like those of Harari, Jones, and Sek. To put a still-contentious issue in perhaps over-simple terms, new forces may severely challenge a "collectivist-institutional orientation," if such a one has been prominent among Poles. Any such decline should be related, in principle, to increases in burnout.

Much the same point about the relevance of cultural profiles, if in more detail and with sharper definition, derives from a series of studies of tedium and coping strategies among Israelis and Americans in a variety of occupations. Tedium is defined as the "experience of physical, emotional and mental exhaustion" (Etzion, Pines, & Kafry, 1983, p. 42), and consequently shares much conceptual ground with burnout.

Overall, this line of research consistently finds lower levels of reported tedium among Israelis than Americans (e.g., Etzion & Pines, 1986; Pines, Aronson, & Kafry, 1981; Pines, Kafry, & Etzion, 1980), and the cultural interpretations deserve detailing for such findings as that conflict between life and work is significantly higher for an American sample of managers (Etzion, Kafry, & Pines, 1982). An Israeli research team places the templates of two cultural profiles over these results, as it were. To begin, Etzion and her associates (1982) suggest that strong social systems of family, friends, and neighbors help support Israelis in times of stress, whereas American culture emphasizes competition and individual achievement. Moreover, due to the volatile political climate, limited geographic mobility, and small size of their country, Israelis have a greater sense of social unity and mutual fate. The researchers also speculate that the greater conflict between life and work among the American sample may be due to the importance of work as a source of social contacts, which are more widely available in

Israel. This line of reasoning may be correct, but it remains more suggestive than established.

In addition, the Etzion team explains that tedium relates to different cross-national preferences about coping strategies. In a study of human service professionals (Etzion et al., 1983), all correlations for Americans between tedium and success of the active coping techniques are negative and significant. For the Israelis, success of an active coping strategy almost always is unrelated to tedium. Again, these tendencies may reflect culturally-determined values. Israelis apparently value active modes of coping for their own sake, while Americans value active techniques only when they prove successful.

Cross-National Research and Operational Measures

The numerous operational measures underlying Table I.2 constitute *the* major obstacle to the interpretation of the 1996 panel of studies, as has been alluded to at several points. Thus, most operational measures focus on *stressors*, as is true of the School Psychologists and Stress Inventory, or SPSI (Burden, 1988) as well as virtually all instruments focusing on teaching (e.g., Tokar & Feitler, 1986). In contrast, a few operational measures direct attention at the resultant *strain* (e.g., Etzion *et al.*, 1983; Maslach & Jackson, 1981a, 1986).

Overall, little is known about the conceptual and mensural overlap of these several operational definitions, whether within a nation or culture or between two or more of them. The single exception to this generalization is the Maslach Burnout Inventory, or MBI (Maslach & Jackson, 1981a, 1986), as discussion in later chapters will establish. The great and growing reliance on the MBI in cross-national research is a hopeful sign of convergence in the burnout literature.

This hardiness of the MBI justifies special confidence in the results generated by the many research designs using this operational measure. Perhaps the most substantial cross-national study using the MBI involved over 1,000 Norwegian and U.S. social workers drawn from randomly-selected samples (Himle, Jayaratne, & Thyness, 1986), and it isolates the typical covariants of the three MBI sub-domains—that is, emotional exhaustion, depersonalization, and reduced personal accomplishment. See also Chapter II. In both samples, for example, challenge of the job emerges as the most common and strongest predictor of all three MBI sub-domains of burnout, and the same is true for job satisfaction and turnover.

However, the same study also suggests some concerns about separately tracking the covariants of each of the three MBI sub-domains. Here, we can only sample some of the findings that pose interpretive problems. Value conflict is a significant predictor of depersonalization in the Norwegian sample, but is associated with lower job satisfaction and turnover in the American group. Relatedly, role conflict emerges as a significant predictor of emotional exhaustion and depersonalization among the Americans, but is associated with decreased job satisfaction for the Norwegians. And this list could be extended, easily and even interminably—for example, Maslach (1976) versus Himle et al. (1986).

Global Burnout seeks a way out of the interpretive *cul de sac* implied by such research. Thus, the observant reader of such research is left with several possibilities—for example, that nature is inherently unruly, or that differences in findings are due to changes in operational definitions. The present approach to testing for such interpretive possibilities involves a focus on a single operational definition of burnout in numerous worksettings.

This may give too much the benefit of a doubt to what follows but, in any case, these and similar interpretive dilemmas usefully frame the two main tasks of subsequent chapters. They describe the phase model's approach to considering simultaneously the three MBI sub-domains; and they test that model's approach in global settings as well as in North America. In effect, these chapters will help resolve these two interpretive ambiguities of existing reliance on the MBI, among other issues of concern.

In sum, such differences suggest either pervasive inter-nation or inter-cultural effects; or they may suggest limitations of the use of the separate MBI sub-domains. Both possibilities may apply at the same time, of course.

Similar concern with operational definition of burnout is infrequent, and, consequently, few comparisons of different operational definitions of burnout have been attempted. For example, Schaufeli and Van Dierendonck (1992) compare the MBI and the Burnout Measure (Pines & Aronson, 1988), which was originally represented as a measure of "tedium" (Pines, et al., 1981). These researchers find some overlap between the measures, but also differences that might be expected to generate diverse patterns of findings.

The present generalization about non-North American research on burnout seems so inescapable, and so crucial, as to merit deliberate underscoring. In the general absence of comparative work on operational definitions, summaries of burnout-related research have to be tentative even when results trend in the same direction. To be sure, the literature summarized above clearly has certain central tendencies, but far greater specificity about operational definitions is required. For example, studies reporting differences/similarities in covariants often rely on research designs using different operational definitions. These different measures complicate interpreting results, especially in those estimating "stress levels" in cross-national school settings (e.g., Burden, 1988; Manso-Pinto, Tokar & Feitler, 1986).

How to interpret those differences/similarities? One might argue that similarities in covariants reflect a burnout-related centroid in nature, if you will, that is pervasive enough to be isolated by even very different operational measures of "stress," "strain," or "burnout." But what of the differences within and between the covariants? They might result from differences in operational definitions, for example, *stressor*-based measures versus those tapping *strain*. No one can say, yet.

Interpretively, this constitutes a wash, and encourages a looseness of usage. Hence, the discussion above fudges in using labels such as "burnout-related" or "stress-related." That constitutes the best-available option for the total burnout literature, but clearly falls far short of the ideal.

No single volume can solve such crucial problems related to operational definition but, even at this early stage of development, the evidence provides real motivation to attempt some narrowing of the unknown and ambiguous. Even given diverse operational measures, in general, the higher the burnout, the worse the associated consequences. A relatively-consistent set of findings seems to be accumulating. This suggests that "burnout" is a major factor in our lives, and the accumulation of relatively-specific findings implies research has been moving along a useful path. This accumulation also urges and legitimates a determined as well as determinative effort to sharpen our insights via determined attention to operational definition.

Two Steps Forward, One Giant Step Remains

In a revealing sense, progress in global settings on the operational definition of burnout may be characterized fairly as two steps forward, and one giant step to go. As for the steps forward, their significance is great. Thus, the 1996 panel definitely shifts its focus toward "burnout," as opposed to the earlier emphasis on "stressors," "strain," or "stress." This has great promise, since one has a better chance of finding what one is looking for when the target is specific.

In addition, no doubt the greatest progress in operational definition in global settings will involve the Maslach Burnout Inventory, or MBI (Maslach & Jackson, 1982, 1986). Useful methodological work has been accumulated on its three sub-domains, and especially in Scandinavian and eastern European countries. This progress was sparked by the 1991 Conference on Burnout in Krakow, Poland, sponsored by the European Network of Organizational Psychology, and numerous reflections of it appear most prominently in an edited volume (Schaufeli, Maslach, & Marek, 1993). Chapter II provides details on the MBI's development.

As useful as these two steps in global research on burnout are, however, the work on operational definition remains severely limited. In sum, research generally supports the three sub-domains posited by the MBI and tapped by its items. But the subsequent use of the MBI sub-domains has been limited to separate tests for covariation with a range of variables: for example, creativity has been tested for non-random associations with each of the three MBI sub-domains—Depersonalization, Emotional Exhaustion, or Personal Accomplishment (e.g, Noworol, Zarczynski, Fafrowicz, & Marek, 1993). But that falls short of a test for the associations with creativity of the three combined MBI sub-domains.

Subsequent chapters will add detail about the limitations of such separatist research designs, but even at this point it should be clear that mixed findings are likely, if results are not seriously misleading. Bluntly, the three MBI sub-domains are proposed as components of a holistic psychological concept, and yet the three sub-domains are all-but-universally tested separately. That will not wash, commonsense suggests. For example, a holistic measure alone will permit clear estimates of burnout, and of its persistence; and that clarity is critical for informing individual and social judgments concerning what should be done to remedy matters, to whom it should be done, and when. Particularistic estimates will not do (e.g., Aström, Nelson, Norberg, Sandman, & Winblad, 1991).

Hence, this volume attempts to take the remaining giant step—defining a holistic phase model of burnout, and testing it in both North American and global settings.

But this puts *Global Burnout* ahead of its developmental curve, as it were. Two further generalizations about our 1996 panel have not yet been introduced; and they require attention.

Cross-National Research on Incidence and Persistence. A next-to-last generalization about the 1995 panel on burnout especially motivates an extension of the existing beachheads, and the point deserves reemphasis. Given the underlying unclarity about operational definitions, no one can make reasonable estimates of how many people experience which degrees of burnout. To be sure, a few studies have made this attempt (e.g., Sek-Yum, 1993), but these are normally difficult to interpret and usually relate to each of the three MBI subdomains, as contrasted with some total measure.

The estimate of incidence has a high priority for informing social and political policies, and hence the relevance of putting the phase model of burnout to a global test. That is, the North American literature suggests the usefulness of the phase model which, in turn, provides an estimate of the degree of burnout experienced by individuals. Simple calculations then permit ballpark estimates of how many people have which degrees of burnout in some unit—a society or an organization. See Chapter VI for details.

Relatedly, if we can estimate incidence, it is both a small step to get useful perspective on how long various degrees of burnout last. The global literature is particularly weak concerning persistence, which gets only rare attention (e.g., Capel, 1991). Here, again, North American experience with the phase model also is instructive. See especially Chapter VI, which adds substantially to the rare data on the persistence of phases of burnout. Clearly, the lack of longitudinal studies helps explain this serious inadequacy of the literature.

Critical Shortage of Ameliorative Applications

One final generalization from the 1996 panel seems justified, even if explanations of the condition must remain tentative. Burnout is widespread, if variously and often-loosely defined. Although the covariants associated with advanced burnout constitute a sad and even tragic litany, conscious amelioration has been infrequently attempted.

Why this gap exists remains problematic, but we cannot overestimate the criticality of its shortfall: much burnout, but little of the literature attempts to reduce advanced burnout, or to prevent it in the first instance. Other observers may come to a different count, but we see only two cases in the 1995 global studies' panel that can be considered ameliorative, even by generous count (i.e., Belfiore, 1994; Schaufeli, 1996). Of course, much burnout commentary gives advice and offers prescriptions about how to alleviate burnout, but we do not include such commentary as "rigorous research," however wise these prescriptive commentaries may be. Moreover, only one of those two non-North American studies makes any effort to rigorously compare treatment effects in a longitudinal research design.

In sum, the growth curve for amelioration is up in the 1995 panel of global burnout studies, but up only a tad, and that from a very low base. Compared to the 1990 sub-panel, *any* ameliorative studies during the 1990-1996 interval would constitute growth.

Chapter VIII returns to the point, and reviews the sparse ameliorative research on burnout. This sparseness is usefully speculated on here, as another way of motivating the reader to persevere through the bulky text which follows. Perhaps basically, lack of data about the incidence and persistence of burnout credibly help explain the lack of ameliorative research. *Global Burnout* will help fill those two crucial gaps, and especially in connection with incidence. This understates the matter, in fact. All readers of *Global Burnout* will leave it with a heightened sense of the magnitudes of burnout incidence and persistence. The estimates are that impressive, even mind-boggling.

In addition, almost all burnout research provides little leverage for amelioration. That is, leading roles in burnout research are played by those who focus basically on the individual, while this analysis presents a strong case that burnout has major roots in organization features—managerial practices, policies and procedures, cultures, and structures. This point applies on definite balance, even as it does not hold for all researchers at all points-in-time. For example, even early burnout prescriptions recommend organizational palliatives such as job rotation, which allows people to "warm-up" to the most stressful aspects of their work, and then cool-down from them. That is often good advice, but is quite limited and constitutes no news. After all, baseball umpires have followed a rotational regimen for as many decades as this group of authors can remember—and some of us are getting a bit of age on us. But the first possible explanation of underwhelming attention to amelioration nonetheless applies—quite broadly, and most of the time.

Perhaps even more directly, the global literature on burnout remains in the early stages of developing a case for the usefulness of interventions to reduce burnout because of a basic characteristic commented on more than once in this early discussion. Directly, the numerous measures of burnout reflected in the global literature inhibit or preclude cumulative estimates of incidence and persistence of burnout. Relatedly, the dominance of particularistic measures such as the three MBI sub-domains also provides no useful base for estimating how many people have which degree of the holistic "it" referred to as burnout, or how long people retain that status. In turn, no realistic sense of the relevance and urgency of ameliorative applications can be expected. A bit of internal advertising for *Global Burnout* is in order, then, and can claim a substantial reasonableness. As noted earlier, and as will be emphasized at several points later in this book, the phase model attempts a holistic estimate of burnout as a basic way of helping move beyond the lack of attempts to ameliorate burnout.

This message has been delivered before, we authors realize. So why risk redundancy? Our rationale is simple. Some things deserve being repeated because they are so useful, or so likely to be forgotten otherwise.

NEXT STEPS TOWARD GLOBAL BURNOUT?

So what to do now? And how to do it better, especially in connection with detailing the epidemiology of burnout?

These ten generalizations about research on global burnout at once encourage moving forward as well as guide that movement in important particulars. Overall, if with qualifications, the generalizations motivate the expansion of perspective from North American ——> global burnout; but those generalizations urge against just any old extension.

The motivating forces are direct. Thus, the increased attention to burnout in non-North American settings suggests that the target is a global disease, and this fact can powerfully leverage any developments in future research— whether positive or negative. In short, even large sunk investments can be justified by the possibility of world-wide applications. In addition, in general, the global burnout literature reflects the expected pattern of covariants—physical as well as emotional symptoms, negative reactions to work, and so on. Moreover, extensions of burnout methods and findings to arenas beyond work suggest the centrality of burnout in human affairs.

The preceding discussion also implies ways for sharpening the sense of mission-and-roles for *Global Burnout*. These approaches involve five challenges to measurement, as well as imply certain conventions for dealing with these challenges.

Five Challenges to Measurement

Directly, the discussion above informs and motivates a vigorous exploration of burnout, mostly in the sense of highlighting what is necessary but does not now exist for coming to a substantial understanding of some socially- and personally-critical issues. These issues include:

- Estimating how closely a person approaches "going around a corner?"
- What consequences are associated with different degrees of strain-ready-to-break?
- Why do such differences exist?
- Is burnout long-lasting or episodic? Or both?
- What can be done about reducing burnout?

As advertised, five elements get attention in this list of gaps-needing-filling. First, most of the early attention to burnout has been episodic and anecdotal, if at times compelling and even convincing. Studies of the latter kind have been made by specialists in organizational development and change (e.g., Mitchell, 1977), but the general *ad-hoc*-ness gets reflected in the diversity of operational definitions of burnout, which encompass a very broad and often unclear range of phenomena. With burnout meaning almost anything and everything to various observers, research and experience are, as Cherniss (1980b, p. 16) warns, not likely to mean much specifically when it comes to generating theoretical formulations of increasing power.

Fortunately, this book does not have to be the first explorer of unknown territory. It rests primarily on seminal developmental work on measurement (Maslach & Jackson, 1982), which we seek to extend in several ways. Newton wrote of standing on the shoulders of others as *the* prerequisite for seeing more in nature, and the observation definitely applies here.

Second, the early work on burnout has involved people in the helping professions. These include social workers (Barad, 1979), religiously-oriented samaritans (Collins, 1977), law-enforcement officials (Maslach & Jackson, 1979), lawyers in legal-services offices (Maslach & Jackson, 1978), day-care workers (Daley, 1979; Pines & Maslach, 1980), and organizational intervenors or change agents (Mitchell, 1977; Weisbord, 1978). A longer list could be developed easily.

This focus rests on a solid rationale, even though later analysis demonstrates that too much should not be made of the association between burnout and the people-serving professions. The overall evidence shows that burnout is where you find it; that is, everywhere, whether at high levels of organization or low, in various demographic aggregates, in this country and that, and so on. Nonetheless, we authors do not propose to neglect the solid— perhaps even the special—connection between the helping professions and burnout. As Maslach and Jackson explain (1981, p. 1), people in such professions "are often required to spend considerable time in intense involvement with [troubled people, and these exchanges commonly become] charged with feelings of anger, embarrassment, frustration, fear or despair." The resulting chronic tension and stress can be emotionally draining, which leaves the person "empty" and "burned out."

The association between burnout and helping professions also highlights a critical aspect of the disease, wherever it is found—the need for help from others to break out of the inward-and-downward-spiraling characteristic of burnout. For burnout seems to be accompanied by a curious myopia, perhaps even an incapacity. As Freudenberger (1977, p. 26) notes, those who suffer from it do not see "themselves as the angry, rigid, cynical and depressed human beings others are having difficulty working with." Rather, they find themselves "fatigued, depressed, irritable, bored and overworked," as well as contributing less, while often working longer and having to contend with a growing array and intensity of physical symptoms. Their strong and common tendency is to externalize their plight. As Freudenberger (1977, p. 26) concludes, they "often fail to see their situation as stemming from inside themselves. Instead, they find fault with everything and everyone around them, complaining about the organization and reacting cynically to whatever is suggested or attempted by others."

Third, the common view of burnout often suggests that it has an off/ on character: "I was burned out on this project yesterday, but I'm OK today."

Perhaps. However, this view is at least inelegant, and the evidence below supports the conclusion that most burnout does not seem to be a temporary condition. In any case, only rare attention has been given to what may be called "progressive burnout" and its persistence (e.g., Cherniss, 1989).

Global Burnout determinedly seeks to provide that attention, and for major reasons. With the hope of usefully reframing a central theme, to explain, the neglect of degrees of burnout and their perhaps-variable persistence disregards major theoretical and practical possibilities. For example, different phases of burnout might respond to different ameliorative efforts or designs. A successful focus on progressive burnout also might well encourage its prevention, or at least its remediation, because a valid and reliable measuring instrument would permit intervention before "things get too bad." We encourage the reader to test this capability of the phase model, as the evidence unfolds. But there should be no mistake about what *Global Burnout* seeks. The seeking of "hot spots" dominates in the motivation underlying the development of the phase model of burnout. And the metaphor of "going around the bend" or "snapping" implies the relevance of identifying individuals at early stages in their progression to full-scale burnout.

Fourth, the available literature—as Perlman and Hartman clearly show in their review article (1982)—is unequivocal only concerning the precursors of burnout. Bluntly, *anything* can be a precursor of burnout for *somebody* at *some time*. Indeed, as Maslach observes (1978a, p. 115), "What is most emotionally painful for one...person may not pose any special problems for the next." Consequently, one person's stressor at T_1 can be a positive motivator for another person, or even for the initial person at T_2. Concepts of burnout are typically nested in this prototypic model:

Among other advantages, this environmental view provides for the frequent occurrence and even universality of burnout, as well as its persistence. In this sense, the disease basically refers to an accumulation of stressors great enough to propel individuals beyond their comfortable coping limits, and thus powerful enough to create strain, the struggle against which uses great amounts of energy. The overall picture suggests a vicious, downward spiral. Managing strain absorbs energies that could go into everyday living, and any coping deficits worsen the strain, which in turn exhausts greater energies in bare maintenance. As the vernacular puts it: "It's hard to design a drainage system for the swamp when you're up to your hips in alligators." And perhaps harder still to contemplate the meaning of life, or to write poetry.

In a manner of speaking, burnout phases deal with the bottom-line of each specific individual's experienced balance of *eu-stress* over *dis-stress*, *whatever the ranges and magnitudes of stressors to which specific individuals are exposed, and whatever their coping skills.*

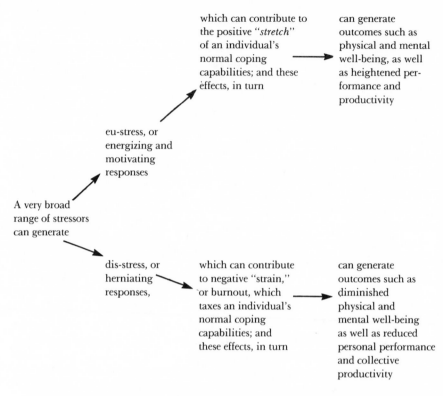

which can contribute to the positive *"stretch"* of an individual's normal coping capabilities; and these effects, in turn ⟶ can generate outcomes such as physical and mental well-being, as well as heightened performance and productivity

eu-stress, or energizing and motivating responses

A very broad range of stressors can generate

dis-stress, or herniating responses, ⟶ which can contribute to negative "strain," or burnout, which taxes an individual's normal coping capabilities; and these effects, in turn ⟶ can generate outcomes such as diminished physical and mental well-being as well as reduced personal performance and collective productivity

The criticality of the effort cannot be overstated. *If* one can develop a valid and reliable bottom-line measure, *then and only then* can one test whether certain classes of precursors are dominant in inducing or reinforcing such an effect. And those base-lines of incidence and persistence constitute the beginnings of wisdom on which an arsenal of remedial and especially preventive approaches can be built—an arsenal involving behaviors, attitudes, policies, practices, and so on.

Most research has approached the problem more or less the other way around, focusing on the precursors of burnout, or on the "personal psychological factors" (Fischer, 1983, p. 41) that may constitute a "sufficient cause" for specific events to trigger eu-stress, dis-stress, or no reaction in a specific person. In the conventional view, burnout derives from the *presence* of strain-inducing stressors that can overwhelm a person's coping capabilities. A second covey of observers shifts the focus to the *absence* of positive motivators—job features like autonomy, variety, and significance (Jayaratne, Tripodi & Chess, 1983), commitment, and moral purpose in work (Cherniss & Krants, 1983), or organizational support (Farber, 1983, pp. 242-243).

To put it baldly, the dominant focus has not been on the bottom-line measurement of burnout and, in the present view, this bias encourages a welter of conflicting findings. There once existed no way to make reasonable choices about burnout or its amelioration, especially given the reliance by various studies on different measures of burnout in different populations, and also given the focus on small panels of variables. In short, both "presence" and "absence" orientations suffer from the same basic ambiguities. Some of these ambiguities inhere in the variability of burnout precursors, from person to person; and some of them are exacerbated by idiosyncratic features of specific studies. In general, the main problem is that, using such a model, there is no end of possible precursors or features that can be associated with the phenomenon.

The present approach does not seek to finesse forever the study of precursors—absent or present—but it does assign them a distinctly-secondary priority. Rather, in *Global Burnout*, the first priority goes to isolating a single burnout measure that—if reliable and valid—will serve to accurately show the variation in stressors, in coping skills of individuals, and so on. The bulk of this book supports the view that this first priority has been met, and that substantial progress has been made on detailing a set of precursors and consequences.

Fifth, the available literature suggests a dreary catalog of *outcomes* associated with advancing burnout, but often is neither comprehensive nor specific enough in describing these outcomes. Particularly lacking are statements about organizationally-relevant outcomes *and* about their variation in relation to specific degrees of burnout. For the most part, this shortfall derives from two sources: the clinical or even anecdotal character of most of the available literature, and the tendency to adopt an on/off view of burnout.

Ample incentive exists for detailing such links between specific degrees of burnout and a varied range of organizationally relevant outcomes. Burnout has been associated with a broad range of noxious outcomes—for individuals and, by implication, for their employing organizations (Cherniss, 1980b; Freudenberger, 1980; Maslach, 1982a, 1982b). Detailing these implications, in ways that are clearly understandable as well as collectively consequential, remains a largely-unmet challenge that *Global Burnout* deals with. Hence, for example, the test below of the linkage of the phases of burnout with the use and costs of medical insurance.

An Environmental Model, Again

This volume, then, addresses the five preceding critical shortfalls. They constitute the major analytical targets and will be approached by the simple

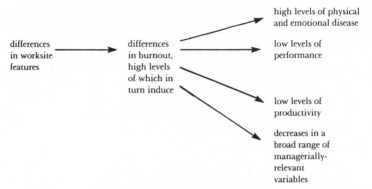

Figure I.1. Enviromental model underlying this research

environmental model in Figure I.1. The model provides for four classes of consequences, obviously, which are linked with differential burnout, as activated by differences in worksites. This environmental model is most satisfactorily tested in the next three chapters, but never completely.

The attraction of the environmental model lies not in its novelty but rather in its general acceptance (e.g., Harrison, 1981; Jayaratne, Tripodi & Chess, 1983). This study adds to this attraction: it tests the phase model of burnout at numerous worksites, worldwide. These provide a range of data, both in self-reports concerning many worksite features or physical and emotional health, as well as objective archival information about worksite descriptors as well as about performance appraisals, productivity, and turnover. This is conventional stuff, but too little explored in the burnout literature.

A long tradition of research on organizational behavior also suggests important linkages between features of the worksite with individual responses at work. This book takes guidance from the long line of research by a distinguished collection of students of human behavior—Likert, Argyris, and so on—who have highlighted how worksite structures and styles can have profound practical and moral consequences. As Harrison (1981, p. 43) expresses the core agreement of this tradition of research: "role strain and attitudes toward the work itself are near the core of the burnout problem."

Several Specific Guides for Global Burnout

How will these challenges be approached in *Global Burnout*? Right or wrong, this volume builds on seven fundaments. In outline, they urge that:

- The operational definition underlying assignments to phases of burnout has strong support in both North American and global settings.

- Research with a number of North American populations justifies a strong expectation that the phase model of burnout isolates a specific pattern of association with a large panel of covariants. As the phases advance I ——> VIII, simply, so also do conditions tend to worsen or deteriorate for individuals and their organizations
- This expected pattern will be illustrated, early on, and then used as the standard of judgment for a range of key questions. For example: Are measurement conventions different from those used in the phase model more suitable for analysis?
- The pattern of burnout findings also will be tested in a number of global worksettings. Some basis for optimism existed about such global extensions of the phase model, beyond the available North American literature, and this volume indicates that this initial optimism was not misplaced.
- The strategy is to keep as many things constant as possible for the purpose of reducing indeterminacies in interpreting observed effects. The things held "constant" include the basic operational definition of the phase model, the research design, and often the panel of covariants or marker variables tested for association with the phase model.

Overall, the desire to transcend the prototypic "boom and bust" cycle common in behavioral research has been a conscious one since the earliest work on the phase model, and persists. To describe that last and all-too-typical condition briefly, some research on Theme A creates excitement about some "positive findings." Soon, numerous variations in design and especially operational definitions are introduced, and the results soon scatter over a very broad range: some studies replicate the original "positive" findings, others isolate only random effects, and (sooner or later) studies will report "negative" effects. Then, "bust" replaces "boom."

This cyclicality should hardly surprise, but has predictable and even tragic consequence. Variations in results seem likely, given the propensity to innovate (indeed, proliferate) operational definitions. And this typically leaves observers with *the* question being left open, despite real industry: Are the "mixed" results due to the lawlessness of nature that defies our best efforts, or are they results of mere variations in operational definitions?

The point is a simple one but, time after time, the boom-and-bust cycle is repeated (e.g., Golembiewski, 1962; Miller & Friesen, 1984). Not here, however, if we can avoid it.

- The analytic methods will permit identifying micro-variations in observed effects, and these methods are thus "transparent." The times favor other methods of analysis—for example, LISREL routines—

which are said to be powerful but are summative and "opaque" concerning micro-effects.

Essentially, then, the focus in *Global Burnout* is not on causal linkages, but more elementally on the usefulness of the operational definition underlying the phase model. This is meant in the sense of putting elementals first, and keeping them there until they get substantially resolved. In short, research on burnout can be powerfully informed and directed by a valid and reliable operational definition. No agreement presently exists about a holistic burnout measure, and testing the applicability of the phase model in both global as well as North American settings will powerfully inform a judgment about whether or not the phase model fills the bill.

NOTES

1. The generalizations here usually follow the model in Golembiewski, Scherb, and Boudreau (1993, pp. 219-227), while they also add generalizations and much detail to that source.

2. The 1996 panel is *not* comprehensive. Separate surveys are underway in geographic and language arenas not tapped by this panel. For example, Maria Cseh is surveying native language publications in eastern Europe, primarily Hungary and Romania.

Chapter II

Essentials of Phase Model of Global Burnout: Three Sub-Domains—Here, There, Everywhere

Substantial progress has been made toward resolving the measurement challenges introduced in Chapter I, and the present mission is to detail the major senses in which this is the case. There are two basic geographic arenas from which supporting evidence will be drawn: North American worksites, and especially the United States; and several locations from the rest of the world, mainly eastern Europe and Asia.

The more-general reader may choose to skim some of this material, but in conscience that reader cannot be encouraged to merely jump to Chapter III. A full record must be established to serve as a solid foundation for interpreting numerous studies that provide proof supporting the phase model. So we urge the general reader to hang-in-there, as convenient as it would be to skip to later chapters. Chapter II provides a necessary foundation for all that follows.

By way of introduction, five emphases constitute the vitals of Chapter II. In order, attention gets directed at:

- three MBI sub-domains underlying the phase model of burnout;
- the validity and reliability of estimates of the three sub-domains, both in North America but especially in populations from other countries
- the features and usefulness of the phase model of burnout, which at once encompasses and transcends the three sub-domains while it also generates a range of advantages for measurement
- the phase model as countercultural in stress research; and
- evidence reinforcing the basic view of the phase model as environmental.

MASLACH BURNOUT INVENTORY, OR MBI

The phase model of burnout fundamentally rests on the early version of the Maslach Burnout Inventory (Maslach & Jackson, 1981). The original version of the MBI consists of 25 items, which tap three sub-domains:

> *Depersonalization*, high scores on which distinguish those who tend to view people as things or objects, and who tend to distance themselves from others;
> *Personal Accomplishment* (reversed), high scores on which identify respondents who see themselves as performing poorly on a task they evaluate as not being particularly worthwhile and which has negative influences on coworkers; and
> *Emotional Exhaustion*, high scores on which come from individuals who see themselves as operating beyond their comfortable coping limits, and as approaching "the end of the rope" in psychological and emotional senses.

Extensive factor analyses with a variety of public-sector and non-profit populations (Maslach & Jackson, 1981) assigned MBI items to the three sub-domains, and later analysis will test the adequacy of these assignments in several ways.

The MBI has been variously modified by its originators (e.g., Maslach & Jackson, 1986), but those changes will *not* concern us here. Our overall purpose is to keep as many things as equal as possible in exploring the phase model of burnout. Hence, the insistence on retaining the original MBI items in the construction of the phases of burnout. This is not common practice. Driven by creativity, or whatever, most behavioral scientists prefer to generate successive modifications of measures, and often entirely new ones. In the present view, this basically serves to complicate the interpretation of results. Mixed findings are likely (e.g., Miller & Friesen, 1984), and it typically is unclear whether this reflects nature's complexity or even chaos, or whether this is merely an effect of differences in operational definitions of the avowedly-same domain.

Whatever else, *that* problem will not trouble this research.

Upfront and Retained Modifications

The preceding paragraph is not exactly accurate in that, at the earliest stages of work with the phase model, two of the present co-authors made certain modifications in the MBI items were made. And, strictly speaking, these modifications of the original are maintained in the many pieces of research dealt with in the remainder of this book.

Three modifications deserve explicit attention. Thus, some propose that the MBI be restricted to people-helpers (e.g., Evans & Fischer, 1993; Friesen & Sarros, 1989) and, as noted, the phase model rejects this position.

Specifically, all MBI items are revised so that the term "clients" is replaced by terms that relate to fellow workers in all organizations.

Two other modifications of the MBI instrument also deserve special attention. Thus, while the original MBI items ask for two ratings on each item—one for frequency and one for intensity—our respondents get simpler instructions:

> III. Write a number in the blank to the left of each statement below, based on this scale: To what DEGREE is each of the statements LIKE or UNLIKE you?
> Very much 1   2   3   4   5   6   7   Very much
> UNLIKE me   LIKE me
> Enter one NUMBER in the blank to the LEFT of each statement. Make certain you use LOW numbers to describe statements which are *unlike* you and HIGH numbers to describe statements LIKE YOU.
> _____   148. I feel emotionally drained from my work.

In addition, we drop two items from the original MBI instrument, and also convert two EE items to DP, based on a detailed item analysis. Details are available elsewhere (e.g., Golembiewski & Munzenrider, 1988, esp. pp. 19-20). See also Appendix C.

Evidence about Modifications

Four strands of evidence suggest the serviceability of these three modifications, which distort neither Maslach's intent nor her findings. First, in a reanalysis of Maslach's data, Ahmavaara's technique (1954) estimates that the intensity and frequency factorial structures share about 96 percent of their variance, in both pattern *and* magnitude (Golembiewski, Munzenrider, & Carter, 1983). Indeed, the authors are not aware of even a single reference in the literature that does not lead to the same conclusion.

In sum, little or nothing is lost by the present convention of neglecting the intensity-versus-frequency distinction. Maslach herself no longer urges the intensity/frequency instructions, and her 1986 MBI uses 0-6 response stems tapping frequency.

Second, although the data are omitted here to conserve space (Golembiewski, Munzenrider, & Stevenson, 1986, p. 15), the *alpha* reliabilities for the three "modified" versus "original" MBI scores increase, on balance, after the two item deletions. The modified reliabilities are quite acceptable for present purposes: at Site B, they are .76, .72, and .86 for Depersonalization, Personal Accomplishment, and Emotional Exhaustion, respectively; and other applications of the MBI usually generate similar or higher coefficients, which are acceptable for research purposes. In addition, in the early modifications, any deletions or shifts in items in all cases but one item lower *alpha* reliabilities. Finally, the individual items correlate diversely with sub-domain scores. This implies a synergistic effect of each of the three batches of items, as distinct from a single collection of items. This feature discourages a simple addition of the three sub-domains or of the several items, as occasionally happens (e.g., Schaufeli, Keijsers, & Miranda, 1996).

Third, and consistent with the preceding point, a relatively clean factorial structure emerges when three factors are called for, as in Sites A and B whose labels indicate a North American worksetting. See Appendix A for details about all worksites in North America. Appendix B describes all global worksites, which are identified by country—as Japan A, Japan B, and so on. At Site B, for example, communalities (H^2) are high and reflect at a glance how much of an item's variance is included in the factor analysis. The lowest value is 18 percent, and many are much higher. This indicates the salience of the retained items to the three-factor construct of burnout.

Fourth, the three sub-domains have correlations that leave most of the variance unaccounted for. This reinforces the usefulness of the three components. Evidence from Site B in this regard is like evidence from other worksettings. One coefficient indicates that 31 percent of the variance is shared by one pair of the off-diagonal sub-domains, and the two other coefficients do not attain 9 percent (Golembiewski & Munzenrider, 1988, p. 22). This common pattern of intercorrelations suggests that the three sub-domains make relatively independent contributions to defining the content of "psychological burnout."

THREE-FACTOR STRUCTURE, GLOBALLY

A key issue associated with the MBI items—perhaps *the* key issue—involves the question of whether separate MBI administrations isolate the same dimensions in different settings. In sum, convincingly, the three-factor structure seems very durable in different settings. This conclusion is consistent with the four pieces of evidence just reviewed about the usefulness of the MBI sub-domains and, together, the findings provide powerful support for the present measuring conventions.

An Overview of Sub-Domain Congruence

No one can propose without qualification that the three MBI sub-domains apply globally, but the accumulating evidence definitely leans in that direction. Although the evidence varies in quality, the three-factor view of the MBI dominates. Thus, Kim establishes (1990, pp. 26-29) that virtually all investigations support the validity of a three-domain model of burnout, even when different methods of analysis are employed. Broadly, numerous studies of concurrent validity highlight the usefulness of the three MBI sub-domains, (e.g., Golembiewski, Munzenrider, & Stevenson, 1986; Golembiewski & Munzenrider, 1988), although a few propose that Depersonalization is dispensable (e.g., Gaines & Jermier, 1983). Both correlational and factor analytic approaches support a similar conclusion, on definite balance (e.g., Golembiewski & Munzenrider, 1988, pp. 22-23; Kim, 1990, pp. 77-103). In addition, most studies argue for a cosmopolitan application of the three MBI sub-domains—they are seen as appropriate across nations, as well as across professions (e.g., Himle, Jayaratne, & Thyness, 1989; Green, Walkey, & Taylor, 1991; Schaufeli & Janczur, 1994). To be sure, opposition voices exist, but they are in a definite minority (e.g., Firth, McIntee, McKeown, & Britton, 1985; Garden, 1985; Pedrabissi, Rolland, & Santinello, 1993).

Specific Tests for Sub-Domain Congruence

Detailed tests provide useful complement to this generalized view, with Ahmavaara's (1954) technique again permitting direct estimates of the specific patterns and magnitudes of congruence at pairs of worksites in two of the four tests detailed below. His technique rests on factor analysis of each population—here, specifically, Principal Factor Analysis followed by Varimax rotation. Ahmavaara's technique produces two measures of congruence of each pair of factorial structures:

- a product-moment coefficient, which estimates the congruence of "patterning" between any two factorial structures.
- An intraclass coefficient, which compares two structures not only with respect to "patterning" but also relative to "magnitude." The coefficient estimates the degree to which the loadings in one matrix are higher or lower than in the other, as well as assesses their similarity of profile.

In principle, Ahmavaara's technique distinguishes one matrix as "target" and the other as "problem," and differences in coefficients are possible. Analyses of all pairs here are run both ways, and only negligible differences exist in the coefficients generated for any pair. Below, typically, data are reported for only one of the two possible analyses. Estimates in this sub-section always consider Site B as the "target."

The present criterion of "similarity" is conservative: as noted, estimates of congruence in the .80s indicate "similar" structures, and the two Ahmavaara coefficients are best read, when squared, as estimates of the variance shared by two factorial structures. Note also that the basic inputs to Ahmavaara's procedure are correlation matrices from each of a pair of factorial analyses. Hence, the number of subjects does not directly enter into the interpretation of the two primary Ahmavaara outputs, but N always will be a factor in judging the stability of all factor analyses. Typically, these factor analyses involve 10 times as many subjects as MBI items, *at a minimum*. The subject-to-item ratio at a maximum approximates 50-100:1.

In effect, the four sub-sections immediately support the conclusion proposing the worldwide applicability of the three MBI sub-domains. Four separate lines of research enhance the clarity of our perspective on reliability and validity of the three MBI sub-domains.

Selected North American Populations

The initial focus goes to six North American populations—with Site B's factorial structure being paired and tested for congruence with five other worksites. They are:

- Maslach's original composite population, $N = 2,000$
- Site G, middle-level and senior Canadian managers, $N = 244$
- Site H, Canadian hospital employees excluding doctors, $N = 399$
- Site I, employees of midwestern U.S. division of a corporation of retirement communities, $N = 942$
- Site M, employees of a U.S. corporation of nursing homes, $N = 2,389$

Ahmavaara's coefficients reveal that MBI applications in these North American settings isolate very similar factorial structures, as Table II.1 reflects. In sum, the 5 pairs of factorial structures share about 85 percent of the variance, on average, considering both pattern and magnitude of the factorial structures.

Table II.1. Congruences of Selected North American Factorial Structures, Ahmavaara's Technique, with Site B ($N = 1,535$) as Target

	Intraclass Correlation Coefficient	Product-Moment Coefficient
Maslach's Original Population vs. Site B	.86	.86
Site G vs. Site B	.88	.88
Site H vs. Site B	.87	.88
Site I vs. Site B	.97	.97
Site M vs. Site B	.96	.96

This constitutes convincing evidence that in an array of North American populations the three MBI sub-domains are not artifacts of a specific locus. In sum, people in a range of settings seem to "see" the same conceptual dimensions in the MBI items. Patently, this implies the centrality in nature of the "something" measured by the MBI items as well as the usefulness of the present scoring conventions.

Similar Factorial Scores in Three Settings

A second line of research also supports our reliance on the three MBI sub-domains. Although it is impossible here to do anything but to illustrate the evidence, the factorial scores generated by MBI items typically seem similar. Consider one triangular example of this similarity involving Maslach's original population, Japan C, and Site B which hosted much early developmental work on the phase model. In preview, earlier discussion emphasizes the similarity between Maslach's population and Site B, among others. Table II.2 closes the loop, as it were, by demonstrating the similarity of factorial scores in the two other comparisons in our focal trio.

Clearly, the factor scores in these comparisons leave little room for unexplained variance. Admittedly and unavoidably, the exemplars are narrowly selective. But the findings do not appear to be atypical (e.g., Munzenrider, 1986), and many other triangulation exercises would generate results similar to those just outlined.

Table II.2.   Correlations Between MBI
Factorial Scores in Three Populations

	Maslach Original Population		
	Depersonalization	*Personal Accomplishment*	*Emotional Exhaustion*
I. Japan C vs. Maslach Original			
Japan C			
Depersonalization	0.91	-0.33	0.26
Personal Accomplishment		0.94	-0.25
Emotional Exhaustion			1.00
II. Japan C vs. Site B			
Japan C			
Depersonalization	.95	-.28	.13
Personal Accomplishment		.93	-.34
Emotional Exhaustion			1.00

Congruence of MBI Sub-Domains In A Global Panel

A third line of research definitely raises the ante. In effect, the relevance of the three MBI sub-domains is tested in a significant way, if again a limited one. In sum, the relevant North American results in Table II.1 seem to closely parallel findings in other national settings. Several individual studies support this conclusion (e.g., Schaufeli & Van Dierendonck, 1992), but here the focus will be on 8 national samples, including six from global worksettings. Respondents in the latter cases were given the MBI items as translated by social scientists with appropriate first-languages. Translations did not pose great problems, but some adjustments were required. For example, the Japanese and Mandarin languages contain no direct equivalent for the usage "being at the end of one's rope," which is part of an MBI item. In the Mandarin version, for example, the replacement became "Shanqiong-Shuin—where the mountains and rivers end." Consequently, although "translate, then retranslate" expressed the ideal, that was beyond our (or anyone's) reach on a few items.

On clear balance, the several cross-national comparisons below suggest that respondents to the MBI items "see" substantially the same dimensional universe despite the underlying differences between national loci, work settings, organizational cultures, and macro-cultures. Here analysis compares data from six countries, with Ahmavaara's coefficients again providing the basic guidance for estimating the congruence between pairs of factorial structures.

Table II.3 provides useful, if far-from-comprehensive, perspective on the cross-national congruence of responses to the MBI items. In that table, the intraclass correlation coefficients approximate .74, on average, including the several obvious outliers associated with Korea. This falls below the .80 standard which experts propose for indicating similar factorial structures. However, the coefficients involving Korea probably reflect the fact that the number of respondents ($N = 60$) is too small to support stable factorial results. Here, the ratio of cases-to-items is only a bit larger than 2-to-1. In any case, eliminating the Korean coefficients raises the mean beyond .8.

Two technical details complete this review. Thus, the product moment correlations are quite similar and, although they are not reproduced in Table II.3, they require only trivial qualifications of the results summarized above. Moreover, which of the pair of factorial structures is "problem" and which is "target" can effect the coefficients generated by Ahmavaara's technique, but those effects are minuscule in the present case. To conserve space, the results of these problem —> target switches are not reproduced here.

Table II.3. Congruence of Selected Cross-National MBI Factorial Structures, Ahmavaara Technique, Intraclass Correlation Coefficients Only

Population in Target Space	Population in Problem Space						
	Site B (N = 1535)	Site H (N = 399)	China A (N = 196)	Japan A (N = 914)	Japan C (N = 352)	Korea A (N = 61)	Poland A (N = 181)
Site H	.88						
China A	.83	.71					
Japan A	.84	.81	.67				
Japan C	.81	NA	NA	NA			
Korea A	.70	.65	.53	.66	NA		
Poland A	.90	.83	.76	.80	NA	.49	
Yugoslavia A (N = 100)	.79	.80	.71	.73	NA	.52	.72

47

MBI Sub-Domains in European Settings. Reinforcing the evidence about the centrality of the MBI sub-domains reflected in Table II.3, other approaches also imply that these dimensions are generic rather than culturally- or nationally-specific. The best evidence comes from Europe, and can be summarized with safety. Using methods that differ from the approach underlying Table II.3, the evidence nonetheless supports the same conclusion: the three MBI sub-domains seem to be isolated by virtually all studies (e.g., Schaufeli, Maslach, & Marek, 1993, pp. 179-180, 207-211, 217-236). Although not all researchers agree (e.g, Evans & Fischer, 1993), the evidence nonetheless reinforces Table II.3 and the associated discussion.

PHASE MODEL OF BURNOUT

Given such an apparently-solid foundation in the three MBI sub-domains, as modified, this analysis seeks to extend and improve upon the two usual ways of relying on the MBI sub-domains. Early on, Maslach and her many followers basically were in a bivariate mode: they sought to assess the associations of each of the three sub-domains, separately, with a range of personal as well as (if to a far-lesser degree) organizational variables. This approach still dominates. Indeed, only a few studies even calculate a total MBI score (e.g., Golembiewski & Munzenrider, 1981; Schaufeli, Keijsers, & Miranda, 1996), let alone test for covariants of such a measure.

More recently, the three sub-domains have been entered into various multivariate data-processing schemes (e.g., as provided by LISREL). Researchers hope to get vital information about the three sub-domains—for example, about alternative sequences in possible causal linkages (e.g., Burke, 1989; Leiter, 1988; Wolpin, Burke, & Greenglass, 1990). See also Chapter VII.

Research with the phase model of burnout takes an approach that is both holistic and transparent to the observer. In effect, this tradition—now well over a decade old—makes a trinitarian use of the original MBI items, as modified for present purposes.

Specifics about this compound usage follow. Basically, the phase model attributes-for-testing a specific order of both sequence and virulence to the three MBI sub-domains—in turn, Depersonalization, Personal Accomplishment, and Emotional Exhaustion. Beyond that, the phase model utilizes norms from Site B to distinguish High from Low scores on each sub-domain, and then defines the phases in burnout in terms of the 8 possible High/Low combinations of these scores on the three sub-domains.

Details of these phase assignments will be presented soon, but note here a preliminary caution. Just as easily, and perhaps more accurately, the "phases" could have been called "degrees" or "levels." Indeed, perhaps the phase model should have been labeled differently.

But that die has been cast. All of the labels can be seen as imperfect when viewed critically; and no terminology will completely prevent confusion. The only defense against misunderstanding here is, rather, a conceptual one. The phases measure what the following discussion describes—nothing more, nothing less—despite the various connotations associated with terms such as "phases," "degrees," or "levels."

Virulence and Potencies of MBI Sub-Domains

Essentially, the phase model both posits and then assesses the relative potencies of the three proposed contributors to burnout. This section seeks to be clear about that assumption, as a prelude to the detailed testing that preoccupies the chapters to follow.

A straightforward rationale underlies the assumed potencies of the three MBI sub-domains in what may be called an *idealized chronic progression.* Broadly, Depersonalization is seen as the earliest and least-potent contributor to burnout. In general, Emotional Exhaustion is the most potent contributor, and Personal Accomplishment is intermediate. Later analysis will provide much detail about a second progression—*acute onset.*

The relative potencies of the three MBI sub-domains in chronic onset derive from several sources, with years of organization-watching providing most of the inspiration for such a view. Consider upwardly-mobile persons, and especially those in an autocratic organization, as one way of gaining perspective on the present view that depersonalization represents the most-common and least-virulent initiator of progressive burnout. Early organizational progress for such persons often will be defined largely in rational-technical terms, which can encourage depersonalization. We refer here not only, or even mostly, to getting-ahead by "stepping on others." Indeed, some degree of "objectivity" or "detached concern" (Lief & Fox, 1963) seems necessary or at least useful for effective performance in many occupations and professions. Beyond some undefined point, however, depersonalization can undercut personal accomplishment. Perhaps the prototypic case involves the depersonalizing salesperson promoted to manager. In episodic contacts with "sales targets," certain attitudes and behaviors of salespersons may be useful or at least not troublesome—a focus on people that is narrow and instrumental, "snow job" skills that reflect little regard for the interests of potential "marks," a certain elasticity with regard to facts, and so on.

This line of conceptual development can be extended easily, consistent with theory and especially experience. In a managerial job, such depersonalizing features often undermine systems and human performance. To illustrate, a deepening depersonalization may deprive a manager of needed information, and this shortfall may result in poor decision making. Poorer performance may result, reasonably, and this can result in strain surpassing an individual's normal coping limits. In turn, both can induce the energy deficit encompassed by the notion of emotional exhaustion.

The hypothetical sequencing of the three MBI sub-domains as contributors to escalating burnout in chronic onset can also be illustrated by reference to two other critical sorts of situations: when the individual at work experiences too heavy a load, or is otherwise overstimulated; and when the individual faces an environment containing too little stimulation and challenge (Cherniss, 1980b, p. 45). In both cases, the individual may feel a loss of autonomy and control, which reasonably can threaten or diminish his or her self-image. At early stages, individuals may actively seek a constructive way out, but persistence of the condition may eventually encourage treating other people as objects. That is to say, one begins to treat others as one is being treated. The resulting depersonalization could then cycle in ways that diminish one's sense of personal accomplishment, and this eventually can lead to growing emotional exhaustion.

A summary may help here. Relying on the MBI sub-domains, one can easily see how job stress and strain often result in counter-productive coping by individuals. Depersonalization suggests a failure to develop the appropriate levels of detached concern (Lief & Fox, 1963) useful or even necessary in many work settings. Detached concern seeks a precarious balance: being accessible to others and being concerned about them, but in ways that permit one to employ the required objectivity and skill in situations that might otherwise immobilize. That this balance is often not realized gets convincing support from the many awkward approaches to inducing some degrees of distance between self and other—for example, as between a service-supplier and clients. Counterproductive approaches include "negative labeling" (Maslach, 1978a, pp. 57-58), as when professionals see clients as unworthy or inferior (Wills, 1978, pp. 958-959), and this encourages "blaming the victim" (Ryan, 1971).

Maslach (1978b, p. 113) proposes that a sad and self-defeating chain-of-effects in human-service organizations often results from such losses of concern for clients: "...clients are viewed as somehow deserving of their problems and are often blamed for their victimization. Consequently, there appears to be a deterioration in the quality of care or service that they receive." From the care-providers' perspective, "this failure to cope can be manifested in a number of ways, including low morale, impaired performance, absenteeism, and high turnover." The wording would have to be changed a bit for jobs not in the people-helping category, but much the same point applies broadly at work as well as to all of life.

These simplified dynamics can be integrated in a mini-theoretical network. Literally, persons so poised cannot win for losing. Excerpts from Freudenberger (1974, pp. 160-162) emphasize a heightened tendency to reach angry flash-points generated by growing irritation and frustration, and exacerbated by personal rigidity and stubbornness, which the person experiencing burnout tends to see as something imposed by external forces. Freudenberger adds that people in such a state often become "...the house cynic" [who] blocks progress and constructive change...because change means another adaptation [for which they are] just too tired...." Longer hours often are spent at work, but less gets accomplished. Freudenberger (1977, p. 27) sketches a tragic maladaptation: the affected person desperately needs support and caring but, often because of intensified preoccupation with work and lengthening hours, tends to withdraw from others. In sum, greater effort and diminishing returns come to dominate. This going-nowhereness often follows a period of hectic effort, in a broad range of settings in life—at work, in one's family, and so on.

Norms for High and Low

If this conceptual way of viewing the dynamics of the three MBI sub-domains makes sense, *the* operating problem becomes the development of economical and valid ways of differentiating "a little" from "a lot." As a first step, the phase model of burnout distinguishes High from Low scores on each of the three MBI sub-domains. Operationally, the medians for the three sets of raw MBI scores at Site B provide the empirically-grounded estimates of High versus Low. These became the "universal norms" (Golembiewski, Munzenrider, & Stevenson, 1986, pp. 24-25)—18, 26, and 23, for Depersonalization, Personal Accomplishment (reversed), and Emotional Exhaustion, respectively. To put it another way, while dismissing the risk of being perceived as fussy:[1]

- a High score on Depersonalization is 19 or larger on the MBI items; 18 or lower is a Low score
- a High score on Personal Accomplishment (Reversed) is 27 or greater; 26 or less is a Low score
- a High score on Emotional Exhaustion is 24 or more; 23 or less is a Low score

Those universal norms underlay most of the analyses that follow, though they may be invisible to even conscientious readers. We emphasize the point because researchers are not always clear about cutting-points when employing their variations of the phase model. This suggests the view that the cutting-points are arbitrary and of no consequences; but this is wrong-headed. Readers will be alerted on those occasions when the text employs alternatives to the universal norms, usually for the purpose of testing relative usefulness.

The opposite view here is that such norms are consequential and even critical. Hence, we again repeat the point: the cutting-points for the universal norms are set at 18, 26, and 23 for Depersonalization, Personal Accomplishment (Reversed), and Emotional Exhaustion, respectively.

Why deliberately adopt these limiting conventions about universal norms? Basically, *the* purpose in research with the phase model is to provide direct comparisons of many replicative studies, pejoratively labeled "convenience populations," based on the practical fact that many small-scale replications will be required to legitimate later funding of key studies of large and rigorously-selected populations whose findings could claim direct generalizability. In addition, *as long as the universal norms work,* they permit consistent estimates of who has which degree of burnout. If the universal norms clearly fail in replications, then it will be necessary to go back into the data sets to construct alternative sets of norms.

Until now, these "local norms" have not received major attention because the universal norms tended "to work," both in North America as well as abroad. However, it was not a pure case of out of sight, out of mind. The present researchers did keep their eyes on one variety of "local norms"— the medians for each convenience population studied—and we also published some comparisons between the local and universal norms (e.g., Golembiewski, Sun, Lin, & Boudreau, 1995). But more of this later, as in Chapter VII.

In a few words, as this book will show, the first-cut reliance on universal norms has "worked" beyond all early expectations, not only in North American populations but also in a growing number of populations from worldwide locations.

This unexpected finding provides solace for the initial choice of universal norms, of course, which had to swim against strong conceptual currents. Schaufeli and Van Dierendonck (1995, p. 1088) well express those countercurrents related to nationality as well as to clinical diagnosis. They urge caution "when using cut-off points for the classification of burnout levels." Indeed, they note, it "does not make sense to use cut-off points in one country to classify subjects in another country." Schaufeli and Van Dierendonck conclude:[2]

And, it does not make sense to use cut-off points that are obtained for a "normal" working sample to classify subjects as clinically "burned out." Yet, by using clinically derived, nation-specific cut-off points we can learn more about the incidence of burnout in working populations. Moreover, cross-national research on burnout can clarify this construct and at the same time provide greater insight into the relationship between cultural norms and stress.

Schaufeli and Van Dierendonck take a reasonable position, and especially for those who assume dominant cultural effects, but that position does not clearly relate to the phase model. Thus, the phase model deliberately seeks to test the universality of what these two researchers reject—the general applicability of one burnout measure and its effects, and only subsequent analysis will establish whether or not that "makes sense." Moreover, "nations" are certainly not homogeneous, and huge proportions of the variance between people in different loci are inexplicable in terms of such gross social categories (e.g., Pinker, 1994). In any case, we emphasize research use of the phases, rather than individual diagnosis,[3] with the focus on whether or not the progressive phases isolate a consistent pattern of similarities/differences in covariants, both in North American as well as in global worksettings. Paramountly, the phase model is viewed in an environmental context. Hence, when applications of the model are made to ameliorate burnout, the focus is on intact workgroups rather than individuals. Primarily, the phase model views burnout as environmental rather than as individual-rooted (e.g., Golembiewski, 1990). See also Chapters VII and VIII.

The key issue for the present authors/researchers, then, always was whether or not replications involving many convenience populations, *relying on the universal norms*, would generate similar patterns of covariants. The results of those replications would be determinative, and those results fill this volume. So, the present authors always felt that we would see whether the assumptions built into the phase model were basically workable. No *final* estimate of workability will ever be possible, but now is a good time for an interim assessment. Lacking the *key* study of a global population chosen randomly, we nonetheless have a substantial number of convenience populations whose cumulative findings seem revealing to us. Conveniently, also, if the universal norms prove insufficient, analyses always can be re-run to test the usefulness of alternative norms.

Assignments of Individuals to Burnout Phases

Given the universal norms, a simple decision rule generates an 8-phase model of burnout. That is, Emotional Exhaustion is considered most characteristic of advanced phases of burnout, and Depersonalization is considered least virulent. Each person is assigned a High or Low status on the three MBI sub-domains and, in turn, those three assignments permit determining one's phase of burnout based on this simple model:

	Progressive Phases of Burnout							
	I	II	III	IV	V	VI	VII	VIII
Depersonalization	Lo	Hi	Lo	Hi	Lo	Hi	Lo	Hi
Personal Accomplishment (Reversed)	Lo	Lo	Hi	Hi	Lo	Lo	Hi	Hi
Emotional Exhaustion	Lo	Lo	Lo	Lo	Hi	Hi	Hi	Hi

In sum, phases are expected to have different covariants even though their total MBI scores are similar. For example, Phases II, III, and V will have similar MBI total scores, since each has one High and two Low statuses on the three MBI sub-domains, each of which is estimated by responses to approximately the same number of items. Phases IV, VI, and VII also have similar total scores. Detailed analysis of Site B assignments establishes that the scoring conventions generate subpopulations that meet such expectations, all-but-universally (Golembiewski & Munzenrider, 1988, esp. p. 28).

Note also, finally, that on a few occasions a set of collapsed phases is utilized. These distinguish: Low Burnout (Phases I, II, and III); Moderate Burnout (Phases IV and V); and High Burnout (Phases VI, VII, and VIII). Typically, the collapsed version is utilized for populations with a small N, or for those populations in which one or more phases contain few or no assignees.

Reliabilities of Sub-Domains and Phases

So what do we have? Are the three MBI sub-domains, and the phases of burnout built upon them, reliable? Perspective on early evidence about this central methodological feature comes from five observations at Site K over a seven-week interval (Golembiewski, Deckard, & Rountree, 1987). Changes in N mostly reflect availability of individuals at testing times rather than turnover or refusal to participate. Chapter VI provides further details, but a summary will do here. Note the summarized results probably provide a conservative estimate of test-retest reliability, since measurement error as well as "real change" are involved, and also because Phase IV and V (as later evidence will show) seem transitional.

In any case, the reliability over time of MBI scores can be estimated by the correlations between scores on each of the three MBI sub-domains at five points in time. The coefficients average .58, .55, and .72 for Depersonalization, Personal Accomplishment, and Emotional Exhaustion, respectively. These coefficients imply that several scores share 33, 31, and 52 percent of their variance, respectively, for Depersonalization, Personal Accomplishment, and Emotional Exhaustion.

However one evaluates these MBI sub-domain scores over time, the estimates above are no doubt conservative. Recall that sub-domain scores are used only to make High vs. Low assignments, and this implies a substantial margin for measurement error that would not exist if direct covariants of the raw scores were the basic target for analysis.

As for the phases, their congruence at the five points in time also can be estimated. Knowing the initial phase assignment of an individual is powerful in predicting subsequent assignments. On average, compared to chance, the *gamma* statistic (Mueller et al., 1970, pp. 279-292) implies that knowledge of a person's initial assignment reduces one's error in predicting subsequent assignments by about 55 percent. Significantly, also, *gamma* seems to vary little between comparisons of proximate vs. distal administrations. Thus, the four most-proximate observations (T_1 vs. T_2, T^2 vs. T_3, and so on) have a *gamma* $\overline{X} = .5423$, while the four most-distant observations average .5395. See also Chapter VI.

Although no one can say for sure, such estimates suggest a substantial stability of phase assignments over time. No doubt, for example, some natural change in phases can be expected over even a 7-week observational period. For present purposes, such "natural change" would be reckoned as unreliability.

While suggestive, however, estimates of stability for both sub-domains and phases alike are *not* the central concern. That status is reserved for covariants of the phases; and this discussion is almost ready for the relevant tests of that central concern, but not quite yet.

Two other features of the phase model require introductory attention. In turn, the sub-sections below: introduce the trinitarian concept of change which the phase model seeks to illuminate; and develop the sense of mode of onset of burnout which was hinted at earlier but still requires some detailing.

Apparent Advantages of the Phase Model

In effect, several potential advantages of the phase model already seem clear. Basically, the phase model promises a way to measure burnout in large aggregates, while also classifying all individuals in terms of the virulence of their particular cases. The phases also highlight three specific contributors to a person's particular level of burnout, and this permits targeting ameliorative interventions, *if* the phases are valid and reliable. For example, a person assigned High on Depersonalization would not obviously be a prime candidate for the same intervention as the individual with advanced emotional exhaustion. Although the total MBI scores of two individuals are similar or even identical, their phase assignments often will differ.

Although it will not be until Chapter VII that all the pieces can be brought together, the phase model has several other advantageous features, and perhaps primarily those associated with the several varieties of what have been labeled the trinitarian concepts of change (e.g., Golembiewski, 1992). Merely to mention the point here in passing, the phases seem to constitute a surrogate for *gamma change*—that is, transformational change. Gamma is distinct from alpha (or incremental) change.

This apparent surrogacy for gamma constitutes a major conceptual bonus for the phase model, although the available developmental work still requires careful caveats. But more of this, much more, in Chapter VIII. Here, note only that the phase model requires logically at least one point of transforming change or difference—that is, the point, or zone, at which "some degree" of burnout becomes "too much." Conveniently, to rely on the general vocabulary introduced in Chapter I, that location may be thought of as indicating where "snapping" or "going around the corner" become reasonably-probable concerns. The ability to estimate which individuals are at such a point, or fall in such a zone, has profound practical and theoretic significance. Ditto for the question of what proportion of individuals in any population do so. That is clear even at this early point. Progress via the phase model toward making such an estimate will receive summary attention later, especially in Chapter VI.

Phases and Modes of Onset

To shift conceptual gears, also note what the phase model *does not propose to do*. It neither proposes nor requires that individual cases of full-term burnout progress in order through each of the eight phases. Indeed, this would be psychologically awkward or impossible. For example, the movement from Phase II to III obviously requires some improbable psychological contortions. Hence, this analysis seeks only to test whether the phases are progressively virulent, whenever and however they occur.

Relatedly, the phase model permits a convenient distinction between the modes of onset, relying on common medical usages. *Chronic burnout* reflects a kind of water torture mode of onset, which can be characterized as I —> II —> IV —> VIII. Descriptively, in this variant of onset, the individual moves to *High* on Depersonalization, then to *High* on Depersonalization as well as on Personal Accomplishment (Reversed), and finally adds to that High pair another *High* on Emotional Exhaustion.

A family of *acute* flight-paths also are proposed. For example, pathway I —> V —> VIII describes one reaction to the sudden loss of a mate, which precipitously swamps the individual's coping skills/attitudes, thereby creating a substantial emotional deficit (V). Short of quick recovery, one can easily imagine cases in which a person assigned to V might be motivated to withdraw from others (VI). Or, an initial I might experience this pathway: I —> V —> VII, where a mourner seeks to lose self in work but performs poorly. In both cases, an VIII assignment might follow if the coping proves ineffective. Or a VI or a VII might recover, but most likely in different ways. Numerous other acute flightpaths can be distinguished (e.g., Golembiewski & Munzenrider, 1988, esp. pp. 176-177), but the details need not detain us here.

TEST OF PHASE MODEL AS ENVIRONMENTAL

Switching to a more macro-view, let us complete this primer on phase model elementals with a basic contrast. Evidence in subsequent chapters often will test the sense of the phase model as environmentally rooted, in contrast to putting the onus on the individual. The latter interpretation dominates in much burnout commentary—sometimes explicitly, but usually implicitly.

What can be said of the phase model as "environmental." Here, we provide early evidence that the phase model is reasonably rooted in worksite features that influence burnout variations which, in turn, induce consequences relevant to individuals and organizations. The present illustration focuses on one test of a model whose proposed outcome variable is a construct labeled Emotional Agitation. In sum, this model is proposed for testing (Deckard, Rountree, & Golembiewski, 1988):

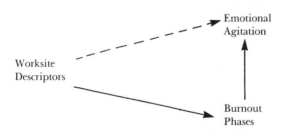

Solid lines indicate the anticipated "direct causal path" between the worksite descriptors, the burnout phases, and Emotional Agitation. The broken line indicates a supplementary linkage.

Some measurement details are necessary. Three scales from the Index of Organizational Reactions (or IOR)—Amount of Work, Kind of Work, and Financial Rewards—detail worksite descriptors commonly seen as major stressors at work (Rountree & Deckard, 1983). These three scales are added to form a composite measure of work stress. "Agitation" derives from a factor analysis (Zuckerman, Lubin, & Rinck, 1984) involving the 132 words on the Multiple Affect Adjective Check List (Zuckerman & Lubin, 1965). High scores on Agitation characterize individuals who express strong agreement that words like the following characterize "how you felt in recent days": annoyed, irritated, agitated, impatient, angry, discouraged, and disagreeable.

Two rounds of testing provide support for the present operational definition of burnout. First, as the discussion above requires, Emotional Agitation increases as the phases progress from I to VIII, with the association at Site L being substantial but hardly perfect. Specifically, one-way analysis of variance finds nonrandom variance somewhere in the distribution of Agitation scores arrayed by phases ($P < .001$). But far more powerful evidence also exists about the direction as well as magnitude of the differences. Specifically, 85.8 percent of the paired-comparisons are in the expected direction, and 25 percent of those comparisons achieve $P < .05$ by the Least Significant Difference test, as modified for unequal sub-sample sizes. That is, persons assigned to Phase I report less Agitation than those in Phase II; assignees to Phase II report being better off than those in III, and so on.

Second, path analysis also confirms the pattern of relationships consistent with an environmental model of burnout. Worksite descriptors seem to dominate on the predicted direct path. Specifically, the present descriptors correlate .51 with the burnout phases (r_{12}), which accounts for 26 percent of the variance. The other two correlations (r_{13} and r_{23}) both are .27, and hence each accounts for about 7.3 percent of the variance. Moreover, as the predicted pathway for an environmental model of burnout requires, the two path-proofs correspond quite closely to the two other correlations (r_{13} and r_{23}). The path-proof for work descriptors and Agitation sums to .273, as compared to the .274 correlation between the two. For burnout and Agitation, the figures are .271 and .273, respectively.

This adds a bit of support to the environmental model on which *Global Burnout* rests. More will follow in subsequent chapters.

PHASES AS COUNTERCULTURAL

This progressive testing is of especial moment because, even at this early stage of analysis, it should be patent that the phase model runs counter to most current research fashions in the stress-related literatures. Here, we elaborate this central point. Exhibit II.1 begins this compound task by summarizing the dominant fashions associated with research on stress-related phenomena, and this outline can rest on detailed developments of the several characterizations (e.g., Golembiewski & Munzenrider, 1988; Newton, 1995). The label "stress-related" in Exhibit II.1 seeks a deliberate flexibility. It encompasses pre-stress formulations (e.g., Cannon, 1932) as well as the explicit stress formulations (e.g., Selye, 1946, 1976), and also encompasses those related to burnout.

Exhibit II.1. Summary of Leading Ideas in Stress-Related Literature

- usually rooted in the physiological and intrapsychic reactions of individuals, both in what may be called the pre-stress literature (e.g., Cannon, 1932), in work explicitly targeting stress-related phenomena (e.g., Selye, 1976), as well as in much of the early burnout research.
- often conceived as an inescapable cost of modern living—as in Selye's (1946) General Adaptation Syndrome—that the adaptive responses well-suited to the early stages of human development have become increasingly maladaptive and damaging to individuals. Especially in its more extreme formulations, this view can trivialize or even normalize high and increasing levels of stress, or can even encourage blaming the victim as an inadequate coper
- typically reflect little or no sense of collective contributions of employees or the employing organization to stress-formulation, its modes of expression, or its remediation, despite compelling but infrequent research to the contrary (e.g., Hochschild, 1983; Katz & Kahn, 1966, Pollert, 1981).
- consequently, or at least consistently, stress concepts feature awkward pairings or shortfalls:
  - isolated individual employees and management. The common practical reality—and perhaps the intent (Newton, 1995, esp. 121)—is that management remain the sovereign stakeholder. However, multiple stakeholders—for example, unions, professional associations, and governments—can play countervailing roles.
  - broad social policies about work and family may be relevant, if not crucial, in stress reactions
  - some designs for structuring work may contribute to strain by heightening boredom and reducing a sense of mastery or control
  - multiple stakeholders can play—for example, unions, professional associations, and government—in countervailing roles between employees and management
- in concept, the work itself—its structure as well as governing policies and procedures—tends not to be conceptually integrated with either the production or amelioration of stressors and strain. This reflects the prevailing balance of power at the worksite, as well as the relative value placed on management's vs. labor's experiencings of stressors. In the common view, the character of the worksite is given, essentially, and employees do the reacting and adapting.
  Consequently, the onus typically falls on the individual employee, who at best is armored or vaccinated by cognitive or skill inputs to better identify and cope with stressors, as via the stress management workshops usually attended by people who are and typically remain "strangers." This contrasts with members of intact work teams.
- this completes the cycle of sanitation or depolitization of stress-related phenomena, and with profound consequences—in Newton's formulation (1995, p. 87), the common ideation reduces the "...organizational issues affecting the collective to a question of individual differences in stress appraisal and coping ability [and] implying that both individual and the organization outcomes of stress are self-evidently pathological and thus in need of treatment rather than elimination in ways that might reduce the stress-potential of the worksite."

A major reason for focusing on burnout is both direct and consequential: the phase model is not only informed by the leading ideas in Exhibit II.1 but often seeks to extend, moderate, or even reject them. Using burnout phases as the guiding concept, then, can help skim the cream from the stress literature while minimizing its limited as well as limiting aspects.

In sum, the leading ideas in Exhibit II.1 are nuanced, if that is the appropriate term. Thus, they in effect attempt to finesse rather than take into explicit account various environmental differences, including shifts in the balance of labor/management power or differences in the subjective experiences of worksites by (for example) labor and management or by the two genders.

This basic nuanced simplicism does not surprise, since "the organization" usually has been considered the given to which individuals must adapt. This was true in the Hawthorne studies, the early Human Relations movement, and so on, for reasons that are not obscure (e.g., Baritz, 1960). In effect, Exhibit II.1 reflects one preferred political distribution of power—or perhaps better said, a conceptual depolitization that intends a kind of forfeit-by-definition. In sum, the individual is seen as the basic problem to be fixed in Exhibit II.1.

Global Burnout takes a different track than the traditional view abstracted in Exhibit II.1. Thus, basically, the phase model is rooted in the analysis of experienced subjectivities and inquires whether generalizations apply, in North America as well as worldwide. Indeed, they do apply, as later chapters will show, and with a regularity and magnitude that will surprise, if not startle.

How can we reconcile the prominence of these generalizations about burnout and its covariants worldwide, given that culturally-relative ideation provides such a powerful predisposition to expect major differences by countries? We authors believe, and much evidence suggests, that the experienced subjectivities of burnout and of their consequences are similar in most global worksettings, because work is similarly designed in most places, with common consequences, on definite balance. It also follows, then, that doing something fundamental about burnout in the context of the phase model will require basic environmental changes—that is, changes in organizational and social structures, policies, and procedures. In a few words, the phase model sees the burned-out individual as reacting rationally to an environment that poorly serves human needs. Here, the primary focus of attention is on which common structures, policies, and procedures need fixing.

Specifically, the findings associated with the phase model in *Global Burnout* in major particulars poorly fit the leading ideas in Exhibit II.1. In order of their development in the text, the major differences include these:

- As earlier analysis of the MBI sub-domains of burnout has shown, worldwide, respondents tend to structure their subjective experiences of burnout in very similar ways. This implies a collective and social-psychological sense of burnout. In opposition, Exhibit II.1 attributes an individual and physiologic bias to the traditional stress-related literature.

- As Chapter III will show, worldwide, numerous marker variables strongly tend to map on the phases of burnout in regular and robust ways. Broadly, these marker variables describe employee responses to worksettings—to their styles and underlying managerial policies, procedures, and structures. This implies tendencies that are both trans-subjective as well as trans-cultural, even as they encompass the possibility that differences in worksite features as well as broad cultures can result in different distributions of phases. In brief, in contrast to Exhibit II.1, work $<\longrightarrow>$ burnout.

- Chapter IV establishes that the phases I $\longrightarrow$ VIII usually are associated with degrading health conditions and potentialities. This ties burnout into the heart of the classic stress-related literature, and also implies work $<\longrightarrow>$ burnout associations.

- In Chapter V, various system costs of burnout will be detailed, with an emphasis on North American settings but including several global settings. These system costs relate to: performance appraisal; productivity measures; turnover; and the use of medical insurance.

- As Chapter VI details, the burnout phases have a substantial incidence and persistence. Incidence estimates are high for both North American and global settings, overall, despite some real differences in magnitude that can be attributed to such features as micro-organization cultures as well as broad cultures of societies or nations. However, persistence estimates are restricted to U.S. settings. No other operational measure of burnout provides similar estimates, as critical as they are for management and public policy.

  In multiple senses, the data about incidence and persistence highlight the poverty of Exhibit II.1, which conclusion is reinforced by the catalog of dour covariants associated with the phases I $\longrightarrow$ VIII. In the context of this virulence, incidence, and persistence, Exhibit II.1 can be said to be both cavalier as well as puny.

- Chapter VII deals with several key issues in phase research that remain open. Of special relevance are several emphases at odds with Exhibit II.1 They include: the inadequacy of an individual level of analysis; the relevance of gender in the phase model; and approaches to ameliorating burnout that focus on changes in worksites as well as changes in the values, attitudes, and skills of individuals.

- Chapter VIII concludes *Global Burnout* with a review of a number of generalizations drawn from research on the phase model. These generalizations cover a broad range but, on balance, focus on change as well as the theory of change, as they relate to the burnout phases.

NOTES

1. One can never be too careful! For example, the earlier *Phases of Burnout* (Golembiewski & Munzenrider 1988, p. 28) contains a central typographical error despite multiple readers.

2. Reproduced with permission of authors and publisher from: W.B. Schaufeli, & D. Van Dierendonck. A cautionary note about the cross-national and clinical validity of cut-off points for the Maslach Burnout Inventory. *Psychological Reports*, 1995, 76, 1083-1090. © *Psychological Reports* 1995.

3. Even where applications of the phase model occur, the clearly-articulated view of this team of researchers is that reductions in high concentrations of persons assigned to advanced phases is primarily a matter of environmental change rather than of changes in individual attitudes or skills (Golembiewski & Munzenrider, 1988, esp. pp. 218-243; Golembiewski, 1990, esp. pp. 155-175).

Chapter III

Worksite Descriptors and the Phase Model: Mapping Patterns in North America, and Worldwide

Judging from the clinical literature on burnout, its covariants include a broad and noxious range, personal as well as organizational (Cherniss, 1980b; Freudenberger, 1980; Maslach, 1982a, 1982b). Consequently, the quality of workinglife should contribute to the level of burnout and, in a feedback way, the character of the worksite also will no doubt be adversely affected by persons in advanced phases of burnout.

This again highlights the essential motivator of *Global Management*. To put the point briefly, even tersely: we will never be able to determine the validity of any generalizations, nor estimate the magnitudes of their effects, unless we have a meaningful measure of burnout.

The phase model proposes such a bottom-line measure of burnout, and accumulating evidence permits a substantial test of its efficacy. Anecdotally, several investigators report results "remarkably similar to [the phase] model" (Gryskiewicz & Buttner, 1994, p. 751). Hence, this critical synthesis of the phase approach.

How to begin? The section below identifies a set of features commonly used to assess the quality of a worksite, and also predicts the pattern of associations of these variables with the phases of burnout. Once that is done, tests at numerous worksites will assess whether the apparent covariants in fact "map" on the phases in the expected ways.[1] Site B will get immediate attention, in effect testing the phase model in a North American population. In addition, a summary table will augment the detailed analysis of Site B, by way of reinforcing its results by tests of the usefulness of the phase model in other North American settings using a large panel of variables.

Later, we again test these North American findings, this time from a global perspective. Several worldwide studies will be reviewed in similar ways, again highlighted by a summary table of findings.

This approach to assessing concurrent validity has a simple purpose. If the selected variables vary regularly and expectedly, phase by phase, this will support the present approach to identifying progressive phases of burnout. If that does not occur regularly, this will be the correct time to start again in defining an operational measure of burnout different than the phase model.

NOTES ON METHODS AND METHODOLOGY

This choice of a basic research design is not arbitrary, but neither is it ideal. In the long run, rigorous analytic methods and advanced conceptual/operational definitions will contribute to ever-more comprehensive theoretical development, but that balance-point has not yet been achieved. Hence, the following introductory comments, which sketch the general case and then add methods-specific details.

Methodological Specificity

Our basic case is direct. Given operational definitions of unestablished validity and reliability, to simplify a bit, we propose that the more rigorous one's analytic methods, the worse. Put directly, rigorous methods in the given case can lead only to firmly-held but probably-invalid and unreliable conclusions.

The implied message for today's research on burnout should be clear enough. Today, the onus should be on the quality of operational definitions, rather than on how elegantly the resulting data are manipulated. Problems going into analysis, in short, will generate imponderables coming out of analysis. Daft's (1984) vocabulary may help characterize this approach. In short, the research story on the phase model of burnout begins with an "organic approach." As this story unfolds, the "mechanistic" side of the story will be emphasized.

Hence the present emphasis on ANOVA and then on the non-randomness of all possible paired-comparisons for each marker variable that achieves $P \leq .05$, overall, when arrayed by the phases. The Least Significant Difference test, or LSD, as modified for unequal sub-sample sizes, is the choice for these paired-comparisons, although the Scheffé test under many conditions may provide the "tougher" test.

The goal is what might be called "high analytic visibility." Specifically, do the eight phases of burnout isolate significant differences on a large panel of marker variables? And if so, which (if any) of the phases have greater (or lesser) discrimination? The reason for high analytic visibility is patent. In essence, *Global Burnout* seeks to test the validity and reliability of one operational definition of burnout, and to do so in overt and even obvious ways. The virtue of replicative consistency is often overlooked in bursts of real or feigned creativity but, flatly, that neglect typically implies waste-work that does not help build empirical theory. Absent a valid and reliable operational definition, analysts are doomed to trying to accomplish the analytic equivalent of hitting moving targets. This obvious point has received periodic attention (e.g., Golembiewski, 1962; Miller & Friesen, 1984), but the bulk of attention in empirical research has focused on the caboose of findings rather than on the engine of operational definition. Commonly, the results vary in succeeding studies of putatively the same concepts, given great...ah...flexibility in underlying operational definitions. This variability often is attributed to the recalcitrance or non-lawful character of the relationships in reality, although the simpler explanation is that different operational definitions just cannot be expected to generate consistent findings.

Terse Specifics about Methods

A few words usefully elaborate on how the chosen analytic methods will contribute to the goal of high analytic visibility. As for the rationale supporting ANOVA and LSD, they not only help establish overall non-random variance but they also permit assessing the ability of marker variables to track on specific pairs of phases in the expected ways. Simply, this permits highlighting the details of the usefulness of the phase model.

Other powerful analytic technologies do not provide such visibility, for various reasons. Here, we are suggestive rather than exhaustive, considering only LISREL. Its routines make significant demands on data-sets that typical data-sets cannot meet. Moreover, those routines cannot improve on the quality of the operational definitions fed into them for analysis. This is another case of X in, X out. Here, the X refers to measurement garbage, to orthogonal dimensions of reality, and everything in-between.

ORGANIZATIONAL COVARIANTS AT NORTH AMERICAN SITES

The key initial test of the phase model took place at Site B—which is described in Appendix A—and analysis focuses on 16 variables. All based on self-reports, these variables selectively profile the worksites of respondents from a large federal agency in several particulars thought to be relevant by most observers. These variables are discussed here briefly, along with expectations about their likely relationships with burnout.

Marker Variables at Site B

The panel of "marker variables" includes two classes. One class consists of *Assorted Scales*, of which all but one should decrease as burnout progresses Phases I —> VIII. Inverse associations should be expected for five variables:

- Trust in supervision (Roberts & O'Reilly, 1974)
- Trust in fellow employees (*ad hoc*)
- Job involvement (White & Ruh, 1973)
- Willingness to disagree with supervisor (Patchen, 1965)
- Participation in decisions re work (White & Ruh, 1973)

An additional scale should show an increase as phases of burnout advance. Job Tension (Kahn et al., 1964) should increase, Phases I —> VIII. The rationales for the two sets of expectations are transparent.

The marker variables at Site B also include the *Job Diagnostic Survey*, or *JDS*. Among other uses, its scales estimate satisfaction with ten facets of work (Hackman & Oldham, 1980), all of which should decrease as burnout progresses. The scales deal with:

- Meaningfulness of work
- Responsibility for results
- Knowledge of results
- General satisfaction
- Internal work motivation
- Growth
- Job security
- Compensation
- Coworkers
- Supervision

Solid theoretical reasons support both the selection of these 10 marker variables, as well as our expectations concerning their variation with the phases. Hackman and Oldham (1980) provide substantial and convincing justification for the worksite relevance of JDS, and no great prescience is required to establish their inverse linkages with advancing phases.

The mini-networks of theory underlying the Assorted Scales are similarly obvious. Consider here only Job Tension, which taps several important classes of stressors—for example, those related to role ambiguity and conflict—that should impact on the burnout phases, and quite directly. Significant moderators of this direct relationship have been isolated (e.g., French & Caplan, 1973), but these are not measured at Site B and remain obvious subjects for fine-tuning this kind of analysis, if the phase model proves generally serviceable.

Table III.1.   Covariation of Phases of Burnout and Marker Variables Via One-Way Analysis of Variance, Site B

| | Progressive Phases of Burnout | | | | | | | | | |
	I LoLoLo N =352	*II* HiLoLo 107	*III* LoHiLo 193	*IV* HiHiLo 124	*V* LoLoHi 107	*VI* HiLoHi 176	*VII* LoHiHi 109	*VIII* HiHiHi 367	*F-* *Ratio*	*F-* *Probability*
Marker Variables										
Participation	17.8	16.3	15.2	14.9	16.2	14.9	13.5	13.0	46.793	<.001
Job Involvement	34.7	32.9	31.8	29.7	30.9	29.8	25.4	24.7	72.227	<.001
Trust in supervision	15.9	14.4	15.1	13.1	14.6	12.7	12.2	12.2	23.196	<.001
Trust in employees	19.6	17.7	17.6	17.0	17.4	16.1	15.0	14.7	32.726	<.001
Willingness to disagree with supervisor	14.6	15.6	13.7	14.6	16.4	15.3	15.0	14.9	2.996	<.01
Job tension	17.0	19.1	18.2	19.9	21.0	22.2	22.0	23.1	49.240	<.001
Job Diagnostic Survey (JDS) Scales										
Meaningfulness of work	23.0	21.2	20.9	19.4	20.1	19.5	17.7	16.4	64.940	<.001
Responsibility for results	36.4	33.6	33.9	32.1	33.6	31.9	30.2	29.1	51.462	<.001
Knowledge of results	23.0	21.5	21.9	10.4	21.2	19.8	10.3	18.9	32.840	<.001
General satisfaction	28.4	26.4	26.0	24.2	23.1	22.2	19.9	19.2	97.183	<.001
Internal work motivation	35.7	33.7	33.2	31.9	34.4	32.9	31.1	29.9	37.987	<.001
Growth satisfaction	23.1	21.5	20.7	19.3	20.0	18.6	16.4	15.5	73.738	<.001
Satisfaction with security	10.9	10.5	10.6	10.3	9.7	9.2	9.2	8.6	21.085	<.001
Satisfaction with compensation	10.4	10.1	10.2	8.7	8.7	8.4	8.6	8.2	18.987	<.001
Satisfaction with coworkers	18.3	17.5	17.1	15.9	17.6	16.0	15.5	13.9	76.314	<.001
Satisfaction with supervision	17.1	15.7	15.9	14.1	14.7	13.5	12.5	12.2	38.385	<.001

Notes: * Degrees of freedom = 7, 1537.

Source: From Robert T. Golembiewski and Robert F. Munzenrider, *Phases of Burnout: Developments in Concepts and Applications*, reprinted with permission of Greenwood Publishing Group, Inc., Westport, CT. Copyright (c) 1988, p. 35.

67

Overall, that is, we expect that the phases will isolate robust patterns of association with marker variables like the present set, *if the phases constitute a reliable and valid operational definition.* Although various moderating variables may influence such patterns, they are not expected to distort or camouflage them—but *if and only if* the phase model is useful. If that usefulness cannot be established, it will be necessary to abandon the phase model and to move on.

Covariation at Site B

Five points contribute to the conclusion that at Site B a regular and robust pattern of association links burnout with the 16 worksite descriptors. See Table III.1 for the original data. First, note that all the possible covariants have acceptable measurement properties. Thus, Cronbach (1951) *alphas* for the variables average .79, and in only two cases fall below .70—specifically, .68 and .69. These *alphas* are acceptable for research purposes.

Second, for each of the 16 variables arrayed by the phases, all cases contain nonrandom variance, as determined by one-way analysis of variance. All observed trends are in the expected directions: that is, Job Tension increases, phase by phase, and all other variables decrease. In short, all organization features "map" appropriately on the phases of burnout.

Third, the paired-comparisons of variables X phases support expectations impressively—indeed, massively. See especially Table III.2, along with its summary in Table III.4, row 2. To summarize, phase by phase, analysis of all possible paired-comparisons indicates that over 90 percent of all the 448 differences fall in the expected directions; over 55 percent of all differences attain statistical significance; and only 2 differences of 448 are in an unexpected direction as well as statistically significant (0.5 percent).

In sum, Table III.2 is definitely not overburdened by deviant cases.

Eta^2 permits quite a precise estimate of the variance accounted for by phases X worksite descriptors: 17.1 percent, on average.

Fourth, the data suggest that almost all of the phases discretely map significant as well as regular differences on the target variables. The record for significant paired-comparisons suggests the point, of course, and focusing on the "distance" between phases documents the same point in greater detail. Table III.2 details all possible paired-comparisons, and the aggressive reader can verify that even the proximate pairs of phases meet expectations about marker variables X phases. This implies a substantial sensitivity of the phase model, of course. Thus, Phases I vs. II, II vs. III, and so on are "1;" Phases I vs. III and II vs. IV illustrate "2;" and so on. The usefulness of the full 8-phase model will be supported by large proportions of expected and statistically significant differences, more or less

Table III.2.   Statistical Significance of Paired-Comparisons of Burnout Phases X Marker Variables, Site B

	I vs II	I vs III	I vs IV	I vs V	I vs VI	I vs VII	I vs VIII	II vs III	II vs IV	II vs V	II vs VI	II vs VII	II vs VIII	III vs IV
Assorted scales														
Participation	X	X	X	X	X	X	X				X	X		
Job involvement		X	X	X	X	X	X	X			X	X	X	
Trust in supervisor			X		X	X	X					X	X	X
Trust in employees	X	X	X	X	X	X	X					X	X	
Willingness to disagree with supervisor														
Job tension	X		X	X	X	X	X				X	X	X	
Job Diagnostic Survey (JDS) scale														
Meaningfulness of work	X	X	X	X	X	X	X				X	X	X	
Responsibility for results	X	X	X	X	X	X	X					X	X	
Knowledge of results	X	X	X	X	X	X	X					X	X	X
General satisfaction	X	X	X	X	X	X	X			X	X	X	X	
Internal work motivation	X	X	X		X	X	X					X	X	
Growth satisfaction		X	X	X	X	X	X	X			X	X	X	
Satisfaction with security				X	X	X	X			X	X	X		
Satisfaction with compensation			X	X	X	X	X	X	X	X	X	X	X	X
Satisfaction with coworkers	X	X	X		X	X	X	X		X	X	X	X	X
Satisfaction with supervision			X	X	X	X	X			X	X	X	X	X

	III vs V	III vs VI	III vs VII	III vs VIII	IV vs V	IV vs VI	IV vs VII	IV vs VIII	V vs VI	V vs VII	V vs VIII	VI vs VII	VI vs VIII	VII vs VIII
Assorted scales														
Participation		X	X					X		X	X	X	X	X
Job involvement		X	X				X	X	X	X	X	X		
Trust in supervisor		X	X	X					X	X	X			
Trust in employees		X	X			X	X		X	X			X	
Willingness to disagree with supervisor	X													
Job tension	X	X	X	X		X	X	X				X		
Job Diagnostic Survey (JDS) scale														
Meaningfulness of work		X	X	X				X			X	X	X	X
Responsibility for results		X	X	X				X			X	X	X	X
Knowledge of results		X	X	X				X				X		X
General satisfaction	X	X	X	X		X	X	X			X	X	X	X
Internal work motivation		X	X					X		X	X		X	
Growth satisfaction		X	X	X			X	X			X	X	X	X

(continued)

Table III.2. *(Continued)*

Satisfaction with security		X	X	X	X		X		X	
Satisfaction with compensation	X	X	X	X						
Satisfaction with coworkers		X	X	X	X		X	X	X	X	X X
Satisfaction with supervision		X	X	X			X		X	X	

Note: X indicates a paired-comparison of differences on a variable that attains or surpasses the .05 level, based on the Least Significant Difference test, as modified for unequal size of subpopulation.

Source: From Golembiewski and Munzenrider (1988, pp. 36-37). Reprinted with permission of Greenwood Publishing Group, Inc., Westport, CT.

evenly distributed among the seven possible distances. In contrast, if small distances show "low" proportions of paired-comparisons that are statistically significant as well as fall in the expected direction, the phase model will have less to recommend it.

The data for several sites appear in Chapter VIII and, overall, they demonstrate that neighborly as well as remote phases tend to map discrete segments of the ranges of all target variables. At Site B, this conclusion holds most clearly for the five most distant pairs of phases (3 to 7)—where over 76 percent of all paired-differences fall in the expected direction as well as attain statistical significance. Moreover, even distances 2 and 1 generate 41 and 20 percent records, respectively, of significant differences in mapping the marker variables on paired-comparisons.

Fifth, the 16 target variables do not merely measure the same domain in multiple ways. A factor analysis (Varimax rotation), not reproduced here to conserve space, implies three major domains (Golembiewski & Munzenrider, 1988, p. 40). One factor accounts for 45 percent of the common variance on the initial statistics, to which the other two factors add some 16 percent. Twelve of the 16 worksite descriptors have loadings on the first factor greater than .3. The second factor seems distinguished by its focus on supervisors versus peers, as well as by security versus job contributors to satisfaction. And the third factor suggests an emphasis on satisfaction with a good-paying job paired with a willingness to raise contentious issues with supervisors.

This factor analysis supports the concurrent validity of the phase model at Site B. In general, the phases should covary indirectly with the three factor scores, although the conceptual case is least clear for Factor III. And so they do, as Table III.3 shows. One-way ANOVA indicates significant variation in all three factor scores, with over 76 percent of the paired-comparisons being in the expected direction, and with nearly 40 percent of them attaining statistical significance. Three of 84 cases falling in an opposite direction also achieve the .05 level, which approximates 4 percent.

Table III.3. Summary Data on Factor Scores X Phases, Site B

Factor Labels	F-Ratio	F-Probability	Pairs in Expected Direction	In Expected Direction and Statistically Significant	Pairs in Contrary Direction	In Contrary Direction and Statistically Significant
I. High Energy, Positive Job Features	79.5	<.0000	96.4%	71.4%	3.6%	0%
II. High Trust, Tension-Avoiding	25.0	<.0000	92.9%	42.9%	7.1%	0%
III. Active, Disagree with Supervisor	3.7	<.0005	39.3%	3.6%	61.7%	10.7%
Totals			76.2%	39.3%	23.8%	3.6%

Source: From Golembiewski and Munzenrider (1988, p. 41). Reprinted with permission of Greenwood Publishing Group, Inc., Westport, CT.

In addition, as Table III.3 also details, the pattern of covariation of phases X worksite descriptors at Site B is more robust for the first two factors than for the third. For Factor III, to illustrate, only 39 percent of the paired-comparisons fall in the expected direction and less than 4 percent attain P < .05. In contrast, for the first two factors, those proportions achieve formidably-larger proportions which approximate 95 and 62 percent, respectively. Again, for the first two factors, none of the 5.4 percent of the comparisons falling in an opposite direction attains statistical significance. Given the more solid measurement status of the first two factors, these results are expected and add to the consistency of the pattern of covariants of the phases.

North American Studies

A substantial number of worksites have been studied with research designs similar to that detailed for Site B, and with similar results. Table III.4 conveniently summarizes the degrees to which the phase model maps in expected ways on a substantial panel of marker variables, phase by progressive phase.

Note that Appendix A provides information about the North American worksites referred to in Table III.4. Appendix B describes global work settings. These two appendices are unevenly detailed. Brief attention goes to those sites that receive only limited attention in the text—for example, concerning the distribution of the phases of burnout in some specific work setting. Detailed attention in Appendix A or B goes to those cases on which this book relies heavily.

Now, back on the track of applications of the phase model of burnout in

North American work settings. Table III.4 does not exhaust all possible worksites, but it does summarize a sizeable collection of North American studies of the work-related covariants of the phase model of burnout. Moreover, just as Table III.5 does not exhaust North American studies, neither does it appear to misrepresent them. For example, Chapter IV presents data from a number of worksettings, both in North America and elsewhere, related to health-related covariants of the phases. And Chapter V adds to the list of covariants by focusing on various systemic features—performance, productivity, and costs such as those associated with the use of medical insurance.

The results do not require hedged conclusions. Considering the variables summarized in Table III.4, nearly 93 percent, achieve statistical significance and fall in the expected direction. Note also that, on average, well over 80 percent of all paired-comparisons fall in the expected direction. Consistently, excepting only Site VVb, no less than 16.4 percent of the paired-comparisons achieve $P \leq .05$ as well as fall in the expected direction, with most studies falling in the 30-60 percent range. Random forces alone can be expected to generate only 5 percent of such cases. Relevantly, also, the pattern seems *least* robust for the measures most open to methodological questions: See Sites VV a and b, as well as JJJ. In the latter case, single-item covariants isolate the least-impressive pattern, which is consistent with the greater heterogeneity reasonably associated with such variables.

In short, the data suggest a strong and expected pattern of covariation with the phases, both in the case of Site B as well as in summaries of 13 other North American work settings. Both public and business organizations are represented and, although tentativeness is appropriate, no major differences trouble our interpretation.

Table III.4. Selective Summary, Worksite Descriptors X Phases, North American Studies

Sites	Operational Definitions of Worksite Variables	Researchers	Status of † Marker Variables	Summary, Paired-Comparisons, Marker Variables X Phases, in %			
				In Expected Direction	In Expected Direction and Statistically Significant	In Contrary Direction	In Contrary Direction and Statistically Significant
1. Site A	6 original marker variables; 10 Job Descriptive Index scales; and 6 from Job Description Scale	Golembiewski, Munzenrider, & Carter (1983)	19/20 significant in expected direction, $P \leq .05$; 2 variables expected to vary randomly due to local conditions. eta^2 = .134.	84.8%	16.4%	15.2%	1.0%
2. Site B	6 original marker variables; 10 Job Descriptive Index scales	Golembiewski, Munzenrider, & Stevenson (1988)	16/16 significant in expected direction, $P < .01$	90.2	55.1	9.4	0.5
3. Site L	5 scales from Index of Organizational Reactions (IOR); 3 scales from Work-Related Psychological Sense of Community (PSC)	Deckard & Rountree (1985)	8/8 significant in expected direction, $P < .000$.	84.3 (IOR) 78.6 (PSC)	51.4 (IOR) 29.8 (PSC)	15.7 (IOR) 21.4 (PSC)	1.2 (IOR) 1.4 (PSC)

Note: † On all tables, P value refers to the highest probability observed

(continued)

Table III.4. (Continued)

Sites	Operational Definitions of Worksite Variables	Researchers	Status of † Marker Variables	Summary, Paired-Comparisons, Marker Variables X Phases, in %			
				In Expected Direction	In Expected Direction and Statistically Significant	In Contrary Direction	In Contrary Direction and Statistically Significant
4. Site K	10 scales from Work Environment Scale, and 8 from Index of Organizational Reactions	Rountree (1984); Golembiewski & Rountree (1986)	17/18 significant in expected direction, $P < .000$; 1/18 in expected, direction, $P = .04$. About 11.7 percent of variance is explained, on average.	81.5%	58.9	18.5	8.9
5. Site NN	14 scales relating to work setting; work outcomes; emotional and physical well-being	Burke & Greenglass (1989)	12/14 significant in expected direction, $P < .01$.	81.1%	26.0	18.9	NA
6. Site OO	Job Involvement, Self-Esteem, and GHQ	Aldinger (1993)	3/3 significant in expected direction, $P < .0000$; eta^2 approximates .13.	88.1%	67.9	11.9	0.24

(continued)

74

Table III.4. (Continued)

Site	Measures	Citation	Results				
7. Site SS	13 scales dealing with: role issues; somatic distress; and facets of satisfaction	Kilpatrick, Magnetti, & Mirvis (1991)	12/13 significant in expected direction, $P < .0000$; on average, about 17 percent of the variance is explained.	83.2%	43.6	16.8	1.1
8. Site VV	a. supervisory rating of performance	Bower (1994); Golembiewski, Bower, & Kim (1993)	0/1 significant in expected direction, $P = .466$.	57.1%	0.0	42.9	0.0
	b. three measures of family functioning	Golembiewski, Bower, & Kim (1993)	0/3 significant in expected direction, $P = .11$, .11, and .23.	88.2%	0.0	11.8	0.0
9. Site AAA Time 1	12 scales: Participation; Job Involvement; 4 work facets; 5 satisfaction facets	Munzenrider (1995)	11/12 significant in expected direction, $P < .05$; on average, about 15 percent of the variance is explained. Only Satisfaction with Compensation is NS.	81.3%	34.3	18.7	0.0
10. Site AAA, Time 2		Munzenrider, Aiegenfuss, & Lartin-Drake (1996).	11/12 significant in exxpected direction, $P < .0115$; 16 percent of variance is explained	79.5	20.8	20.5	0.0

(continued)

Table III.4. (Continued)

| | | | | | Summary, Paired-Comparisons, Marker Variables X Phases, in % | | |
| | | | | | | | |
Sites	Operational Definitions of Worksite Variables	Researchers	Status of † Marker Variables	In Expected Direction	In Expected Direction and Statistically Significant	In Contrary Direction	In Contrary Direction and Statistically Significant
11. Site AAA, Time 3	Munzenrider, Ziegenfuss, & Lartin-Drake (1996).		11/12 significant in expected direction, P < .0063; on average about 18 percent of variance is explained	77.4	25.0	23.6	0.0
12. Site JJJ	8 scales and and 6 single items. Scales include leadership credibility; change motivation; meaningfulness of work; and feeback adequacy. Single-items tap: autonomy; job satisfaction; etc.	Gabris Ihrke (1995b)	14/14 significant in expected direction, P < .04	*Overall* 72.5%	38.0	27.5	0.0
				Scales Only 76.8%	35.6	23.2	0.0
				Single-Items Only 66.6%	41.2	33.4	0.0
13. Site KKK	5 Job Descriptive Index facets of satisfaction; streesful life events; and daily hassles	Rahim, Golembiewski, & Munzenrider, 1996	7/7 significant in expected direction, P <. 0002; on average, 10 percent of variance is explained.	71.0%	22.4	29.0	3.6

ORGANIZATIONAL COVARIANTS AT GLOBAL SITES

With growing frequency, replicative studies of the phase model of burnout also have been completed in global worksettings. A number of these studies utilize our "standard replication package," which is re-introduced immediately below. Whatever marker variables are utilized, the goal of all these global replications is to test the reach-and-grasp of the phase model. *The* question is direct: Do the marker variables map on the phases in expected ways, in different countries and perhaps different cultures?

The working answer for worldwide studies at a few points requires some qualifications, as will be shown, but the expected mapping is typically observed. In sum, the marker variables deteriorate as the phases progress I —> VIII.

Two sets of details are required to provide a frame for these worldwide studies, as well as to suggest the nature of the required qualifications. In turn, attention goes to the marker variables and then to the findings in global settings.

Marker Variables

Available global replications usually rely on a "standard replication package"—the MBI items and several marker variables to test the concurrent validity of the phase model of burnout. There have been several such packages, which include some or all of these marker variables:

- Job Tension
- Job Involvement
- Job Satisfaction
- General Health Questionnaire: GHQ I for Total Score; and GHQ II for estimating normals/cases when the criterion is non-psychotic psychiatric symptoms that justify clinical intervention
- Helplessness

Global Findings

Table III.5 summarizes the results of available replicative studies using the phase model of burnout. Two conclusions apply, overall. Obviously, these studies isolate the same pattern of covariants of the phase model as do North American studies, overall. Clearly, also, the pattern in Table III.5 tends to be somewhat less pronounced than for the exemplars in Table III.4, on balance.

Fifteen cases do not permit unqualified interpretation, of course, but the weight of evidence in Table III.5 patently favors the concurrent validity of the phase model. In overview, almost all data arrays isolate significant variation in every variable considered, and no case isolates non-random variance in less than 7 of 12 variables. This accounts for 76 variables out of 84, or more than 90 percent. In addition, no study reports less than 70 percent of the paired-comparisons in the expected direction, with the average being about 80 percent. In addition, the proportion of paired-comparisons that achieve significance, as well as fall in the expected direction, is always substantially greater than can be expected by chance, and often is far greater. That proportion is never less than twice that proportion, and averages over four times as much.

Even the least-robust case—Belarus E—tends to fit the pattern. Moreover, the small number of cases in that population also encourages reliance on the collapsed phases—I-III, IV and V, and VI-VIII—and they clearly reflect a sharper pattern than do the full 8 phases. The same sems to hold for Israel A and China B, where the collapsed phases also reflect a more robust pattern than the full eight phases.

Subsequent chapters provide other consistent studies of covariants in global worksettings. This is especially the case with Chapter IV, but all chapters following that one also provide useful perspective on the phase model in global worksettings.

This summary of consistent covariants of the phase model in global work settings attracts attention, for common shoptalk is likely to emphasize cultural relativity rather than consistent results in different nation states or cultures. The implied issues will be dealt with at numerous later points inthis volume. Provisionally, a simple interpretation of Table III.5—like that relevant to Table III.4, but a bit less robust—seems apt. The phase model seems to apply globally, but its generic character may be moderated by such features as differences unique to specific organizations. In the global worksettings, in addition, the findings in Table III.5 also provide room for the possible effects of national populations and possibly cultures or mosaics of sub-cultures. Table III.5 leaves room for site-specific effects, clearly enough; but the phase model of burnout seems to tap major generic features common to all worksites tested, again clearly enough.

RETROSPECTIVES ON MAPPING COVARIANTS OF THE PHASES, WORLDWIDE

This may seem like crying hunger with a loaf of bread under one's arm, but the pattern of covariation associated with the phases probably represents an understatement of the relationships in nature. Put positively, the findings

Table III.5. Summary, Worksite Descriptors X Phases, World-Wide

Sites	Operational Definitions of Worksite Variables	Researchers	Status of Marker Variables	In Expected Direction	In Expected Direction and Statistically Significant	In Contrary Direction	In Contrary Direction and Statistically Significant
1. Belarus A	Standard Replication Package	Golembiewski, Boudreau, & Levin (1996)	5/5 significant in expected direction, $P < .007$; mean eta^2 = .099.	70.7%	11.4	29.3	0.7
2. Belarus B	Standard Replication Package, plus self-rated productivity	Boudreau, Zhilina, Zhilina, & Faiferman (1996a)	6/6 significant in expected direction, $P < .0000$; mean eta^2 = .210.	68.5%	27.4	31.5	7.7
3. Belarus C	Hardiness	Boudreau, Zhilina, Zhilina, & Faiferman (1996a)	1/1 significant in expected direction, $P < .0000$, mean eta^2 = .188.	75.0%	10.7	25.0	0.0
4. Belarus D	Standard Replication Package, plus self-rated productivity	Boudreau & Levin (1996a)	6/6 significant in expected direction, $P < .0002$, mean eta^2 = .097.	73.8% _Full Phases_	20.2	26.2	1.8
5. China B	Standard Replication Package	Golembiewski & Luo (1996)	5/5 significant in expected direction, $P < .0001$; mean eta^2 = .159.	82.1% _Collapsed Phases_ 10.0%	18.6 / 66.7	17.9 / 0.0	0.0 / 0.0

(continued)

Table III.5. (Continued)

Sites	Operational Definitions of Worksite Variables	Researchers	Status of Marker Variables	In Expected Direction	In Expected Direction and Statistically Significant	In Contrary Direction	In Contrary Direction and Statistically Significant
6. Belarus E	Standard Replication Package, plus self-rated productivity	Boudreau & Levin (1996b)	For full phases, 3/6 significant in expected direction, P < .01, and two others approach significance. For collapsed phases, 4/6 achieve significance.	Full Phases 73.8% / Collapsed Phases 100.0%	2.4 / 22.2	26.2 / 0.0	0.0 / 0.0
7. Belarus F	Hardiness	Boudreau & Levin (1996c)	1/1 significant in expected direction, P < .0002, eta^2 = .143	100.0%	10.4	0.0	0.0
8. Canada A	Standard Replication Package, plus self-rated productivity	Duplicea and Hubert (1996)	6/7 significant in expected direction, P < .0146	85.7%	17.9	14.3	0.0
9. Ghana A	Standard Replication Package	Fiadzo (1995); Fiadzo, Golembiewski, Bradbury, & Rivera (1995)	5/5 significant in expected direction, P < .001, eta^2 = .122.	73.6%	14.3	26.4	2.2
10. Israel A	Standard Replication Package, plus self-rated productivity, hardiness, and a burnout measure	Pines and Golembiewski 1996	Full Phases 7/8 significant in expected direction, P < .0304 Collapsed Phases 8/8 significant in expected dir-	76.3% / 91.7%	22.8 / 54.2	23.7 / 8.3	0.9 / 0.0

Table III.5. (Continued)

11. Japan B	Job Involvement		1/1 significant in expected direction, $P < .0000$, $eta^2 = .167$.	82.1%	28.6	17.9	7.1
12. Japan C	Standard Replication Package, plus self-rated productivity	Golembiewski, Boudreau, Goto, & Murai (1993)	6/6 significant in expected direction, $P < .005$; mean $eta^2 = .136$.	81.5%	10.7	18.5	1.2
13. Saudi Arabia A	Participation in Decisions at Work, Job Involvement, and Job Tension	Al-Ebedah (1995)	3/3 significant in expected direction, $P < .002$; mean $eta^2 = .150$.	77.4%	35.7	22.6	0.0
14. Taiwan A	Job Involvement, Helplessness, Work Satisfaction, and Job Tension	Golembiewski, Sun, Lin, & Boudreau (1995)	4/4 significant in expected direction, $P < .0000$; mean $eta^2 = .117$.	86.6%	37.5	12.5	1.8
15. Taiwan B	Standard Replication Package	Lin, Sun, & Golembiewski (1996)	5/5 significant in expected direction, $P < .0001$; $eta^2 = .159$.	85.7%	43.6	14.3	2.9

above are presented as straight-vanilla, but we know some data sets have features that distort or camouflage relationships between marker variables and burnout. For example, of the 22 total data sets summarized in this chapter, four stand out as the least-robust exemplars of the expected pattern—Belarus A, Belarus E, China B, and Japan C—and they all are populations having one or more phases having small numbers of assignees. This condition exists for different reasons, but it commonly admits the possibility that artifactual features can help explain the differences-in-a-common-pattern reflected above.

Subsequent analysis, and especially in Chapters VII and VIII, will provide useful perspective on several probably-intervening features. They include gender as well as small cell size, among other features. Consistently, to whet the readers' appetites a bit, the same four populations—Belarus A, Belarus E, China B, and Japan C—have high representations of females as well as contain some phases with few assignees. But more of this later.

NOTE

1. The convention adopted here is that the data used come from the major published source, wherever applicable. In a few cases—for example, Japan C—the data cited may differ in incidentals from updates, which in general result from adding cases to the reported N, after they were very late in arriving from field settings.

In Japan C, N here is 352 while an update includes 411 cases. No substantial differences in results were observed in the update.

Two purposes underlay this convention. Thus, we seek to facilitate cross-checking by readers of results here with published sources, which often contain additional detail and analysis. In addition, some convention had to be adopted for including materials in this book, and perhaps especially because even minor adjustments in a single study would require tedious recalculations in six major tables in Chapter VI.

Of course, if a reanalysis had generated a different pattern of results, both it and the original would have been reported. That was not necessary, however.

Chapter IV

Human Costs of Burnout:
Health-Related Indicators
Around the World

The burgeoning literature on burnout suggests that noxious physiological and emotional effects will accompany high levels of strain. Thus, Cherniss (1980, pp. 15-16) expects that greater incidences of a long catalog of psychophysical disturbances will be associated with increasing burnout; Freudenberger (1980) emphasizes that great psychological distress is a common concomitant of great strain; and Maslach and Jackson (1981, pp. 99-101) propose that high rates of headaches, lingering colds, backaches, gastro-intestinal disturbances, and other indicators of impaired physical functioning will occur along with the emotional shortfalls associated with advanced levels of experienced burnout.

A general appreciation of this linkage of physical and emotional distress with burnout requires no great inferential leaps. Advanced burnout implies that an individual experiences a collection of stressors that cause so much strain that normal coping skills/attitudes do not suffice. Thus overextended, the individual is left vulnerable to various upsets, including those generated within the body or mind as well as those caused by invading microbes that find that the body's normal defenses have become less robust.

And truth be told, the literature is all-but-unanimous in proposing such linkages of burnout, however defined operationally, with various measures of emotional and physical functioning—again, whatever their operational definitions. Exceptions are rare (e.g., Burke & Greenglass, 1989, p. 55), and this chapter will not add to their slim total.

The credible linkages of the phases of burnout with physical and emotional distress require detailed proof, however, and for several reasons. To begin, the general literature on burnout shows more agreement than evidence. For example, most of the literature is anecdotal, involves numerous operational definitions, and it often involves very small populations. Moreover, we wish here to assemble research on the phases of burnout which, of course, those committed to other operational definitions have attended to only in bits-and-pieces. Such reasons motivate this test for the health covariants of the phases of burnout throughout the world.

This chapter is neither exhaustive nor uniform, but it marshals some impressive evidence from several parts of our spaceship earth supporting the view that the criticalities of emotional and physical health seem to vary with the phases, worldwide. Five emphases illustrate the emerging North American and global data-sets. In turn, the sections below deal with: physical symptoms; several affective states; mental health; objective estimates of health such as weight and cancer risk; and blood chemistry.

PHASES AND PHYSICAL DISTRESS

To illustrate the common regular covariation of the first of several health-related domains, data come from the regional offices of a U.S. agency, conveniently labelled Site B and described in Appendix A. Health status is estimated by self-reports to a conventional list of physical complaints (Quinn & Shepard, 1974; Quinn & Staines, 1979). Respondents are offered four possible stems: Often, Sometimes, Rarely, and Never. The response stems are used in connection with 19 indicators of well-being, with the scoring being uniform so that "Often" is coded 4 and "Never" gets a 1. The several physical symptoms are not detailed here, but four factors and a total score get most attention. The score Total Symptoms has a Cronbach's *alpha* of .89.

Findings Concerning Physical Symptoms

Although the magnitude of their patterning varies between individual symptoms as well as between clusters of them, as will be shown later, the phase model isolates a marked pattern of association with physical symptoms. This claim for the usefulness of the phase model rests on two kinds of evidence: a one-way analysis of variance involving the eight phases and Total Symptoms scores; and a factor analysis of the 19 symptoms, coupled with an analysis of the resulting factors arrayed by the phases of burnout.

Individual Items, ANOVA. The ANOVA findings require no hyperbole. They reflect a high probability of nonrandom variation in the array of Total Symptoms by phases. Most specifically, over 96 percent of all paired-comparisons vary progressively: that is, Total Symptoms for Phase I < Phase II < Phase III, and so on. In addition, 60.4 percent of the 28 paired-comparisons are also statistically significant at the .05 level, as judged by the Least Significant Difference (LSD) test, modified for unequal sample sizes (Golembiewski & Munzenrider, 1988, p. 70). For other details about the paired-comparisons, consult Tables IV.3 and IV.4 below.

In sum, the more advanced one's burnout phase, the worse the profile of physical symptoms; and the covariation of Total Physical Symptoms and phases is not a puny one. Specifically, eta-square reveals that Total Symptoms and the phases share some 16 percent of their variance.

Factor Analysis of 19 Symptoms. On closer inspection, some health symptoms vary more robustly with the phases than other symptoms. Factor analysis of the 19 symptoms identifies specific clusters that add depth and specificity to that general observation, and the results establish that the 19 symptoms do not simply elicit generalized "feel good/bad" responses from respondents. Details are omitted here, but Table IV.1 summarizes the results of the standard tests used in *Global Burnout*.

What does this closer look reveal? Table IV.1 summarizes the patterns of association involving the five aggregates of symptoms, whose *alphas* average more than .80, and the eight phases of burnout. Note that in all five cases statistically significant variation exists, overall, and especially so for the two clusters labeled Factor I and Total Symptoms, in that order. Simply, as arrayed in 5 different ways, clusters of physical symptoms worsen as burnout phases progress from I through VIII, substantially in all cases but not uniformly so.

How to circumscribe "substantially?" A few summaries do the job. For one thing, more than 90 percent of all paired-comparisons fall in the expected direction, as Table IV.1 shows. Moreover, 43.6 percent of all 140 paired-comparisons are large enough and regular enough to attain the .05 level of statistical significance. The present results are striking, since only 1 in 20 statistically-significant cases are expected by chance. Clearly, random variation does not characterize the data.

This aggregate record obscures a bit even as it reveals a lot, however. As Table IV.1 shows, two clusters of symptoms again stand out as having the most marked associations with the phases of burnout—Factor I and Total Symptoms. In sum, for those two clusters over 96 percent of their paired-comparisons fall in the expected direction, phase by phase; over 62 percent of those expected differences in paired-comparisons achieve statistical significance; and all of the tiny remnant of 3.6 percent of the contrary cases reflect random variation only.

Table IV.1. Summary of Paired Comparisons of Five Clusters of
Physical Symptoms Versus Burnout Phases

	Summary of Differences, in Percentages			
	In Expected Direction	In Expected Direction and Statistically Significant	In Contrary Direction	In Contrary Direction and Statistically Significant
Total symptoms	96.4	60.4	3.6	0.0
Factor I: General enervation and agitation	96.4	64.3	3.6	0.0
Factor II: Cardiovascular complaints	92.9	42.9	7.1	0.0
Factor III: Noncardiac pains	92.9	17.9	7.1	0.0
Factor IV: Sleeplessness	71.5	32.1	28.5	0.0

Source: Golembiewski and Munzenrider (1988). Reprinted with permission of Greenwood Publishing Group, Inc., Westport, CT.

The other three clusters of symptoms also show a regular increase in reported symptoms, by progressive phases of burnout, but less dramatically so. Directly, for both Total Symptoms and Factor I, the phases account for an average of 18.0 percent of the variance. The other three factor X phase combinations account for somewhat less than 5.7 percent of the variance. A scanning of Table IV.1 also establishes that these three clusters of symptoms have fewer paired-comparisons falling in the expected direction, although the pattern is relatively sharp even in those cases, phase by phase.

In some part, the record for Factor III also may reflect its low *alpha* coefficient.

How Bad Is Bad? How severe are the physical symptoms reported at Site B? Two comparisons provide useful perspective on this crucial estimate. Thus a 1972 national sample of respondents (Quinn & Shepard, 1974) provides self-reports about all 19 of the symptoms studied at Site B, and these responses can be compared with phase results, if tentatively, given the time gap between the 1972 survey and the 1982 survey at Site B. Fortunately, comparisons closer in time are possible on most of the 19 symptoms. A 1977 survey (Quinn & Staines, 1979) provides data less distant from the Site B survey, but for only 12 of the present list of symptoms.

So we take three comparative approaches to providing perspective on the central question: How bad is bad? Each approach has its limits for present purposes but, because they provide reinforcing findings, their basic message can hardly be denied. Physical health varies with burnout, and the phases isolate robust associations with several measures of well-being.

Comparison with 1972 National Sample. At an aggregate level, we can begin with a bold generalization: the levels of symptoms reported at Site B are markedly higher than in the 1972 survey. In all 19 cases, significantly greater proportions of Site B respondents report experiencing each symptom "Sometimes" or "Often." What is the magnitude of "significantly greater?" Overall, an average of 28.2 percent of the Site B respondents chose these two indicators of the frequency with which they experienced the 19 symptoms. In comparison, 19.7 percent of the 1972 national sample chose the same response stems. Statistical analysis shows that one would go broke in betting that those differences are due to random factors only ($P < .001$).

Comparison with 1997 National Sample. For the 1977 national survey, only 12 symptoms are included. What do these 12 comparisons show, in sum? All available cases reflect much the same pattern as the example for "feel fatigued" in Table IV.2. That is to say, the two national samples do not seem to differ systematically or significantly over the interval, 1972-1977. The 1972 and 1977 data provide similar bases of comparisons with 1982 data from Site B.

Table IV.2. "Feel Fatigued," Site B and in Two National Samples

		Percent Reporting "Feel Fatigued"			
	Number	*Never*	*Rarely*	*Sometimes*	*Often*
All respondents Site B	1,575	32.3	39.0	21.5	7.2
Phases I-III, Site B	653	42.1	40.7	15.5	1.7
Phases VI-VIII, Site B	652	21.2	36.8	29.0	13.0
1972 National sample (Quinn & Shepard, 1974)	2,149	58.6	26.2	12.0	3.3
1977 National sample (Quinn & Staines, 1979)	1,081	58.8	25.7	12.2	3.3

Source: Golembiewski and Munzenrider (1988, p. 76). Reprinted with permission of Greenwood Publishing Group, Inc., Westport, CT.

Phases, Symptoms, and Phases.   To involve the phase model in synthesis of results about the physical symptoms, two summaries encapsule a more detailed analysis available elsewhere (Golembiewski & Munzenrider, 1988, pp. 70-77). First, Site B respondents report a greater incidence of all symptoms than 1977 and 1972 respondents. The example in Table IV.2 is typical for all 12 available symptoms: almost 29 percent of Site B respondents report "feeling fatigued" either "Sometimes" or "Often," while the comparable percentage in the 1977 national population is 15.5. See the last row in Table IV.2.

Chapter VI will provide one explanation of this difference. The distribution of advanced phases at Site B is large; and symptoms increase as the phases progress I —> VIII. But this gets ahead of the present analysis, and necessary details will be reviewed later.

Second, Table IV.2 also illustrates that the symptoms seem quite sensitive to differences in burnout at Site B. Specifically, only 17.2 percent of the respondents classified in Phases I-III report that they "Sometimes" or "Often" feel fatigued. For those in Phases VI-VIII, the comparable percentage is 42, which nearly triples the proportion in both national samples. We authors deliberately chose a less-extreme case. For most other symptoms, the differences are even greater.

In sum, "bad" at Site B seems pretty bad indeed. Table IV.2 implies that a prime conclusion seems beyond serious doubt. In short, the phases seem significant in understanding differences in symptomology.

And What of the Global Pattern? The same general pattern characterizes health-related findings from populations in several nation-states, and Table IV.3 summarizes the results of several studies in a convenient form. The three variables featured in Table IV.3 deal with aspects of mental or emotional health—with GHQ providing a summary estimate of status, and with Helplessness and Hardiness providing perspective on significant aspects of personal orientations to dealing with one's world.

Several other points set the table for the analysis to follow. Details about operational definitions of health status appear at several places in this text, and can be accessed via the Subject Matter Index. See also the next section. The researchers are listed in the References and, in most cases, their findings have been published. As noted earlier, only universal norms are utilized here. Several other studies are consistent with the present analysis, please note, but are not detailed because they use different operational definitions, or because they are reported in a format different from the one used here (e.g., Burke & Deszca, 1986).

Table IV.3. Selected Summaries, Health Status in Global Work Settings

Sites	Operational Definitions of Health Status	Researchers	Status of Health Variables	In Expected Direction	In Expected Direction and Statistically Significant	In Contrary Direction	Statistically Significant and in Contrary Direction
1. Belarus A	General Health Questionnaire GHQ I; Helplessness	Golembiewski, Boudreau, & Levin (1996)	2/2 in expected direction, $P <$ .007, eta^2 = .124	75.0%	17.8	25.0	1.7
2. Belarus B	General Health Questionnaire, GHQ I	Boudreau, Zhilina, Zhilina, & Faiferman (1996b)	1/1 in expected direction, $P <$ .000, eta^2 = .272	64.3%	28.6	35.7	0.0
3. Belarus C	Hardiness	Boudreau, Zhilina, Zhilina, & Faiferman (1996a)	1/1 in expected direction, $P <$ .000, eta^2 = .188	75.0%	10.7	25.0	0.0
4. Belarus D	General Health Questionnaire, GHQ I	Boudreau & Levin (1996a)	1/1 in expected direction, $P <$ .000, eta^2 = .178	85.7%	35.7	14.3	3.6
5. Belarus E	General Health Questionnaire, GHQ I	Boudreau & Levin (1996b)	0/1 not significant	100.0%	-	0.0	-

(continued)

Table IV.3. (Continued)

6. Belarus F	Hardiness	Boudreau & Levin (1996c)	1/1 in expected direction, $P <$ .0002, eta^2 = .143	100.0%	10.7	0.0	0.0
8. China B	General Health Questionnaire, GHQ I	Golembiewski & Luo (1996)	1/1 in expected direction, $P <$ .000, eta^2 = .167	85.7	17.9	14.3	0.0
9. Ghana A	General Health Questionnaire GHQ I	Fiadzo (1995)	1/1 in expected direction, $P <$ .001, eta^2 = .091	71.4	7.2	28.6	0.0
11. Japan C	General Health Questionnaire, GHQ I	Golembiewski, Boudreau, Goto, & Murai (1993)	1/1 in expected direction, $P <$ .000, eta^2 = .103	75.0	7.2	25.0	0.0
12. Taiwan B	General Health Questionnaire, GHQ I; Helplessness	Lin, Sun, & Golembiewski (1996)	2/2 in expected direction, $P <$ .000, eta^2 = .147	92.9	44.4	7.1	0.0

In sum, worldwide, Table IV.3 makes a strong case supporting the unattractive covariation of phases and various indicators of health status. In all but one case—Belarus E—health status shares non-random variance with the phases at twelve worksettings in seven nation states, which are scattered across the world and exist at different macro-stages in their economic, political, and social development. Moreover, on average, no fewer than 3 of every 4 paired-comparisons of health status X phases fall in the expected direction. On average, something like one-fifth of all paired-comparisons do fall in a direction contrary to expectations but, in support of a definite pattern of association of health status X phases, these contrary paired-comparisons are almost-always random. Most revealing, the paired-comparisons in the expected direction also attain statistical significance in far-greater proportions than chance allows—from a minimum of 40 percent more (Japan C), to a high of some 800 percent more (Taiwan B), than can be expected by chance association.

Belarus E, the single case in which only random variation is observed, does not provide a real challenge to the conclusion above. That population is quite small, $N = 86$, and even so 3 of every 4 paired-comparisons, on average, fall in the expected direction.

Indeed, Table IV.3 may provide an estimate that is both strong *and* conservative. This is an attractive combination, obviously, and Table IV.4 supports it. Specifically, several of the 12 worksites represented in Table IV.3 have smallish Ns and/or phases with such small numbers of entries that one or a few outliers might distort or camouflage relationships. For a few studies, Table IV.4 collapses the 8 phases into 3 categories, as one approach to compensating for sparsely-populated cells. The effect is clearly supportive of the phase model. Note that, with Belarus E again being an outlier, Table IV.4 shows that every paired-comparison falls in the expected direction and, on average for the collapsed phases, something like 7 of every 10 paired-comparisons attain statistical significance as well as fall in the expected direction.

PHASES AND AFFECTIVE STATES

Part of the judgment concerning the conceptual usefulness of the burnout phases will rest on tests of whether they "anchor" appropriately in conditions emphasized in the clinical literatures. For example, many observers assume that advanced burnout implies high rates of depression (e.g., Deckard, 1985), for obvious conceptual reasons. And a useful operational definition of burnout should consistently isolate such covariation.

Table IV.4. GHQ I Means vs. Collapsed Phases of Burnout

	F-ratio	F-Probability	Eta^2	In Expected Direction	Statistically Significant and in Expected Direction	In Contrary Direction	Statistically Significant and in Contrary Direction
1. Belarus A (N = 312)	25.55	< .0000	.15	80.0%	40.0	20.0	0.0
2. Belarus D (N = 460)	35.02	< .0000	.13	100.0%	100.0	0.0	0.0
3. Belarus E (N = 86)	NS	.1927	-	100.0%	-	0.0	-
4. China B (N = 259)	16.77	< .0000	.16	100.0%	66.7	0.0	0.0
5. Japan C (N = 352)	12.46	< .0000	.07	100.0%	33.3	0.0	0.0
6. Site PP (N = 231)	32.99	< .0000	.24	100.0%	100.0	0.0	0.0

Note: Site PP by Scheffé test; others by Least Significant Difference test, as modified for unequal subsample sizes.

How might appropriate tests be designed? For example, tests of this clinical "anchoring" might proceed in several ways. For example, as in a following section, some measures of proneness to psychiatric illness might be assessed for covariation with the phases.

The focus here is on specific affective states that seem clinically relevant, whether or not an individual is aware of them. The purpose here is exploratory, and weighty reasons imply the likelihood that contingencies may distort even robust associations in nature. That is, some feeling-states may be identified more easily than others, and individuals may be more in-touch with some affective states. Also, some feeling-states may variously "lead" or "lag" specific phases of burnout and, hence, some covariations may reveal themselves only in longish time-frames.

Introduction to Affective States

All data come from a survey of 10 facilities in one region of a corporately managed chain of life-care retirement communities, identified in Appendix A as Site L (Deckard, 1985). Numerous analytic details supplement this summary (Golembiewski & Munzenrider, 1988, pp. 185-194).

A few points need introduction. Basically, in addition to the phases, this section employs eight scales developed from the Multiple Affective Adjective Checklist, or MAACL. These scales come from two lines of research.

Five of the eight MAACL scales used here come directly from the long tradition of research begun by Zuckerman and Lubin (1965). Initially, the MAACL relied on an empirical method of item selection, while factor analysis was later used to select items and identify scales (Zuckerman, Lubin, & Rinck, 1984). The investigators conclude that the two strategies are of comparable validity. Originally, MAACL focused on "three of the clinically relevant negative affects: anxiety, depression, and hostility," using a list of 132 adjectives as stimuli on which respondents could report how they feel "today" or "now." This contrasts with assessments in other time-frames such as "Generally" or "Occasionally." That is, MAACL sees affect *as a state* rather than as a trait. Later, two summary scales were added to the initial MAACL trio: Positive Affect (or Euphoria), and Dysphoria. Their bare designations are revealing enough for present purposes.

This analysis also deals with three additional scales derived from the MAACL. The underlying research utilizes a new response stem for MAACL—how respondent "felt in recent days" rather than "today"—and conservative research practice encouraged a verification by factor analysis of the structure of responses to these stems. Analysis generates five factors with eigenvalues greater than 1.0, and the first three and easily-interpretable factors are labeled Genial, Despondent, and Agitated.

We expect that the eight targeted affective states will vary regularly and robustly with the phases. For two scales—Positive Affect and Genial—scores should decrease, phase by phase. For the other six scales, scores should increase, phase by phase.

The rationales are transparent. For the six negative affective states, the decreasing emotional slack associated with the phases should induce growing emotional deficits or deficiencies. Decreased slack means that one is closer to "snapping" or "going around the bend," in a loose manner of speaking. For the two positive affective states, phase by phase, decreases are expected because of the greater energy-drain of coping with advanced burnout.

Measurement details support analysis of these scales. For example, reliability estimates seem adequate for research purposes. Except for one case—Genial, whose Cronbach's *alpha* is .63—the coefficients range from .75 to .90.

Findings About Phases and Clinically-Relevant Affects

The findings suggest a definite pattern of associations of the expected kind, but the magnitudes of the associations permit various interpretations. The table is not reproduced here, but it reflects a regularity in pattern for MAACL-derived scales by progressive phases of burnout (Deckard, 1985, p. 85). In sum, as expected, the six negative affects all increase, Phases I —>

VIII; and Positive Affect and Genial decrease. Moreover, all eight cases reveal a very high probability ($P < .000$) that nonrandom variation exists somewhere in the overall distributions of scores by phases. In addition, nearly 88 percent of all possible paired-comparisons fall in the expected directions, and no statistically significant deviant cases exist. Most revealingly, 19.2 percent of all paired-comparisons achieve statistical significance, using the Least Significant Difference test, as modified for unequal subpopulations. The record of significantly different paired-comparisons varies little between: all eight MAACL scales (19.2 percent); the five traditional scales (18.6 percent); and the three scales constructed for present purposes by factor analysis (20.2 percent).

In sum, the 3 classes of clinically-relevant affective states generate familiar and similar profiles of statistically-significant paired-comparisons falling in the expected directions. In summary terms, between 3 and 4 times more statistically significant paired-comparisons exist than one can expect by chance. Note also that the two positive affective states produce a substantially greater proportion of statistically-significant differences, phase by phase, than the six negative affective states: 32.1 vs. 17.9 percent, respectively.

Some Interpretive Possibilities

These results do not permit unequivocal interpretation, but a trio of possibilities merit attention. First, one cannot easily explain-away the results as reflecting measurement inadequacies. The phases reliably isolate differences in burnout with marker variables often used in studies of affect; and the MAACL also has proved sensitive to variations in feeling-tone— for example, those induced by natural experiments or drugs (e.g., Lubin & Zuckerman, 1969). Deckard (1985) expresses disappointment that the associations she isolates are not more massive, to be sure, but the pattern of her results requires no revisionism concerning phase model measurement conventions.

Second, one could argue that specific individual characteristics dilute associations, such as differences in Social Desirability, or SD (Crowne & Marlowe, 1964). SD measures the tendency to temper observations by a concern for social approval. High SD scorers should experience some difficulty in attributing to self the more negative MAACL adjectives, and hence they might generate artefactually-low scores on some scales. Patently, a substantial proportion of high SD scores could reduce the magnitude of any observed associations without destroying the pattern reported above.

A simple research design tests, if indirectly, for an SD effect on the covariation of phases X MAACL measures. Let us distinguish two clusters of MAACL-derived scales, as a way of beginning a test of this possibility.

We isolate Positive Affect, Genial, and Agitated from the remaining five scales, on the general principle that those three seem to involve the *least unattractive* self-descriptions and, hence, should pose fewer problems for high SD scorers.

The evidence supports our line of supposing. Consistent with the SD concept, the three "attractive" MAACL scales generate 29.8 percent statistically-significant differences in paired-comparisons in the expected direction, while the five "unattractive" scales average 12.9 percent. Similarly, as noted earlier, a substantial difference also exists in the record of statistically significant paired-comparisons for the two "positive" scales—Positive Affect and Genial. The record for this affective duo differs substantially from that for the six "negative" states: 32.1 and 17.9 percent, respectively.

Third, the results do not permit making a judgment concerning whether the affective states are "leading" or "lagging" indicators. Only a longitudinal research design can help make such judgments, and the present one-shot design no doubt combines cases of "entrance" to more-advanced phases of burnout with cases of "exit" to less-advanced phases. Consequently, no specificity about leading/lagging indicators is possible. But the possibility nonetheless remains that interactions between phases and affective states may be distorted by the unspecified "directions" of individual movement through the phases.

PHASES AND MENTAL HEALTH[1]

Let us now raise the ante, in effect. The popular and technical literatures both reflect all the signs of a blizzard of publications dealing with burnout and, like the reviews above, they invariably anticipate associations with diminished physical health and flagging feelings.

However, a central concern receives infrequent explicit attention. Do persons with advanced burnout have impaired mental health? The question has obvious theoretic and practical relevance, and the approach in this section builds on, as well as moves substantially beyond, the discussion surrounding Tables IV.3 and IV.4 about "clinically-relevant affects."

Moreover, cross-cultural or cross-national replications of relevant research designs are even more rare. A few exceptions do exist, and this section highlights several of them.

This section adds to a slim literature, then, and in two central regards. Specifically, this section initially deals with mental health in Japan C, as it relates to the phases, and then reports on several replications of those results. But several matters need preliminary attention before dealing directly with Japan C and the other cases.

Associations of Burnout and Health

Near-consensus provides this section with a solid take-off point. To risk redundancy because the point is so powerful that it deserves repetition, virtually all theorists and all empirical evidence agree that useful measures of burnout should covary with states of health. This agreement can be reviewed under two sub-heads—the first dealing with physical health, and the second with mental health.

Physical Health.   As for physical health, the evidence is great and even overwhelming: indicators of diminished well-being increase with advancing burnout. In addition to the reviews of studies in the opening section of this chapter, supporting evidence comes from almost all independent observers (e.g., Burke, Shearer, & Deszca, 1984; Deckard, 1985; Shinn & Mørch, 1983), in the United States, Canada, and elsewhere. These independent researchers employ different operational measures of burnout and of physical health, and this adds weight to the substantial consistency of the results. The targeted covariants must be powerful, persistent, and pervasive.

Although most of the available studies dealing with the covariants of physical health and burnout use self-reports, some recent research employs "hard" or objective indicators which also isolate a similar pattern of association between the burnout phases and various health-related measures. Later discussion of two separate populations—approximating 200 and 800 members, respectively—provide replications and partially-reinforcing results (Golembiewski & Munzenrider, 1991c, 1993a, 1993b, 1995).

Mental Health and Phases.   Consistently, some research also associates progressive phases of burnout with deteriorating mental health, and this section adds to that critical mass. Primarily, this section illustrates and reinforces such linkages in Japan C. But this section goes substantially beyond Japan C. Replications from North America also exist: specifically, three studies in American public agencies indicate a close association of burnout phases with non-psychotic psychiatric symptoms. Two of the populations are small, although substantial proportions of the variance are accounted for. In addition, again using common measurement tools, several global studies that replicate the expected pattern also get attention below.

The basic purpose of this section needs underscoring, although the message has already been delivered several times. Designs testing the covariation of the phases with both physical and emotional health rest on a simple if basic conceptual linkage. Health status serves as both a contributor to burnout as well as a consequence of it. Hence, robust associations of health-related states should be isolated by any tolerably valid and reliable operational measure of burnout. Failure to observe them here will cast real doubt on the adequacy of the conceptual and operational bases of the phase model.

Methods

Six useful introductions to methodology and methods follow, which all relate (naturally enough) to the phase model of burnout as applied in Japan C. In turn, discussion relates to: research population; a few measurement details concerning the phases; the General Health Questionnaire; a distinction between active and passive modes of coping with burnout; demographics in Japan C; and our approach to translation of the MBI items.

Research Population. Japan C respondents ($N = 352$) come from two Japanese islands, Hokkaido and Honshu, heavily emphasizing health-care providers and females. See Appendix A for details. So, if the present purpose were to contrast the degree of burnout among all Japanese and American workers, the characteristics of Japan C would be very suspect. Here, however, the main purpose is to assess whether several marker variables covary with different phases of burnout in Japan C in ways consistent with observations from numerous North American settings. For present purposes, in effect, methodological lemons can contribute to lemonade.

Results of similar research designs in several North American settings also are summarized in this section. This expands on the discussion surrounding Table IV.3 and IV.4.

Burnout Phases. Early chapters provide details, and we here persist in relying on the universal norms only. Cronbach *alphas* in the present sub-population imply reliabilities acceptable for research purposes: specifically, .73 for Depersonalization; .73 for Personal Accomplishment (Reversed); and .76 for Emotional Exhaustion.

In addition, two forms of the phase model test for the possible effects of small sub-sample size. The two clusters of phases involve:

- all 8 phases; or
- 3 collapsed phases: Low burnout (phases I-III); Medium (phases IV-V); and High (phases VI-VIII).

The collapsed phases will provide a supplementary but useful test of the stability of any associations, both in North American and global worksettings where N is small or some phases have few entries in the full model.

98 / *Global Burnout*

General Health Questionnaire. The GHQ permits a judgment about which respondents have mental health symptoms that, if diagnosed on the basis of clinical interviews, would justify clinical interventions. The scale seeks to identify respondents with symptoms of non-psychotic psychiatric illness, based on the respondent's current mental state (Goldberg, 1972, p. 2). The GHQ uses the following format (Goldberg, 1972, p. 143):

HAVE YOU RECENTLY

7. _____ been able to concentrate on whatever you're doing?

(0)	(1)	(2)	(3)
Better than Usual	Same as Usual	Less than Usual	Much Less than Usual

This research uses the 30-item version of the GHQ developed for U.S. contexts (Goldberg, 1972, pp. 26-37, 55-57, 140), and two scoring variants are employed in connection with Tables IV.3 and IV.4 as well as in subsequent discussion:

- GHQ I, a total score for the four response stems illustrated above. *Alpha* is .91.
- GHQ II, which assigns a (0) for each item scored 0 or 1 and a (1) for each item scores 2 or 3 on the response stems above. The sum is used to distinguish "cases" from "normals," using as a cutting point ≥ 4.

GHQ II intends to isolate individuals who present symptoms that on the basis of individual diagnosis during clinical interviews would be classified as "psychiatric cases" rather than "normals" (Goldberg, 1972, p. 56), and the GHQ II does so with substantial fidelity. Specifically, after administering the GHQ blind to those already diagnosed for mental illness, Goldberg estimates about 20 percent misclassifications of normals/cases.

Active and Passive Respondents. Substantial evidence (e.g., Golembiewski & Munzenrider, 1988, esp. pp. 208-218) indicates that individuals in any of the eight phases can adopt one of two modes of coping. Thus, some individuals remain "actives": that is, they continue to confront their environment, and even contest it. Other individuals can be classified as "passive": that is, either quickly by personal predisposition or by a withdrawal after extended struggle, they adopt a submissive posture toward their environment. The latter persons are acted upon, in useful simplification, rather than acting on.

Several surrogates have been used to estimate mode (e.g., Golembiewski, Hilles, & Daly, 1987), and this study relies on a well-known measure of Job Involvement, or JI (White & Ruh, 1973). It contains 9 items, has attractive measurement properties, and has often been used in research with the phases. Here, *alpha* = 0.92.

For present purposes, JI scores are distinguished as High and Low, using as a cutting-point a norm from a large population (Golembiewski & Munzenrider, 1988, pp. 209-213). Total scores can cover the range 9 to 45, and the cutting-point for a High assignment is a JI score of 30 or greater.

Demographics. Several demographics also are available and they, along with the active/passive distinction, will be useful in the discriminant analysis concluding this section. These demographics include:

- gender (dummied)
- organization level: 4 categories
- age
- hours worked per week

Approach to Translation. All items used in this research in Japan C were translated by two of the investigators (Goto and Murai), for whom Japanese is their first language. The basic approach utilized was: translate, then retranslate and compare with the original. This ideal was not always realizable: that is, there are no Japanese analogs for such MBI usages as "at the end of my rope."

Hypotheses

Three hypotheses will be tested first in Japan C and later in several other worksettings, and support for them is consistent with the view that the phase model—concept, operational definition, and developing network of relations—applies cross-nationally. Failure to support the hypotheses is consistent with two views: that burnout research is nationally- or culturally-bounded; and/or that the phase model is not valid or reliable.

Hypothesis I. As the phases progress I —> III, GHQ I will increase.

GHQ I estimates mental health, which should covary directly with any valid and reliable measure of burnout. Thus research findings are all-but-unanimous on this association (e.g., Burke, Shearer, & Deszca, 1984), even given numerous operational definitions of health and burnout. The careful reader will remember that Tables IV.5 and IV.6 already provide summary support for Hypothesis I.

The conceptual grounds for this expectation appear solid. Thus, progressive burnout implies psychological strain that is reasonably associated with chemical changes in the body, as well as with the onset of various symptoms of ill-health (e.g., Steffy & Jones, 1988). No doubt a reinforcing loop also exists: that is, poor health no doubt often contributes to a sense of heightened burnout as well as derives from it.

Hypothesis II. As the phases progress I ─> VIII, the proportion of non-psychotic, psychiatric "cases" will increase.

The conceptual linkage is just like that detailed above for physical symptoms. That is, burnout and psychiatric symptoms are each linked by reinforcing loops of effects.

Hypotheses III. As the phases progress I ─> VIII, the proportion of "actives" will decrease.

Conceptually, the direction of this association has two major contributors, by hypothesis. Progressive burnout seems reasonably associated with increasingly-frequent withdrawal resulting from unsuccessful coping over a period of time. Perhaps less commonly, individuals may have genetic or learned predispositions to passivity—as in helplessness, hopelessness, or low robustness (e.g., Garber & Seligman, 1980). Such individuals probably have a greater tendency to be strained by whatever stressors they experience.

Findings

The associations of the two forms of the phases and the two GHQ estimates seem both regular and marked. The advancing phases tend to covary with indicators of worsening mental health in ways that imply only a very small probability of random effects. Three points detail this conclusion. In turn, separate sub-sections deal with: associations between the phases and GHQ I in the United States and Japan; the proportions of "cases" and "normals" in each phase; and whether or not "actives" and "passives," phase by phase, generate different patterns of association with GHQ II.

A concluding analysis will estimate the relative effects on GHQ II of several demographics as well as the phases, relying on discriminant analysis. This analysis employs the canonical discriminant function technique to assess the phases' ability to predict group memberships of "cases" and "normals."

Findings About Hypothesis I.   GHQ I reveals the expected pattern for the two ways of arraying the phases, in Japan C as well as in other global and North American populations. Consistent with our usual format, summaries for the two geographic loci are provided separately.

Japan C and Global Worksettings.   Tables IV.3 and IV.4, already presented, provide the data relevant to Hypothesis I from several global populations. For the full 8 phases (Table IV.3), Japan C reflects the least robust pattern of relationships, but even it isolates non-random variation between the phases and GHQ I. Specifically, in Japan C, paired-comparisons between GHQ I and the phases fall in the expected direction in 75 percent of the cases and the overall distribution surpasses $P < .000$. About 40 percent more of the differences between paired-comparisons achieve $P \le .05$ than chance allows.

Since several of the phase distributions in Table IV.3 have small numbers of cases, as noted above, the ANOVA analysis was run again for 3 collapsed phases. One pattern characterizes both Japan C and the other global settings, as Table IV.4 makes plain. In sum, a more robust pattern of associations in the expected direction exists for the collapsed phases than for the full 8 phases. This suggests a heterogeneity of variance in the full phase model, due to small sub-sample sizes. For example, three of Japan C's phases contain less than 10 entries. The population was substantial, but a very large proportion of respondents were assigned to the three most-advanced phases.

North American Settings.   Hypothesis I also clearly holds for the selected North American populations shown in Table IV.5. The patterns range from noteworthy to almost-exceptionless support (Site OO). Along with the preceding tables, Table IV.5 implies strongly that cultural differences are not sufficient to camouflage or distort the association between the phases and GHQ I. Indeed, the North American and global patterns seem quite similar.

To be specific, Table IV.5 summarizes two kinds of information about emotional status. Part I presents data about a few selected North American sites, which reinforces the record for global worksettings summarized in Table IV.3. Part II in Table IV.5 presents another way of estimating the covariation of the phases and emotional status. The MAACL scales referred to in Part II were introduced earlier.

Two common features of Table IV.5 also deserve emphasis, and they at once provide support for the phase model while raising basic questions. In sum, Hypothesis I gets substantial support in Japan C as well as in global and North American worksettings. That is, on average, over 90 percent of the paired-comparisons fall in the expected direction. However, the proportions of paired-comparisons that achieve statistical significance vary

Table IV.5. Summary, Mental Health Estimates by Phases, Selected North American Worksettings

Sites	Definitions of Worksite Variables	Researchers	Status of Marker Variables	In Expected Direction	In Expected Direction and Statistically Significant	In Contrary Direction	In Contrary Direction and Statistically Significant
I. Overall Health Estimates							
1. Site 00	General Health Questionnaire, GHQ I	Aldinger (1993)	1/1 significant in expected direction, $P <$ .0000.	100.0%	71.4	0.0	0.0
2. Site PP	General Health Questionnaire, GHQ I	Golembiewski, Scherb, Lloyd, & Munzenrider (1992)	1/1 significant in expected direction, $P <$ .0000. $Eta^2 = .26$.	92.9%	14.3	7.1	0.0
3. Site ZZ	General Health Questionnaire, GHQ I	Billingsley, 1990; Golembiewski, Munzenrider, Scherb, & Billingsley (1992)	1/1 significant in expected direction, $P <$ .0000. $Eta^2 = .14$.	90.3%	12.9	9.7	0.0
II. Scales Estimating Emotional Status							
1. Site I.	8 scales based on Multiple Adjective Affect List	Deckard (1985)	8/8 significant in expected direction, $P <$ .000.	88.8%	19.2	11.2	0.0

widely—from about 13 percent to over 70 percent. Two factors may be involved. First, 2 of the 3 less robust patterns (Sites PP and ZZ) come from smallish populations that leave some phases relatively unpopulated, and this may accentuate the relevance of a few deviant cases. Second, 2 of the 3 less-robust proportions of significant paired-comparisons come from populations with large representations of females. Chapter VII directs special attention to some of the issues implied by this feature of phase research, which also has relevance at several points in *Global Burnout*.

Findings About Hypothesis II. Further, in both Japan C as well as in selected global and North American settings, Hypothesis II seems apt, as Tables IV.6 and IV.7 show. In sum, with a substantial regularity, the proportion of "cases" tends to increase as the phases progress I —> VIII. The pattern is basically the same for the 3 collapsed phases, not reproduced here to conserve space, as it is for the full 8 phases underlying Table IV.6 and IV.7.

Global Worksettings. The generalization about "cases" increasing as the phases progress I —> VIII gets support from Table IV.6 and the 6 global worksettings about which it reports. For Japan C, see row 6. Over 78 percent of the paired-comparisons are in the expected direction, and chi-square indicates that non-random variance exits. Table IV.6 also reports

Table IV.6. "Cases" by Phases, in Japan C and Other Global Worksettings

	Phases of Burnout							
	I	*II*	*III*	*IV*	*V*	*VI*	*VII*	*VIII*
1. Belarus B,[a] (*N* = 777) "Cases," in percent =	55.6%	70.0	71.7	80.3	0.0	69.0	64.3	90.3
2. Belarus D,[b] (*N* = 458) "Cases," in percent =	17.5%	35.5	38.5	43.7	37.5	78.8	52.0	66.1
3. Belarus E,[c] (N = 87) "Cases," in percent =	56.2%	20.0	47.1	75.0	33.3	100.0	83.2	76.9
4. China B,[d] (N = 259) "Cases," in percent =	42.3%	60.0	71.4	60.7	77.8	84.0	85.7	71.1
5. Ghana A,[e] (N = 327) "Cases," in percent =	27.3%	35.0	37.8	45.7	35.7	56.1	31.3	72.3
6. Japan C,[f] (N = 400) "Cases," in percent =	44.4%	50.0	40.0	70.1	83.3	72.6	60.0	78.5

Notes: [a] $Chi^2 = 50.87, P < .0000$, Cramer's V = .26.
[b] $Chi^2 = 50.52, P < .0000$, Cramer's V = .33.
[c] $Chi^2 = 12.44, P = .087$, Cramer's V = .38.
[d] $Chi^2 = 27.49, P < .001$, Cramer's V = .32.
[e] $Chi^2 = 27.87, P < .001$, Cramer's V = .32.
[f] $Chi^2 = 19.42, P = .0069$, Cramer's V = .22.
All degrees of freedom = 7.

Table IV.7. "Cases" by Phases, in Selected North American Worksettings

	Phases of Burnout							
	I	*II*	*III*	*IV*	*V*	*VI*	*VII*	*VIII*
1. Site 00 (N = 1106)								
N by phases =	186	55	143	71	101	111	137	302
"Cases," in percent =	16.1%	30.9	21.0	57.7	42.6	54.5	54.0	66.9
					Chi^2 for 7 df	=	73.43	
					Probability	=	< .0000	
					Cramer's V	=	.396	
2. Site PP (N = 213)								
N by phases =	64	20	41	18	12	16	9	33
"Cases," in percent =	14.1%	25.0	19.0	16.7	50.0	37.5	66.7	57.6
					Chi^2 for 7 df	=	32.56	
					Probability	=	< .0000	
					Cramer's V	=	.391	
3. Site ZZ (N = 161)								
N by phases =	66	12	33	13	4	23	14	29
"Cases," in percent	18.2%	25.0	28.3	38.5	50.0	69.6	42.6	51.7
					Chi^2 for 7 df	=	20.28	
					Probability	=	.005	
					Cramer's V	=	.355	

other relevant data, similar in pattern to Japan C but variably regular. For China B, for example, over 82 percent of the paired-comparisons fall in the expected direction. For Belarus B, in contrast, somewhat less than 61 percent do so.

Chi-square values for Japan C in Table IV.6 support non-random variation in the array of "cases" by phases, but less than 5 percent of the variance is accounted for. Chi-square results for almost all other worksettings are consistent with those for Japan C. For Ghana A, for example, 75 percent of the paired-comparisons show that the proportions of "cases" increase Phases I —> VIII and Cramer's V implies that nearly 12 percent of the variance is accounted for this pattern. Only one case does not achieve significance (*P* = .087), and that exception has a small population. Cramer's V implies that 5-15 percent of the variance is explained in the 6 cases.

North American Worksettings. As a review of Table IV.7 implies, the pattern in North American populations at once differs in details from Japan C and the other global worksettings, while basic similarities also seem to exist. Specifically, 84.5 percent of all paired-comparisons in Table IV.7 are in the expected direction vs. 78.6 percent in Japan C; and the estimated variance explained in all of the North American populations approximates 15 percent while the Japan C estimate is 4.7 percent. At the same time that these gross regularities exist, the slopes of the global curves in Table IV.6 seem clearly distinguished from the curves in Table IV.7.

In any case, Hypothesis II gets general but variable support. This may reflect cross-cultural or cross-national differences, or it may be an artifact of the sometimes-smallish populations available for analysis. But our favorite hypothesis is that the three exemplars in Table IV.7 involve military or quasi military populations, with presumably-special training and socialization that emphasizes emotional stability. In this context, the trends in Table IV.7 are especial attention-getters.

Findings About Hypothesis III. The data from Japan C provide statistically-significant but gentle support for the proposition that the proportions of "passives" increase as the phases progress. Table IV.8 provides summary data for Japan C, whose distribution is almost certainly

Table IV.8. Actives, by Full Phases, in Percent

		Phases of Burnout							
		I	*II*	*III*	*IV*	*V*	*VI*	*VII*	*VIII*
1.	Belarus A[a]	76.1%	65.9	47.5	53.8	100.0	63.2	55.6	55.3
2.	Belarus B[b]	88.9%	60.0	9.2	82.2	100.0	51.9	21.4	24.3
3.	Belarus D[c]	75.0%	77.4	42.8	44.7	87.5	39.4	40.0	42.5
4.	Belarus E[d]	87.5%	80.0	56.3	41.7	33.3	0.0	33.3	53.8
5.	China B[e]	40.8%	40.0	14.3	17.9	44.0	32.0	0.0	15.8
6.	Ghana A[f]	97.1%	100.0	83.3	63.9	95.5	84.4	76.5	66.0
7.	Japan A[g]	92.3%	94.7	72.5	59.6	100.0	82.3	67.4	47.4
8.	Japan B[h]	72.2%	61.9	28.6	17.7	66.7	67.8	25.0	25.3
9.	Japan C[i]	66.7%	80.0	40.0	62.5	83.3	82.8	63.6	39.4

Notes: [a] $Chi^2 = 12.47$, $P = .086$, and Cramer's V = .201.
[b] $Chi^2 = 79.71$, $P < .0000$, and Cramer's V = .322.
[c] $Chi^2 = 31.89$, $P < .0000$, and Cramer's V = .264
[d] $Chi^2 = 13.17$, $P = .069$, and Cramer's V = .391.
[e] $Chi^2 = 16.04$, $P = .025$, and Cramer's V = .249.
[f] $Chi^2 = 32.97$, $P = .0003$, and Cramer's V = .343.
[g] $Chi^2 = 80.68$, $P < .0000$, and Cramer's V = .290.
[h] $Chi^2 = 90.99$, $P < .0000$, and Cramer's V = .426.
[i] $Chi^2 = 44.18$, $P < .0000$, and Cramer's V = .341.
All degrees of freedom = 7.

non-random and where 11.6 percent of the variance in modes and phases is explained. But only 60.7 percent of the paired-comparisons are in the expected direction.

The eight other global cases in Table IV.8 reflect a similar pattern. Six of the distributions are non-random, and account for 5-20 percent of the variance. The percentage of "actives" also decreases, phase by phase, in a bit over 6 of every 10 paired-comparisons.

Global and North American Populations. Chapter VIII gives substantial attention to the active/passive distinction, because the point raises issues that would swamp the present focus on mental health and the phases. Note here only that the active $\longrightarrow$ passive proportions seem generally associated with Phases I $\longrightarrow$ VIII movement, although cross-national or cross-cultural factors may influence the slopes of the curves. But more of this much later.

Japan C and Discriminant Analysis

As a useful final step in this section, we test 5 demographic variables and the phases for their ability to correctly classify respondents as "cases" and "normals" in Japan C. Discriminant analysis shows that 5 of 6 variables tested—phase assignments, gender (dummied), organization level, age, hours and active/passive—are statistically significant in accounting for variations in GHQ II, but phases and gender play the major roles in Japan C.

Greater specificity is both possible and convenient. Pedhazur (1982) advises—as a rule-of-thumb—that analysts consider as meaningful only structural coefficients $\geq .30$. In the single canonical discriminant function here, the correlations are:

phases	.70171
gender	.57537
organization level	.25093
age	.24292
active/passive	-.18137
hours worked per week	-.17080

By the Pedhazur rule, then, GHQ II meaningfully covaries with two variables—the phases and gender.

One other analytic detail provides a useful sense of the magnitudes at issue here. Thus, the canonical correlation for the first canonical discriminant function is .2954, which permits the estimate that the significant discriminating variables account for 8.7 percent of the variation in GHQ II.

Discussion

The present findings extend research on the association of health and the burnout phases in two useful ways: the focus here is on mental health, which extends the more-common emphasis on physical health; and the prime locus of this research is Japan C which—along with several other North American and global settings—introduces a useful cross-national or cross-cultural thrust. As in virtually all available studies, the results indicate noteworthy deterioration of health with advancing phases. In general, tests of three hypotheses reinforce as well as replicate other studies, in both global and North American settings.

The interpretation of results also should be qualified, however, and especially by four caveats. First, the Japanese respondents have an awkward distribution of phase assignments: to be precise, four phases have cell counts approximating 10 or fewer. Obviously, this skewedness may attenuate associations, and results with collapsed phases encourage this point of view. Moreover, Tables IV.3 and IV.4 report sharper patterns of covariation in North American vs. global loci.

Second, it may be that this variability-within-a-pattern reflects cultural features. In effect, these cultural forces are not so powerful as to destroy the basic pattern of associations, but seem sufficient to dilute those relationships.

Third, the difference in magnitude may reflect the need for fine-tuning of the dependent variables—GHQ I and II. Specifically, the 30 GHQ items were chosen for American respondents, and they may be applicable in different senses or degrees to respondents in other global settings. To be balanced about this possibility, however, other evidence tethers such speculation. Typically, for example, *alpha* coefficients for the MBI sub-domains as well as for marker variables are substantial in all research settings considered in this section. In Japan C, for example, Cronbach's $alpha$ = 0.92 for GHQ I, which implies that Japanese respondents saw the items in internally-consistent ways.

Fourth, and perhaps paramountly, it may be that the present results reflect the variable applicability of the "universal norms" underlying the High/Low distinctions for the three MBI sub-domains which, in turn, define the 8 phases of burnout. As advertised, the authors of this book persist in using these norms as the cutting points, based on a large ($N = 1,535$) population from a U.S. federal agency (Site B). So far, the authors see no convincing evidence for abandoning this working bias.

But other opinions must be taken into account: some students urge different norms (e.g, Burke, 1989; Lee & Ashforth, 1991). Typically, such observers prefer "local norms"—for example, the median scores on the three

MBI sub-domains for each specific data-set. This key issue will get detailed attention below, especially in Chapter VII.

Caveats notwithstanding, practically, the present results add a definite urgency to research with the phase model, and especially in Japan. Two reasons dominate. Thus, very high proportions of Japanese respondents fall in the most advanced phases of burnout. In Japan C, moreover, 74.7 percent of all respondents are classified as "cases;" the percentage for China B is 63.7. The specific proportions may be an artefact of our measuring conventions but, in any case, their magnitudes are lower but still startling in the selected North American cases. There, an average of 20-plus percent are classified as VIIIs, on average, and there also perhaps 30 percent of all respondents are classified as "cases," using our standard conventions. The resulting challenges may be "big" or "bigger," then, but all available evidence urges ameliorative efforts in all of the worksites detailed here, but moreso in some worksites than others.

The challenge for officials in organizations seems the same, then, whatever the norms: help members stay in the less-advanced phases or, if it is too late for that in specific cases, help people move toward the less-advanced phases. The situation is especially serious because three available worksites—Site 00, PP, and ZZ—are military or police populations which do (and should) place a special premium on the emotional stability of their members. Even in those loci, the estimates of "cases" as well as "passives" seem associated regularly with Phases I $\longrightarrow$ VIII.

TOWARD PHASES AND
OBJECTIVE ESTIMATES OF HEALTH[2]

This section focuses on two generalizations, with the goal of building upon and beyond them, respectively. As should be clear from the sections above, both in North America as well as in global settings, the phases consistently isolate meaningful proportions of variance on self-reports about well-being. However, most studies using physiological measures of health show weak or no effects (e.g., Steffy & Jones, 1988). To those observers who see self-reports as inferior measures, the apparent covariation with stress or burnout operational definitions merely represents common methods variance, autocorrelation effects, and similar contaminants.

Consequently, testing the phase model against objective health-related measures requires little justification. Directly, most of the literature assesses a self-report measure in terms of other self-reports. Careful researchers must acknowledge that resulting associations may derive from common methods variance. In any case, reliance on multiple measures—both "objective" and "hard" as well as "subjective" and "soft"—seems reasonable.

What we intend here is both ambitious and limited. In this section, 8 health-related covariants will extend the assessment of the concurrent validity of the phase model, with most of these covariants resting on objective indicators or having major non-subjective components. Again, positive findings will reinforce the usefulness of the phase model as an operational definition for estimating the degree of burnout that individuals experience at work. However, the word "toward" in the section title is used deliberately. This section constitutes a useful step, but only an early one down a long trail that winds far into the future.

Population

Site D, $N = 783$, is a sub-set of one year's participants in a corporate wellness program, with all data gathered at registration. All respondents are employees of a firm in a personal products firm, they represent all hierarchical ranks, and participants perform the full range of activities from research through marketing and finance. Wellness participation was voluntary, as was participation in this research. See also Appendix A.

Let us dispose of a possible early objection. There is no reason to anticipate major biasing effects here due to self-selectivity. The present design tests for covariation between an estimate of burnout and various health-related measures. So, even if a healthier-than-normal population did volunteer here—the usual assumption, of course—the present results would *not* be artefactual. Rather, this situation constitutes a conservative test of any associations, given a reasonable number of cases in all phases. Table IV.9 establishes that Site D generates just such a distribution. No phase has fewer than 45 assignees. Note also that Chapter VI will show that Site D has about perhaps 10 percent fewer assignments to the three advanced phases than the average North American worksetting on which phase data are available to the present authors. In this sense, Site D respondents are substantially "healthier" than available data circumscribing "normal."

But why use the descriptor "conservative?" The rationale is direct. If healthier individuals do volunteer, that will attenuate scores on the health-related measures. This, in turn, should increase the difficulty of establishing non-random covariation with the phases.

Table IV.9. Phase Model and Distribution of Phase Assignments, Site D

	Phases of Burnout								
	I	II	III	IV	V	VI	VII	VIII	
$N =$	244	48	133	55	50	71	45	137	$= 783$
$\% =$	31.2	6.1	17.0	7.0	6.4	9.1	5.8	17.5	

To be sure, the situation would be very different were the focus (for example) on assessing the efficacy of a program for stress reduction, in which case it would follow that the enrolling population probably would have a special interest in reducing stress, or keeping it at low levels, and both characterizations could bias results. In such cases, a control group of non-enrollees is indicated. No such clear argument applies in the present case although, as usual, evidence of positive associations should be interpreted cautiously and as part of the evolving research on the phase model.

Methods

Three introductory emphases describe the ways and means employed by this test of the concurrent validity of the phase model of burnout. These emphases include: brief descriptions of several health-related measures; expected association with the phases; and a note on statistical analysis. In addition, note that reliability estimates support the present use of the MBI sub-domains. Depersonalization has a Cronbach's *alpha* of .8125, Personal Accomplishment of .7409, and Emotional Exhaustion of .8827.

Health-Related Measures.   All relevant data were gathered and analyzed for corporate purposes by a firm doing wellness diagnoses, and were made available "blind" to the researchers for detailed analysis. However, all testing of employees used conventional principles and practices. Guidelines for the last four measures listed below are drawn from leading health sources—the National Mental Health Association, U.S. Dietary Guidelines for Americans, American Cancer Institute, American Cancer Society, and American Heart Association. The estimates include:

- *weight* in pounds
- *body mass index*, a ratio of weight in kilograms divided by height in meters squared, with lower ratios considered more desirable
- *percent body fat*, with desirable ranges distinguished for men (12-16 percent) and women (20-24 percent)
- *stress/coping index*, on which high scores indicate an unfavorable state as assessed by responses to 6 items that tap: overall stress; incidence of stress signals; energy levels; adequacy of sleep; degree of happiness; and status of social support systems (Breslow Study, Alameda County, CA).
- *exercise score* is based on self-ratings of the number of workouts per week assessed by a single item.
- *nutrition score* is based on guidelines from the National Institute of Health, which encompass several "hard" and "soft" variables: four

objective blood factors—total cholesterol (C), LDL-C or "bad" cholesterol, HDL-C or the "good" variety, glucose, and triglycerides— as well as self-reports on 11 survey items that assess amount of breads and grains eaten, fats used in cooking, and sweets eaten.

- *cancer risk*, follows National Institute of Health recommendations and is based on several risk factors including: smoking status, alcohol consumption, high fat diet, low fiber intake, family history, and hemocult analysis.

- *cardiac heart disease risk* is based on the cholesterol education program of the National Institute of Health, and combines several risk factors: smoking, blood pressure, high stress, exercise levels, family and personal histories, any presently-experienced symptoms, and levels of total cholesterol (C), HDL-C, LDL-C, triglycerides, and glucose.

Individuals are assigned to four categories: extra low ($N = 252$); low ($N = 75$); moderate ($N = 272$); and high ($N = 184$).

The eight measures, then, incorporate both "hard" and "soft" estimates. The first three measures are "hard," and three others give major weight to objective indicators (nutrition score, cancer risk, and cardiac heart disease risk). Three other measures incorporate self-reports from a survey, while the stress/coping and exercise measures rest solely on self-reports. This mixed character of measures constitutes an important test of the phase model.

The present eight are not the only health-related measures, of course. But they are common ones in health inventories; and they do constitute a useful test of the concurrent validity of the phase model.

Expected Association with Phases. Rationales could be developed for each health-related measure, but only a single exemplar is provided here, and briefly. For example, high levels of experienced stress seem to create physiological conditions seen as precursors of cardiac heart disease risk (e.g., Haynes & Feinleif, 1980). Again, then, a useful operational definition of burnout should isolate a pattern of non-random associations between the phases and experienced stress.

One further detail remains. In all tests below, the 8 health-related measures are expected to worsen as the phases progress. Consequently, the stress/ coping index will increase, phase by phase; similarly, the risks of cancer and cardiac heart disease are expected to increase with the progressive phases; and so on.

Statistical Procedures. As an initial exploration, this study uses one-way analysis of variance to determine whether non-random variance exists somewhere in the distribution of the various health-related measures, arrayed by phases of burnout. This reliance on bivariate analysis makes no assumptions about the ordinality or rank-ordered character of the progressive phases. As elsewhere, when ANOVA achieves or surpasses $P \leq$ .05, tests will be run of the statistical significance of each pair of differences. The Scheffé procedure will be utilized in this section to test all possible paired-comparisons. This test is probably more conservative than the Least Significant Difference (LSD) test used elsewhere in this volume.

Next, stepwise regression analysis provides a comprehensive picture of the association of the phases with the health-related measures. In effect, the technique enters three independent variables—phase assignments, age, and gender—in the order in which they contribute to explaining the variance in each health measure. This extends the analysis well beyond ANOVA and Scheffé, with the beta scores and ΔR^2 providing an estimate of the proportion of variance explained by each independent variable. In this analysis, unlike most analyses in this book, the stepwise regression procedure assumes the ordinal character of the phases. Specifically, the progressive phases I, II...VIII are entered as 1, 2...8 in the stepwise regression.

Note also that *alpha* coefficients or other tests of internal reliability of the last four health-related measures listed above are not available. Confidentiality safeguards kept researchers distant from the original data-set, and the firm providing the wellness survey does not include reliability estimates in its data-processing protocols.

Findings

Table IV.10. Intercorrelations of Marker Variables

	Weight	Body Mass Index	% Body Fat	Stress-Coping Index	Exercise	Nutrition	Cancer Risk
Body Mass Index	.83**						
% Body Fat	.05	.39**					
Stress-Coping Index	.002	-.01	.05				
Exercise	.023	-.08	-.19**	-.10*			
Nutrition	-.10*	-.13**	.01	-.02	-.36**		
Cancer Risk	.13**	.15**	.10*	.08	-.27**	-.36**	
Cardiac Disease Risk	.46**	.46**	-.02	-.02	-.16**	-.11*	-.25**

Note: * designates 2-tailed significance at .01 level, and
** does so at .001 level.

In general, any associations of the health-related measures with the phase model cannot be attributed to the unidimensionality of measures. Table IV.10 provides the product-moment correlations for the 8 health-related measures. Although over 64 percent of the coefficients attain $P \leq .01$, that reflects population size more than large coefficients and extensive shared variance. Indeed, only one coefficient exceeds .4, and mean R^2 approximates .065. Obviously, that leaves ample variance unaccounted for, and suggests the multi-dimensionality of our panel of 8 health status variables.

Trends by Phases. Overall, the phases isolate the expected pattern. As Table IV.11 shows, 5 of the 8 cases either show non-random variation somewhere in the distributions of the health-related measures arrayed by the phases, or closely approach usually-accepted levels of statistical significance ($P = .066$ for Exercise). Moreover, as Table IV.12 shows, finer-grained analysis supports the phase model. That 152 of 224 (or 67.9 percent) of all possible paired-comparisons show an increase in health risk, phase by progressive phase; and this is more markedly the case with the 83 of 112 cases (or 74.1 percent) associated with the four variables that attain $P \leq .05$, overall. Finally, statistical significance is achieved by 9.8 percent of all paired-comparisons of the four variables attaining overall significance, while 5 percent of such cases could be expected if chance only were operating. Except for Stress-Coping Index, only small proportions of the variance are explained.

Table IV.11. Phases vs. Health-Related Measures

	F-ratio	Probability	Eta^2
Weight	1.03	.404	———
Body Mass Index	0.81	.578	———
Percent Body Fat	2.44	.018	.02
Stress-Coping Index	20.33	.001	.15
Exercise	1.91	.066	.02
Nutrition Score	2.72	.008	.02
Cancer Risk	1.19	.308	———
Cardiac Disease Risk	2.09	.042	.02

Table IV.12. Patterns of Association,
Phases and Health-Related Measures

	Proportions	%
Paired-Comparisons in Expected Direction (All Measures)	152 of 224	67.9
Paired-Comparisons in Expected Direction (4 Significant Measures)	83 of 112	74.1
Paired-Comparisons in Expected Direction and Statistically Significant (All Measures)	11 of 224	4.9
Paired-Comparisons in Expected Direction and Statistically Significant (4 Significant Measures)	11 of 112	9.8

Trends by Age, Gender, and Phases. More specific analysis is necessary because (for example) we know that gender has direct associations with some of the covariants in the present panel—that is, percent body fat trends greater for females than males, and weight as well as body mass index also are linked to gender and age. In fact, these known regularities may help explain the failure of the first two variables in Table IV.11 to attain significance.

Stepwise regression permits the required specification, and Table IV.13 summarizes the results for the 8 health-related covariants, the 8 phase model, gender, and age.[3] Among the three independent variables, the phases and gender are both statistically-significant contributors in 6 of 8 cases, and age in 5 of 8. For the significant cases only, mean R^2 contributions attributable to gender approximate .14, for age .06, and for the phases .03.

Discussion

In sum, two findings receive support from the data. Thus the concurrent validity of the phase model is supported by yet another panel of covariants, in general, although age and gender clearly explain more of the variation in the health-related measures than do the phases. Moreover, 6 of the 8 present measures are either "non-subjective" or have major "objective" components. Hence, this test usefully supports the phase model, and especially in connection with stress-coping, cancer risk, cardiac disease risk, nutrition, excercise, and body fat.

Table IV.13. Stepwise Regressions, Three Independent Variables on Health-Related Measures, N = 783

Weight

Order of Independent Variables[a]	Beta[c]	R²	ΔR²
Gender[b]	-.51**	.27	.27
Age	.15**	.29	.02
Phases	NS		

Body Mass Index

Order of Independent Variables[a]	Beta	R²	ΔR²
Age	.23**	.06	.06
Gender	-.18**	.09	.03
Phases	NS		

% Body Fat

Order of Independent Variables[a]	Beta	R²	ΔR²
Gender	.65**	.40	.40
Age	.41**	.56	.16
Phases	.08**	.57	.01

Stress/Coping Index

Order of Independent Variables[a]	Beta	R²	ΔR²
Phases	.36**	.13	.13
Gender	.07*	.14	.01
Age	NS		

Exercise

Order of Independent Variables[a]	Beta	R²	ΔR²
Phases	-.11**	.01	.01
Age	NS		
Gender	NS		

Nutrition

Order of Independent Variables[a]	Beta	R²	ΔR²
Age	.18**	.03	.03
Phases	-.12**	.05	.02
Gender	.12**	.06	.01

Cancer Risk

Order of Independent Variables[a]	Beta	R²	ΔR²
Phases	.08*	.01	.01
Age	NS		
Gender	NS		

Cardiac Disease Risk

Order of Independent Variables[a]	Beta	R²	ΔR²
Age	.38**	.15	.15
Gender	-.36**	.28	.13
Phases	.10*	.29	.01

Notes: [a] The order in which independent variables are admitted to step-wise equations differs for specific covariants.
[b] Gender is dummied as 0 (male), 1 (female).
[c] A negative sign on the partial beta indicates that being female decreases the predicted score.
* indicates $P < .05$.
** indicates $P .01$.
NS indicates an insignificant covariant not admitted to stepwise equation.

Several caveats also are in order. First, the present population clearly does not eliminate concerns about generalizability even as it represents distinct improvements in several particulars over earlier research with the same design. Specifically, the underlying pilot study (Golembiewski & Munzenrider, 1991a) can be criticized on two grounds: it encompassed only a smallish minority ($N = 204$) of all participants in an earlier Be Your Best program; and the participating population was in turn a minority of the eligible population. This replication eliminates the first threat to generalizability, and substantially reduces the second.

Second, that pilot study (Golembiewski & Munzenrider, 1991c) also generates the sharper pattern of results. In that earlier research, in sum, 81.4 percent of all ANOVAs achieve significance, and the mean eta-square for those non-random cases approximates 10 percent. Moreover, only the phases there attain statistical significance on each health-related variable in all step-wise regressions, while gender and age are non-significant in 4 of 14 cases involving them.

These differences require further analysis. Among numerous other possibilities, the pilot study reflected problems with homoscedasticity, while the present health-related variables do not seem to present problems with their variance, possibly excepting the Stress-Coping Index.

Third, the phase model is the subject of debate (e.g., Burke, 1989; Leiter, 1988, 1989; Golembiewski, 1989), with perhaps the most salient issue involving the sequence of the MBI sub-domains. As noted, the phase model assumes this sequence in chronic onset: Depersonalization, Personal Accomplishment, and Emotional Exhaustion. Alternatively, Maslach and her associates seem inclined toward a model where high levels of emotional exhaustion will, *if* sufficient depersonalization subsequently occurs, lead to low levels of personal accomplishment. Other observers question the universal norms we use for High/Low assignments (e.g., Burke, 1989). See also Chapter VII.

Comparative analyses of alternative models of the phases alone will provide constructive resolution of the conceptual and measurement issues in contention, but relevant work is still at early stages. Available research—in this volume, as well as in other sources (e.g., Golembiewski & Munzenrider, 1991b; Kim, 1990)—generally supports the special usefulness of the present version of the phase model. See also Chapter VII, which directs attention to several consistent features of the phase model, as they are informed by the knowledge and experience underlying this book.

Fourth, the associations here clearly are not as marked as for other covariants of the phase model, and this difference may be interpreted in several ways, one of which relies on the "funnel of causality" used to explain results concerning voting behavior (Campbell et al., 1960, pp. 23-24). In this view, the phases measure a contemporary condition and hence are reasonably related to proximate features, whether measured by self-reports— of physical symptoms, job satisfaction, and so on—or by objective measures like turnover. In contrast, the present measures relate to variously distal and probabilistic health-states, and remain "further out" on the funnel of causality than the phases. Only a longitudinal research design can provide perspective on the phases as leading indicators, and the results above come from a one-shot study.

The funnel of causality provides guidance concerning the present findings as well as about a way to test them. Following the funnel line of argument, no dominant associations with the phases should be expected here. Hypothetically, also, the associations will increase in longitudinal studies, *if* present burnout levels in fact anticipate future health-statuses.

TOWARD PHASES AND BLOOD CHEMISTRY

That word "toward" appears again in connection with this last of five health-related tests of the phase model, and that appearance is not accidental. Blood chemistry should be even more distal from burnout than the "objective" or "hard" measures of health just considered, and hence this section constitutes an even-longer "reach" than the preceding discussion.

So let's get on with it. Again, the encouraging results of a pilot study got us started (Golembiewski & Munzenrider, 1993a). Our motivation is direct, both in this replication as well as in the pilot study. Eventually, research on burnout will develop an operational measure that will be validated by testing its concurrent validity in terms of numerous self-reports and objective indicators that researchers for theoretical and empirical reasons relate to variations in burnout. Both "hard" and "soft" indicators should be utilized. But "eventually" is not yet "now."

In the interest of completeness at the risk of repetition, a reasonable scaffolding of expectations and research findings supports a replication of the pilot study of the covariation of the phases and several estimates of blood chemistry. The sections above provide encouragement, and the psychological $<\longrightarrow>$ physical association has long been recognized (e.g., Eastwood, 1975). More pointedly, work such as that of Mechanic and Angel (1987) also shows the way. They had data about back pain from a large number of respondents for whom extensive self-report data were available, along with the results of extensive medical examinations. This simultaneity permitted the development of an index estimating the extent to which reported back pain exceeded physical findings. Mechanic (1994, p. 113) highlights two major findings of this significant research, which controls for numerous conventional demographics. Thus, those with a "depressed mood" reported more complaints and revealed on examination more physical bases for those complaints, as is consistent with the discussion in this chapter. Mechanic adds that the "most interesting finding" involves a distinction between older persons. The general tendency of older persons to report less pain was, given comparable status as determined by physical examination, statistically significant *only* for that older sub-sample also reporting "higher levels of psychological well-being." This also is consistent with the interpretation in this chapter.

How certain is our present "grasp?" We are part of the way there. In general, self-reports have dominated in estimates of burnout as well as in almost all of the marker variables employed to assess concurrent validity. As this book demonstrates, robust and regular associations usually exist. In contrast, efforts to use objective measures—in the stress literature (e.g., Steffy & Jones, 1988), as well as in the previous section—usually result in weaker patterns of associations with target variables, or in no consistent findings. As Steffy and Jones conclude about their own research and that of others (1988, p. 887): "The findings...have not suggested as strong a relationship between workplace stresses and physiological indicators of stress as have studies employing subjective dependent measures of stress....These results are disappointing, given the assumption that physiological measures are more objective and reliable than self-report measures."

No firm interpretation is possible of efforts to encompass "hard" and "soft" variables in burnout research. Thus, one can argue that the mixed findings indicate the inferior status of available burnout measures. Alternatively, one can argue that no relationships exist. Or, one can emphasize the various problems in reliably generating "hard" data, as in fine-tuning the testing procedures required by physiological assays (e.g., Steffy & Jones, 1988, p. 688). Hence, even negative findings do not settle all important issues.

These indeterminacies challenge next steps, but do not intimidate them. This fifth test of health-related features of the phase model has three emphases. In turn, attention gets directed at: population and methods; findings concerning blood chemistry and the phases; and a discussion of results.

Population and Methods

Three introductory themes provide perspective on the present research design and methods. In turn, these themes deal with: the populations of respondents; eight measures related to blood chemistry; and a brief review of analytic methods.

Population.   The host of this fifth test of health status and the phases—ite EEE, $N = 743$—is a health-care firm located in the United States. For details, see Appendix A.

For reasons like those detailed in the previous section, there is no reason to expect spurious positive effects. The present design constitutes a conservative test, then, and requires only a reasonable number of cases in all phases, and Table VI.1 establishes that this condition is met.

Some Measurement Details.   Relying on the numerous details already presented about the MBI sub-domains and the phases, we need only note the acceptable Cronbach *alpha* coefficients of the three MBI sub-domains. The coefficients for Depersonalization, Personal Accomplishment, and Emotional Exhaustion are, respectively, .8125, .7409, and .8827. In the very large majority of cases, the MBI was completed shortly after blood samples were taken.

Two other measurement issues require greater attention. They deal, respectively, with: two approaches to estimating circulatory health; and brief but important notes about statistical methods.

Many physiologists have proposed that valid and reliable covariants of stress are available. These indicators include blood pressure, serum cholesterol, and triglyceride serum (e.g., Haynes & Feinleib, 1980; McIlroy & Travis, 1981). Such indicators are commonly seen as causally involved in various stress-related diseases and disorders, especially of the circulatory system (e.g., Ramsey, 1982).

This analysis focuses on two kinds of measures of blood chemistry to test the concurrent validity of the phase model of burnout, with all data gathered at Site EEE by a firm doing corporate wellness diagnoses. All hematologic results come from a certified and licensed clinical laboratory working under the supervision of a board-certified pathologist. The data were delivered "blind" to the researchers. Blood pressures were taken at the workplace by professional staff before blood samples were drawn. Volunteers were encouraged to fast before the sample-taking.

Two emphases introduce this approach to estimating circulatory health. Immediately, eight features of blood chemistry and the circulatory system get attention. Later, an aggregate Profile of circulatory health is described.

Measures of Circulatory Health.   The eight measures can be introduced briefly, along with brief comments about their expected associations with experienced stress and work-related outcomes. These measures include:

- *Systolic blood pressure.* Elevated levels suggest stress-related disorders, prominent among which are hypertension and coronary diseases.

- *Diastolic blood pressure.* Medical opinion considers this a more valid and reliable indicator of stress-related disorders than systolic readings.
- *Serum cholesterol.* This fat-like substance can collect in arteries and increase the risk of coronary disease. Research is not conclusive about the association of worksite stressors with serum cholesterol (e.g., Howard, Cunningham, & Rechnitzer, 1986), although early work suggests such an effect (e.g., Friedman, Rosenman, & Carroll, 1957).
- *LDL cholesterol* is now widely considered "bad" because, in its presence, cholesterol deposits tend to develop in the arteries. LDL-C seems a better indicator of coronary disease than total cholesterol.
- *HDL cholesterol.* HDL-C has a good reputation, and apparently guards against coronary disease by helping remove deposits from the arteries. As noted above, LDL-C seems to be associated with potentially-harmful deposits.
- *Ratio of Total Cholesterol to HDL-C.* Some recent work suggests this ratio may be the most useful single indicator of stress, as well as a more revealing antecedent of coronary disease (e.g., Hendrix, Ovalle, & Troxler, 1985). Lower ratios are more desirable.
- *Triglycerides.* Elevated levels not only indicate fat in the blood which can impair circulation, but high concentrations of triglycerides also seem associated with other abnormal lipid levels. Triglyceride levels seem associated with such stressors at work as job dissatisfaction and role ambiguity (e.g., Howard, Cunningham, & Rechnitzer, 1986).
- *Blood glucose.* High levels of sugar can indicate diabetes, and imply increased risk of diseases of the heart and blood vessels. More broadly, the "stress reaction," in anticipation of fight/flight responses, sends chemical signals that release glucose as well as (for example) cholesterol. Our evolution may be our undoing in this regard. Thus, the release presumably *was* functional in past epochs, but contemporary conditions make those responses largely inappropriate (e.g., Fox & Mathews, 1981, esp. pp. 560-580).

Profile of Circulatory Health.   In addition to these eight estimates, this analysis also tests a Profile score against the phases. Figure IV.1 presents details and, basically, it provides three kinds of information:

- recommended levels for each of the 8 measures
- five intervals on each of the measures that permit estimating an individual's specific status as poor —> excellent
- weights for each of the measures that estimate their relative significance to cardiovascular health

Cardiovascular Health Categories

Hematologic Measures	Recommended Levels	Poor	Below Recommended Range	Recommended Range	Above Recommended Range	Excellent	Weight
Systolic Blood Pressure	< 140	160 or >	150	140 – 135	125	110 or <	5
Diastolic Blood Pressure	< 90	100 or >	95	90 – 85	75	65 or <	10
Cholesterol	< 180 mg	290 or >	230	180 – 170	155	140 or <	10
HDL Cholesterol Males: > 45		25 or <	35	45 – 55	65	75 or <	10
HDL Cholesterol Females: > 55		35 or <	45	55 – 65	70	80 or <	
LDL Cholesterol	< 130 mg	175 or >	145	130 – 120	110	100 or <	10
Ratio Chol/HDL-Chol	4.0 or less	7.0 or >	5.5	4.0 – 3.5	3.25	3.0 or <	20
Triglycerides	< 100 mg	275 or >	175	100 – 75	50	20 or <	5
Glucose	< 115 mg	180 or >	125	115 – 110	90	60 or <	10

Figure IV.1. Eight Hematologic Measures, Recommended Levels, and Weights in Cardiovascular Health

Figure IV.1 is generated for present purposes from several sources, and especially from information provided by the firm doing the wellness diagnosis at Site EEE. The recommended levels come from standard sources about which substantial agreement exists; and several medical doctors have reviewed Figure IV.1 and report no egregious errors. However, no independent empirical support of the Profile is available, which will be tested here for the first time. In outline, the Profile has four features:

- for each measure, each individual can be assigned a gross status—(0) to (4) for the degree of meeting each recommended range.
- each hematologic measure is assigned a weight— 5, 10, or 20— consistent with our sense of its generally-accepted contribution to cardiovascular health.
- again on each measure, each individual can be assigned a specific status that takes into account both a measure's weight and an individual's rating on that measure—for example, a 220 Cholesterol reading is scored as 10 X 1, or 10.
- aggregating all 8 weighted scores for each individual provides an overall estimate of a person's cardiovascular health—X of 320 possible points.

Analytic Methods. Causality cannot be established here, of course, and should not be inferred. For preliminary purposes, any associations can be interpreted either as possible antecedents or as consequences of burnout. Of course, we can be definite about whether the covariation is random or not.

Two tests of associations with the phases of burnout are run. In turn, analysis will emphasize: multivariate tests of associations of the 8 hematologic estimates with three possible independent variables—age, gender, and the phases; and bivariate as well as multivariate tests involving the Profile of cardiovascular health.

Subsequent analysis takes the 9 health-related variables, as well as age, gender, and phases into simultaneous account. This analysis encodes the progressive phases I, II...VIII as 1, 2...8 in the stepwise regressions.

This stepwise regression subjects the data to a first-pass for the purpose of sorting-out demographic versus phase contributions to blood levels. The method provides two useful perspectives on each type of contributor: the *order* in which the various measures enter (or do not enter) the equation estimating the apparent importance of each factor for predicting the various blood measures; and the partial betas associated with each factor indicate the *relative importance* of each factor while controlling for other predictors.

Table IV.14. Interrelations, 9 Estimates of Circulatory System Health

	Systolic Blood Pressure	Diastolic Blood Pressure	Cholesterol	HDL Cholesterol	LDL Cholesterol	Ratio: Chol/HDL Cholesterol	Triglycerides	Glucose
Diastolic B-P	.7243**							
Cholesterol	-.2477**	.2658**						
HDL Cholesterol	-.1628**	-.1855**	.0951*					
LDL Cholesterol	.2596**	.3135**	.9151**	-.2033**				
Ratio: Chol/HDL Chol	.2978*	.3417**	.4349**	-.7314***	.7082***			
Triglycerides	.2529**	.2244**	.4649**	-.3654**	.3291**	.6365**		
Glucose	.2271**	.2021**	.3153**	-.1349**	.3109**	.3151**	.2898**	
Profile	-.4120**	-.4768**	.6687**	.5935**	.9083**	-.5977**	-.5977**	-.3844**

Note: * designates 2-tailed significance at .01 level, and
** at .001 level.

123

Using the phases as an independent variable does not satisfy the strict requirement for regression analysis that independent variables be measured as continuous variables—for example, interval or ratio levels of measurement. A phase "score" is, strictly speaking, an ordinal measure, and we typically treat it as a nominal variable. Nonetheless, we here consider that the phases approximate continuous properties, and the beta weights we calculate will give us a good indication of the merit of this convenience.

Findings

As a useful preliminary, the intercorrelations in Table IV.14 of the estimates of the health of circulatory systems suggest that this analysis does not simply measure one domain nine different ways. As expected because of how it is constructed, the Profile has substantial correlations with the 8 other measures: in fact, the absolute mean correlation approximates .605. The 28 other coefficients are all significant due to the large N, but 14 share less than 10 percent of their variance while 23 of the 28 cases share less than 20 percent.

Three patterns of association of the nine cardiovascular measures with the phases are expected, *if* the phase model constitutes a valid and reliable measure of experienced stressors. Thus, HDL-C should vary inversely with the phases: that is, higher estimates should be associated with less-advanced phases. Moreover, high levels of the seven other estimates of blood factors indicate increasing health risks. Hence, higher levels of these seven measures are expected for the more advanced phases of burnout. Finally, larger Profile scores imply better health, and consequently should be inversely associated with the phases.

Associations with Age, Gender, and Phases.   When each of the raw hematologic measures is considered simultaneously along with three possible covariants, all eight cases have significant predictors in stepwise regressions. See Table IV.15. Age or gender or the phases—or all three in two cases—have significant associations with the blood measures. Cumulatively, about 13.4 percent of the variance is accounted for in the significant cases, on average.

Viewed another way, the phases contribute significantly to two of the eight measures of circulatory health. Both of these cases explain only a small percentage of the variance, as Table IV.15 demonstrates.

Weighted Associations, or Profile.   The final approach to testing for associations of the phases employs Profile scores. This approach generates mixed results, but assigns no major role to the phases.

Table IV.15. Stepwise Regressions, Three Independent Variables on Circulatory Health Measures, Site EEE.

Order of Independent Variables[a]	Systolic Blood Pressure				Diastolic Blood Pressure				Cholesterol				HDL-Cholesteraol		
	Beta[c]	R^2	ΔR^2		Beta	R^2	ΔR^2		Beta	R^2	ΔR^2		Beta	R^2	ΔR^2
Gender[b]	.19**	.04	-	Gender	.26**	.07	-	Age	-.34**	.11	-	Gender	.17**	.03	-
Age	-.19**	.07	.03	Age	-.26**	.13	.06	Gender	.09**	.12	.01	Phases	NS		
Phases	NS			Phases	NS			Phases	NS			Age	NS		

Order of Independent Variables[a]	LDL Cholesterol				Ratio: Chol/HDL				Triglycerides				Glucose		
	Beta[c]	R^2	ΔR^2		Beta	R^2	ΔR^2		Beta	R^2	ΔR^2		Beta	R^2	ΔR^2
Age	-.33**	.11	-	Gender	.49**	.25	-	Age	-.25**	.06	-	Age	-.26**	.07	-
Gender	.24**	.17	.06	Age	-.24**	.30	.05	Gender	.23**	.11	.05	Gender	.23	.12	.05
Phases	NS			Phases	-.10**	.31	.01	Phases	-.09**	.12	.01	Phases	NS		

Notes: [a] The order in which independent variables are admitted to step-wise equations differs for specific covariants.
[b] Gender is dummied as 0 (male), 1 (female).
[c] A negative sign on the partial beta indicates that being female decreases the predicted score.
* indicates $P < .05$.
** indicates $P < .01$.
NS indicates a non-significant covariant not admitted to stepwise equation.
[d] N varies from 756 to 772.

125

Table IV.16. Stepwise Regression, Three Independent Variables
on Profile Scores, Site EEE

	Partial Beta	Adjusted R^2	ΔR^2
Gender	.41**	.18	-
Age	-.33**	.28	.10
Phases	-.09*	.29	.01

Note: * indicates $P = .004$.
  ** indicates $P < .0000$.

Stepwise Regression for Profile.   Gender and age contribute significantly
to explaining the Profile scores, as do the phases. Table IV.16 reflects the
results of this analysis, and it shows that the phases explain about 1 percent
of the variation in Profile scores.

Discussion

The underlying details about the covariation of the phases of burnout
with the nine measures of cardiovascular health may be summarized by two
conclusions. First, the phases attain significance in 3 of the 9 tests detailed
above. Second, the phases here explain only small proportions of the
variance in those cases in which statistical significance is observed.

In sum, the present results add some indeterminacy to the literature on
the phase model which, in general, has been quite consistent. That is to
say, the present results stand at some odds with almost all other phase
research that also utilizes objective or "hard" variables—for example,
significant associations with the phases have been observed for turnover
(Golembiewski, Hilles, & Daly, 1987), performance appraisals (Golembiewski & Munzenrider, 1988, pp. 85-89), and the use of medical insurance.
Even in such cases, the findings can be mixed. Thus Jackson and Manning
(1996) show that the reliance on medical insurance by those in advanced
phases increases significantly when total dollars are concerned, but the
regularity does not appear when the frequency of usage is targeted (Manning
& Jackson, 1996). Perhaps intervening variables are at issue here. See also
Chapter V.

The present results also are not consistent with research testing many
"soft" or self-report covariants of the phases, as this book illustrates in
almost-all particulars studied. Typically, 15-25 percent of the variance is
explained when self-report data are tested for covariation of marker variables
with the phases.

Three interpretations of the present results are possible. Obviously, to
begin, the measures of cardiovascular health here may be only marginally

useful, if not the wrong ones. The Profile is initially suspect, since it was created for *ad hoc* purposes and is supported by no replication.

Some evidence supports this point of view, in fact, but it is conjectural. Thus, Fried (1988, esp. pp. 362-363) reports that blood measures like those above are more revealing concerning "acute stress" while (for example) catecholamines may be more relevant for the "chronic stress" most associated with burnout as measured by the phase model. This possibility is well-taken, but recall the phase model accommodates both chronic and acute onset. So Fried's point at least does not apply in a direct and unmediated sense. See also the data in Chapter VI about the persistence of the burnout phases.

In addition, to take an opposed position, some researchers (e.g., Melamed, Kushnir, & Shirom, 1992) have reported positive associations between burnout and measures like those above. The mixed and modest associations reported here, in this context, imply questions about the phase model or, alternatively, about the research design in this section as well as about its methods of gathering as well as analyzing the data.

These two possibilities are difficult to assess. Thus, the first possibility "explains" the present findings but only by neglecting the large and growing inventory of findings supportive of the phase model, many of which are detailed in this book. It seems unlikely we can have both.

Third, as was suggested at the end of the previous section, the full body of results is understandable in terms of a concept like the "funnel of causality," introduced in voting analysis some years ago (Campbell, Converse, Miller, & Stokes, 1960, pp. 23-24). They explain: "We wish to account for a single behavior [voting] at a fixed point in time [election day]. But [that behavior] stems from a multitude of prior factors. We can visualize the chain of events with which we wish to deal as contained within a *funnel of causality*."

Relying on the concept of a causal funnel can help explain both "positive" and "negative" findings associated with the phase model. That is, some covariants are proximate to burnout phases—for example, job satisfaction, turnover and especially intent to turnover, and performance appraisals—whether "hard" or "soft" measures are utilized. Substantial evidence supports just such an interpretation, as this volume establishes. In contrast, covariants like those in this section will be distal to future effects—for example, high blood pressure to subsequent health—and cannot be expected to show up markedly in associations with today's burnout estimates. In general, only longitudinal analysis can isolate such distal connections, which would reveal more marked covariation over time *if* the phase model is valid and reliable. This possibility is arguably greater in populations like the present one, which is youngish and hence further removed from the experienced or observed consequences of today's phases on the blood chemistry of individuals and their future health.

Perhaps, however, these interpretations stand in need of dose of optimism. Thus, a pilot study (Golembiewski & Munzenrider, 1995) revealed *no* significant associations. The present analysis remedies several deficiencies in that pilot, and the results just reviewed suggest that analysis seems headed in a productive direction. So, the research glass is definitely X-nths empty; but it also seems 1 minus X-nths full!

NOTES

1. This section derives from Golembiewski, Boudreau, Goto, and Murai (1993).

2. For other details, see Golembiewski and Munzenrider (1993a).

3. Some analysis uses the exact ages of respondents, while other analysis groups ages in five 10-year intervals. This reduces the differences between. The number of categories used to estimate the three independent variables. In general, age is coded in 5 categories, gender in 2, and the full phase in 8. No substantial differences are observed in the results based on the two ways of aggregating age.

Chapter V

System Costs and Burnout Phases: Performance, Productivity, and Use of Resources

Outputs are a central purpose of collective life, and they may be viewed as coming in three major varieties—individual performance, collective productivity, and the utilization of resources. This chapter directs attention to each of these aspects of output via four surrogates. These include: individual performance, as measured by appraisals; two measures of productivity; and the magnitude of the resources exhausted by burnout, as estimated both by employee turnover and the use of medical insurance.

A brief introduction precedes detailed analysis of the phase model from these three crucial perspectives.

MOTIVATIONS FOR FOCUSING ON PRODUCTIVITY, PERFORMANCE, AND USE OF RESOURCES

Two factors motivate attention to system costs. Most burnout covariants considered so far rely on self-reports, and therefore some observers will devalue them as reflecting only "subjective reality." This view seems overstated to the authors, and solid evidence suggests that self-reports may even be the evidence of choice in many cases (Howard et al., 1980). But the alleged superiority of "hard data" has a broad currency; and all models should be tested against a broad range of indicators. Moreover, if nothing else, the three perspectives below—on performance, productivity, and use of resources—are important attention-getters, and they "make the world go around" for many people, much of the time.

These analyses will add to the needed evaluations of the phase model, then, although they also leave much undone. Major efforts have been made to generate "hard" or "objective" measures so as to complement self-reports in tests of the regularity and robustness of their association with the phases, but this energy has achieved only modest results.

Not that we and others usually failed in the conventional sense. In a dramatic case, indeed, an independent team of researchers succeeded beyond virtually anyone's expectations in identifying associations of the phases with a very important "hard" measure in a healthcare setting—arguably including the "hardest" measure—that was uncomfortably regular and robust. The host organization involved thus far has exercised its contractual right to withhold permission to publish the data, one hopes for the purpose of doing something to ameliorate advanced phases of burnout and to change the eminently unsatisfactory outcomes closely linked with them. The healthcare setting generated data that associated burnout phases of staff with the mortality of clients. The association was not due to random factors, one can be almost-absolutely certain.

Nor does this chapter exhaust the needed approaches to estimating the systemic costs of burnout. Useful evidence is added, and especially in connection with global settings, but not always with "objective" or "hard" data. Nonetheless, the "system costs" of burnout remain the weakest link in the argument concerning why we should pay real attention to burnout. Nonetheless, this chapter spotlights real tests of the generality and comprehensiveness of the phase model in organizations. Specifically, attention focuses on three questions:

- Do burnout phases covary with personal performance, as judged by influential others?
- Do burnout phases covary with differences in collective productivity, as measured by "cold numbers"?
- Do burnout phases covary with self-ratings of productivity?
- Do phases covary with the use of medical insurance?

An important limitation requires up-front acknowledgment. Most data come from North American settings, but global worksettings do provide some useful (if limited) perspective.

BURNOUT AND PERFORMANCE APPRAISALS IN NORTH AMERICAN SETTINGS

The literature suggests three critical links between burnout and individual performance, though large shortfalls exist concerning when and how often these linkages exist. These three alternative, but not necessarily mutually exclusive, links may be expressed in these terms:

- High achievement has high costs, one of which is advanced burnout (Freudenberger, 1980; Maslach, 1982).
- Low achievement has high costs, one of which is advanced burnout (Edelwich & Brodsky, 1980).
- The association of achievement and burnout is contingent—that is, it depends on the specific mixes of personal features, job characteristics, worksite norms, and so on.

This section reviews some data relevant to these alternative views of the association of performance and burnout. This is done without pretending to resolve questions concerning which explanation applies and how often, but with the hope of extending a useful dialog. In any case, four emphases characterize this approach to performance. In turn, the focus shifts from notes about hosts and methods, then to two sets of findings and, finally, to several implications of those results.

Notes about Hosts and Methods

This analysis emphasizes findings from Site B, with an assist from Site A. For details about the worksites, see Appendix A. In turn, this review has four major foci. Thus, the association of performance appraisals with worksite descriptors gets initial attention; then burnout phases become focal; later, physical symptoms are targeted; and, finally, several implications conclude this review of performance appraisal.

Performance Appraisals and Worksite Descriptors

Several details help frame this discussion of findings, with an assist from the discussion of worksite descriptors in Chapter III. Consistent with the phase model, this analysis targets the proposition that low achievement (as measured by in-house performance appraisals) is associated with high costs. Costs here are defined in terms of degrees of psychological burnout, as well as in terms of deficits in a substantial array of variables assessing the quality of worksite and individual reactions to it. Higher scores almost always imply more of the quality in question, whether the scale involves facets of satisfaction or job tension. Where appropriate, one-tailed estimates are involved.

One caution about the two research sites requires emphasis. Performance appraisals at Site A come from organization records, while those at Site B are based on respondent self-reports. Overall, any misreporting probably would "sweeten" recollections at Site B, and hence may dilute any associations there with burnout and other variables.

Findings at Site B. Findings at Site B reveal statistically significant but modest associations between worksite descriptors and performance appraisal, as measured by self-reports. In fact, Table V.1 shows that all 16 marker variables achieve statistical significance, with all the descriptors worsening as performance appraisals shift from "Outstanding" through "Minimally Satisfactory." In addition, 99 percent of the paired-comparisons are in the expected direction, and over 62 percent of those differences achieve statistical significance as determined by the Least Significant Difference test, modified for unequal subsample sizes.

The pattern is more regular than robust, however. Eta^2 calculations indicate that an average of 2.5 percent of the variance is accounted for.

Findings at Site A. The association here has a pattern and magnitude similar to those just reviewed (Golembiewski, Munzenrider, & Stevenson, 1986, p. 91), with the major difference that at Site A performance appraisals come from archival records rather than self-reports. Overall, the findings reinforce the conclusion that worksite descriptors are distal covariants of performance appraisal, rather than main effects. Worksite features directly seem to influence burnout and, as the next sub-section details, variations in phases seem to impact performance.

Performance and Burnout Phases

What can be said of the association between performance and the phases? The findings generally support the phase model, and suggest a trinity of covariants: worksite descriptors, burnout, and performance. But the associations must be qualified, in part due to the "grade inflation" at both sites as well as to sometimes-small sub-sample sizes.

Findings at Site A. The relevant data are available elsewhere (Golembiewski & Munzenrider, 1988, p. 88), but here note only that the regular association of high levels of burnout with poorer performance appraisals should be viewed in the light of two technical points. Due to the small sizes of several cells, the eight burnout phases are collapsed into three categories. This is not ideal. In addition, two sets of appraisals are available. Appraisal I was made in the succeeding six months or so centering around the first survey at day 1. Appraisal II data come from a similar interval around day 365, when the second survey was administered.

Table V.1. Self-Reported Performance Appraisals and
Three Classes of Variables, Site B

	Highly Outstanding	Fully Satisfactory	Minimally Satisfactory	F-Ratio	F-Probability
A. Worksite Descriptors					
Participation	16.5	15.8	14.2	13.1	33.003	.001
Job Involvement	30.8	29.9	29.1	27.7	4.942	.002
Trust in supervisor	14.9	14.5	13.0	10.3	24.179	.001
Trust in employees	18.0	17.2	16.6	13.8	13.095	.001
Willingness to disagree with supervisor	15.8	15.7	13.7	13.3	18.688	.001
Job tension	18.9	19.7	21.0	23.7	19.274	.001
Experienced meaningfulness of work	20.7	19.8	19.4	18.6	5.317	.001
Experienced responsibility for work	33.9	32.7	32.3	29.5	10.173	.001
Knowledge of results	22.0	21.1	20.3	19.3	15.072	.001
General satisfaction	24.8	23.9	23.3	20.3	9.583	.001
Internal work motivation	33.4	32.9	32.7	31.3	2.735	.042
Growth satisfaction	20.4	19.5	18.9	16.6	9.319	.001
Job security	10.1	10.0	9.7	8.4	5.829	.001
Compensation	9.6	9.1	9.1	8.4	3.037	.028
Coworkers	16.7	16.6	16.1	14.9	7.375	.001
Supervision	15.7	14.8	13.9	10.8	22.339	.001
B. Symptoms Scores					
Total symptoms	37.2	37.3	37.7	41.1	2.618	.050
Factor I: General enervation and agitation	19.0	19.2	19.3	21.3	3.415	.017
Factor II: Cardiovascular complaints	6.5	6.5	6.7	7.5	3.097	.026
Factor III: Noncardiac pains	8.0	7.5	7.7	8.2	3.041	.128
Factor IV: Sleeplessness	3.8	4.1	4.0	4.4	3.076	.027

Source: Golembiewski and Munzenrider (1988, p. 86). Reprinted with permission of Greenwood Publishing Group, Inc., Westport, CT.

Some individuals are appraised twice, and a few do not get appraised in either period. Moreover, not all individuals are classified into burnout phases at days 1 and 365. Consequently, the total Ns vary.

At Site A, in any case, all three categories—Day 1 burnout with appraisal I, Day 1 burnout with appraisal II, and Day 365 burnout with appraisal II—show statistically significant covariation. The more advanced an individual's phase of burnout, the poorer the performance appraisal. Of course, nearly two-thirds of all employees get "excellent" appraisals at Site A. But only a bit over 45 percent of those in the three most advanced phases do so, while the percentage increases to nearly 70 percent for those in the other phases. Looked at from another angle, those with "Excellent" appraisals are four or five times more likely to be assigned to Phases I-III than to VI-VIII. For poorer appraisals, the ratio drops to 2:1, approximately.

However, the association is moderate in strength. The square of Cramer's V indicates that only approximately 5 percent of the variance is accounted for, on average.

The point is speculative, in conclusion, but the substantial "grade inflation" at Site A might well dilute any association between burnout and performance appraisals. In this sense, data from Site A may generate a conservative estimate of the degree of association between performance appraisal and the phases.

Findings at Site B. Data from Site B also suggest an inverse association between performance appraisals and the phases of burnout, on balance, but the interpretation here must be cautious.[1] The one-way analysis of variance only approaches statistical significance ($P = .078$), and the data are not reproduced here to conserve space. Eta^2 indicates that about 1 percent of the variance is accounted for.

These associations of burnout and performance appraisals at Site B also may be conservative. Appraisals there came from self-reports rather than organization records, and inaccurate recollections may distort appraisal differences between the least-and most-advanced phases of burnout.

Discussion

With limitations, then, individual performance has the expected association with the phases, and this estimate may be conservative. As noted, local "grade inflation" does not provide an ideal test of associations with burnout. Relatedly, performance appraisals are generated by evaluation processes whose participants, character, and quality no doubt vary across a broad range. This variability might create spurious associations, of course, but the dilution or distortion of relationships in nature seems far more likely. Hence, the modest relationships sketched here suggest that regularities in nature were possibly distorted or moderated by many variables controlled at Sites A or B.

Neglect is the major limitation on the conclusion about a linkage between burnout and appraisals. Few relevant studies exist, and some of them generate inconclusive findings (e.g., Golembiewski, Bower, & Kim, 1994). Moreover, problems of operational definition tend to trouble the interpretation of these few relevant studies, and no one can be certain about the degree to which results reflect nature or methodological inelegancies. See also the discussions below of quantitative estimates of productivity in North America, as well as of self-ratings of productivity in several global settings.

BURNOUT AND PRODUCTIVITY

We now turn to a second measure of system output; and the focus is first North American, and then global. The summaries below are reinforced by detailed analyses elsewhere.

Measuring Productivity in A North American Setting

Via detailed productivity records, Site B provides rare bottom-line data which, on initial reviews, seemed a God-send to test the usefulness of the phase model of burnout. This rarity is no less unfortunate because it is understandable. Relevant data are rarely kept in a form useful for present purposes, and access to that data is difficult to arrange even in those few cases where useful data are available.

Notes About Host and Method. When it comes to measuring productivity, Site B departs from the stereotype about public agencies. That division of a federal agency has a long-standing interest in such measurement, with much time and energy being devoted to accumulating and disseminating a broad range of data on productivity. This point is usefully amplified. Two following sub-sections introduce quantitative and qualitative measures of productivity, and the third sub-section elaborates several of their limitations.

Six Measures of Qualitative Productivity. Site B's parent agency requires several qualitative measures of productivity. Their focus is on evaluations generated by management as well as by clients.

Headquarters Ratings of Management and Quality. The headquarters staff of Site B performs a yearly and widely-reported review of each of the 50-plus work stations, and this activity is used to generate three measures of the quality of performance focusing, respectively, on management, quality, and a combined rating.

Omitting details, management and quality at each work station are rated by headquarters' staff as "Excellent," "Favorable," or "Needs Improvement." For present purposes, these staff-produced ratings are coded as 3, 2, and 1, respectively, for each of the two measures. For each work station, the combined rating sums the management and quality codes, and hence scores can range from 2 to 6.

Clients' Criticism Scores. Independently of the work stations, headquarters staff also solicits the reactions of clients concerning the character and quality of the services provide. For present purposes, three aspects of these reactions are included under the general rubric of clients' criticism scores:

- "Poor" ratings, or percent of respondents rating service as "Poor," with other response stems being "Excellent," "Good," or "Fair"
- "Not courteous" ratings, or percent of clients noting that division employees were discourteous
- "Poor" plus "Not courteous" ratings, combined.

Measures of Quantitative Productivity. Each month, each station within Site B provides headquarters with data about the numbers of individual services performed, as well as about the total hours devoted to the station's work. For each station, an automated system churns out various indices, primary among which are measures of overall productivity and direct-labor effectiveness. The results of this number-crunching are widely disseminated.

Both key ratios rest on an engineering approach to work. All direct services are enumerated—let us say there are 46 of these activities, such as "initial screening interview," with each having a "standard time." To illustrate, answering each incoming phone call is assigned a standard time of four minutes. Simple but laborious calculations convert activities X standard times into "standard man-hours" (SMH). For each of the division's work stations across the country, directly, the frequencies with which the various services are performed during a month are multiplied by the appropriate standard times. The sum of these several multiplicands generates standard hours for each work station, and these in turn provide a measure of the total work accomplished.

The calculation of overall productivity makes another use of standard hours. SMH is divided by "total available hours" to generate a ratio. The question it asks is direct: how much did a station do with all the time resources allocated to it?

Direct-labor effectiveness uses the same numerator, SMH, but seeks to remove all "indirect" hours from the denominator. Direct hours include total available hours *minus* supervision, clerical overhead, leave and so on. The central question this second ratio seeks to answer is: how much did direct-service providers at each station accomplish with the time resources available to them?

Major Concerns about Productivity Measurement

The present productivity data are not ideal (Golembiewski, Munzenrider, & Stevenson, 1986, pp. 104-109), that much seems certain. Three major concerns illustrate why.

Conventions for Estimating Work-Station Burnout. An issue with levels of analysis clearly exists. All measures of productivity relate to work stations, some with over 100 employees. Other data of concern here—such as those on burnout—come from individuals and relate to individuals.

Differences in levels of analysis cannot be reconciled. The prime accommodation to recalcitrant realities involves assigning each work station to one of four classes, based on the degree of burnout reported by employees. The conventions clearly are arbitrary:

- Low stations, where 50 percent or more of the respondents are classified in Phases I through III;
- Bipolar stations, where 40 percent or more of the respondents are classified in each of the two sets of extreme phases—I through III or VI through VIII;
- Mixed stations, where respondents are more or less equally distributed among the three major clusters of phases—the two sets of extreme phases as well as IV plus V; and
- High stations, where 50 percent or more of the respondents are classified in Phases VI through VIII.

All but two work stations can be classified in these ways. The headquarters group is excluded, because no productivity data are available for it, and a low response rate to the survey eliminates another work station. In summary, the four major classes of work stations have these distributions of employees in the three clusters of phases (Golembiewski & Munzenrider, 1988, pp. 9-96):

Work Station Burnout	Number	Percent of Employees, by Phases		
		I-III	IV and V	VI-VIII
Low	14	58.8	13.6	27.6
Bi-polar	15	43.2	12.6	44.2
Mixed	5	31.8	34.5	33.6
High	19	23.6	15.4	61.0

Failure to Isolate Immediate Work Groups. These assignments seem relatively clean but, among other limitations, the conventions for aggregating individual data at the level of work stations do not identify "immediate work groups" or the clusters of first-reports of any supervisor. These may constitute the most relevant unit of analysis in burnout (Golembiewski, 1983b; Rountree, 1984), as well as in all organizational analysis. At Site B, the smallest stations most closely approximate *a* group, but some stations have over 100 employees and no doubt contain numerous distinguishable (if not hostile) clusters of employees.

Briefly, then, our aggregating convention lacks precision, as is established by considering a hypothetical work station with 60 percent of its members classified in Phases VI-VIII. Assuming four immediate work groups of equal size in this station, many distributions of advanced burnout could result in a 60-percent record for the entire work station. Such differences cannot be distinguished in the present data, but they can cause profound mischief in interpreting results in complex worksettings like Site B. The point has been clear in principle for a long time (e.g., Golembiewski, 1962, pp. 34-68), but is no less troubling to virtually all organizational analysis, including this one. For a formal attempt to bring the issue of level of analysis to the forefront of researchers consciousness, see Schneider (1985).

Possible Ceiling Effects. Policies in Site B's agency also pose problems for interpreting productivity effects. To be specific, a station can rank *too high* as well as *too low* on the two quantitative measures—overall productivity and direct labor effectiveness. Any variances greater than ± 10 percent of the "national average over a period of several consecutive months should be investigated or analyzed," an agency bulletin prescribes.

The rationale seems obvious. The policy seeks to inhibit a work station from "making good numbers" by lowering the quality of services. For good or ill, this policy stayed in place throughout the period of data-gathering, and was rescinded later.

Findings Concerning Productivity and Phases. So what can be said about the covariants of productivity at Site B, given the chilling effects of these several limitations? Expectations and findings relate, in turn, to burnout as well as performance.

Expectations About Productivity and Burnout. Expectations here are best-guesses only. For obvious reasons, High Burnout work stations—defined earlier as having 50 percent or more of their memberships in Phases VI-VIII—should be characterized by low productivity, as variously measured. However, if ceiling effects do exist, they could moderate or even hide any associations between productivity measures and other variables. In addition, high burnout in cases no doubt can be associated with high productivity, but that effect is presumably not one that will hold over the long run or for large numbers of individuals in the same or similar worksettings.

Expectations about productivity levels in Low work stations—as defined above as having at least 50 percent of their membership in Phases I-III—defy such easy prediction, but high productivity constitutes a best-guess. However, the Low work stations may contain laissez-faire immediate work groups, where burnout is low while performance is casual, and energy levels at work are low.

More directly, Bi-Polar stations—those with 40 percent or more of their employees classified in *both* Phases I-III and VI-VIII—are expected to be intermediate in productivity.

The remaining work stations—the Mixed—are eliminated because no clear rationale for productivity effects seems reasonable. On the one hand, Mixed stations suggest low levels of productivity. Why? With approximately one-third of their employees in each of the three clusters of burnout phases, the potential for deflecting energy from work seems substantial. Moreover, their high proportions of members in Phases IV and V—"high" for this and all other populations studied—suggest transitional dynamics that could be major energy-absorbers. See also Chapter VI.

Where do these considerations leave us? Basically, seven stations will not be included in the following analysis. The excluded units encompass the five Mixed stations, the management group, and one unit with a very low response rate. Productivity expectations are:

Work Station Burnout	Expected Productivity
Low	High
Bi-polar	↕
High	Low

Work-Station Productivity and Burnout. Table V.2 summarizes an ANOVA test of these expectations about productivity and burnout in 46 work stations. Five points highlight aspects of the findings, and they all suggest—but do not establish—that burnout and productivity are related inversely. First, productivity seems to worsen as burnout increases.

Specifically, Low burnout work stations score lowest on all three of the clients' criticism scores, where "low" is favorable; and they also score highest on six of the other seven measures of productivity where "high" is "good." Overall, 86.7 percent of the paired-comparisons are in the expected directions, although the differences are small in many cases.

Second, the differences achieve or approach statistical significance in only a minority of cases. One case shows non-random variance; two of the 10 cases achieve $P < .10$; and three additional cases attain $P < .30$. The first three cases refer to Management and Combined ratings by the headquarters staff, and those cases explain about 14 percent of the variance.

Third, no paired-comparisons achieve statistical significance in the one case of $P < .05$. This may be due to small Ns and unstable variances.

Fourth, the quantitative measures show higher productivity in the first quarter than in the preceding fiscal year. Credibly, this may reflect ceiling effects in the yearly data.

Fifth, the High work stations tend to have the lowest productivity. This is true in seven of ten total comparisons, and the High stations also tie for lowest productivity in two of the three other comparisons. However, only one of these differences achieves statistical significance.

Table V.2. Means of Ten Productivity Measures, Arrayed by Three Categories of Work Station Burnout ($N = 48$)

Productivity Measures	Low (14)	Bi-Polar (15)	High (19)	F- Ratio	F- Probability
Overall productivity					
First quarter, 1983	83.4	82.5	81.2	0.390	0.67
Fiscal year 1982	80.1	79.9	77.8	0.805	0.42
Direct-labor effectiveness					
First quarter, 1983	113.1	113.0	110.1	0.405	0.67
Fiscal year 1982	107.1	107.5	104.9	0.554	0.57
Headquarters rating, Fiscal 1982					
Management	2.6	2.2	2.2	2.422	0.09
Quality	2.5	2.2	2.2	2.027	0.14
Combined	5.1	4.4	4.4	3.406	0.04
Clients' criticism scores, Fiscal 1982					
"Poor" ratings, percent	1.9	2.0	2.2	0.054	0.92
"Not courteous," percent	0.2	0.3	0.5	1.273	0.29
"Poor" and "not courteous" combined, percent	2.1	2.3	2.7	0.226	0.79

Source: Golembiewski and Munzenrider (1988, p 98.). Reprinted with permission of Greenwood Publishing Group, Inc., Westport, CT.

Global Perspective on Productivity in ICU Settings

The issues emphasized throughout this volume, as well as directly above, have global applications. Consider a major recent study of Intensive Care Units, or ICUs, in Dutch hospitals (Schaufeli, Keijsers, & Miranda, 1995). Those researchers based their work on the long-standing conclusion that "burnout" was listed among the top research priorities for ICUs (e.g., Lewandowski & Kositsky, 1983), which in turn must rank among the few most-strategic hospital worksettings. Researchers began with a clear sense of the mixed findings of the sparse available research, including not only the Site B effort analyzed above but several others as well (Roelens, 1983; Lazaro, Shinn, & Robinson, 1985; Randal & Scott, 1988). Only the Site B study employed objective measures of performance. To simplify for present purposes, the researchers employed three outcome measures (Schaufeli, Keijsers, & Miranda, 1995, pp. 264-265):

- *Objective effectiveness*, or the degree that goals and objectives are met, and was estimated here by a standard mortality ratio, or SMR; this estimate of clinical effectiveness is adjusted for several patient characteristics such as the severity of the illness, age, and so on
- *Objective Efficiency*, or the cost of meeting goals and objectives, here estimated by the length of stay at an ICU; and
- *Perceived Unit Effectiveness* (PUE), a 5-item subjective estimate of the degree to which goals and objectives are attained.

How did things work out? The care with design and the welcome emphasis on "hard" or objective measures generated mixed results, including ones that elicited surprised reactions from the researchers. Figure V.1 provides a convenient overview, but at the cost of excluding researchers' valuable treatment of the "use of technology."

Let us summarize this composite of mixed results and surprises, if only briefly and incompletely. Thus, as expected, Burnout is associated significantly with Objective Efficiency, but curiously not with the other two outcome measures. We will have the researchers speak to their own sense of surprise in three basic particulars (Schaufeli, Keijsers, & Miranda, 1995, p. 267):

- "Quite surprising, and somewhat counterintuitive, burnout is positively related to the units' efficiency; in ICUs where nurses report higher levels of burnout, patients stay for a shorter period."
- "Nurse burnout is [not significantly related] to [either objective or perceived] effectiveness; in ICUs as where nurses are more burned out

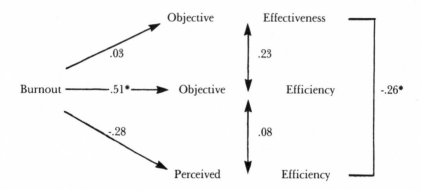

Note: N.B. * designates a statistically-significant association, relying on a "standardized LISREL solution."

Source: Based on data from W. B. Schaufeli, G. J. Keijsers, & D. R. Miranda, "Burnout, Technology Use, and ICU Performance," pp. 259-271, which appeared in S. L. Sauter & R. Murphy, *Organizational Risk Factors for Job Stress.* Washington, D.C.: APA. (1995, esp. pp. 266-267). Copyright © 1965 by American Psychological Association, Washington, D.C. Adapted with permission.

Figure V.1.   Findings About Burnout and Outcomes

about as many patients die according to the SMR as in ICUs where nurses are less burned out." [We authors add: and *vice versa.*]

- "Somewhat surprising, the nurses' perceived unit effectiveness is unrelated to ICU efficiency and negatively related to objectively assessed ICU effectiveness."

No one can confidently explain these mixed results or the surprises,[2] but it may prove instructive to suggest several possible contributions to an explanation. First, fundamentally, mixed results and surprises encourage reconceptualizing and experimenting with other operational definitions such as the phase model. Nature may be too unruly and chaotic to support generalizations, of course, but burgeoning evidence concerning burnout implies the opposite. Certainly, the bulk of the results of *Global Burnout* stand uncomfortably beside the Dutch ICU results.

Second, changes in expectations may help, as in the case of higher burnout being associated with Objective Efficiency. The latter is estimated by length of stay in ICU, and one can construct a rationale that can moderate the surprise even as it raises serious issues. Thus, some units may "push" for short ICU stays to such a degree and in such ways as to generate strain for nurses.

Third, the three researchers use an additive measure of burnout. The MBI items are used to create scores for individuals on the three sub-domains, which are then aggregated at the ICU level. This volume encourages a reanalysis of the data using a phase formulation, and there is no reason to expect an isomorphism with any additive MBI scores. The mixed results and surprises, in short, may derive more from measurement features than from reality.

Fourth, the three researchers focus on *each* ICU as the unit of analysis, and that apparently means parts of several individual hospitals are the units. This may leave many individuating features unspecified, personal and cultural, along the lines of the limitations of focusing on the regional office as the unit of analysis in the Site B research. From the text, moreover, it is unclear whether 19 or 20 such "units" are involved (e.g., compare p. 263 with p. 266 in Schaufeli, Keijsers, & Miranda, 1995).

Self-Rated Productivity in Global Settings

Going global helps a bit in testing for covariation between the phases and output, but only a little. Worldwide settings do not resolve the need for "objective" or "hard" indicators because, if anything, the measurement problems there are more daunting than in North America. But studies in a global setting at times do include a self-report item for each respondent to rate productivity along a 0-100 point continuum. Major autocorrelation effects seem unlikely,[3] and the self-reports from global worksites will add to our understanding of phase X productivity covariants.

Results generally support the view that productivity estimates deteriorate as the phases progress I —> VIII.

Moreover, no paired-comparisons falling in a contrary direction achieve significance. In addition, when $P \leq .05$, noteworthy proportions of significant paired-comparisons are typically reported. In Table V.3, that proportion surpasses 20 percent of all possible paired-comparisons, which is substantially more than chance alone allows. Eta^2, varies from trivial proportions of explained variance to 15 percent or so.

Finally, the less-robust cases in Table V.3 typically present one or more difficulties: for example, Israel A has four phases with few entries. See also chapters VII and VIII.

Table V.3. Summary of Representative Studies,
Self-Rated Productivity X Phases, Worldwide

| | | | | | Paired-Comparisons, in % | | | | |
Sites	N =	Researchers	F =	Probability =	In Expected Direction	In Expected Direction and Statistically Significant	In Contrary Direction	In Contrary Direction and Statistically Significant	eta^2 =
1. Belarus B	795	Boudreau (1995)	7.0855	<.0000	75.0	25.0	25.0	0.0	.060
2. Belarus C	460	Boudreau & Levin (1996a)	4.1274	.0002	53.6	10.7	46.4	0.0	.061
3. Canada A	130	Duplicea & Hubert (1996)	1.9243	NS (.0713)	75%	—	25.0	—	.100
4. China B	259	Golembiewski & Luo (1996)	0.551	NS	71.5	-	28.5	-	-
5. Israel A	100	Pines & Golembiewski (1996)	1.9422	NS (.0732)	67.9%	—	32.1	—	.144
6. Japan C	387	Golembiewski, Boudreau, Goto, & Murai (1993)	9.9769	<.0000	78.6	21.4	21.4	0.0	.158

USE OF RESOURCES AND
SYSTEM COSTS OF BURNOUT

This final theme adds to our knowledge of what burnout means for performance in human systems, even as new questions are raised. Two emphases develop the point: one deals with turnover; and the second emphasis deals with the reliance on medical insurance by employees. In its own way, each demonstration reflects on the use of resources and how advanced phases of burnout imply system costs. Usefully, also, both measures involve "hard" or "objective" indicators, and thus provide a valuable addition to the literature on the phase model of burnout.

Phases and Turnover

The case for a direct association here seems strong, on theoretic as well as experimental grounds, but little research is available. See also Chapters I and VIII. The illustrative focus here is on one action research design at Site T that decreased burnout, while major reductions in employee turnover also occurred. For details on Site T, see Appendix A.

The design and its consequences have been reported on fully (e.g., Golembiewski, 1990, esp. pp. 155-175), so Table V.4 summarizes major milestones in the action research, as well as periodic estimates of burnout and turnover. The presenting conditions can be sketched: the targeted corporate HR group was doing well in developing programs of change throughout the organization, but its members were suffering high rates of turnover (as many were aware), and high proportions of them fell in advanced phases of burnout (as became clear on diagnosis). Interventions— broadly described as sociotechnical in character—were begun at Day 115. Improvements in phase distributions were maintained after interventions were concluded, along with downward shifts in turnover. Significantly, both effects were maintained despite major macro-system changes in the host organization.

The causal linkages underlying Table V.4 are credible, and were supported by several observations during an experimental design that targeted both burnout and turnover at Site T. Interventions sought to improve interaction among HR members as well as to provide structural reinforcement for that improvement. Absent such interventions, depersonalization would tend to remain at high levels, if not worsen; personal accomplishment would be hindered; and emotional exhaustion might well grow. Hence, one predicts, many HR members would develop an intent to relocate, which could be acted upon when opportunity permitted. Only one piece of the local rationale remains. The HR group

Table V.4. Summary, Burnout and Turnover, Site T

			Turnover Rates %	
		% in Phase VIII[a]	Total Corporation[b]	Human Resources Staff
Day 45	Observation I	14%	13%	37%
Day 115	Begin interventions			
Day 200	Observation II	22		
Day 265	Conclude major interventions			
Day 295	Observation III	14		
Day 425	Observation IV	7	12	20
Day 575	Last Survey	0		
Day 820			15	13
Day 1185			15	14

Notes: [a]These figures relate to matched respondents only, $N = 14$. The figures for all respondents are: 19, 27, 11, 17, and 5 percent, respectively. $N = 31$-35.

[b]Listed by approximate date of public release, and refer to the previous full year.

Source: Golembiewski, Hilles, and Daly (1987). Reprinted with permission of Sage Publications.

had developed a growing reputation for helping an organization move into a major developmental orbit, and hence many HR employees experienced opportunity mating with intent. After the interventions, intent to leave a punishing situation was reduced, presumably, and hence turnover decreased as the profile of phases improved. If anything, after the interventions, the opportunity to move remained relatively constant and high, if it did not increase.

Phases and Use of Medical Insurance

Given the strong and consistent evidence about the decreases in physical and emotional health as the phases progress I $\longrightarrow$ VIII, one resource of special interest to management credibly will increase with advancing phases: health insurance costs. Data about such usage are very difficult to obtain, but the linkages seem obvious and well worth the effort to establish. As Jackson and Manning observe (1995, p. 32) in the study targeted in this subsection:

> ...one type of variable which has been lacking from previous studies of stress and burnout is health care utilization. Stress is frequently cited as a risk factor for various physical ailments (Ganster & Schaubroeck, 1991), which suggests that it should likewise lead to higher utilization of health care. Preliminary evidence suggests that indeed workplace stress is associated with higher levels of health care utilization (Manning, Jackson, & Fusilier, in press).

These researchers add that advanced burnout seems logically associated with high costs of medical insurance. Jackson and Manning add: "...However, no link has been established in the literature between burnout and health care utilization. It is the goal of this paper to empirically examine this relationship."

Not all issues have been laid to rest, but a valuable start has been made. Four major emphases provide support for this compound conclusion. In turn, attention goes to: their population; marker variables and other measures; selected findings; and a brief discussion of the findings of the research by Jackson and Manning.

Population. $N = 238$ in this seminal study, with 80 men and 158 women. Respondents come from two work settings: 110 were employed in a small manufacturing division of a large chemical corporation, and 128 came from a large insurance company. Average age was 36.4 years, with a range from 21 to 64.

Measures. Three marker variables are used, along with the MBI instrument to assign phases. Surveys at the worksites, and archival health insurance data obtained from the insurer, provide the basic data. Claims data were aggregated over the interval of a year, and the survey data were collected during the last quarter of that interval.

Four basic introductory points about measurement are useful. Health care utilization is estimated here in two ways, which are briefly considered immediately below. Note that all insurance premiums are paid by the employer. Then, a self-report scale tapping Strain at Work is described. Finally, a few comments describe the authors' use of the MBI items in assignments of employees to phases of burnout.

Direct Costs of Medical Treatment. This "hard" or objective variable is operationalized in a highly-reliable way by the actual dollar costs of the health care provided to each employee. Insurance records provide the data, which reflect all medical costs except for those presumably-rare cases in which employees preferred not to reveal their use of personal funds to pay for services.

This variable is of patent interest to management, for several reasons. To be selective, the cost of health care is a significant expense for most businesses, including the two represented in this research. More broadly, humanist concerns also are relevant to most managements, and high medical costs represent a reasonable signal of the mischief or even damage that work does to employees.

Number of Health-Care Claims. The second health-care estimate is useful because it may—although it need not—relate to the number of times an employee's work is interrupted by medical problems. The second operational definition is direct: the total number of insurance claims, for each individual, for all possible reasons covering the gamut from visits to a health-care provider's office to prescriptions filled.

Strain at Work. Jackson and Manning also utilized one self-report measure. They standardized four strain-related scales, and summed them to form a composite index with an *alpha* coefficient of .79. The composite index includes:

- Job-Related Tension Index (Kahn, Wolfe, Quinn, Snoeck, & Rosenthal, 1964)
- Job Satisfaction (Manring, 1979)
- Negative Affect (Sipprelle, Gilbert, & Ascough, 1976)
- Somatic Complaints (Adams, 1981).

Factor analysis indicates that these four components load on a single factor, which accounts for 62.1 percent of the variance.

The estimate of Strain at Work serves several purposes in the Jackson/Manning research. Paramountly, for present purposes, if Job Strain and the burnout phases prove to be unrelated, that will provide presumptive evidence of major problems with the population, research design, or the phase model. Expectations are strong that a stout linkage should exist between Strain at Work and burnout phases, for practical as well as theoretic reasons. See especially Chapters III and IV.

MBI Sub-Domains. Jackson and Manning observe that their study "adheres as closely as possible to the Golembiewski and Munzenrider approach in order to produce a test of the [universal norm] phase model." A number of technical details, far beyond present purposes, limit the direct comparison of the Jackson/Manning phases and those of the model's originators. But these differences do not seem to disqualify the test of three reasonable covariants of the phases, although those differences may dilute associations.

Findings. Two points summarize the findings of this important study by Jackson and Manning. First, as Table V.5 shows, the Strain Index closely tracks the phases, and fits comfortably in the tradition of findings detailed above. This provides presumptive evidence of the usefulness of our operational definitions of phases.

Table V.5. Summary, 3 Marker Variables X Phases, ANOVA, Site BB

			Paired-Comparisons, Marker Variables X Phases, in %			
Marker Variables	*F-ratio*	*Probability =*	*In Expected Direction*	*In Expected Direction and Statistically Significant*	*In Contrary Direction*	*In Contrary Direction and Statistically Significant*
Strain Index	30.25	.01	92.9%	71.5	7.1	0.0
Health Care Costs	2.06	.05	67.9%	21.4	32.1	3.6
Health Care Claims	1.24	NS	75.0%	-	25.0	-

Source: Based on Jackson and Manning (1995, pp. 36-37).

149

Second, the two cost measures provide generally-positive but mixed evidence. Thus, both Costs as well as Claims tend to increase, phase by phase, as Table V.5 shows; and over four times more paired-comparisons involving Costs attain statistical significance than chance allows. However, only Costs attains usually-acceptable levels of statistical significance. Claims as arrayed by the eight progressive phases do fall in the expected direction in three of every four paired-comparisons, but that distribution may reflect random factors only.

In sum, "hard" and "soft" estimates of the costs of burnout in the Manning/Jackson research yield supporting but qualified results. That is, the Strain Index mirrors typical findings with the phase model. Moreover, the two "hard" estimates are directionally consistent with the preponderance of findings based on the phase model, but only Costs reflect non-random differences at Site BB.

Discussion.   In several senses, qualifications hedge these results. Of greatest significance, perhaps, the population is not only small and has three cells with 10 or so assignments, but Site BB reports a very favorable distribution of phases. Indeed, Table V.6 reflects one of the half-dozen or so least-advanced distributions of the phases ever recorded. See Tables VI.1 and VI.2 for comparative data. More or less, Table V.6 has 50 percent more cases in the three least-advanced phases, and 50 percent less in the trio of most-advanced phases, than the evidence in Chapter VI leads us to expect in North American settings, on average. For the record, moreover, global populations compare even less favorably to the Jackson/Manning distribution, overall.

This distribution may have significant implications for interpreting the Jackson/Manning results. If nothing else, that population experiences restricted burnout effects and that, in turn, may distort relationships by attenuating the ranges of health insurance costs/usage.

Table V.6.   Frequency of Phases at Site BB

	Phases of Burnout							
	I	*II*	*III*	*IV*	*V*	*VI*	*VII*	*VIII*
Depersonalization	Lo	Hi	Lo	Hi	Lo	Hi	Lo	Hi
Personal Accomplishment (Reversed)	Lo	Lo	Hi	Hi	Lo	Lo	Hi	Hi
Emotional Exhaustion	Lo	Lo	Lo	Lo	Hi	Hi	Hi	Hi
Frequency =	64	12	70	12	21	20	15	24
Percentage =	26.9	5.0	29.4	5.0	8.8	8.4	6.3	10.1

Source: Frequencies taken from Jackson and Manning (1995, p. 36).

In addition, the Site BB population also may be unrepresentative in other ways—for example, in having a lower proportion of high-cost medical claims. Relevant data about non-responders are not provided, but one can easily empathize with Jackson and Manning. Health-care data are very difficult to obtain, in any case, and presumably impossible for those claimants who do not grant explicit permission.

Moreover, Claims data may have been gathered over an interval that was too short. One year may be an inappropriately-short interval, especially given the fact that many variables other than burnout no doubt influence the decision to make a medical expenditure or to file a medical insurance claim. A longer time-frame, in effect, might allow intervening variables to be "more or less equal" than does a year's interval.

It remains conjectural, to be sure, but another critical issue with the Jackson/Manning research involves the interval by which burnout "leads" or "lags" health consequences. The phase model assumes that the phases are lead health effects but, even if one accepts this view, no one knows the "average duration" of such a leading effect. Recall, also, the earlier discussion of the "funnel of causality."

Indeed, from one perspective, the strength of their findings is surprising. Directly, the Jackson/Manning design implies that medical costs *lead* burnout, and this basic design feature may well camouflage or distort associations with the phases. Let us develop this critical point in some detail, even at the cost of repetition of earlier arguments. As noted, Jackson and Manning gather their phase data in *the last quarter of the interval for which they provide cost data.*

This leading role seems unlikely. The environmental model does expect feedback loops between health status and the phases, but emphasizes this causal linkage: phases —> health status. Consequently, although Chapter VI implies that a substantial consistency of phase assignments probably will exist from year to year, we authors expect diluted associations between the phases and health status in the research design utilized at Site BB.

A final possibility also deserves highlighting, by way of balance. The view is inconsistent with almost all of the results reviewed here, but nonetheless deserves notice. As Jackson and Manning conclude (1995, p. 40):

> [Perhaps] the phase model itself is not yet articulated in its most complete and correct form, or even...is simply invalid. The considerable research by Golembiewski and others cited above has demonstrated that the model has considerable relevance to the relationship of stress with burnout. The fact that the strain index scores in the present data set matched so closely the model's prediction adds weight to the evidence of validity of the model, especially with respect to stress variables. However, the failure of the present study to predict health care costs and number of claims equally well also raises questions about whether this linkage is complicated by other factors.

SYSTEM COSTS AND BURNOUT AS ENVIRONMENTAL MODEL: ANOTHER STIMULANT FOR CONFIGURATIONAL ANALYSIS

These details concerning several approaches to system costs of the phases, just concluded, plus the earlier analysis of individual costs, are suggestive and encourage further research, but they are also limited. The results generally support the simple schema below, where solid lines indicate direct relationships and broken lines indicate feedback linkages:

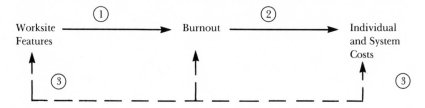

Let us develop the sense of this schema in two ways. Thus several caveats get initial attention, and then analysis shifts to a generic reason why the associations look through a dark or distorted glass, as it were.

Several Caveats

To begin, the data support—but could be far stronger at critical points—an environmental model. Supporting discussion appears elsewhere (e.g., Golembiewski & Munzenrider, 1988, pp. 77-81, 103-107), and will not be repeated here. But some illustrative review will serve a useful purpose. In this chapter and especially in others, generally-stout linkages seem to exist at ① , as is required by the environmental schema.

The ② linkages do not seem as robust, in general, and especially for systems costs. Nonetheless, they do not disappear. This dual condition could be explained in part by the uneven quality of performance measures, for example; or perhaps the pattern above reflects as-yet-unperceived methodological shortfalls in the phase model.

Finally, the strengths of several ③ linkages support their proposed status as feedback loops rather than main-line effects. But several other interpretations are possible, as Chapter VI will show in more comprehensive ways than are convenient here.

Configurational Analysis

Briefly, future analysis can enrich one feature that may powerfully dilute or distort the relationships above—specifically, differences between the properties of immediate organization units or between individuals. The point is not novel (e.g., Golembiewski, 1986), and has been framed in compelling terms by Miller and Friesen (1984). They focus on an ironic question: Why is it that, the more effort we devote to an area of organizational analysis, the less we seem to know? That is, initial analysis may isolate what seem robust patterns of relationships, and a kind of boomtown atmosphere gets generated for a while. However, replicatory studies typically rain on everyone's parade: some replications may support or even extend the initial results but, on balance, cases of nonrandom variation and contrary results come to dominate.

Miller and Friesen are not surprised (1984, pp. 15-17). Indeed, in general, it could hardly be any other way. We not only lack reasonable typologies for distinguishing (for example) between organizations and groups, but little interest exists in developing such typologies. Rather, investigators tend to assume that a group is a group, and that an organization is an organization. Even gentle "configurational analysis" reveals the fragility of such convenient assumptions, however. For example, Mintzberg (1975) distinguishes five kinds of organizations, at a general level: simple structure, machine bureaucracy, professional bureaucracy, a divisionalized form, and *adhocracy*. Friesen and Miller ask rhetorically about the common failure to make such configurational distinctions (1984, pp. 14-15): "Now assuming…that at least a good proportion of organizations tended to adopt these or some other configurations of their structural parameters—what would happen if different kinds of organizations were mixed in research samples and then relationships gauged…?"

Much the same question may be asked in connection with many kinds of groupings: immediate work groups, various reference groups, and so on. One size does not fit all of them, either (e.g., Bowers & Hausser, 1977). So what happens when findings from an undifferentiated collection of groups are combined?

One need not grope for an answer. To illustrate, with an emphasis on the organizational level, a machine bureaucracy might well tend toward advanced centralization, while a professional bureaucracy might generally favor decentralization, or even chaotic localism. Consequently, apparent contradictions in existing findings might be reconciled after differentiating organizational configurations in different data batches.

Following through on this insight will preoccupy much work (e.g., Bowers & Hausser, 1977; Kets De Vries & Miller, 1984; Miller & Friesen, 1984), and only general orientations for guiding "configurational analysis" exist (e.g., Golembiewski, 1986). But noting the bare insight does useful and multiple duty in connection with the phase model, as four points establish:

- Burnout phases and their covariants appear dominant in nature, otherwise the general failure to distinguish unit differences would distort or hide relationships.
- Burnout research ties into classical issues in the behavioral sciences, which it highlights and cannot finesse.
- The phase model seems to provide a useful and even strategic launching platform for extensions reaching toward such classical issues as configurational analysis.
- This volume will make some forays of its own into configurational analysis related to burnout—conceptually and in applications—in Chapters VII and VIII.

NOTES

1. Far more detailed discussion is available (Golembiewski & Munzenrider, 1988, pp. 93-103).

2. Another analysis by Dutch scientists confirms these surprising finding (Keijsers, Schaufeli, LeBlac, Zwerts, & Miranda, 1995).

3. Although caution is appropriate concerning overlays of the self-report ratings with the MBI's Personal Accomplishment, note that the latter also taps the worthwhileness of work in addition to the judgment of how well a person sees self as performing. Moreover, direct tests (e.g., Golembiewski, Boudreau, Goto, & Murai, 1993, pp. 13-14) typically show that Personal Accomplishment and self-rated productivity are significantly correlated but share only a minority of their variance—for example, 21.6 percent in the case of Japan C.

Chapter VI

Magnitudes of Burnout, Worldwide: Estimating Incidence and Persistence Via the Phase Model

The recent flurry of attention to burnout leaves numerous questions unanswered, even as it raises the consciousness of many about what seems one of the contemporary worksite problems—indeed, perhaps *the* major concern. Here the focus is on three questions, approached from different but related perspectives. In preview:

- What are ideal levels of burnout? And tolerable levels?
- What is the actual incidence of advanced burnout?
- How long does burnout persist?

Numerous replications of phase model findings, both in North America and especially in other countries, permit working answers to these central questions, and for the first time with some confidence. In sum, the detailed review above permits three broad-gauge conclusions. They can be stated boldly:

- Most people idealize low levels of burnout, and see far less of it than seems to exist.
- Distributions of the phases far surpass these ideal or tolerable levels, in virtually all North American and global worksettings investigated.
- Phases seem to have extended levels of persistence over time, and especially for the least- and most-advanced phases.

No other operational definition of burnout can lay a similar claim. Some operations have received great attention, like the three particularistic MBI sub-domains, but they do not permit an estimate of who has which degrees of burnout. And some would propose that this is the way it should be, because it will be a long time before valid and reliable estimates are justified. We differ, respectfully. At the very least, no other operational definition of burnout can assemble the support for their reliability and validity that *Global Burnout* provides for the phase model.

HOW BAD SHOULD BURNOUT BE? HOW BAD IS IT?

What does the common wisdom say about the ideal and tolerable incidences of burnout? As a convenient benchmark, many hundreds of managers have been asked about the distribution of phases of burnout they expect to find in their organizations, and also about the distribution they prefer. These "actual" and "ideal" distributions almost universally take on a "one hump" shape, a "normal distribution," for almost all managers at all levels.

However, one difference between managers seems clear enough. Their responses fall into two clusters: these clusters can be labelled as "organizational humanists" and "organizational realists," respectively.

The humanists constitute the smaller cohort, and they want to shift their normal curve decisively toward the least-advanced phases, with the goal in practice of eliminating almost all cases of advanced burnout. The ideal of the humanists is zero advanced burnout, or a very small percentage. Humanists can differ in the actual distributions of burnout they perceive.

The organization realists constitute the much larger cluster of managers, and their one-hump curves for ideal and actual distributions of the phases are similar in shape to those of the humanists, but trend more toward the advanced phases. The realists observe that organization membership requires doing uninteresting or difficult things by all members—at least some of the time for everybody, and for many members much or all of the time. Hence, estimates of actual burnout for realists can range up to 30 percent or so in the three most-advanced phases. Given what appear to them intractable realities, the realists estimate that the best that can be done is perhaps 20 percent or so in the three most-advanced phases—that is, Phases VI through VIII.

These are rough estimates of actual and ideal conditions, of course, but they merit two data-based reactions. Thus, the two ideals do not differ much from one another. Moreover, the two ideals are wildly less than of the levels of burnout that seem to exist, in North American as well as elsewhere. The distributions of phases in nature are substantially higher than both realists and especially idealists estimate as existing.

HOW LONG DOES BURNOUT LAST?

The sting of burnout, no matter what proportions of people have it, is often mitigated by guesses about how long "it" lasts. Not so long, say some, with a few even implying that burnout merely comes and goes. Others see a long, long trail awinding (e.g., Cherniss, 1995; Freudenberger, 1980).

Concerning persistence, the phase model of burnout can make another major contribution. Little longitudinal research exists, and almost all of that on small populations (e.g., Cherniss, 1989, 1995), as well as for short intervals (Boudreau & Hackson, 1990). This is a significant shortfall, because persistence has major theoretical and practical relevance. The reasons are obvious: if burnout basically comes and goes, practitioners lose interest in it; and theorists are likely to move on in their search for centroids in nature.

INCIDENCE AND PERSISTENCE OF BURNOUT: INTRODUCING A UNIQUE DATA BASE

If we were to rely on informed estimates of burnout as it exists at the "average" worksite, things would not be too bad. For sure, previous chapters detail a long litany of dour covariants of advanced phases. But most estimates of advanced burnout fall in a narrow and low range. And many see burnout as transient, if not mercurial.

So the situation in this common view of burnout is not exactly a slam-dunk. But neither is it far removed from that status, in general.

If the phase model is even approximately applicable, however, this informed opinion is not very accurate. The evidence from the phase literature suggests that, all in all, things are pretty bad, in the two following ways, which we repeat for emphasis:

- Burnout seems to have a high incidence in organizations. Many people seem to have "it" in advanced degrees.
- Burnout seems to have a high persistence. "It" seems to last for extended periods for people in most organizations.

To repeat: only the phase model provides credible support for these two generalizations.

So how bad is burnout, really? The data on incidence come in two general varieties, both from North America as well as global settings. The first source provides a bare estimate of the distribution of the phases, with the survey form containing only MBI items. An *ad hoc* network provided many such snapshots of burnout phases.[1] Observers attempted no rigorous assessments of the hosts—their cultures or climates, structural arrangements, and so on.

The second source of data about the incidence of phases involved detailed research designs, and on occasion confronted respondents with as many as 600 or 700 items. Many of these studies have been referred to in previous chapters.

This chapter aggregates both kinds of sources of data about incidence, distinguishing them only as having North American loci or as representing other worldwide locations. Appendices A and B, respectively, provide details about the numerous worksettings that here provide data about incidence of the phases.

Incidence in Numerous North American Settings

Table VI.1 summarizes data on incidence from a large number of North American locations. In most cases, only summary data about phase assignments were available to the present authors (see Row A). Overall, we try to be careful, if not scrupulous, that universal norms are used to make phase assignments (see Chapter II). Hence, Table VI.1 also isolates—see Row B in Table VI.1, Direct Data Access—those cases in which the present authors directly made the phase assignments. Asterisks in Table VI.1 identify the cases of Direct Data Access.

No cases are included[2] in which it is known that phase conventions were not followed. For example, Greiner (1992, p. 373) reports that he uses local norms and, consequently, the distribution of phases he reports does not appear in Table VI.1.

Row C in Table VI.1 reports cases for which we have only summaries of phase distributions calculated by others.

We will return to the associated issues at several points but, generally, ample reasons support the view that Table VI.1 reflects conservative estimates, if anything. For example, as noted, the universal norms derive from an organization experiencing many stressors and much strain, and hence those universal norms probably set a high standard for High assignments on the three MBI sub-domains.

If with caveats that later discussion will be able to substantially address, in sum, Table VI.1 encourages two reactions. They are:

- A rush to judgment seems justified, on obvious grounds, about several major points.
- But, then again, restraint is appropriate in some regards.

Table VI.1.   Incidences of Phases in North American Work Settings

Locus[a]	Researchers	N =	Phase Assignment, Sub-Ns/%							
			I	*II*	*III*	*IV*	*V*	*VI*	*VII*	*VIII*
1. Site A*	Golembiewski, Munzenrider, and Carter (1981)	296	121 40.9%	31 10.6	23 7.7	14 4.7	41 13.9	27 9.1	22 7.3	17 5.8
2. Site B*	Golembiewski, Stevenson, and Munzenrider (1986)	1535	352 22.9%	107 7.0	193 12.6	124 8.1	107 7.0	176 11.5	109 7.1	367 23.9
3. Site C*	Golembiewski and Munzenrider (1991)	200	20 9.8%	1 0.5	102 52.0	13 6.4	6 2.9	3 1.5	30 14.7	25 12.3
4 Site D*	Golembiewski and Munzenrider (1995)	783	244 31.2%	48 6.1	133 17.0	55 7.0	50 6.4	71 9.1	45 5.8	137 17.5
5. Site E*	Golembiewski, Munzenrider, and Carter 1981	229	84 36.7%	21 9.2	42 18.3	6 2.6	20 8.7	17 7.4	17 7.4	22 9.6
6. Site F	See Note 1.	36	9 25.0%	3 8.3	4 11.1	2 5.6	2 5.6	4 11.1	3 8.3	9 25.0
7. Site G	Cahoon and Rowney (1984)	244	79 32.4%	42 17.2	35 14.3	20 8.2	15 6.1	22 9.0	0 0.0	31 12.7
8. Site H*	Boudreau (1986, 1996a)	396	92 23.2%	20 5.1	87 21.8	32 8.1	22 5.3	36 9.1	29 7.3	86 20.5
9. Site I*	Loo, 1994	135	3 2.2%	0 0.0	54 40.0	19 14.1	0 0.0	2 1.5	13 9.6	44 32.6
10. Site J	Boudreau and Golembiewski (1989, p. 64)	728	157 21.6%	16 2.2	150 20.6	36 4.9	66 9.1	26 3.6	122 16.8	155 21.3
11. Site K	Rountree (1982)	2,123	435 20.5%	0 0.0	365 17.2	252 11.9	0 0.0	447 21.1	347 16.3	277 13.1
12. Site L	Deckard (1985)	864	195 22.6%	59 6.8	126 14.6	70 8.1	76 8.8	80 9.3	83 9.6	175 20.3
13. Site M	Rountree (1982)	2389	694 29.1%	0 0.0	0 0.0	337 14.1	0 0.0	442 18.5	227 9.5	689 28.9
14. Site N	See Note 1.	64	5 7.8%	7 10.9	23 35.9	17 26.6	3 4.7	3 4.7	0 0.0	6 9.4
15. Site O	See Note 1.	20	5 25.0%	0 0.0	1 5.0	1 5.0	0 0.0	6 30.0	0 0.0	7 35.0

(continued)

Table VI.1. (*Continued*)

16. Site P	Burke, Shearer, and Deszca (1984)	424	78	32	69	17	31	38	24	135
			18.4%	7.5	16.3	4.0	7.3	9.0	5.7	31.8
17. Site Q	See Note 1.	132	71	27	2	1	8	19	2	2
			53.8%	20.5	1.5	0.8	6.1	14.4	1.5	1.5
18. Site R	See Note 1.	114	15	40	0	3	7	40	1	8
			13.2%	35.1	0.0	2.6	6.1	35.1	0.9	7.0
19. Site S	See Note 1.	102	23	15	1	1	19	35	1	7
			22.5%	14.7	1.0	1.0	18.6	34.3	1.0	6.9
20. Site T*	Golembiewski, Hilles and Daly (1987)	31	6	0	1	1	7	7	3	6
			19.4%	0.0	3.2	3.2	22.6	22.6	9.7	19.4
21. Site U	See Note 1	53	16	10	4	7	1	2	3	10
			30.2%	18.9	7.5	13.2	1.9	3.8	5.7	18.9
22. Site V	Burke, in Golembiewski and Munzenrider (1988)	708	165	50	103	35	52	84	56	163
			23.3%	7.1	14.5	4.9	7.3	11.9	7.9	23.0
23. Site W	See Note 1.	36	6	2	2	5	3	3	4	11
			16.7%	5.6	5.6	13.9	8.3	8.3	11.1	30.6
24. Site X	See Note 1.	58	11	4	5	5	1	5	10	17
			19.0%	6.9	8.6	8.6	1.7	8.6	17.2	29.3
25. Site Y*	See Note 1.	78	18	2	9	2	12	2	6	27
			23.1%	2.6	11.5	2.6	15.4	2.6	7.7	34.6
26. Site Z	See Note 1.	25	6	2	4	2	1	5	2	3
			24.0%	8.0	16.0	8.0	4.0	20.0	8.0	12.0
27. Site AA	See Note 1.	38	5	1	6	5	3	2	4	12
			13.2%	2.6	15.8	13.2	7.9	5.3	10.5	31.6
28. Site BB	See Note 1.	17	14	1	1	1	0	0	0	0
			82.4%	5.9	5.9	5.9	0.0	0.0	0.0	0.0
29. Site CC	See Note 1.	16	4	3	4	2	1	1	1	0
			25.0%	18.8	25.0	12.5	6.3	6.3	6.3	0.0
30. Site DD	See Note 1.	772	227	85	105	81	59	64	32	119
			29.4%	11.0	13.6	10.5	7.6	8.3	4.1	15.4
31. Site EE	See Note 1.	637	190	61	69	71	41	68	33	104
			29.8%	9.6	10.8	11.1	6.4	10.7	5.2	16.3
32. Site FF	Deckard, Rountree, and Golembiewski (1986)	111	15	9	5	18	14	11	4	35
			13.5%	8.1	4.5	16.2	12.6	9.9	3.6	31.5

(*continued*)

Table IV.1. (Continued)

Locus[a]	Researchers	N =	I	II	III	IV	V	VI	VII	VIII
					Phase Assignment, Sub-Ns/%					
33. Site GG	See Note 1.	94	17	17	7	11	3	17	2	20
			18.1%	18.1	7.4	11.7	3.2	18.1	2.1	21.3
34. Site HH	Deckard, Rountree, and Golembiewski (1986)	89	19	6	10	10	4	16	3	21
			21.4%	6.7	11.2	11.2	4.5	18.0	3.4	23.6
35. Site II*	Boudreau (1996b)	196	46	13	30	20	15	19	20	32
			23.4%	6.6	15.2	10.2	7.6	10.3	10.2	16.2
36. Site JJ	See Note 1.	91	29	12	6	8	1	15	2	18
			31.9%	13.2	6.6	8.8	1.1	16.5	2.2	19.8
37. Site KK*	Harrison, (1990); Golembiewski, Scherb, and Munzenrider (1984)	984	293	24	13	3	210	215	17	209
			29.7%	2.4	1.3	0.3	21.5	21.8	1.7	21.2
38. Site LL	Burke and Greenglass (1989); Golembiewski and Boss (1991)	622	161	52	63	54	55	78	34	125
			25.9%	8.4	10.1	8.7	8.8	12.5	5.5	20.1
39. Site MM	Burke and Greenglass (1989); Golembiewski and Boss (1991)	622	177	53	72	45	60	68	30	117
			28.5%	8.5	11.6	7.2	9.6	10.9	4.8	18.8
40. Site NN	Burke and Greenglass (1989)	746	186	49	93	51	69	67	54	177
			24.9%	6.6	12.5	6.8	9.2	9.0	7.2	23.7
41. Site OO*	Aldinger (1993)	1106	186	55	143	71	101	111	137	302
			16.8%	5.0	12.9	6.4	9.1	10.0	12.4	27.3
42. Site PP*	Golembiewski, Scherb, Lloyd, and Munzenrider (1992)	213	64	20	41	18	12	16	9	33
			30.0%	9.4	19.3	8.5	5.6	7.5	4.2	15.5
43. Site QQ	Burke and Greenglass (1991)	307	69	21	36	30	27	37	17	70
			22.5%	6.8	11.7	9.8	8.8	12.1	5.5	22.8
44. Site RR	Burke and Greenglass (1991)	307	80	21	30	26	30	38	16	66
			26.1%	6.8	9.8	8.5	9.8	12.4	5.2	21.5

(continued)

Table VI.1. *(Continued)*

45. Site SS	Kilpatrick, Magnetti, and Mirvis (1991)	344	137 39.8%	62 18.0	14 4.1	6 1.7	25 7.3	70 20.3	0 0.0	30 8.7
46. Site TT*	Armistead (1993)	829	190 22.9%	89 10.7	146 17.6	93 11.2	27 3.3	97 11.7	49 5.9	138 16.6
47. Site UU	Novelli (1990)	626	13 2.1%	5 0.8	201 32.1	94 15.0	2 0.3	32 5.1	58 9.3	221 35.3
48. Site VV*	Bower (1994); Golembiewski, Bower, and Kim (1994)	308	80 26.4%	25 8.3	20 6.6	21 6.9	35 11.6	42 13.9	27 7.3	58 19.1
49. Site WW	Golembiewski and Deckard (1994)	216	80 37.0%	9 4.2	0 0.0	1 0.5	60 27.8	63 29.2	1 0.5	2 0.9
50. Site XX	Seltzer and Lynn (1994)	178	53 29.8%	16 9.0	16 9.0	17 9.5	18 10.1	20 11.2	11 6.2	27 15.2
51. Site YY	Seltzer and Lynn (1994)	180	54 30.0%	18 10.0	10 5.6	16 8.9	16 8.9	30 16.2	9 5.0	27 15.0
52. Site ZZ*	Billingsley (1990); Golembiewski, Munzenrider, Scherb, and Billingsley (1992)	160	33 20.5%	12 7.5	32 20.5	13 8.1	4 2.5	23 14.3	14 8.7	29 18.0
53. Site AAA*	Munzenrider (1995)	432	136 31.5%	20 4.6	43 10.0	18 4.2	48 11.1	49 11.3	41 9.5	77 17.8
54. Site BBB	Manning and Jackson (1996)	238	64 27.0%	12 5.0	70 29.4	12 5.0	21 8.8	20 8.4	15 6.3	24 10.1
55. Site CCC	Federal executive aggregate	69	12 17.4%	9 13.0	7 10.1	5 7.2	6 8.7	14 20.3	1 1.4	15 21.7
56. Site DDD*	Corporate Well ness population (1989)	204	59 28.9%	18 8.8	30 14.7	11 5.4	19 9.3	23 11.3	13 6.4	31 15.2
57. Site EEE*	Corporate Well- ness population (1991)	743	247 33.2%	54 7.3	116 15.6	61 8.2	39 5.2	49 6.6	37 5.0	140 18.8
58. Site FFF	Federal executive aggregate	79	24 30.4%	9 11.4	12 15.2	8 10.1	4 5.1	10 12.7	3 3.8	9 11.4

(continued)

Table VI.1. (*Continued*)

Locus[a]	Researchers	N =	Phase Assignment, Sub-Ns/% I	II	III	IV	V	VI	VII	VIII
59. Site GGG*	Boudreau (1995)	18	3	2	3	1	2	3	0	4
			16.7%	11.1	16.7	5.6	11.1	16.7	0.0	22.6
60. Site HHH*	Golembiewski and Kim (1987)	78	12	16	4	5	8	21	1	11
			15.4%	20.5	5.1	6.4	10.3	26.9	1.3	14.1
61. Site III*	Polok and Boss (1994)	183	41	10	7	6	24	38	13	44
			22.4%	5.5	3.8	3.3	13.1	20.8	7.1	24.0
62. Site JJJ*	Gabris and Ihrke (1995a)	1,064	199	48	58	35	152	198	111	263
			18.7%	4.5	5.5	3.3	14.3	18.6	10.4	24.7
A. Overall	N =	24,721	6,129	1,476	3,059	2,025	1,764	3,249	1,978	5,041
	% =		24.8%	6.0	12.4	8.2	7.1	13.1	8.0	20.4
B. Direct Data Access	N =	9,172	2,325	585	1,322	613	792	1,028	648	1,849
	% =		23.5%	6.4	14.4	6.7	8.6	11.2	7.1	20.2
C. Summaries of Phase Assignments Only	N =	15,766	3,840	898	1,796	1,424	980	2,238	1,339	3,251
	% =		24.4%	5.7	11.4	9.0	6.2	14.2	8.5	20.6

Notes: [a] See Appendix A for descriptions of the worksettings and research details. Universal norms are used in all cases. Some minor double-counting exists.
* Indicates populations to which authors had direct access to original data.

Some Clear-Enough Implications About North American Incidence

Several significant points seem worth making about Table VI.1, and without hesitation. They involve: the staggering problems implied by the data on incidence; the somber fact that the view is much the same for several categories of distributions of phases; the unacceptability of those estimates of advanced burnout; the surprising "non-normal" distributions of phase assignments; and the basically-chronic character of burnout. Note, again, that all estimates in Table VI.1 and throughout this chapter rest on the universal norms for High/Low assignments on the three MBI sub-domains.

Burnout Seems Epidemic, At Least. This label may seem dramatic, but the data justify histrionics. Specifically, Row A in Table VI.1 labeled Overall shows that over 41 percent of all assignments are to Phases VI-VIII. Comparable proportions derive from the two other ways of aggregating incidences in Table VI.1—those distributions for which we authors had

Table VI.2. Proportions of Units and Respondents in
Two Sets of Extreme Phases, Overall North American Work Settings

Ranges of Those Classified Respondents	Phases I-III		Phases VI-VIII	
	Number of Units Within Range	Percent of All I-III Respondents	Number of Units Within Range	Percent of All VI-VIII
0-10%	—	—	1	< 0.1%
10.1-20	—	—	3	0.4%
20.1-30	6	7.3%	10	7.2%
30.1-40	10	18.6%	19	29.6%
40.1-50	26	40.6%	23	36.2%
50.1-60	12	24.8%	5	26.5%
60.1-70	6	7.7%	1	0.1%
70.1-100	2	1.1%	—	—

access to data (B), as well as those distributions made available to us in one summary form or another (C).

Table VI.2 provides greater specificity, again with a focus on the Overall data, but the view does not get any less ominous. Thus, only 4 of the 62 North American organizations have fewer than 20 percent of their respondents assigned to Phases VI through VIII, and these represent less than one-half of one percent of all VI-VIII assignees. Relatedly, 47 of the 62 organizations have between 30 and 60 percent of their responding employees assigned to the three most-advanced phases, and these cases contain over 92 percent of all assignments to Phases VI through VIII.

These data should surprise, if they do not shock. Recall that even the "organizational realists" estimated only 30 percent or so in those three most-advanced phases, which guesstimate falls far short of reality as viewed through the eyes of the phase model *when the universal norms are used.*

Why is surprise or shock appropriate? In a few words, substantial proportions of all populations tested will suffer the consequences of these covariants of advanced burnout: poor attitudes concerning the character of the worksite; high levels of physical symptoms; poor performance appraisals; lower productivity; and so on and on. The costs of living in organizations with a high proportion of Phases VI-VIII seem substantial.

As if matters were not bad enough as they stand, Tables VI.1 and VI.2 may underestimate the distributions of phases. No one can be certain that those tables are representative. But one can argue cogently that, if anything, they probably underrepresent the "worst" organizations. Presumably, organizations with very high concentrations of the most-advanced phases would be less open to researchers than the present panel. So Tables VI.1 and VI.2 may reflect a conservative view of what exists in the world of organizations. If that is a reasonably-accurate presumption, it goes almost without saying, Tables VI.1 and VI.2 reflect a truly-ominous picture.

The View Seems Stereophonic. In effect, Table VI.1 provides three perspectives on phase distributions in 62 North American organizations. Rows A-C provide these different looks, and they do not vary much. That is, concern seems appropriate—whether the focal panel includes all available phase estimates, whether those estimates were variously quality-controlled by the present authors, or whether those estimates were available to us authors only in summary form.

Burnout Seems Unacceptably High. Beyond any reasonable doubt, Tables VI.1 and VI.2 present a grave normative challenge in their estimates of the incidence of advanced phases of burnout. Whatever one's tolerable level of burnout in organizations, not to mention one's ideal, the estimates implied in Table VI.1 *are far too high for anyone's comfort.* Most estimates of the ideal cluster in the 5-10 percent range for Phases VI through VIII, and the estimates of actual advanced burnout are not that much higher. But even the *most favorable* estimates in Tables VI.1 and VI.2 are greater than managerial actuals, not to mention ideals.

Phase Distributions Seem Bimodal. Overall, the "normal curve" does not represent the distributions of phases: a two-humped curve serves far better. Specifically, all but 19 of the 62 cases in Table VI.2 have over 30 percent of their members in each of the two clusters of three extreme phases. About 75 percent of all I-III assignments come from organizations with at least 40 percent in those phases; and over 62 percent of VI-VIII assignments are in organizations having at least 40 percent of their members in the three most-advanced phases.

This bimodal distribution surprises most observers. They are accustomed to "normal" distributions, which concentrate most cases near the mean. Similarly, those whimsical readers who are into camels no doubt already have concluded that distributions of the phases of burnout deal with bactrians rather than dromedarians, as it were. To explain, the latter species of camels have one hump, while the former have two.

The prime implication of Tables VI.1 and VI.2 for managerial action and policy seems direct. One should not think, in general, of a single approach that will accommodate the situations of most organization members with regard to burnout. Most members of most macro-organizations will cluster in *one of the two sets* of extreme phases of burnout. And management policies must relate to employees where they are. On average, for the phases, at least *two* sets of these policies are required to touch most employees.

The present view contrasts sharply with the common managerial view, which myopically assumes that "normal distributions" dominate in nature—that is, that most cases of burnout fall somewhere in the middle phases. Such a myopia encourages visualizing some single set of policies and procedures relevant to burnout that "imply the greatest good for the largest number." But this calculation seems far too simple, given the phase model and universal norms.

In sharp contrast to the common managerial mind-picture of a "normal" distribution, the burnout distributions in Tables VI.1 and VI.2 suggest the need for at least *two* portfolios of policies and procedures to deal with a two-humped reality. This flies in the face of dominant managerial metaphors,— "*a* smoothly running machine," or "*a* well-integrated team." In sharp opposition, the two-hump distribution of burnout phases suggests two or more clusters of ships passing in the night; and at least for a substantial proportion of those ships, the seas will be stormy.

The point about bactrian distributions is also at direct odds with the opinion of influential observers like Peters and Waterman (1982)—who focus on *an* organizational culture and applaud its alleged salubrious effects. Bimodality of burnout supports the contrasting concept of multiple and interacting sub-cultures (e.g., Shils, 1951), of culture as a mosaic rather than a monolith. Indeed, consistently, growing evidence implies that the immediate work group is the prime locus of burnout, not the macro-organization. Recall the definition of an immediate work group: those persons reporting directly to an integrating superior—presidents and their VPs, or individual supervisors and their collections of operators. Independent studies (Golembiewski, 1983; Rountree, 1984) show a very strong affinity of groups of first-reports for one *or* the other of the two clusters of extreme phases—with some 70 to 80 percent of all respondents coming from immediate work units that have at least a majority of their members classified in either clusters I-III or VI-VIII. See also the analysis of group properties in Chapter VII.

This bimodality can be explained in convincing practical and theoretic terms by the homogenizing forces operating in smallish groups of first-reports, or immediate work groups. Put another way, the total organization does not appear to be the behaviorally-relevant unit for analyzing burnout. The group of first-reports claims that distinction, so far. In the aggregate, knowing the phases of burnout of an individual provides the best prediction of the phases of a majority of all other members of that individual's immediate work group (Golembiewski, 1983; Rountree, 1984).

Two powerful possibilities or probabilities inhere in the basic bimodality. Presumably, local supervisory practices and policies impact most on member burnout, in opposition to the impact of a macro-culture. This does not surprise (e.g., Shils & Janowitz, 1948), but it nonetheless poses complex analytical and practical challenges. Specifically, burnout phases seem to be associated more directly with persisting features of work, rather than with acute onset associated with traumatic life events. See also Chapter VII.

Table VI.3. Proportions of Units and Respondents in Two Intermediate Phases, Overall, North American Work Settings

Range of Those Classified in Phases IV and V	No of Units Within Range	% of All IV-V Respondents
5% or less	1	< 0.1%
5.1-10%	6	2.2%
10.1-15%	20	39.5%
15.1-20%	28	48.6%
20.1-25%	3	6.4%
25.1-30%	3	2.8%
30.1% or greater	1	0.6%

Burnout Seems Basically Chronic. Despite its snapshot character, to develop the possibility/probability just alluded to, the phase data permit some useful speculation about chronicity and acuteness. Consider the low and narrow range of the proportions in Table VI.3 of those classified in Phases IV and V. Specifically, over 88 percent of all IVs and Vs come from units having no more than 20 percent of all respondents in those phases. See also the section below on persistence, which reinforces the infrequency and instability of Phases IV-V assignments.

Both infrequency and instability help distinguish chronic from acute burnout. Thus, Phase IV is seen as central in chronic outset: I —> II —> IV —> VIII. Whence the instability? Phase IV implies difficulties with both relationships and task, which quickly can lead to heightened Emotional Exhaustion. That is, IV can soon eventuate in VIII and, absent sharp improvement, Phase VIII would tend to persist. This line of conceptual development is consistent with the raw percentages in Table VI.1 for those phases—8.2 for IV vs. 20.4 percent for VIII, in Row A.

As for Phase V, it is central in acute onset which, by definition, is induced by some major trauma. Such traumatic life events probably are infrequent, with (for example) Phase I serving as the take-off point for sudden post-trauma movement to V, or an initial II moving to Phase VI. Moreover, remaining at Phase V for extended periods seems unlikely. Absent quick recovery, one prototypic flight-path might well be: I —> V, with possible advance to VI or VII depending on one's coping strategy, and then possibly to VIII. The low incidence of Phase V in Table VI.1—7.1 percent in Row A—is consistent with this line of thought, both in connection with the low frequency of traumatic onset as well as with the probable transiency of Phase V assignments.

But Not So Fast, at Least Not Yet. Nonetheless, let us pull-in the reins on such implications, at least for a while. Paramountly, the adequacy of the High/Low norms for the three MBI domains is critical in any interpretation of the data. In short, all but minor departures from the universal norms will change the phase assignments. The universal norms are based on Site B data, and seem conservative because the norming population probably sets a stiff standard for High scores. Opinions on this central point can differ, and future research may undermine the present judgment. But the universal norms remain for the present, at least, and Chapter VII summarizes the evidence reinforcing this basic choice.

In addition, the "snapshot" design underlying Tables VI.1 through VI.3 requires tentativeness regarding chronic versus acute onset. Only longitudinal analysis will permit specificity concerning several significant questions about the phase model in connection with chronicity and acuteness of onset which, in turn, will have profound implications for theory as well as for treatment.

No such clinical analyses using the phase model are yet available. That is the hard truth, at once tethering interpretations of Tables VI.1 through VI.3, as well as motivating longitudinal research to remedy the limits of that and associated tables.

The third and final caveat also relates to the one-time observations relied on here. Entrance to, and exit from, the advanced stages cannot be distinguished in Tables VI.1 through VI.3. Since entrance may have covariants that differ from exit, at least in degree, the failure to distinguish the directionality of phase assignments can confound the interpretation of present results.

These three caveats must discipline interpretations of Tables VI.1, VI.2, through VI.3, to be sure. However, the several "clear enough" implications about North American burnout provide useful points of departure for epidemiological estimates. They also provide a reasonable rationale for doing a random survey, worldwide.

Incidence of Phases in Global Settings

The findings about the worldwide incidence of phases not only will provide useful context for Tables VI.1 through VI.3, but they also will inform decisions about the phase model's comprehensiveness and the reliability of its estimates. Usefully, in the vast bulk of the global cases, there is no question that phase model measurement conventions were fully applied.

Note also that, as in Table VI.1, the three summary rows in Table VI.4—(A) Overall, and (B) Direct Data Access, and (C) Summaries of Phase Assignments Only—refer to different ways of aggregating incidence data about the phases. That is, Direct Data Access refers to hands-on status by the present authors.

Table VI.4. Incidence of Phases in 21 Global Work Settings

Locus[a]	Researchers	N =	I	II	III	IV	V	VI	VII	VIII
						Phase Assignments N and in %				
1. Belarus A	Golembiewski, Boudreau, and Levin (1996)	312	33 10.6%	18 5.8	55 17.6	65 20.8	11 3.5	26 8.3	17 5.4	87 27.9
2. Belarus B	Boudreau, Zhilina, Zhilina and Faiferman (1996a)	795	9 1.1%	11 1.4	236 29.6	139 17.5	3 0.4	33 4.2	28 3.5	336 42.3
3. Belarus C	Boudreau, Zhilina, Zhilina and Faiferman, (1996b)	200	28 14.0%	26 13.0	34 17.0	47 23.5	4 2.0	14 7.0	7 3.5	40 20.0
4. Belarus D	Boudreau and Levin (1996a)	460	40 8.7%	31 6.7	92 20.0	104 22.6	8 1.7	33 7.2	25 5.4	127 27.6
5. Belarus E	Boudreau and Levin (1996b)	87	16 18.4%	5 5.7	17 19.5	12 13.8	3 3.4	2 2.3	6 6.9	26 29.9
6. Belarus F*	Boudreau, Zhilina, and Zaiferman (1996c)	191	20 10.5%	27 14.1	24 12.6	40 20.9	3 1.6	22 11.5	10 5.2	45 23.6
7. Canada A	Dupicea and Hubert (1996)	130	36 27%	5 3.9	21 16.2	4 3.1	20 15.4	10 7.7	11 8.5	23 17.7
8. China A	Rowney and Cahoon (1987)	196	20 10.2%	13 6.6	7 3.6	17 8.7	7 3.6	50 25.5	9 4.6	73 37.2
9. China B*	Golembiewski, and Luo (1996)	259	71 27.4%	40 15.4	7 2.7	28 10.8	18 6.9	50 19.3	7 2.7	38 14.7
10. Ghana A*	Fiadzo (1995)	287	38 13.2%	21 7.3	37 12.9	36 12.5	44 15.3	46 16.0	17 5.9	48 16.7
11. Israel A	Pines and Golembiewski (1996)	99	43 43.0%	14 14.0	3 3.0	3 3.0	9 9.0	10 10.0	5 5.0	12 12.0
12. Italy A	See Note 1.	10	2 20.0%	1 10.0	1 10.0	2 20.0	0 0.0	3 30.0	1 10.0	0 0.0
13. Japan A*	Boudreau and Golembiewski (1989)	970	26.6 2.7%	19 1.9	51 5.3	144 14.8	14 1.4	62 6.4	46 4.6	608 62.7
14. Japan B*	Boudreau and Golembiewski (1996b)	503	19 3.8%	21 4.2	35 7.0	96 19.1	21 4.2	45 8.9	24 4.8	242 48.1

(continued)

Table VI.4. (Continued)

15. Japan C*	Golembiewski, Boudreau, Goto, and Murai (1992)	411	9 2.3%	6 1.5	16 3.9	17 4.1	6 1.5	62 15.1	11 2.7	264 69.1
16. Korea A	See Note 1.	61	5 8.2%	3 4.9	3 4.9	11 18.0	2 3.4	8 13.0	2 3.4	27 44.2
17. Poland A	See Note 1.	181	30 16.6%	15 8.3	27 14.9	14 7.7	16 8.8	17 9.4	17 9.4	45 24.9
18. Saudi Arabia	Al-Ebedah (1996)	264	40 15.2%	8 3.0	9 3.4	9 3.4	64 24.2	60 22.7	25 9.5	49 18.6
19. Taiwan A	Golembiewski, Sun, Lin, and Boudreau (1995)	623	113 18.1%	25 4.0	78 12.5	67 10.8	66 10.6	86 13.8	44 7.1	144 23.1
20. Taiwan B	Lin, Sun, and Golembiewski (1996)	553	58 10.5%	34 6.1	46 8.3	86 15.6	18 3.3	76 13.7	15 2.7	220 39.8
21. Yugoslavia A	See Note 1.	100	10 10.0%	11 11.0	20 20.0	5 5.0	12 12.0	17 17.0	4 4.0	21 21.0
A. Overall	N = %=	6692	666 10.0%	354 5.3	819 12.2	946 14.1	349 5.2	732 10.9	331 5.0	2495 37.3
B. Direct Data Access	N = %=	4605	345 7.5%	230 5.0	625 13.6	723 15.9	155 3.4	405 8.8	209 4.5	1904 41.3
C. Summaries of Phase Assignments Only	N = %=	2087	321 15.4%	124 5.9	194 9.3	214 10.3	194 9.3	327 15.7	122 5.9	591 28.3

Notes: [a] See Appendix B for descriptions of worksettings and research details. Universal norms are used in all cases.

* Indicates populations to which authors had direct access to original data.

So what does available research have to say about the global incidence of burnout? Table VI.4 provides the best data available, even though they are patently only suggestive. But Table VI.4 has its attractions. To deliberately pose a strict test for the phase model, the table emphasizes loci that are less-frequently represented in the stress-related literature reviewed in Chapter II. And it permits direct comparisons of several loci, given its consistent reliance on the same operational definition of burnout in the form of translations of the MBI items.

Some Clear-Enough Implications About Global Incidence. Given questions about generalizability, Table VI.4 severely heightens concerns about burnout, for four basic reasons. First, as Row A shows, the worldwide incidences provide no comfort to those who see burnout as restricted to western settings. A few specifics permit a direct comparative sense of the global incidence of burnout. Specifically, Table VI.4, Row A, contains 54.7 percent of its respondents in the three most-advanced phases, and 26.3 percent in Phases I-III. This contrasts sharply with Table VI.1 for North American settings, where 41 percent of the respondents are assigned to each of the two clusters of the three most-and least-advanced phases of burnout.

There are outliers in Table VI.4, to be sure, but not many; and most of them are small populations. Among the outliers is China B, where less than 37 percent of the phase assignments fall in Phases VI-VIII. Belarus C and E also can be considered outliers, and their Ns also are small.

Many factors can help explain such variations from a generally-high base, in addition to small sample size. In the case of China B, for example, those with special knowledge explain that Beijing public bureaucrats have been treated very well historically—in terms of income, housing, as well as honors and other perquisites. These observers consequently are not surprised by the relatively-favorable distribution of phase assignments in China B. The local screws are now being tightened, however, and a follow-on survey is planned to test for trends.

Such caveats notwithstanding, burnout reasonably can be said to have a major global dimension.

Indeed, if the phase model is reasonably valid and reliable, we have a global pandemic on our hands. Overall, the most-favorable distributions of phases in Figure VI.4 *begin* at the outer fringe of the average incidences reported in Table VI.1, and many are worse. Much worse. Japanese sites present the most skewed distributions, obviously.

Table VI.5. Proportions of Respondents in
Two Extreme Sets of Phases, Global Studies

Ranges	Phases I-III No. of Units Within Range	% of All I-III Respondents	Phases VI-VIII No. of Units Within Range	% of All VI-VIII Respondents
0-10%	2	7.8%	0	—
10.1-20%	2	5.3%	0	—
20.1-30%	3	14.5%	1	0.1%
30.1-40%	8	54.8%	5	5.7%
40.1-50%	4	17.6%	7	35.0%
50.1-60%	1	0.1%	2	13.2%
60.1-70%	—	—	3	14.2%
70.1% or greater	—	—	2	31.8%

Second, no revisions of substance are required, whichever of the three summary perspectives gets applied to Table VI.4. See Rows A-C.

Third, the data in Table VI.4 certainly add urgency to an aggressive and timely exploration of the incidences of burnout, worldwide. Table VI.4 represents only a start toward what requires doing but, even as it is, two refinements can be made here. Thus, Table VI.5 summarizes the ranges of respondents in the two sets of most-and least-advanced phases, worldwide. The bias here is quite pronounced. In revealing summary, all but six of the global worksettings contain 40 percent or more of their respondents in the three most-advanced phases, while only 7 have 40 percent or more of their respondents in Phases I-III.

Moreover, as for Phases IV and V in global worksettings, Table VI.6 shows a pattern similar to that of North American worksettings. Nearly 90 percent of IV-V assignees come from organizations that have less than 25 percent of their respondents in those two intermediate phases, combined.

Fourth, again, recall that all tables in this chapter rely on universal norms for making High/Low assignments on the three MBI sub-domains. Perhaps, to present one note of possible optimism concerning Table VI.4, norms sensitive to different national cultures, or organizations are more appropriate. These "local norms" may generate profiles of the phases that differ from those resulting from universal norms. Chapter VII directs attention at this central issue, and details some orders-of-magnitude of universal vs. local norms.

But Not So Fast, At Least Not Yet. Despite their mutual reinforcement, Tables VI.1 and VI.4 permit one obvious way of avoiding much of the sting in the raw incidences of the phases. Directly, there seem unacceptably-high incidences of the advanced phases, not only in North America but also elsewhere. However, that may not be so bad *if* phases of burnout come and go, with the consequence that advanced phases do not bedevil very many people for very long, even though many of us will be in advanced phases at any point in time.

Table VI.6. Respondents in Two Intermediate Phases, IV and Vs Overall, Global Work Settings

Ranges	No. of Units Within Range	% of All IV-V Respondents
5% or less:	0	—
5.1-10%	3	2.0%
10.1-15%	1	2.0%
15.1-20%	8	43.6%
20.1-25%	6	41.%
25.1-30%	2	10.5%
30.1 or greater	0	—

In short, what do we know about the persistence of the phases? That knowledge will be very important influencing how we react to Tables VI.1 and VI.4, as well as their back-ups—Tables VI.2 and VI.3 as well as Tables VI.5 and VI.6, respectively.

DOES BURNOUT PERSIST, OR COME AND GO?

Tables VI.1 and VI.4 do not have direct counterparts when we deal with another crucial aspect of how bad burnout is—that is, how long does it last? In sum, data on persistence constitute a weak link in the chain of research on the phase model. Few longitudinal research designs have used the phase model of burnout in North America, and the case is far worse when it comes to worldwide estimates of persistence. Nonetheless, available data seem troubling.

What say those available data, all from North American worksettings? Studies of persistence of the phases permit useful macro- and micro-perspectives, but only with reservations. In any case, Table VI.7 constitutes the largest panel ever assembled: Specifically, Table VI.7 improves on previously-published sources by 50 percent in worksites represented and about 100 percent in total respondents. These improvements encourage attention, but also caution as well as motivation to improve the breed.

Persistence Estimates Over Extended Intervals

Table VI.7 provides generally-consistent results when the T_1 vs. T_2 intervals vary from several months to several years. Five points highlight the general agreement in those data, whose credibility is heightened by the 11 independent worksites represented.

First, "no change" in phase assignments (or Case A) seems to occur in at least 40 percent of the sites, and usually more, on average. The full range is from about 25-46 percent, with only a single outlier on the low side.

Of course, unobserved switches in phase assignments may have occurred between the two observations involved in each site. Table VI.7 really estimates the probability of an individual being found in the same/similar "shelves" at two points in time, and this may hide other migrations between phases in the intervals between snapshots.

Second, Cases B-D relax the criteria for "no change," and they also reflect substantial stability over time in the "shelving" levels of individuals. Table VI.7 implies that individuals either remain in the same or similar phases, or tend to return to them if migrations do occur.

Overall, no one can go very far wrong in expecting substantial stability, as defined in three different ways in at least half of the cases. The best estimate is "stability" in 2 out of every 3 cases, more or less. Specifically, the three ranges are:

Table VI.7. Persistence of Phase Assignments over Various Intervals, in Percent, N = 1411

Kinds of Stability	I. N = 71 (2 months)	II. N = 28 (5 months)	III. N = 76 (7 Months)	IV. N = 89 (1 year)	V. N = 113 (1 year)	VI. N = 307 (2 years)	VII. N = 143 (1 year)	VIII. N = 146 (1 year)	IX. N = 97 (2 years)	X. N = 202 (2 years)	XI. N = 139 (3 years)
A. No Change	38.0	46.4	32.9	25.8	38.9	43.0	44.1	42.5	40.2	43.0	30.2
B. No Change and +/- One Phase	46.5	43.6	47.4	43.8	57.5	54.7	51.1	54.8	54.6	49.0	43.2
C. Stability within Phases I-III	78.6	66.7	64.7	57.1	81.1	71.5	68.1	66.7	68.1	49.8	65.6
D. Stability within Phases VI-VIII	73.5	71.4	64.3	72.5	52.0	66.7	68.6	65.1	64.9	68.6	49.1
E. Stability within Phases IV-V	26.1	37.5	20.0	28.6	14.3	29.9	23.0	26.9	7.6	34.3	30.4
Site Description	health-care setting (Golembiewski, Deckard, and Rountree 1989; see also site FF)	corporate Human Resources group (Site T)	consumer products firm (Site LL #1 vs. Site MM #2)	medical clinic (Site FF vs. HH)	product division of multinational business (Site A vs. E)	teachers (Site QQ vs. RR)	hospital employees (Site AAA-I vs. AAA-II)	hospital employees (Site AAA-II vs. AAA-III)	hospital employees (Site AAA-I vs. AAA-II)	hospital employees, excluding (Site LL #2 vs. MM #2)	follow-up on student cohort (XX vs. YY)

- Case B: 43.2 to 57.5 percent
- Case C: 49.8 to 81.1 percent
- Case D: 49.1 to 73.5 percent

The pattern for Stability Types A-D seems easy enough to interpret. Typically, only one or two outliers fall in the low portion of each range of change, which suggests a narrow clustering. More powerfully still, the outliers indicating greater change come from the longest test-retest intervals. Specifically, two of the four most-marked outliers on measures A-D come from Case XI, while the other two most-marked outliers are from Case X. The reader will note that the cases with the longest observational intervals come toward the end of the array. This is understandable on general principle, and suggests a basic underlying pattern of stability, as somewhat modified by the passage of time.

In the present environmental view, this pattern implies the essential stability of the "infrastructure" at work—of policies, procedures, and structures within whose context work is performed. Consequently, the stability of phase assignments suggests the general persistence of local infrastructures.

Third, although not all of the data are reported here, it seems about equally likely that, on balance, when a change in phase assignment does occur, it will be for the "better" or the "worse." "Better" here is defined as movement to a lower phase, such as an original IV being assigned later to a I. To illustrate with case V in Table VI.7, 26 percent of the second assignments are to less-advanced phases, 35 percent are worse, and about 39 percent of the assignments remain the same.

Fourth, as the logic of the phase model implies, row E in Table VI.7 shows that Phases IV and V are way-stations through which people pass relatively quickly—apparently on *entrance* toward advanced phases, as well as on *exit* from those phases. Unfortunately, unavailable clinical research is required to provide specifics about the entrance/exit distinction. In any case, the range for those remaining in Phases IV and V in Table VI.7 approximates 7 to 38 percent, with three outliers above 30 percent.

Again, as for stability estimates A-D, *a* pattern of change dominates for E. Consistently, two of the three largest estimates of change in estimate E come from the largest T_2-T_1 intervals. Relatedly, outliers also tend to come from small populations—for example, Cases II and IX—where a few deviant individuals, or even one, can have a big impact.

Earlier discussion emphasizes the centrality of Phases IV and V in chronic and acute onset, respectively, and Table VI.7 supports this line of thought although it does not constitute proof. Briefly, Phase IV is considered the gateway to VIII in chronic onset, and probably after a brief period of "shelving." And Phase V is on the direct pathway of those Is who experience some trauma in acute onset. Here, also, a long stay is not expected. Either the emotional impact of the trauma abates, and people deescalate —> I. Or the impact persists or grows, in which case individuals might progress in these alternative ways:

V —> Phase VI, if Depersonalization occurs, and then —> VIII
V —> Phase VII, if an individual copes by jeopardizing Personal Accomplishment, and then —> VIII.

Fifth, and finally, Table VI.7 suggests no marked tendency for rates of stability to decrease over time. The proportions in Phases IV-V vary in a relatively narrow range; and Stability Types A-D seem to fall over time, but only gently.

Of course, caution is appropriate in such interpretations, and for two major reasons. Several of the worksites contain small numbers of cases, and no studies from global worksettings are available. But newly-available data imply that Table VI.7 is firmly in the ballpark.[3]

Persistence Estimates In Micro-Intervals

Reinforcing perspective about the persistence of phase assignments comes from a single site at which multiple MBI testing occurred on a weekly schedule over two months. N varied from 111 to 71 over that interval. Turnover, reassignments, and reduced response rates account, in decreasing order, for this attrition over time (Golembiewski, Deckard, & Rountree, 1989, pp. 65-67).

Table VI.8. Summaries of Various Component "Stabilities"

"Stability" Conventions	Mean "Stability," in percent	"Stable" Assignments for Various Observation Intervals, in %						
		1 Week	2 Weeks	3 Weeks	4 Weeks	5 Weeks	6 Weeks	7 Weeks
I. No Change	47.7%	48.5	44.9	50.7	50.9	61.7	42.4	38.0
II. No Change and + - One Phase	56.2	58.8	53.2	61.0	54.2	70.0	48.5	46.5
III. No Change from Phases I-III	65.3	60.0	57.5	62.5	75.0	78.3	61.1	78.6
IV. No Change from Phases VI-VIII	74.3	75.9	71.8	74.4	74.1	81.5	69.7	73.5
V. No Change from Phases IV-V	41.2	41.1	42.2	45.5	50.0	50.0	33.3	26.1

Source: From Golembiewski, Deckard, and Rountree (1989, p. 74).

Table VI.8 summarizes five estimates of "stability" in phase assignments during 7 weekly assessments, on the model of Table VI.7. Only one apparently-major difference catches the eye. The "stability" in Phases IV and V seems greater than in Table VI.7.

Why? No one can say definitely. However, simply, movement out of Phases IV and V in both chronic and acute onset may simply take longer than is allowed by the research design underlying Table VI.8. The exciting possibility: this feature in Table VI.8 may identify, in effect, critical timing-points.

Let us put that possibility in a more direct form. After Week 6, the data in Table VI.8 may be trending into territory more consistent with Table VI.7.

So Does Time Heal Burnout?

The answer seems clear: one should not count on it, given the available data—warts and all.

NOTE

1. In many cases, the data-sets underlying Table VI.1 have not been published independently but were provided in summary form by an *ad hoc* network of observers. The observers include: Robert A. Aldinger, (Valdosta State University); Gary M. Andrew (Rand McNally & Co.); Sister Marianna Bauder (St. Mary's Hospital & Medical Center); Weyland Billingsley (Georgia School for the Deaf); Leslie S. Boss (Brigham Young University); R. Wayne Boss (University of Colorado at Boulder); Robert Boudreau (University of Lethbridge); Donald Bower, (University of Georgia); Ronald J. Burke (York University); Allan Cahoon (University of Calgary); Diane Carter Carrigan, free-lance consultant; Sister Lynn Casey (St. Vincent Hospital & Health Center); James Michael Corbett (Aspenwood Dental Corporation); Rick Daly (Allergan Pharmaceuticals); Gloria J. Deckard (University of Missouri at Columbia); Eugene Deszca (York University); H. Sloane Dugan (University of Calgary); Mark Dundon (Sisters of Providence Health System); Jane Nelson Fine (St. Mary's Hospital & Medical Center); Terry D. Fine (Aspenwood Dental Corporation); Mike Fuller (University of Calgary); Alan M. Glassman (California State University, Northridge); Esther R. Greenglass, (York University); Roysten Greenwood (University of Alberta); Robert B. Grimm (University of Colorado at Boulder); Alan Guerrie Hornberger (St. Francis Hospital & Medical Center); Conrad Jackson, (University of Tulsa); Tom Janz (University of Calgary); Anne Osborne Kilpatrick, (South Carolina School of Medicine, Charleston); Brad Leach (Sheriff, Boulder County, Colorado); Joseph Lischeron (University of Calgary); Michael Lloyd, Albany, GA; Robert Loo, (University of Lethbridge); Lynn E. Lynn, (LaSalle University); Sandra M. Magnetti, (Tucson VA Medical Center); Michael Manning, (New Mexico State University); Sister Ann Marita (St. Francis Hospital & Medical Center); Franca Maroino (Tesi Spa Consulting Firm); Marco V. Maroino (Tesi Spa Consulting Firm); Mark L. McConkie (University of Colorado at Colorado Springs); David M. Mirvis (Veterans Administration Medical Center, Memphis, TN); Wayne Montgomery (Personal Improvements Programs); Robert F. Munzenrider (Penn State University, Harrisburg); William M. Murray (St. Vincent

Hospital & Medical Center); Eva Maslyk-Musial, Warsaw, Poland; David P. Noffsinger (Aspenwood Dental Corporation); Sue E. Noffsinger (Grand Junction, Colorado); Josip Obradovic (University of Zagreb); Se-Jeong Park (Keimyung University), Taegu, Korea; Michael S. Ross (University of Calgary); Benjamin H. Rountree (University of Missouri at Columbia); Julie I.A. Rowney (University of Calgary); Katherine Scherb, (University of Wisconsin Law School); Patrick Scott (International Trade Association, U.S. Department of Commerce); Joseph Seltzer, (LaSalle University); John Shearer (York University); Jerry G. Stevenson (University of Arkansas at Little Rock); Christopher N. Tennis (University of Colorado at Boulder); David J. Voorhis (Voorhis Associates); and William D. Wilsted (University of Colorado at Boulder).

2.   The careful reader will correctly note that a few studies referred to elsewhere do not appear in Table VI.1 or in other tables in this chapter. They were late entries that could be entered elsewhere, and conveniently. In this chapter, these entries would require onerous recalculations. These few new entries fit well within the framework of this chapter.

3.   For example, Site SS was surveyed again in 1992 after an initial survey in 1989, with 110 matched pairs reponding. The five stability estimates do not depart widely from Table VI.7:

Same Phase:	50.0%
Same Phase +/-	
One Phase:	63.6%
I - III Cluster:	73.8%
VI - VIII Cluster:	72.7%
IV - V Cluster:	22.2%

These data became available too late to include in Table VI.7.

Chapter VII

Open Issues in Approaching Burnout Via the Phase Model, Worldwide

The previous chapters bring to mind the partially-filled glass. You know: is it X-nths full? Or X-nths empty?

The present view is of two minds about these central questions. Thus, the literature on the phase model is substantially more full than empty. Moreover, it also seems to us quite clear what key tests require attention in order to more solidly establish whether X = a very high percentage or only a noteworthy percentage.

Seven key questions get attention in this chapter, and available research will be summarized and evaluated. The key questions are:

- Are the universal or local norms more useful?
- So, how many people have which degrees of burnout? And for how long?
- Does gender play a role in the choice of concepts and operations for the phase model?
- Do alternative ways of sequencing the three MBI sub-domains seem superior to the convention underlying the phase model?
- Are eight phases about right?
- Does the study of burnout begin and end with the individual level of analysis?
- *The* key question for burnout gets concluding attention: what can be done at worksites to reduce burnout?

As has been the bias throughout this book, whenever available, research from global settings will be included in working answers to these questions. Nonetheless, most of the research deals with North American worksettings.

179

The available research badly needs replication, to be sure, but what we have does not stand mute. In general, and despite real qualifications, the available research leans definitely toward supporting the phase model and the conventions on which it rests.

But that is enough pre-selling. Let us sample the available evidence about the open issues, and readers can judge for themselves.

NORMS FOR THE SUB-DOMAINS?

From the origins of the phase model, norms have been seen as central, and so must it also be in this list of key questions. "Universal norms" from Site B have been relied on from the start (Golembiewski & Munzenrider, 1984). This acts on the general theory that—*if* burnout is ubiquitous and robust in nature—it should have associations that transcend differences of space, time, and culture. Nonetheless, "local norms" also have been recognized as possibly useful, and are here defined in terms of the medians on the three MBI sub-domains specific to each responding population.

Several points remain absolutely clear, whatever else. The conventions for differentiating High vs. Low scores on the three MBI sub-domains will have an impact on who gets assigned to which phase of burnout. In turn, obviously, such assignments of individuals will determine the distributions of both the incidence and persistence of phase assignments. Such effects will vary, depending on the many possible combinations of cutting-points. Sometimes, distributions of phase assignments will be "worse" for universal norms; sometimes, local norms will do that job; and at other times, as in Ghana A, the two sets of norms will be similar enough that incidences and persistences of the phases will not materially change.

In any choices between norms, *the* test is whether one set or another isolates the sharper pattern of covariants. Multiple comparisons are utilized, and they are consistent with the several replicative studies detailed above: the universal norms do a good job of isolating the expected pattern of covariation with the phases; and, although there is room for improvement, it seems that the local norms *do not* provide any consistent advantage in isolating sharper patterns of covariation.

Again, data come from North American and global settings. In effect, the analysis deals with a key issue: the degree of cultural boundedness vs. the generic character of the phase model and its covariants.

Universal vs. Local Norms and Phase Distributions

To begin, both in North American contexts and elsewhere, the norms utilized can diversely effect the distributions of phases—either up or down or not at all, depending upon the specific range of each set of local norms. Where the local norms constitute greater barriers than the universal norms—for example, 26 vs. 18 for Depersonalization—the distribution of phases will show a less-advanced profile of burnout. Where the local norms constitute lower hurdles, the universal norms will isolate a higher proportion of advanced phases. Expectations will be less simple when the local vs. universal norms differ in mixed ways, and many combinations are possible (Kim, 1990).

Taiwan B illustrates the general pattern. There, the local norms put the High/Low cutting points at 26, 24, and 29 for Depersonalization, Personal Accomplishment, and Emotional Exhaustion, respectively. Two of these three norms imply a "worse" condition in Taiwan than that implied by the universal norms: these are scores greater than 18, 26, and 23 for Depersonalization, Personal Accomplishment (Reversed), and Emotional Exhaustion, respectively. Specifically, Dp and EE have local norms of 25 and 28 for Taiwan B, while the universal norms propose cutting-points beyond 18 and 23 respectively.

The two distributions of phases in Table VII.1 reflect selected differences in norms. In the first case, Japan C, the two sets of norms are very discrepant: High vs. Low assignments there require scores greater than 26, 30, and 31 vs. 18, 26, and 23, respectively, for the three MBI sub-domains Dp, PA, and EE. Taiwan B involves two sets that are moderately discrepant.

One consequence of differences in norms seems clear in Table VII.1. Over 56 percent of Taiwan B respondents are assigned to Phases VI-VIII under the universal norms, and that proportion drops to about 35 percent when the local norms apply. Both estimates suggest major problems, of course,

Table VII.1. Different Sub-Domain Norms and Distributions of Phases, Selective Cases

	Assignments to Phases, in %							
	I	*II*	*III*	*IV*	*V*	*VI*	*VII*	*VIII*
A. Japan C								
Local Norms	17.3	3.6	15.5	8.3	7.2	14.7	9.3	24.0
Universal Norms	2.3	1.6	3.9	4.1	1.6	15.5	2.9	68.2
B. Taiwan B								
Local Norms	13.5	1.3	34.7	14.1	2.0	4.4	9.0	21.0
Universal Norms	10.3	6.1	8.4	15.3	3.2	13.5	2.7	40.2

but the local norms isolate a less-challenging but still startling state of affairs. The same conclusion applies to Japan C, although the magnitudes are greater because the local norms there differ so greatly from the universal norms. Hence, in Japan C, the proportion of assignments to advanced phases is much lower for the local norms.

Universal vs. Local Norms and Patterns of Covariation

The choice between universal vs. local norms will not be made on abstract principles, but on whether one alternative or another is consistently better at isolating the pattern of covariants we can safely associate with advancing burnout. And here the matter seems clear enough, at least as far as the available replicative studies are concerned: *the basic pattern of covariation is retained in virtually all studies of the covariants of universal vs. local norms.* Directly, this implies that "burnout" is a "centroid" in nature: that is, distributions of burnout phases have similar associations with the same or similar variables, despite differences in such an important measurement convention as the norms, because burnout is such a robust feature of life.

Even granting that burnout is a centroid, a significant question remains: Do the universal or local norms still have greater advantages even though they both usually isolate similar patterns of association?

The findings about this question deserve fine-grained analysis, to which this section now turns, and to which other sections also will contribute. Hence, analysis will be detailed. Fortunately, tendencies in North American studies can be compared with results from several global loci. The degree of consistency between the two arenas of studies will have an important influence on the choice of universal or local norms.

North American Studies. Table VII.2 begins the comparison of the relative usefulness of norms using selected studies from North American settings. No strict criteria apply, but the selections clearly bracket the universal norms with sets of local norms that differ from them in major/ minor degree. The pattern below is representative of the comparisons involving other available sites.

Overall, the pattern of covariants is much the same in all selected settings. Directly, 32 of the 36 tests of variables yielded expected results, $P \leq .05$, for both local as well as universal norms.

However, the selected cases urge no abandonment of the universal norms: indeed, if anything, the universal norms get the definite edge. In the largest population (Site OO), for example, universal norms generate the sharper pattern of covariants in two relevant particulars: 88.1 vs. 80.9 percent of all

Table VII.2. Selected Summaries, Universal vs.
Local Norms, North American Settings

Worksite	Researchers		Summary, Tests of Marker Variables X Phases	Paired-comparisons, in %				Mean eta²
				In Expected Direction	In Expected Direction and Statistically Significant	In Contrary Direction	In Contrary Direction and Statistically Significant	
Site 00	Aldinger (1993)	*Local Norms* (Dp > 18; PA (Rev.) > 28; EE > 26)	3/3 as expected, P < .0000	80.9%	50.0	19.1	0.0	.159
		Universal Norms (Dp > 18; PA (Rev.) > 26; EE > 23)	3/3 as expected, P < .0000	88.1%	67.9	11.9	0.2	.147
Site AAA	Munzenrider (1995)	*Local Norms* (Dp > 15; PA (Rev.) > 24; EE > 22)	10/12 as expected, P < .05	80.0%	33.0	19.9	0.0	NR

(continued)

183

Table VII.2. (Continued)

	Universal Norms	11/12 as expected, P < .05	86.3%	34.3	13.7	0.0	NR
Site BBB*	Manning and Jackson, (1996)	*Local Norms* (Dp > 12; PA (Rev.) > 24; EE > 22)				
		3/3 as expected, P < .05	75.0%	35.7	25.0	4.4	NR
		Universal Norms				
		2/3 as expected, P < .05	77.4%	33.3	22.6	1.2	NR

Note: This data set does not permit an exact replication. For the adjustments made because of different items than are used in other phase research, see Manning and Jackson (1996).

aired-comparisons fall in the expected direction, and 67.9 vs. 50.0 percent of all cases are significant as well as fall in the same direction. For the 16 total comparisons of discriminatory power, similarly, 10 favor the universal norms, 3 imply the greater power of the local norms, and the other comparisons are ties.

Global Studies. Table VII.3 provides worldwide perspective on the relative usefulness of universal vs. local norms, relying on four selected studies deliberately chosen to reflect a broad range of differences between norms. The local vs. universal norms: are identical for Ghana A; they are quite similar for Saudi Arabia A as well as for Belarus and China B; Japan C and Taiwan B present the sharpest differences; and Belarus A is intermediate.

Broadly, do the global comparisons favor either set of norms, given the criterion of isolating the expected pattern for a same/similar covariants? Four points trend toward a provisional conclusion, at least as a first-approximation: Yes, and the advantage remains with the universal norms.

First, both universal and local norms tend to isolate a similar pattern of covariation. The surface similarity is perhaps greatest for China B, but the expected pattern of statistically-significant covariation is isolated in all cases. See "Summary..." column in Table VII.3. Moreover, despite obvious differences, statistically-significant paired-comparisons are isolated in at least 40 percent more cases than could be attributed to chance (Belarus A), and beyond 500 percent more cases that chance allows in Saudi Arabia A and Taiwan B.

A bold conclusion seems appropriate on this first test. Burnout effects are so pronounced, even in different global locations, as to resist camouflage or distortion by substantial differences in norms for High/Low assignments.

Second, the robustness of the patterning clearly varies, and seems greatest in Taiwan B—especially as reflected in the column "In Expected Direction and Statistically Significant." In Taiwan B, nearly 8 times more cases are observed than could be expected if chance alone were operating. Japan C also reflects the sharpest advantage for the local model, especially in connection with the proportion of statistically significant paired-comparisons that fall in the expected direction.

Third, if a choice has to be made, the advantage goes to the universal model, if provisionally, and especially where N is substantial and each phase has at least 10 assignees (e.g., Taiwan B). Consider only one way of keeping score. In effect, Table VII.3 implies 20 possible comparisons of the relative discriminating power of local vs. universal norms—5 worksites compared

Table VII.3. Selected Summaries, Universal vs. Local Norms, Selected Global Settings

| Worksite | Researchers | Summary, Tests of Marker Variables X Phases | Paired-comparisons, in % | | | | Mean eta^2 |
			In Expected Direction	In Expected Direction and Statistically Significant	In Contrary Direction	In Contrary Direction and Statistically Significant	
1. Belarus A	Golembiew-ski, Boudreau, & Levin (1996)	*Local Norms* (Dp > 18; PA > 28; EE > 26) 5/5 as expected, P < .05	58.6	7.1	41.4	0.0	.071
		Universal Norms (Dp > 18; PA > 26; EE > 23) 5/5 as expected, P < .007	70.7	11.4	29.3	0.7	.099
2. China B	Golembiew-ski and Luo (1995)	*Local Norms* (Dp > 20; PA > 25; EE > 20) 5/5 as expected, P < .05	84.3	18.6	15.7	0.0	.164
		Universal Norms 5/5 as expected, P < .0001	82.1	18.6	17.9	0.0	NR

(continued)

Table VII.3. (Continued)

Worksite	Researchers		Summary, Tests of Marker Variables X Phases	Paired-comparisons, in %				Mean eta²
				In Expected Direction	In Expected Direction and Statistically Significant	In Contrary Direction	In Contrary Direction and Statistically Significant	
3. Ghana A	Fiadzo (1995)	_Local Norms_	5/5 as expected, P < .001	73.6	14.3	26.4	2.2	.122
		Universal Norms	Identical with local norms					
4. Japan C	Golembiew- ski, Boudreau, Goto, and Murai (1994)	_Local Norms_ (DP > 26; PA > 30; EE > 31)	6/6 as expected, P < .004	72.8	27.2	27.2	4.5	.188
		Universal Norms	6/6 as expected, P < .005	81.5	10.7	16.5	1.2	.136

(continued)

Table VII.3 (*Continued*)

5. Saudi Arabia A	Al-Ebedah (1995)	*Local Norms* Dp > 18; PA > 26; EE > 26	3/3 as expected, P < .005	82.1	40.5	17.9	0.0	NR
		Universal Norms	3/3 as expected, P < .005	77.4	35.7	22.6	0.0	NR
6. Taiwan B	Lin, Sun, and Golembiewski (1996)	*Local Norms* (Dp > 26; PA > 24; EE > 29)	5/5 as expected, P < .0000	77.1	44.3	22.9	2.2	.144
		Universal Norms	5/5 as expected, P < .0000	85.7	43.6	14.3	2.9	.138

on the five columns at the right of Table VII.3, given that local and universal norms are identical for Ghana A. If at least a 10 percent difference is required to attribute an advantage in any of those four particulars to one of the two sets of norms, this scorecard results:

- Advantage to universal norms: 11 cases
- Advantage to local norms: 4 cases
- Ties: 7 cases
- Not reported: 2 cases

Fourth, it appears that the advantage to universal norms would be greater, except for a probable artifact. For example, Japan C simultaneously assigns an advantage to the local norms while the universal norms generate 4 phases that each contain 10 assignees or less. This may produce a heterogeneity of variance that effects the ability of the phases to isolate marked patterns of covariation. Tests of the "collapsed" phases—I-III, IV and V, and VI-VII—support this line of argument. Although the details are not reported here, the universal norms tend to have far greater discriminatory power for the collapsed phases than the local norms. Of course, the collapsed phases permit less-refined estimates of the degree of burnout than do the full 8 phases, but collapsing is a convenient way to avoid the possible artefactualities of small or empty sub-samples.

Gender distributions also may have a similar effect, as the discussion in the third section below proposes.

SO WHAT ABOUT INCIDENCE OF THE PHASES? AND PERSISTENCE?

These and related considerations about norms suggest an operating guide. Both universal and local norms seem serviceable, but the former usually are moreso than the latter. The implication for incidence seems quite direct: *Since the issue of some more complex and better set of norms is still open, however, reporting the incidence and persistence of phases generated by both universal and local norms seems useful.*

Phase assignments obviously are relevant to individual diagnosis, with clinical treatment being based on each specific assignment. There, different assignments may be consequential, even profoundly so, and assignments to phases for local vs. universal norms may well differ. Hence, clarity about norms is absolutely essential for both diagnostician and the diagnosed.

The pervasive bias of the present investigators is environmental, in contrast, and hence the margin for error is far greater. For us, *advanced distributions* of the phases signal the need for environmental change, with the phase assignments of specific individuals not being of primary concern. Hence, when advanced phase assignments are observed, our bias is to reduce the strain-inducing potential of work—its associated structures, policies, procedures, behaviors, and attitudes. See also Chapter VIII. Or in a best-case scenario, favorable phase assignments dictate maintaining and reinforcing existing dynamics. Much is known about the environmental features supporting both best-case and bad-case conditions (e.g., Golembiewski & Munzenrider, 1988).

We do not seek to somehow armor specific individuals against stressors, as by an emotional vaccination. That can be done, we are confident, but may leave one playing perpetual catch-up, with inoculations being followed by the introduction of new stressors, and so on and on. See also Chapter II.

For most practical purposes, universal and local norms may generate different distributions of the phases in a specific case, but their respective distributions typically will have the same or similar implications concerning the need for ameliorative interventions at the organization level. Illustratively, see Table VII.1.

AND WHAT OF GENDER?

Here, we consider a stubborn exception to a general rule. Almost without exception, both the pattern and magnitude of covariation of marker variables with the phases of burnout usually are impressive. This conclusion is reinforced by the fact that similar findings have been generated by several research teams, relying on data from people in a variety of countries, and using a broad range of marker variables. Moreover, as above, whether the focus is on local vs. universal norms, the phase model seems to fare well.

Two caveats are appropriate. First, blood chemistry covariants seem an exception, perhaps because they are distal versus proximate covariants. Second, we do not consider demographics as "marker variables." The associations between phases and demographics are mixed, overall, and the statistically-significant cases account for small proportions of the variance (e.g., Golembiewski & Munzenrider, 1988, pp. 132-144).

Nonetheless, a few studies provide consistent but less-marked findings. They agree that the conventional phase model "works," but they also suggest that other models "work" just as well as the phase model, or on occasion even somewhat better. These findings certainly cannot be neglected.

What is going on? Here, we test one possible explanation of the major apparent exception to generalizations about the phase model. Specifically, are gender effects operating in major ways? This alternative view is based on two sets of studies. One set may be labeled reconstructionist, and typically involve populations containing a large proportion of females (e.g., Lee & Ashforth, 1990). The second set involves some of the phase research in this volume—for example, Site KK, Belarus B, and Japan C, among others—where females also dominate. In both these categories of studies, the expected pattern of covariation is observed, but the magnitude is typically diminished even as non-random forces still seem to be working in the expected directions.

The reader interested in cross-checking the two appendices with various tables can find a number of cases-in-point. For example, Site L is 75 percent female; Japan C has less than 12 percent males; about 80 percent of Ghana A respondents who identified their gender are females; and the several Belarus sites tend to have 30 percent male respondents. It is noteworthy, but not conclusive, that these cases provide less-robust support for the phase model.

To gain better perspective, we need to go far beyond the implications about gender reflected in overall arrays of marker variables X phases. Hence the following test for gender-related effects in a population of more than 1000 respondents—Site OO. Specifically, the three sections below:

- illustrate the typical pattern of covariation of the phases and several marker variables;
- break-out the genders, and assess the degree to which they isolate the expected pattern of covariation; and
- speculate about the causal network underlying gender-specific differences

This trinitarian analysis goes well beyond what seems relatively certain. Thus, females seem to report greater burnout than males, in general; and both genders with higher organizational statuses tend to report less burnout. The obvious linkage: In general, because of historic biases, women will tend to have lower statuses in most organizations. In both comparisons, however, only small percentages of the variance are accounted for (e.g., Golembiewski & Munzenrider, 1988, esp. pp. 132-144).

Phases and Selected Marker Variables

Table VII.4 reflects the expected pattern of covariation between the phases of burnout and a broad inventory of marker variables. In sum, nearly 9 out of every 10 paired-comparisons at Site OO show the expected pattern; over two-thirds of all cases achieve statistical significance as well as fall in the expected direction; and only a few paired-comparisons fall in a contrary direction, let alone achieve significance.

The universal norms underlie Table VII.4, but substituting local norms preserves the essential pattern while weakening it. In sum, the counterpart to Table VII.4 for Site OO's local norms—detailed in Table VII.2—shows (for example) that 80.9 percent of the paired-comparisons fall in the

Table VII.4. Marker Variables X Phases at Site OO,
Universal Norms, All Respondents

	F ratio	P =	Paired-comparisons, in %			
			In Expected Direction	*In Expected Direction and Statistically Significant*	*In Contrary Direction*	*In Contrary Direction and Statistically Significant*
Job Involvement	25.1	< .0000				
General Health Questionnaire, I	35.2	< .0000	88.1	67.9	11.9	0.2
Self-Esteem	22.7	< .0000				

expected direction, and 50 percent also attain $P \leq .05$. This is no wimpish pattern, to be sure; but it falls markedly short of the pattern for universal norms in Table VII.4.

Gender Effects in Air Force Population

Do noteworthy patterns emerge when males and females are disaggregated? Few studies permit such an exercise, for one of two reasons. Thus, some studies involve historically-female occupations such as social workers, nurses, or K-6 teachers. Or populations in some other studies are basically male, as in cadres of executives or middle managers.

Ergo, most burnout studies will not serve present purposes, but the Air Force (AF) population from Site OO constitutes an exception to these two overall characterizations. That is, it includes more than 1000 respondents, as well as a substantial representation of both genders. Details about the population are presented selectively in Appendix A, and comprehensively elsewhere (Aldinger, 1993).

Three emphases highlight the effects in Site OO of disaggregation by gender. First, as Table VII.5 shows, the AF population generates sub-Ns of females and males large enough to provide double-digit entries in almost all of the 8 cells of the phase model, and this permits confident analyses of patterns of covariation for each gender.

Second, the distributions of the phases at Site OO vary for the universal and local norms, but the overall patterns in Table VII.5 are similar. Commonly, for both sets of norms, females tend to cluster more in the advanced phases than males, with males being more concentrated in the less-advanced phases. Specifically, for universal norms, over 50 percent of the females fall in Phases VII and VIII, while 40 percent of the males do so. Relatedly, again for universal norms, 16.6 percent of the females are in Phases I and II, while over 21 percent of the males are so classified.

Table VII.5.   Phase Assignments, Site OO, By Genders

	Phases of Burnout								
	I	*II*	*III*	*IV*	*V*	*VI*	*VII*	*VIII*	*Sub-Ns =*
A. *Universal Norms*[a]									
Females	19	7	16	6	22	8	28	51	157
Males	144	43	106	49	84	103	102	250	881
									1,038 = *N*
B. Local Norms[b]									
Females	27	11	15	10	24	15	19	36	157
Males	201	76	101	69	69	111	65	189	881
									1,038 = *N*

Notes: [a]Chi^2 for 7 df = 15.7, P < .028; Cramer's V = 0.123.
　　　　[b]Chi^2 for 7 df = 16.2, P < .024; Cramer's V = 0.125.

While statistically significant by chi-square test, however, only a small proportion of the variance is explained in the distributions of phases by genders, for both local and universal norms. Cramer's V permits the estimate that about 1.5 percent of the variance in phase assignments is explained by gender.

Third, disaggregating the AF population by gender isolates patterns of covariation on three marker variables that are similar in general but distinct in details. Comparisons of Tables VII.6 and VII.7 provide suggestive details. Thus, the pattern of covariation is clearly sharper for males, even though the pattern for both males and females is similar. Specifically, for universal norms, the record favors males 84.5 vs. 70.2 percent when the criterion is paired-comparisons in the expected direction. More impressively, still, the advantage is huge for the paired-comparisons that fall in the expected direction and also achieve statistical significance—38.1 vs. 6.0 percent, respectively, for males vs. females on the universal norms. A similar difference favoring males also exists for the local norms—42.9 vs 10.7 percent.

Table VII.6.   Summary, Pattern of Covariants, Male Respondents, Site OO

	Summary of Paired-comparisons, in %				
	ANOVA Summary	*In Expected Direction*	*In Expected Direction and Statistically Significant*	*In Contrary Direction*	*In Contrary Direction and Statistically Significant*
Universal Norms	3/3 cases, P < .0001	84.5	38.1	15.5	0.0
Local Norms	3/3 cases, P < .0001	86.9	42.9	13.1	0.0

Table VII.7. Summary, Pattern of Covariants,
Female Respondents, Site OO

	ANOVA Summary	Summary of Paired-comparisons, in %			
		In Expected Direction	*In Expected Direction and Statistically Significant*	*In Contrary Direction*	*In Contrary Direction and Statistically Significant*
Universal Norms	2/3 cases, in expected direction, P < .0001; 1/3 NS	70.2	6.0	29.8	0.0
Local Norms	2/3 cases, in expected direction, P < .0001; 1/3 NS	75.0	10.7	25.0	0.0

Other comparisons of Tables VII.6 and VII.7 also illustrate gender difference-within-similarities. For example, all 6 cases of the ANOVA runs achieve statistical significance for the male sub-batch, while only 4 of 6 do so for females. To the same point, few contrary paired-comparisons exist for either gender or either set of norms, but even so about half as many contrary cases are associated with males as females.

Replications in Global Work Settings

Only a few available data sets from global locations permit a reasonable replication of the findings from Site OO, usually due to small representations of one gender or the other even in large populations, but consistent gender effects within a pattern of phase covariants seem to exist in almost every data set that permits a reasonable comparison. Consider here only Belarus B, which generates results that do not differ substantially from other global settings—for example, Belarus D.

Table VII.8 summarizes the comparison of gender differences-within-a-pattern, using as covariants the Standard Replication Package described in early chapters; and the pattern seems familiar. For both males and females, covariants of the phases pattern similarly, but the pattern for males is more robust on all of the comparative indicators except for significant paired-comparisons falling in a contrary direction. Indeed, the results for males may be understated. For example, despite the substantial sub-N for males in Belarus B, two or three phases typically have 10 or fewer assignees, which leaves the pattern for the genders vulnerable to a few outliers.

Table VII.8. Summary Pattern of Covariation on
Standard Replication Package, by Genders, in One Global Setting

I. *Belarus B, Males* (N = 460) 6/6 cases in in expected direction, P = .0027, or less, mean eta² = .249	*ANOVA Summary*	*Belarus B, Females* (N = 345) 6/6 cases in expected direction, P = .0107, or less, mean eta² = .186
72.2%	Paired-Comparisons in Expected Direction	63.1%
25.4%	Paired-Comparisons in Expected Direction and Statistically Significant	13.9%
27.8%	Paired-Comparisons in Contrary Direction	36.9%
5.6%	Paired-Comparisons in Contrary Direction and Statistically Significant	3.0%

Discussion

How to interpret such gender-associated differences? Speculation must dominate, and the evidence does not all point in the same direction. Nonetheless, the evidence cannot be neglected, and fairly can be interpreted as supporting three points, on definite balance.

First, the present results are not unique to Site 00 or Belarus B. Although they usually include fewer cases, and hence permit less satisfactory analysis, virtually all other studies provide similar results. For one apparent exception, see China B. There, a Chinese municipal government generates inter-gender results different from the present findings, but several phases there contain such small numbers as to decrease confidence in the generalizability of comparisons of results (e.g., Golembiewski & Luo, 1996).

Second, the AF population does not have a balanced representation of the genders in all particulars. For example, Site OO respondents do not equally represent males and females at the higher military ranks, and—in the AF population as well as elsewhere—the higher the rank or grade, the lower the phase of burnout (Aldinger, 1993, p. 131). Obviously, this is consistent with the tendency of females in the AF population to have more-advanced phase assignments (Aldinger, 1993, pp. 128-130). Other conventional interpretations also apply—for example, that sexism heightens the number and magnitude of stressors experienced by female personnel and, consequently, their levels of experienced strain trend higher than for males.

However, such asymmetries do not in any direct way seem to explain the present findings—that is, a similar pattern of covariation for the two genders, but a more marked one for males. Some inferential leaps are required, with one obvious point-of-departure exploring the possibility that males constitute a more homogeneous population than females. For example, *if* work has strong career salience for most AF men, and if AF women tend to be *either* high *or* low on career orientation, that difference could support an interpretation of the present findings. Such inferential leaps are hazardous with the present research design, but some evidence supporting this ideation does exist (e.g., Golembiewski, 1977).

Third, males and females may differ in systematic senses that account for the present findings. For example, a popular book (Tanner, 1994) proposes that the genders tend to differ in their use of language. An experimental design could explore such possibilities, with subjects responding to some standard stimulus such as a videotape of a work group. Various differences in individual conditions—both between the genders, as well as intra-gender—might then be tested for systemic differences in how the standard stimulus is seen. For example, inter-gender, the homogeneity of responses could be assessed by comparing reactions to the standard stimuli. For example, also, the descriptions might be tested for covariants of any differences.

Or one might test for the effects of monthly cycles for women, as well as of life cycles for both women and men (e.g., Boudreau, 1993). Some research has dealt with intra-gender variations and their mutual influence, as in male responses to hormonal changes in a female partner (e.g., DiMona & Herndon, 1994, p. 261).

AND THE SEQUENCING OF SUB-DOMAINS, PLUS OTHER CONSIDERATIONS?

In effect, we authors raise the ante here. We ratchet the analysis forward in important ways by comparing two sequencings of the MBI sub-domains.

And in that process we also encompass differences in genders and norms, to build on immediately-past discussion.

The central issues here have not eluded scientists, but the evidence remains both rare and mixed. To begin, the sequencing of the three MBI sub-domains in the phase model—as Depersonalization, Personal Accomplishment, and then Emotional Exhaustion, in turn—is rooted in theory and experience, as Chapter II shows, and gets empirical support throughout this volume as well as from independent investigators (e.g., Wolpin, Burke, & Greenglass, 1990). However, statistical evidence inferentially provides support for the Maslach sequence (e.g., Burke, Greenglass, & Konarski, 1996), even though comparisons usually are hedged: for example, "Results support Maslach's [model], although its superiority over the Golembiewski sequential model is not definitive" (Cordes, Dougherty, & Blum, 1996, p. 1).

The tests below do triple-duty, to review by way of introduction. They compare two MBI sequencings; the tests inquire whether the Maslach sequence is more appropriate for females; and they add perspective concerning universal vs. local norms.

Two Sequences, Plus, in A Military Population

The burnout literature seems poised at a point of major breakthrough in theory as well as measurement practices, and perhaps the major issue involves two contending models for integrating the MBI sub-domains—the phase model of burnout, as contrasted with the alternative framework associated with Maslach's work (e.g., Leiter, 1988; Lee & Ashforth, 1991; Iverson, Olekans, & Erwin, 1994). The stakes are substantial, even though Maslach herself at one time believed that any integration of the three MBI sub-domains was in the far-distant future (e.g., Maslach & Jackson, 1986, p. 14).

Beyond the huge elemental of sub-domain sequences, the immediate analysis also directs useful attention to two other factors—norms for High/ Low assignments on the three MBI sub-domains; and gender. Why? As others have observed (e.g., Burke, 1988), and as the first section of this chapter recognizes, the norms used to make High/Low assignments on the sub-domains are critical in evaluating the phase model's attempt to provide an integrative specificity beyond the reliance on the three separate MBI sub-domains. In addition, but getting less public notice, gender may also be relevant in evaluating the two contending models.

To what degrees do the two models—using two sets of norms, and taking gender into account—generate expected patterns of covariation with familiar marker variables? Five emphases review the test at Site OO, a U.S. Air Force base. In turn, attention gets directed at: the two alternative models of burnout; two sets of norms; details about the Site OO population and the scales to which they responded; basic expectations associated with the relative usefulness of the two models of burnout; and a summary of the findings.

Alternative Sequences of Sub-Domains. How to combine the clearly-useful MBI sub-domains into progressive models of burnout? Two models serve present purposes. These models are here labelled the G/M model and the M model which, respectively, refer to the Golembiewski/Munzenrider phase model used throughout this analysis, and to a Maslach model.

G/M Model. As described in detail above, the G/M phase model assumes-for-testing that the three sub-domains are differentially virulent—in order, Depersonalization, Personal Accomplishment, and Emotional Exhaustion. Hence, the eight-phase model familiar to readers of this book can be generated, after assigning each respondent a High/Low status on each of the three MBI sub-domains, relying on universal norms in most of our research.

M Model. Although the theoretical details are nowhere spelled out, Maslach and those of similar persuasion (e.g., Lee & Ashforth, 1991; Iverson, Olekans, & Erwin, 1994; Burke, Greenglass, & Konarski, 1995) propose a different sequencing of the three MBI sub-domains. Basically, they argue that advanced burnout begins with high levels of emotional exhaustion and, when *and* if depersonalization escalates sufficiently, personal accomplishment will fall.

Comparing Two Sequences. These two sequences permit a direct contrast. In brief, the M model may be categorized as EE, Dp, PA. In contrast, the G/M phase model may be characterized as Dp, PA, EE.

If one goes a step further, M phases may be generated following the decision rules introduced in Chapter II. Essentially, the two models generate different set of phases, as this direct comparison shows:

	M Model Phases of Burnout							
	I	*II*	*III*	*IV*	*V*	*VI*	*VII*	*VIII*
Emotional Exhaustion	Lo	Hi	Lo	Hi	Lo	Hi	Lo	Hi
Depersonalization	Lo	Lo	Hi	Hi	Lo	Lo	Hi	Hi
Personal Accomplishment (REVERSED)	Lo	Lo	Lo	Lo	Hi	Hi	Hi	Hi
	I	*V*	*II*	*VI*	*III*	*VII*	*IV*	*VIII*

G/M Model Phases of Burnout

Perhaps this last step puts an unwanted formulation in Maslach's name, but we believe that the M model is a reasonable label. In any case, the two sets of assignments differ in an elemental sense: the rank order correlation coefficient for M and G/M phases is 0.57, which achieves significance ($P = 0.048$, two-tailed) but leaves just under 70 percent of the variance unexplained. Despite the fact that Phases I and VIII are in effect defined in the same operational terms in the two models, then, M vs. G/M comparisons have potential for estimating the relative usefulness of the two patterns of sequencing.

Two Sets of Norms

Both variants of the phase model rely on Hi/Lo distinctions on each of the three MBI sub-domains, and we test two sets of norms here. They were introduced earlier as "universal" and "local" norms, respectively. The former derive from a federal agency ($N = 1,535$), and the latter are defined for present purposes as the three MBI medians at Site OO. In sum, for Site OO:

Universal Norms		Local Norms
> 18	Depersonalization	> 18
> 26	Personal Accomplishment (REVERSED)	> 28
> 23	Emotional Exhaustion	> 26

Note the small differences between local vs. universal norms, which imply the signal character of any consistent differences isolated below. That is, since the Site OO local vs. universal norms do not differ dramatically, any differences between the two variants will provide noteworthy evidence about their relative usefulness. That evidence can hardly be labelled conclusive, of course, but any observed G/M advantage will add to the accumulating evidence about the phase model as *the* operational definition of choice.

Two caveats complete this section, and they both add to the motivation for this analysis. Research with the G/M phase model always utilizes the universal norms, as a deliberate choice to test for the generic character of burnout. Maslach and her supporters typically have focused on correlation analysis of possible covariants of each of the three MBI sub-domains. More recently, the sequencing of the three sub-domains has received emphasis, especially via LISREL techniques (e.g., Leiter, Clark, & Durup, 1994), but again using only particularistic burnout estimates within individual populations. Preliminary norms for individual occupations have been made available by MBI developers (e.g., Maslach & Jackson, 1986, p. 34), but these are not considered here and, in the bargain, provide for particularistic estimates of burnout. Moreover, the decision not to employ these norms respects Maslach's opinion that a holistic set of phases of burnout will be a very long time coming (Maslach & Jackson, 1992).

Measurement Details.   For Site OO, three emphases provide substance about the respondents and the marker variables on the survey administered to them.

AF Population.   All respondents are members of a U.S. Air Force fighter wing—henceforth, AF or FW—who volunteered data in September 1991. Many of the respondents had been deployed earlier to the Persian Gulf, from which they began returning in March 1991. Greater detail is available in Appendix A and especially elsewhere (Aldinger, 1993), but selective descriptors here sufficiently reflect the character of the FW population. The response rate is almost exactly 40 percent of the total personnel assigned to FW Base. FW respondents performed missions-and-roles similar to all other fighter wings, and their demographics mirror those of all personnel at FW Base as well as in the Air Force (Aldinger, 1993, pp. 77-95). For example, FW respondents are about 85 percent male; they represent all ranks up to that of full colonel; respondents include 19 percent Afro-Americans and 2.5 percent Hispanic or Latino; they average 28.5 years of age; and over 6 out of 10 respondents have 9 years or less of Air Force service. About 62 percent of the respondents indicate they are married, and about 8 percent report a divorce.

Three Marker Variables.   In addition to data on burnout, respondents provided data about three marker variables that both experience and theory suggest are common covariants. These marker variables relate to health, job involvement, and self-esteem. A few comments about these measures are helpful.

General Health Questionnaire

GHQ I permits a judgment about the degree to which respondents reveal mental health symptoms that, if diagnosed by interviews, would justify clinical interventions. Chapter IV introduces the instrument in some detail. Here, note only that increasing GHQ I scores indicate poorer health status.

Job Involvement

JI has proved a robust covariant of the phases (e.g., Golembiewski & Boss, 1992), and for what seem obvious reasons. Directly, the deprivations tapped by the phase model—unsatisfactory personal and group relationships at work, doing poorly on a job seen as lacking in value, and experiencing stressors beyond one's coping abilities—imply diminished JI as a way of protecting self. The expected association typically shows up, as (for example) in Chapter III.

Here, as elsewhere in research with the phase model, JI is estimated by a 9-item scale (White & Ruh, 1973). The JI format takes this form:

For **EACH** item please circle the alternative that comes closest to describing your attitude or behavior.

1. For me, the first few hours of work really fly by.

(1)	(2)	(3)	(4)	(5)
Always	**Often**	**Occasionally**	**Seldom**	**Never**

Note that for the present scoring convention, *high* JI scores indicate *low* involvement. This differs from the usual usage, as well as from all other phase research in which JI is used.

Self-Esteem

This measure relates to a central human capacity "to experience ourselves positively, to feel competent and effective at what we do, to feel cared for and valued, and to feel good about who we are" (Jaffe & Scott, 1984, p. 131). This SE definition has obvious theoretic and practical linkages with all of life as well as with Air Force doctrine. SE has a clear conceptual relevance to effective performance, and especially of the "healthy" variety. To highlight one obvious exception, those with low SE may be high performers as a way of compensating for their perceived unworthiness, but this generally would come at high personal costs. In the vernacular, such persons would appear to be working sufficiently hard "to kill themselves," or at least to jeopardize balance in their lives.

Consistently, research shows that SE seems to covary inversely with the phases of burnout (Golembiewski & Munzenrider, 1988, pp. 142-143; Golembiewski & Kim, 1989). The magnitudes of the association do vary, and especially between males and females (Golembiewski, Aldinger, & Luo, 1996), but statistical significance typically is achieved. Here, levels of self-esteem focusing on self-approval or self-acceptance are estimated from responses to Rosenberg's (1965) 10-item instrument. Its items include the following: "I feel that I'm a person of worth, at least on an equal basis with others." The respondents are offered five choices: 1 = strongly agree; 2 = agree; 3 = neutral; 4 = disagree; and 5 = strongly disagree. Here, Rosenberg's 10 items are considered to be a simple additive scale. Four items are reversed to inhibit response set.

Various measurement details encourage reliance on SE as Rosenberg operationalizes it. Thus, a useful review of measurement properties has long been available (Robinson & Shaver, 1973, pp. 81-83). Relevant to construct validity and predictive usefulness, moreover, Rosenberg (1965a) provides the earliest if still the most comprehensive evidence. Other evidence supports SE's unidimensionality, in general. In one factor analysis, to illustrate, a single factor accounts for over 61 percent of the total variance in SE scores (Golembiewski & Kim, 1989).

Basic Expectations and Methods. Let us rephrase our comparative focus on the G/M and M approaches to sequencing the three MBI sub-domains. *The* question is direct. For the two models, to what degrees do the three marker variables track in the expected ways? *Perfect* support for either model of burnout requires that (e.g.) Job Satisfaction varies significantly with the phases, that all pair-wise comparisons decrease significantly, and that all pair-wise comparisons achieve statistical significance as well as fall in the expected direction.

Several comparisons below use these simple criteria. Thus, the usefulness of the G/M model will be informed by considering whether the universal vs. local norms generate a sharper pattern of covariants. This elaborates on the analysis of the first key question considered in this chapter. In principle, the use of the universal norms sets a tough standard: basically, that convention assumes-for-testing that the pattern of covariants will persist in the face of differences between organizational sites, local conditions or traditions, as well as diverse cultures and developmental conditions in different nation states, among many other possibilities.

In practice, the G/M phase model can accommodate both universal and local norms, and replications now routinely report both (e.g., Golembiewski, Aldinger, & Munzenrider, 1996). The analysis below will help assess this pragmatic policy, which has received earlier attention.

Further, the usefulness of the two models also will be tested when the genders are distinguished. The basic issue derives from two observations: that males vs. females tend to generate similar patterns of covariants; but also that the males report sharper, more homogeneous patterns (e.g., Golembiewski, Aldinger, & Luo, 1995). Supporters of the M model often rely on populations that tend to be smallish and largely female (e.g., Lee & Ashforth, 1991), and hence are not suitable for gender breakouts.

Many factors could account for this gender-related difference-within-similarity, and here attention gets directed at the issue of whether the M model is more appropriate for women, on average. Conveniently, to explain, the M model suggests that *relationships* are the immediate gate-keeper to advanced burnout: when emotional exhaustion is advanced, only substantial depersonalization can lead to diminished performance in full-blown burnout. In contrast, the G/M phase model implies that *task* plays more of the gate-keeping role in inhibiting the most-advanced phases of burnout in chronic onset. Depersonalization can increase first and easiest, that approach in effect proposes, and this dilution of relationships can trigger performance deficiencies, with high levels of these two then resulting in heightened emotional exhaustion.

The inferential leap-for-testing is obvious, although it may be ill-advised. Perhaps, just perhaps, depersonalization (read: poorer relationships) may be more central to more women, and hence the M model may better fit their average psychodynamics. In sum, the M model may be viewed as implying that women will surrender only in extremis the protection of relationships and feelings. For many or even most men, alternatively, the G/M phase model might provide a better fit, with diluted relationships being the first to be sacrificed as experienced burnout moves beyond Phase I. Here *task* is the gate-keeper to the movement eventuating in full-blown burnout.

If such gender differences concerning relationships and feelings vs. task do exist—and some evidence suggests that they might (e.g., Tanner, 1994)—this could help resolve this basic contention in the burnout literature: M *or* G/M model? It might be that the G/M phase model better suits populations with large proportions of males, while the M model is more appropriate where females dominate. If so, the focus should shift to M *and* G/M models, depending on gender mixes.

We shall see, and in a population that provides a rare opportunity for the required break-outs. As noted earlier, the large majority of data sets are small enough and/or gender-homogeneous enough to make break-outs awkward. And even large data-sets may deal with occupations that are largely gender-specialized, as in a population of about 1,000 Florida elementary school teachers which approaches 95 percent female (e.g., Golembiewski, Scherb, & Munzenrider, 1994).

Findings. The bottom-line requires few qualifications. Data from the AF population provide greater support for the G/M phase model. Five emphases detail that evidence, which justifies high levels of confidence.

Scale Reliabilities. The *alpha* coefficients seem adequate, or better, for present purposes. In sum, the six scales of interest have these Cronbach *alpha* coefficients:

	Alpha
Depersonalization	.7593
Personal Accomplishment	.7056

Emotional Exhaustion	.8831
General Health Questionnaire	.9364
Self-Esteem	.8482
Job Involvement	.8397

Clearly, all coefficients are acceptable for research purposes. Chapters II, III, and IV provide evidence which also supports the useful measurement properties of these variables.

Marker Variables. Table VII.9 establishes that the AF respondents track all marker variables in expected ways, phase by phase, for the G/M phase model using universal norms to make Hi/Lo assignments on the three MBI sub-domains. Later sub-sections will report on the M model, as well as on local norms.

The support of the G/M model in Table VII.9 is not perfect, but it does approach that condition. In sum, all three cases reveal variance that is almost-certainly non-random ($P < .0000$). Moreover, as Table VII.10, Column A, shows: 88.1 percent of the total 84 paired-comparisons fall in the expected direction; 67.9 percent of all paired-comparisons attain $P \le .05$ by LSD (modified); and a mere 0.24 percent of all paired-comparisons fall in a contrary direction and attain statistical significance. Mean eta^2 equals .147.

G/M Phase Model vs. M Model, Overall. As Table VII.10 shows, comparing columns A vs. C and B vs. D, the G/M phase model does better than the M model in all of the six possible paired-comparisons of the 3 marker variables and the phases. "Better" is understood tentatively, of course, but the differences favoring the G/M model can be attention-getters,

Table VII.9. Means for Marker Variables,
G/M Phases, Site OO, Universal Norms

	Phases of Burnout								F-ratio	F-Prob-ability	eta^2
	I	II	III	IV	V	VI	VII	VIII			
N =	186	55	143	71	101	111	137	302			
GHQ I	48.9	51.0	53.5	55.0	55.2	56.7	60.4	63.6	35.2	< .0000	.172
Job Involvement	20.6	21.1	23.9	25.0	23.9	23.8	27.1	27.8	25.1	< .0000	.227
Self-Esteem	14.2	15.6	16.1	18.8	15.0	16.8	17.4	20.2	22.7	< .0000	.042

Notes: NB. Degrees of Freedom = 7, for GHQ and SE, $N = 1,106$; for JI, $N = 1,086$.

Table VII.10.   Summary, Two Models of Burnout, Site OO

	G/M Phase Model		M Model	
	(A) Universal Norms	*(B)* Local Norms	*(C)* Universal Norms	*(D)* Local Norms
Paired-Comparisons:				
In Expected Direction	88.1%	86.9%	77.4%	71.4%
In Expected Direction and Statistically Significant	67.9	42.9	35.9	41.7
In Contrary Direction	11.9	13.1	22.6	28.6
In Contrary Direction and Statistically Significant	0.2	0.0	1.1	2.4
Summaries of ANOVA, Marker Variables X Phases	—as expected in all cases, $P < .0000$ —eta^2 = 0.141, on average	—as expected in all cases, $P < .0000$ —eta^2 = 0.150, on average	—as expected in all cases, $P < .0000$ —eta^2 = .129, on average	—as expected in all cases, $P < .0000$ —eta^2 = .147, on average

as in the critical particular of generating paired-comparisons that are significant as well as fall in the expected direction (67.9 vs. 35.9 percent). The M model also generates more than twice the proportion of paired-comparisons falling in a contrary direction; and, although the absolute members are small, the M model isolates approximately 5-10 times more contrary cases achieving statistical significance than the G/M model.

Universal vs. Local Norms.   Overall, Table VII.10 also suggests the greater usefulness of the universal norms associated with the G/M phase model. For example, columns (A) and (B) show that the universal norms identify a sharper pattern of covariation in 2 of 3 summaries of paired-comparisons. The deviant finding relates to a minuscule edge—0.0 vs. 0.2 percent—for the local norms in generating fewer cases that fall in a contrary direction while also attaining $P < .05$ by LSD test, as modified.

The two ANOVA summaries are quite similar. Columns (C) vs. (D) in Table VII.10 reflect a similar pattern favoring the universal norms, this time used in connection with the M model.

Only provisional interpretations are appropriate, but the consistencies attract attention. Several of the comparisons of local vs. universal norms in Table VII.10 do involve small differences, but this is expected where local

Table VII.11. Summary, G/M Phase Model, by Local
and Universal Norms, and by Gender, Site OO

Paired-Comparisons:	Universal Norms		Local Norms	
	Male	*Female*	*Male*	*Female*
In Expected Direction	84.5%	70.2%	86.9%	72.6%
In Expected Direction and Statistically Significant	38.1	7.1	42.9%	10.7
In Contrary Direction	15.5	29.8	13.1	27.4
In Contrary Direction and Statistically Significant	0.0	0.0	0.0	0.0
Summary of ANOVA, Marker Variables X Phases	—as expected in all cases, $P < .0000$ eta^2 = .141, on average	—as expected in 2/3 cases, $P < .0000$ 1 case is Not Significant	—as expected in all cases, $P < .0000$ eta^2 = .150 on average	—as expected in 2/3 cases, $P < .0000$ 1 case is Not Significant

and universal norms do not differ radically which, of course, is the case with Site OO. Only additional studies will provide perspective on whether greater support for the universal norms is provided by those populations with substantial differences between the two sets of norms.

Gender Effects. Considering both sets of norms, Tables VII.11 and VII.12 provide little support for the hypothetical view that the G/M and M models fit better for male and female sub-groups, respectively. Rather, given a few exceptions, the G/M phase model seems more discriminative for both genders than the M model when tracking the 3 marker variables across the phases.

Two summaries of Tables VII.11 and VII.12 reflect the major findings relevant to gender. First, for both norms and both models, males have the sharper pattern of covariation with the 3 marker variables. Specifically, 8 of the 12 comparisons in Tables VII.11 and Table VII.12 favor the males, and 2 additional comparisons are ties. In addition, the differences often are substantial. Consider, especially, the male vs. female proportions of paired-comparisons that fall in the expected direction while also attaining statistical significance—38.1 vs. 7.1 percent, 42.9 vs. 10.7 percent, 35.7 vs. 4.7 percent, and 40.5 vs. 9.5 percent, to extract the appropriate values from Tables VII.10 and then VII.11, respectively.

Second, the G/M model—for both norms as well as for the two genders—tracks the expected covariation better than the M model. The comparisons involve Tables VII.11 vs. VII.12. In sum, 11 of the 12 comparisons favor

Table VII.12. Summary, M Model, by Local and
Universal Norms, and by Gender, Site OO

Paired-Comparisons:	Universal Norms		Local Norms	
	Male	*Female*	*Male*	*Female*
In Expected Direction	76.2%	66.7%	72.6%	61.9%
In Expected Direction and Statistically Significant	35.7	4.7	40.5%	9.5
In Contrary Direction	23.8	33.3	27.4	38.1
In Contrary Direction and Statistically Significant	2.4	0.0	2.4	1.2
Summary of ANOVA, Marker Variables X Phases	—as expected in all cases, P < .0000	—as expected in 2/3 cases, P < .0000 1 case is Not Significant	—as expected in all cases, P < .0000	—as expected in 2/3 cases, P < .0000 1 case is Not Significant
			1 case is Not Significant	

the G/M model, with one tie. The relative advantages are not as substantial as those for males vs. females, even as they are consistent. To detail those differences, but only for one indicator, all paired-comparisons in the expected direction favor the G/M phase model—specifically by 84.5 vs. 76.2 percent, 70.2 vs. 66.7 percent, 86.9 vs. 72.6 percent, and 75.0 vs. 61.9 percent. Again, the comparisons involve Table VII.11 and VII.12.

A final consideration is relevant to Table VII.11. On average, the eta-square estimates for G/M phases and the M model differ in a narrow range, in effect indicating that 13-16 percent of the variance of burnout X marker variables is explained in comparisons involving males vs. females as well as universal vs. local norms. This advantage sometimes favors the M model, and in other cases favors the G/M phase model. That all cases involving males achieve overall statistical significance, while only 4 of 6 involving females do so, obviously discounts any advantage in mean eta^2 associated with females since that statistic is reported only for non-random tests of covariation.

Two Sequences In Global Populations

No available global data set can replicate the analysis of the North American military population analyzed above, but some perspective on the generalizability of the findings about sequences can be gained, if with qualifications. Two studies are chosen—China B and Taiwan B—because they both measure the same panel of variables, in the same part of the world.

Table VII.13.   Summary, Paired-Comparisons, in Percent

	In Expected Direction	Statistically Significant and in Expected Direction	In Contrary Direction	Statistically Significant and in Contrary Direction
I. China B				
G/M Model, Universal Norms	82.1	18.6	17.9	0.0
M Model, Universal Norms	82.1	17.1	17.9	0.0
G/M Model, Local Norms	84.3	18.6	15.7	0.0
M Model, Local Norms	82.1	18.6	17.9	0.0
II. Taiwan B				
G/M Model, Universal Norms	85.7	43.6	14.3	3.0
M Model, Universal Norms	81.4	43.6	18.6	2.9
G/M Model, Local Norms	77.1	44.3	22.9	2.5
M Model, Local Norms	73.6	32.9	26.4	6.4

The two studies differ in one special particular: findings from both support the phase model of burnout at statistically-significant levels, but Taiwan B generates a much more regular and robust pattern. Analytic details about China B and Taiwan B can be found in the text at several points above, as well as in Appendix B.

Table VII.13 provides a number of comparative details about the two global studies, and supports a short but useful catalog of particulars. Overall, the comparisons in Table VII.13 clearly do not reflect large differences but, on narrow balance, the trend favors the G/M Model, whether the comparisons are within-norm or between-norms. To illustrate, consider only one question: Which model does better at isolating the pattern of covariation expected of the phase model? Of the 20 possible comparisons, 9 favor the G/M Model, 10 are identical, and 1 favors the M Model.

Discussion

This section makes two further basic contributions to comparative research on burnout. Thus, two models are compared while keeping other things constant so as to reduce the confounding or camouflaging effects that bedevil comparative studies. In addition, the results favor the G/M model, on average, and these seem conservative estimates of relative advantage. To explain, in the phase model format, Phases I and VIII assignments are LoLoLo vs. HiHiHi, respectively, for both G/M and M models, despite the different conceptual sequencings of the MBI sub-domains. In addition, on average, Phases I and VIII contain half or more of all respondents. These two features will attenuate any variance, obviously, and this attenuation implies the heightened salience of any consistent differences.

Several Caveats. Despite this probably-conservative estimate of relative advantage, several caveats remain appropriate. First, replications involving numerous data sets are needed. Appropriate data sets are rare, simply.

Second, the results concerning gender also require detailed follow-up, both to replicate the results above but even moreso to extend analysis to other possible explanations of differences between the genders. The present findings confirm differences in patterns of covariation associated with the genders, while they also discourage the convenient interpretation that the G/M phase model and the M model better suit males and females, respectively.

Third, the present populations may not even be representative of other occupational and professional categories, let alone all geographic loci. Again, this encourages targeted replications.

Fourth, replications are especially needed in cross-national and cross-cultural settings. Early cross-national research reveals a strong, even dominant, generic component in the phase model's pattern of covariants. This will surprise many. We are certainly better equipped by the literature to accept propositions about the culture-boundedness of behavioral research, to expect cultural relativity to dominate. Nonetheless, early cross-national research has generated similar results in populations from several nation states—for example, Japan, Taiwan, China, Belarus, Ghana, and Saudi Arabia, as well as North American settings. To be sure, the results all leave some room for culture-specific effects, and especially in the different distributions of the phases in several nation states, as Chapter VI shows. But major generic effects seem beyond dispute.

More on Gender. Caveats notwithstanding, the comparisons above seem significant for all behavioral research and theory, and especially for gender. Why the consistent differences-within-a-pattern between female and male respondents, on average? Some factors may be situational, and at least in practice remediable by determined managerial practices and policies. For example, the present differences *may* reflect the historic pattern of lesser representation of females in senior ranks, but that explanation is almost certainly only a partial one. That is, status accounts for only a tiny fraction of differences in phase assignments, both in the FW population as well as elsewhere.

Profoundly, in contrast, the present results may reflect systemic male/female differences that are resistant to change, or even opaque to it. The emphasis on basic differences between the genders is growing—in the determinedly-scientific literature (e.g., Shaywitz & Shaywitz, 1995), in trendy popularizations (e.g., Tanner, 1994), as well as in many adaptations in-between (e.g., Moir & Jessel, 1989). In any case, any gender differences isolated by the phase model will require major changes in the ways behavioral research is designed and interpreted, and not only in the burnout literature.

Specifically-targeted research designs are required, but some general sense of the suggested approach is illustrated by the data in Table VII.14, which distinguishes three age categories of a large population of female teachers in elementary schools.

Table VII.14. Summary for Site KK, Females Only, Organization Climate Measures by Age, Universal Norms, and Full Phases

	45 or less (N = 700)	*46-55* (N = 197)	*> 56* (N = 78)
In Expected Direction	74.0%	69.9	61.2
Statistically Significant and in Expected Direction	17.9%	7.7	3.6
In Contrary Direction	26.0%	30.1	38.8
Statistically Significant and in Contrary Direction	1.5%	0.0	0.0
ANOVA Summary	all 7 cases as expected, $P < .0000$	6 of 7 cases as expected, $P < .05$; 1 case not significant	4 of 7 cases as expected, $P < .05$; 3 cases not significant
Eta^2 for Statistically Significant Cases, on average	.139	.151	.265

Overall, as age increases, the sharpness of the pattern of covariation gets diluted, even unto obliteration. Why remains speculative, because the age categories in Table VII.14 can be considered only a rough surrogate for the many possible differences between females—for example, pre-vs. post-menopausal. In effect, that table provides evidence that can be viewed from several interpretative perspectives, including these:

- women at the ends of their workinglives tend more than males to distance their affective selves from their experiencing of worksites;
- all people at the end of their workinglives tend to distance their affective selves from their experiences at worksites;
- younger vs. older women in today's workforce identify with their work in different ways: today more as a career; in earlier years as a temporary interlude before marriage or childbirth and after the empty nest;
- almost all women 56 or older will be post-menopausal, which may in multiple senses differentiate them as observers and/or reactors to their worksites—somewhat from women who are 46-55, and far moreso from women who are younger still.

All these interpretations pose problems, and all of them (and more) may apply simultaneously, but we now have no real basis for making these judgments. Moreover, available data do not permit a choice between these possibilities.

AND HOW MANY PHASES ARE NEEDED?

The present phase model began life as the simplest combination of three sub-domains differentiated as High and Low. Directly, $2^3 = 8$ phases. While at first considered only a place to start, that simple model has held up well, as the chapters above establish for North American as well as global settings.

But are eight phases about right, too many, or too few? Here we gently approach this issue from an intentionally-limited perspective. In preview, the "distances" between the phases will be arrayed in terms of the proportions of seven categories of paired-comparisons that fall in the expected direction as well as achieve statistical significance. This approach cannot answer *the* key question: How many phases are needed to encompass the differences and similarities in nature? But the present approach will give us a sense of whether the model of 8 phases is in the ballpark or not.

By way of introduction, there are seven such "distances": for example, I vs. VIII is scored a 7, II vs. VIII is a 6, and so on. Again, four estimates of the several kinds of paired-comparisons are of interest: differences in the expected direction; differences in the expected direction that are statistically significant; the kinds of contrary paired-comparisons. The perfect phase model would have 100 percent of all possible paired-comparisons falling in the expected directions, and 100 percent of those also will achieve statistical significance. For obvious reasons, the greater the proportions of the smaller distances that are "hits" on the present criteria, the greater the sensitivity of the full 8 phases. If "hits" do not occur on even the larger distances, so much the worse for the phase model, as presently conceptualized.

As usual, attention goes to both North American and worldwide settings. In principle, every study of the phase model could be used for comparative purposes. Here, conveniently, only four examples will get attention. The populations differ in many regards—in their loci, and in that one example is the founding piece of research (Site B) on the phases and the others come from the most recent studies. See also Appendix A.

How Many Phases in North American Settings?

Exemplars from among the earliest and most recent studies in North American settings alike provide similar evidence of the degree of appropriateness of the 8-phase model. Data from Site B and Site 00 get explicit attention, although in differing degrees of detail.

Site 00 does not present a picture of perfect fit, but Table VII.15 shows that this Air Force population approaches the ideal. A few selected points illustrate the case. Thus, few contrary cases are observed, only a small percentage of them attain statistical significance, and all those contrary cases fall in the smallest "distances." This is as it should be for a useful model, of course, with the bigger "distances" providing the less-stringent tests of usefulness.

Table VII.15. Summary, Patterns of Covariation for Paired-Comparisons, Overall and by Specific "Distances," Site OO

	Overall (in %)		"Distances" between Paired-Comparisons						
			7	*6*	*5*	*4*	*3*	*2*	*1*
In Expected	88.2	%	100	100	100	100	86.7	83.3	76.2
Direction		#	(3/3)	(6/6)	(9/9)	(12/12)	(13/15)	(15/18)	(16/21)
In Expected	67.9	%	100	100	77.8	66.7	60.0	61.1	38.1
Direction and Statistically Significant		#	(3/3)	(6/6)	(7/9)	(8/12)	(9/15)	(11/18)	(8/21)
In Contrary	11.9	%	0	0	0	0	13.3	16.7	23.8
Direction		#					(2/15)	(3/18)	(5/21)
In Contrary	0.3	%	0	0	0	0	0	5.6	4.8
Direction and Statistically Significant		#						(1/18)	(1/21)

The pattern at Site OO for paired-comparisons falling in the expected direction also suggests a pretty good fit of observations to the 8-phase model. Thus, 10 of 16 cases of "distance" reflect perfect fit; and all but 1 of 16 cases show that at least 60 percent of all paired-comparisons fall in the expected direction *and* attain statistically significance.

How many phases seem appropriate for the differences/similarities at Site 00? Observers may differ, and there certainly is no one-best estimate inherent in Table VII.15. But even a determined contrarian could not make a case for fewer than (let us say) 6 or 7 phases. At the same time, the case for more than 8 phases does not seem strong, if the basic phase conventions are retained. Note that the most convenient extension of the present approach— High, Medium, and Low categories for each of the three MBI sub-domains— involves 27 phases. Only gentle investigations of 27 phases have been attempted, for diverse practical reasons.

The situation is very similar for Site B, although the relevant table is not reproduced here to conserve space (Golembiewski & Munzenrider, 1988, p. 38). However, a brief summary will be useful. Overall, at Site B, the record for paired-comparisons on 16 marker variables demonstrates that neighborly as well as remote pairs of phases tend to map discretely on all target variables. This conclusion holds most clearly for the five most "distant" pairs of phases (3 to 7)—where over 76 percent of the total paired differences are in the expected direction *and* attain statistical significance. Moreover, even distances 2 and 1 generate 41 and 20 percent records of significant differences. This suggests that even very close neighbors in the 8-phase model can be described in terms of significantly different degrees of 16 marker variables. Looked at another way, an average of 90.2 percent of all paired-comparisons are in the expected direction, and that proportion is nowhere lower than 78 percent for the smallest distance—that is, 1.

How Many Phases in Worldwide Settings?

Again, appropriate data sets are rare, but a useful beginning can be made in approaching a working answer to this major question. The Taiwan B and China B data-sets seem broadly representative of studies from global worksettings, and they are both reported in Table VII.16. That makes for a busy table, but such data have not been previously reported, in contrast to North American studies. So if Table VII.15 constitutes overkill, reasonable intentions are at fault. Other studies could be added, but they come to much the same compound finding detailed above.

The interpretation of Table VII.16 seems clear enough. The persistent reader can follow the format above to develop the detailed case supporting an 8-phase model of burnout. As a hint, even for "distances" 1 and 2,

Table VII.16. Summary, Patterns of Covariation for Paired-Comparisons, Overall and by Specific "Distances," Taiwan A and China B

	Overall (in %)	"Distances" between Paired-Comparisons						
		7	6	5	4	3	2	1
Taiwan A								
In Expected Direction	85.7%	100%	100	100	85.0	80.0	71.4	80.0
In Expected Direction and Statistically Significant	43.6%	100%	100	73.3	34.3	31.0	25.7	8.6
In Contrary Direction	14.3%	0.0	0.0	0.0	15.0	20.0	28.6	20.0
In Contrary Direction and Statistically Significant	3.0%	0.0	0.0	0.0	0.0	2.8	5.7	2.9
China B								
In Expected Direction	82.1%	100	100	93.3	90.0	84.0	73.3	71.4
In Expected Direction and Statistically Significant	18.6%	100	60.0	46.6	5.0	20.0	0.0	5.7
In Contrary Direction	17.9	0.0	0.0	6.6	10.0	16.0	26.7	28.6
In Contrary Direction and Statistically Significant	0.0	0.0	0.0	0.0	0.0	0.0	0.0	0.0

over 70 percent of the paired-comparisons are in the expected direction. In addition, all but two of the 28 comparisons contain a greater proportion—typically, a much greater proportion—of statistically-significant paired-comparisons in the expected direction than chance alone justifies.

One significant issue remains. Why, in sum, is the pattern for "distance" in Table VII.16 similar to that in North America, but less markedly so? No one knows for sure. Cultural features may help account for such differences but, on the available evidence, in moderate degree only. In any case, the data in Table VII.16 provide no support for the next-most convenient phase model—$3^3 = 27$ phases, for each of the three MBI sub-domains considered as High, Medium, and Low. The same may be said for a 16-cell variant—the 8 phases, with each distinguished as active and passive. See Chapter VIII for some detail as to why such a format seems worthy of analysis.

Local norms may prove to be one surrogate for taking cultural differences into greater account, but the focus on "distances" contributes little to that conclusion. Specifically, were the local norms counterpart for Table VII.16 reproduced here, its interpretations would be a scaled-down version of that for Table VII.16. To suggest the point, the local norms have 77.1 percent of the paired-comparisons falling in the expected direction, versus 85.7 percent for the universal norms. That is, the local norms version of Table VII.15 would provide a bit less-forceful support for 8 phases than the present table for universal norms, but support there nonetheless would be.

AND WHAT LEVEL OF ANALYSIS?

Most literature on burnout is steeped in the individual level of analysis, and that seems reasonable but may be misleading. Let us look again at this significant issue, adding to the perspective already available in Chapter II.

Patently, to begin, burnout is felt by individuals, and that datum has powerfully influenced analysis as well as remediation. For example, "stress management workshops" remain popular, and they seek to "armor" or "inoculate" individuals so that they can better deal with stressors before they accumulate into the strain we label "burnout." Obviously, in sum, the individual level of analysis dominates in this view.

In important senses, however, what seems reasonable in concept may be misleading, and may even "blame the victim." Specifically, the environmental view underlying the phase model encourages also looking at supra-individual levels of analysis, and the results of the admittedly-small amount of derivative research encourage movement toward two orienting generalizations:

- Theoretically, it is simplistic to fixate burnout analysis at the individual level of analysis
- Practically, fixation on the individual level of analysis may worsen matters at the organizational level, and to the degree, paradoxically, that individual remediation "works."

Let us see how and why, overall, these orienting generalizations apply. The focus is first directed at group properties, and then more broadly at culture.

Burnout Linkages to Group Properties

This literature is slim, curiously. The immediate work-group has received major and long-standing theoretical and empirical attention in the management literatures (Golembiewski, 1962; Likert, 1977), but burnout has typically been viewed from an individual perspective. As Carroll and White note (1982, p. 41): "Unfortunately, most writers on the subject of burnout tend to overemphasize either personal variables [the need to over-achieve,...and so on] or [worksite] variables (such as noise levels...and...obstacles)."

Hence, the motivation for exploring the present theme is strong. Evidence supporting a group locus will urge major rethinking of typical approaches to burnout, both as locus for research as well as target for intervention. Such perspectives can be helpful in many areas of management, and perhaps especially in training and development activities.

A bit more precisely, the discussion gets directed along two lines. The general case will focus on whether work groups seem to have an affinity for homogeneous levels of burnout. Later analysis will test for specific differences in the properties of groups whose members report different levels of burnout. The purpose of both general and specific approaches is the same: they encourage an approach to burnout at multiple levels, including but not restricted to the individual level of analysis.

General Case: Work-Unit Affinity for Extreme Scorers. Only two organizations have been studied in detail, but immediate work groups tend to have an affinity for one *or* the other extreme set of phases, *although not both.* An "immediate work group" is a "group of first-reports," recall, each of which encompasses all subordinates reporting to a common superior, at whatever level—vice presidents to a president, first-line supervisors to middle managers, operators to a first-line supervisor, and so on.

The details tell a simple story. Rountree (1984) isolates 186 immediate task groups in 23 local settings, with $N = 1,393$ employees. He distinguishes three clusters of phases: Low (Phases I-III); Moderate (Phases IV-V); and High (Phases VI-VIII). He notes (1984, pp. 245-246): "...the affinity of work groups for extreme scorers seems substantial....Consider that 87.5 percent of all [Highs] are members of work-groups having at least 50 percent of all their members in those three most-advanced phases." Lows show a similar but less marked tendency, and less than 10 percent of all Moderates are in work-groups where they constitute a majority. Golembiewski (1983a) reports similar results, while relying on a different design.

Specific Case: Phases and Properties of Immediate Work-Units. Again, relying on Rountree's (1984) array of work groups helps answer this central theoretical and practical question: Do the properties of immediate work units relate in reasonable ways to differences in the burnout of their members? The bottom-line? Yes, they do, and clearly so.

Isolating A Class of Immediate Work Units. Rountree's array rests on a major convenience. Specifically, a random sample of 12 High burnout (HiBo) groups is selected from those having 50 percent or more of their members in Phases VI through VIII. And 12 Low cases (LoBo) also are selected from the smaller number of work-groups having 50 percent or more of the members in Phases I through III. N = 185 employees. These seem credible surrogates for the larger collection of immediate work-groups and all responding employees, and require very consistent differences between HiBO and LoBO work groups to achieve statistical significance.

WES as Identifying Group Properties. Form F of the Work Environment Scales (Insel & Moos, 1974) describes the properties of the two categories of work-groups. Table VII.17 identifies the ten WES scales, clusters them in three dimensions, and sketches the proposed associations of the scales with burnout. As the predictions suggest, each WES scale is scored so that a high score indicates a greater degree of the environmental

Table VII.17. Work Environment Scales, Predicted Associated with Burnout, and Observations[a]

I. Classes of WES Dimensions	II. Predicted Associations with WES Dimensions	III. Observations Concerning Predictions
A. *Relationships*		
1. Involvement	1. LoBo > HiBo	1. Supported[b]
2. Peer Cohesion	2. LoBo > HiBo	2. In expected direction and approaches significance
3. Supervisory support	3. LoBo > HiBo	3. Supported
B. *Personal Growth*		
4. Autonomy	4. LoBo > HiBo	4. Supported
5. Task Orientation	5. LoBo > HiBo	5. In expected direction but not significant
6. Work Pressure	6. HiBo > LoBo	6. Supported
C. *System Maintenance and Change*		
7. Clarity	7. LoBo > HiBo	7. Supported
8. Control	8. HiBo > LoBo	8. In expected direction but not significant
9. Innovation	9. No clear associations	9. Not significant
10. Physical Comfort	10. LoBo > HiBo	10. Supported

Note: [a] Based on several sources: Rountree (1984); Golembiewski and Rountree (1986, esp. pp. 27-29); Golembiewski and Munzenrider, (1988, pp. 158-164).
[b] "Supported," based on *t*-test, $p \leq .05$.

feature at issue. WES descriptions are available elsewhere (Golembiewski & Munzenrider, 1988, pp. 162-163), but the labels in Table VII.17 are revealing enough for present purposes. Note also that Cronbach's *alpha* averages .713 for the WES dimensions, with only one coefficient falling as low as .65. Other information about validity and reliability also suggests the instrument's usefulness (Moos & Insel, 1982).

In effect, the WES variables permit both partial replication and extension of earlier research. Specifically, involvement, work pressure, and clarity correspond to common marker variables used in phase research. Several WES scores—for example, peer cohesion, task orientation, and innovation—are seldom employed in phase research.

Findings about Work-Unit Properties and Burnout. Table VII.17 also provides evidence that differences in burnout seem associated with distinct patterns of properties in immediate work-groups, consistent with the predicted associations. Compare columns II and III. Four points highlight the major contributors to this conclusion.

First, six WES dimensions isolate expected and significant differences between the HiBo and LoBo samples. Involvement, supervisory support, autonomy, clarity, and physical comfort are significantly higher in LoBo than HiBo; and work pressure is higher for HiBo than for LoBo. These associations suggest two conclusions: that the phases vary with worksite features in expected ways; and also that few or no cases of *laissez-faire* supervision exist in the LoBo units.

Second, a seventh WES score falls in the expected direction and closely approaches statistical significance—peer cohesion ($P = .085$).

Third, as expected, only random variation characterizes innovation. This result fits the notion that burnout can derive from understimulation as well as overstimulation, a point emphasized in Chapter I but often neglected in the literature.

Other explanations may apply. Thus, the *alpha* for Innovation (.65) does not impress. Moreover, the conceptual space tapped here does not appear to be unidimensional.

Fourth, two variables—task orientation and control—trend in expected directions, but do not closely approach significance ($P = .149$ and $P = .124$, respectively).

Burnout Linkages to Organization Culture

Let us ratchet the argument toward a still-broader level of analysis. In preview, these three features of research on burnout suggest a strong case for culture-relevant covariants of the phases:

- individual reports suggest cultural differences
- properties of immediate contexts reflect cultural differences
- direct cultural descriptors have been related to discrete phase distributions

The following three sections, in turn, briefly support these three implications of available research. A fourth and concluding section emphasizes the several sources of analytic and applied leverage that inhere in burnout $<->$ culture associations.

INDIVIDUAL REPORTS SUGGEST CULTURAL DIFFERENCES

Differences in the phases suggest, but they do not establish, that associated differences exist in the relevant social or cultural contexts at work. Illustratively, among many features, Is and VIIIs provide these two contrasting pictures of their worksites:

Those in Phase I see their worksite as providing:

- substantial participation
- low job tension
- substantial willingness to disagree with supervisor
- a strong tendency to enhance involvement
- great potential for many facets of satisfaction

Those in Phase VIII see their worksite as providing:

- little participation
- high job tension
- general unwillingness to disagree with supervisor
- a strong tendency to limit involvement
- low potential for many facets of satisfaction

The observer can easily visualize very different contexts or cultures required to trigger such differing perceptions of worksites. The right column suggests a "culture of opportunity," and the left column encourages the label "culture of restraint." Cox (1993, pp. 169-170) characterizes such cultures as "high prescription" and "low prescription," respectively.

Properties of Immediate Contexts Suggest Cultural Differences. More directly, early work implies that distributions of phases are associated in predictable ways with group properties that seem to reflect differences that are reasonably labeled "cultural." For example, those in advanced phases see their immediate work-groups in such contrasting ways:

Work-Group Property	High Concentrations of Phases I-III	High Concentrations of Phases VI-VIII
Peer Cohesiveness	Higher	Lower
Involvement	Higher	Lower
Task Orientation	Higher	Lower
Work Pressure	Lower	Higher
Supervisory Support	Higher	Lower

In powerful support of these two profiles, a successful attempt to reduce the proportion of employees in Phases VI-VIII resulted in predicted improvements in both group properties such as those above as well as sharp reductions in burnout (Golembiewski, Hilles, & Daly, 1987; Golembiewski, 1990).

Such variations in group properties associated with different distributions of phases suggest cultural differences, but the contrast above doubtless is too simple. Thus, more than two cultures may prove necessary to comprehensively describe natural-state workgroups (e.g., Bowers & Hausser, 1977). By implication, in any case, two powerful results of research on burnout phases—their persistence, and the affinity of immediate work-groups for those in extreme phases—in different ways suggest a significant connection between persisting cultural features and burnout.

Direct Cultural Descriptors. As an exemplar of what can be done, but seldom has been done, Janz, Dugan, and Ross (1986) associate cultural features directly with the phases. These researchers used the Corporate Culture Survey, which characterizes collectivities in terms of Shared Values, Power, and Rules. In turn, these permit calculating a Culture Index, of CI. For departments, CI correlates -.82 with the percentage of employees in Phases VI through VIII. That is to say, high proportions of employees in advanced phases of burnout tend to be imbedded in cultures at work that feature a low degree of shared values as well as a heavy reliance on power and rules in operating systems. There is no surprise in this.

Multiple Levels of Analysis

In sum, the sparse available literature implies multiple points of theoretical and practical leverage for the phase model, and four get highlighted here. First, linkages of levels of analysis are crucial in the development of any comprehensive theory, but convenience often encourages myopia. For example, this section implies that burnout is responsive to the properties of the worksite—styles of supervision, group climates, and cultural features—consistent with the dominant tradition in organization analysis (e.g., Likert, 1977). Broadly, the mating of individual <—> context has proved invaluable in many areas of inquiry and application—delinquency, criminal recidivism, Organization Development, and so on—but the basic lesson seems to require costly relearning when it comes to burnout, as well as in general (Golembiewski, 1962, esp. pp. 34-68).

Second, multiple levels of analysis help spotlight the strategic significance of the immediate group of first-reports, a theme that keeps reemerging in the history of behavioral analysis (e.g., Shils, 1951), but which also periodically goes into eclipse (e.g., Lakin, 1979). Right now, to apply the point, "culture" dominates in the popularization of Peters and Waterman (1982), who distinguish only "tight" and "loose" cultures, and those only barely. In contrast, the present position suggests a more complicated view of culture—a kind of "building up" of a total culture as a mosaic of numerous "local cultures." Most of the current literature suggests the "trickling down" of a monolithic or total culture, in sharp contrast with that central management theorist of the just-passing age—Chester I. Barnard.

The focus on some kind of "primary group" provides numerous advantages in both research and applications. Practically, the data above imply the limits of "stranger" workshops for stress management, which have been popular over the last decade or so. In a nutshell, and in sharp contrast with the conventional wisdom, the intact work group seems the more reasonable target for designs to ameliorate burnout. Indeed, workshops for individuals may have paradoxical effects, even counterproductive ones. For example, any skills in managing stress that individuals acquire in stranger workshops may result only in making their worksite *more* stressful for back-home colleagues: the experiences increase the tolerance of some individuals for stress but do not reduce worksite stressors, and may also encourage management to provide new or augmented stressors (Golembiewski & Munzenrider, 1988, esp. pp. 164-165). The point gains salience from the possibility—for which some support exists (Golembiewski & Munzenrider, 1988, p. 165)—that those in advanced phases of burnout seem unlikely volunteers for stress management opportunities.

The critical demonstration is still in the tedious process of collecting cases of precisely who elects to attend "stranger" stress management workshops. We predict those in the least-advanced phases are the most-probable volunteers, and for two reasons. Those in advanced phases may be unaware of their condition, or they simply have too little energy.

We shall see.

Third, the focus on burnout <—> culture may help with a vexing issue in behavioral analysis. The evidence increasingly suggests the appropriateness of a plural concept that differentiates changes in state from changes in degree within a state (e.g., Golembiewski, Billingsley, & Yeager, 1976; Golembiewski, 1990). However, the existing formulations have a number of deficiencies. For example, change in state is now defined by complex statistical conventions that do not yield an easily interpretable "direction" for change. Some evidence suggests that variations in the distribution of phases of burnout might reasonably serve as a surrogate for estimating changes in state, as opposed to degree, with the former being the essence of gamma change and similar concepts (Golembiewski, 1990). Among other conveniences, the distributions of phases suggest a desirable direction for change—for example, fewer VIIIs and more Is seem in general a reasonable objective of social and managerial policy. See also Chapter VIII.

Fourth, the burnout phases seem to serve as measures of individual and also collective states. In the latter case, for example, distributions of the phases may serve as a useful surrogate for the states of collectivities, and especially so if immediate work units are distinguished.

AND WHAT OF APPLICATIONS TO AMELIORATE BURNOUT?

This chapter concludes with a significant question, perhaps *the* query. The stakes are great, to judge from the present evidence about the incidence, persistence, as well as adverse covariants of the advanced phases of burnout. As we can manipulate work realities to reduce burnout, then we will not only meet huge and perhaps-growing practical urgencies but we will also enrich basic theoretical knowledge.

So, how have we been doing? Curiously, not well, or even much: the burnout literature has scarcely begun to deal with amelioration. This may sound harsh, but it is merely accurate. The judgment applies substantially to North America, and even moreso to global settings. Overall, only a few studies even describe the dynamics of what might be called "natural change"—that is, getting a burnout reading at T_1, doing so again at T_2, and then trying to describe what happened in-between to account for change or stability (e.g., Cherniss, 1989; Seltzer & Miller, 1994; Wolpin, Burke, & Greenglass, 1994). Even less energy has been devoted to conscious or planned change.

The focus below is on this second category of studies of change. The best/worst case prognosis for the *status quo* is unattractive. Continued general avoidance will do nothing to resolve debates about methods or methodologies, and its *best* outcome is a kind of orbiting-in-place. At worst, failure to give priority to ameliorative applications at the worksite can lead to the boom-and-bust character of much research in the behavioral and organizational sciences. Of course, that boom-and-bust cycle is front-and-center on the list of consequences that this book seeks to avoid.

So this analysis will move on concerning remediation, but with a conscious tentativeness. Again, the dual focus is on North American and global settings. Differences exist, as will be shown, but the overall condition has an unpleasing symmetry. For example, Schaufeli (in press) details the common and severe limitations of the ameliorative literatures, both North American and global. He observes: "... The reviewed studies [usually] use different samples, procedures, time frames, measurement instruments, and training methods. Besides many studies suffer from methodological inadequacies, such as the lack of control groups. ...In addition, the number of subjects included is very small."

Amelioration in North American Settings

Table VII.18 provides three selective summaries that provide perspective on different types of amelioration: the first is a comprehensive effort involving three hierarchical levels beginning at the vice presidential level in a health-care products firm; the second exemplar reflects more of a quick-and-limited effort that focuses on the interaction between pairs of people; and the final illustration deals with a complex and volatile environment within which broad-ranging sociotechnical interventions were made. That is, diagnosis in the first case indicated a chronic burnout problem in a relatively-complex system. The second exemplar focused on two sets of role-holders at middle management levels who were experiencing some start-up concerns about communicating in the face of hierarchical, professional, and perhaps gender differences. And the final ameliorative effort utilized a broad range of interventions—in interaction, in policy as well as in procedures, and also in structure—to influence a broad range of outcomes in a hospital ward.

The details of these ameliorative efforts have been published elsewhere, and substantial confidence in the exemplars seems appropriate for at least four reasons. Thus, all illustrations are rooted in the theory, designs, and experiences developed over the past several decades in what is usually known as Organization Development, or Organization Development and Change. The convenient labels are OD and ODC, respectively. In addition, the patterns of effects are not only almost always in the expected directions, but they usually achieve statistical significance. Moreover, the three exemplars build on relatively-discrete values (e.g., Golembiewski & Rountree, 1996a) which are broadly applicable in all organizations. Finally, the three types of designs have been replicated at several other sites characterized by the full range of presenting conditions—roughly distinguished as:

Table VII.18. Selective Summaries, North American Efforts to Ameliorate Burnout

Presenting Conditions	Source	Diagnostic Tools	Design Elements	Major Consequences
I. chronic conditions developed over time in a staff headquarters unit, $N = 14$-37.	Golembiewski, Hilles, and Daly (1987); Golembiewski (1990)	• surveys • group properties • burnout phases • turnover analysis • worksite features	• interpersonal skill-building • action research re survey findings • policy change • longitudinal: observation of effects several times over 2 year period following several months of data gathering and intervention • comparison group	• major and persisting decreases in turnover • substantial and persisting reductions in phase assignments • major and persisting improvements in targeted group properties • sharp improvements in reactions to supervision • effectiveness of action planning persists beyong the off-site setting
II. start-up issues involving 10 sites of a chain of retirement communities, $N = 20$	Golembiewski and Rountree (1991)	• surveys • group properties • burnout phases • reactions to supervisors	• relationship building between two hierarchical roles • action planning • short pre-vs. post-test of efficacy of offsite experience • control group	• sharp reductions in phase assignments • sharp improvements in group properties and reactions to supervision • effectiveness of action planning persists beyond the off-site setting

(continued)

Table VII.18. *(Continued)*

Presenting Conditions	Source	Diagnostic Tools	Design Elements	Major Consequences

III. medical-surgical ward in a hospital. N's vary widely for various sub-groups	Golembiewski and Rountree, (1996a), (1996b)	• surveys
		  — Emotional Exhaustion
		  — numerous organization and group properties
		  — from all major stakeholders: patients, nurses, and doctors
		  — nursing cost
			• building norms concerning confrontation and dispute resolution at interpersonal and group levels
			• redesigning worksite policies and structures to reinforce new norms for interaction
			• longitudinal: some observational frames cover intervals extending to a year or more
			• control group
				• sharp improvements in Emotional Exhaustion and almost all of 30-plus organization/group properties
				• sharp increases in stakeholder's attitudes about hospital experiences
				• major reduction in nursing costs

- chronic problems in a complex system, of major consequence and largely interaction-centered;
- transitional issues focused on easing the early development of more fluid-relationships between individuals in pairs of roles experiencing tension around start-up; and
- complex mixes of social and technological issues in a volatile and tension-arousing context.

Even though the exemplars no doubt represent type-situations commonly encountered in practice, experience with them hardly qualifies as frequent. Directly, there are few ameliorative efforts in the literature. No one can be very specific of the definition of "few," but one stark comparison implies that one will not go very far wrong in accepting a restricted definition. Specifically, Kilpatrick (1986) isolated 661 published studies about burnout, of which about 20 percent provide some "how to" advice about managing burnout. However, at that time, only four of those contributions to the literature dealt with conscious interventions to ameliorate or prevent burnout (Anderson, 1982; Haack, 1980; Pines & Aronson, 1983; Slutsky, 1981). This proportion underwhelms, and seldom tests the phase model.

The situation, especially in North American settings, got better by the mid-1990s, but no reasons for celebrating exist. Most relevant issues of theory, experience, and skills remain open. All applications in Table VII.18 test aspects of phase theory and its measurement conventions.

Amelioration in Global Settings

The emphasis in Table VII.19 is also selective, but is close to exhaustive because there seems very little global literature to choose from that deals with the amelioration of burnout. There may exist a horde of ameliorative efforts in global settings but, if so, it has escaped our diligent search. We are not alone in this estimate. For example, Schaufeli notes (1996, in press): "Unfortunately, only a few studies evaluate the effectiveness of burnout prevention programmes for people helpers." No global studies that we have found deal with the phase model, although a growing number of researchers note that it constitutes an alternative to their approaches.

Despite this short supply, it seems safe enough to hazard five generalizations about global studies of ameliorating burnout. First, few longitudinal studies exist, with short pre-vs. post-test designs dominating in those few studies with explicit observational frames and some concern for rigor. This bias sets strict limits on the interpretation of even insightful attempts to ameliorate or prevent burnout.

Table Summaries, Global Efforts to Ameliorate Burnout

Presenting Conditions	Source	Diagnostic Tools	Design Elements	Major Consequences
I. nurses and doctors (N = 8) pioneering homebased care for terminally-ill cancer patients in Italy, concerned about burnout due to lack of support in nonhospital settings and exacerbated by great demands on demands on staff "motivation and emotional investment"	Belfiore (1994)	• consultant anticipates likely problems, as reinforced by staff willingness to invest in a program of burnout prevention amelioration	• 20 sessions of "art therapy" to facilitate expressions of personal and institutional force fields • by implication, relationships and empathy can be surfaced in the process of making and discussing pictorial representations of staff experiences • no pre-vs. post-test measures • no explicit action planning	• gives "an account of how the creative and group process unfolded" • pictorial examples imply that interventions touched basic concerns of staff
II. 3-day workshop for community nurses, N = 64, in the Dutch province of North Holland	Schaufeli (1996)	• surveys • 3 MBI sub-domain scores • tedium • psychological strain • somatic complaints • short pre-versus post-test design (30 days)	• relaxation training • didactic and cognitive stress management skills • enhancement of a more realistic professional role	• significant effects observed for Emotional Exhaustion, tedium, psychological strain, and somatic complaints • random effects reported on Personal Accomplishment and Depersonalization

Second, global research reflects less concern with linkages between description and prescription—for example, "action research"—than do North American studies. This is seriously limiting, and implies the early developmental stages of worldwide concern with ameliorating burnout. Patently, this sparse record constitutes a very poor-fit with the worldwide incidence of burnout phases reported in Chapter VI.

Third, the slim global remedial literature seldom utilizes holistic estimates of burnout, as via the phase model or "tedium" (Pines, Aronson, & Kafry, 1981). Holistic estimates permit interpretations of findings beyond such partial surrogates for burnout as the three MBI sub-domains.

Fourth, the global literature on ameliorating burnout suffers from a kind of double deficit. Directly, there is a definite tendency among prominent researchers working in global settings to fixate on "people helping" roles. In contrast, the work with the phase model seeks to encompass people in all organizational settings. At times, one can usefully narrow one's field-of-view to get a finer resolution-in-depth, but there is no compelling evidence that this has been the case in burnout. In any case, ameliorative designs remain rare even in the narrowed view of burnout as a problem of people-helpers only.

Fifth, the planned change efforts in the global panel do not provide any clear test of the phase model or its various measurement conventions.

Chapter VIII

Phase Model of Burnout:
Some Working Conclusions, Worldwide

Well, that is *Global Burnout*, for now. Other relevant studies are underway, but they will have to see the light-of-day later and in other sources. Every project has an end, even if a provisional one. Now is that point-in-time for this version of developments relevant to the phase model.

The phase model has been subjected to substantial prodding and probing, under conditions that increase the probabilities that—even if all things have not been held equal—major factors have been relatively constant. Hence our insistence on preserving the set of original MBI items, for example, despite the real temptations over the years to develop a different set of items. Hence, also, the persisting decision to see how far a reliance on the universal norms could take the phase approach, both in North American as well as global settings.

So what has been learned about the phase model that we can confidently recommend for future research designs? Eighteen points usefully frame generalizations about theory and findings with which we are substantially comfortable. These generalizations are not closed, as Chapter VII reflects. However, to us, the evidence justifies substantial confidence about them as working answers. The interrogative targets in Chapter VII summarize the evidence supporting some of these generalizations, but they derive more basically from the initial half-dozen chapters of *Global Burnout*.

MBI SUB-DOMAINS SEEM VALID

Overall, the evidence about the usefulness of the three MBI sub-domains seems convincing. See Chapter II, especially. This is especially the case because the evidence comes from originators of the phase model as well as from independent researchers, and also because it applies to North American and global settings. A few researchers propose that the three MBI sub-domains have serious shortfalls, but these commentators constitute only a small minority.

NORMS: UNIVERSAL *AND* LOCAL

The developmental work on the phase model insisted on using "universal norms," which were developed at Site B and probably were conservative because worksettings in that division of a federal agency were often emotionally arousing for employees and clients alike. The working assumption goes something like this: if the clinical and popular literatures are even remotely accurate, burnout effects will be pronounced, widespread, and beyond distortion by features or cultures that presumably would be reflected in local norms. Typically, burnout researchers define "local norms" in terms of median scores, for each population, on the three MBI sub-domains.

The evidence—especially in Chapters III through V as well as VII— definitely inclines to two generalizations. The evidence supports the phase model and, if more qualifiedly, also the universal norms associated with them.

Such considerations urge a strong working conclusion. The phase model seems a reliable and valid operational definition and seems to work better in tandem with the universal norms.

However, this working conclusion needs to be qualified in some significant ways. Consider only that the universal vs. local norms often will generate different distributions of the phases of burnout, and with important practical implications, as in assessing the urgency of mounting an ameliorative effort. In most cases, as in Taiwan B, the two distributions differ but only in the sense that the universal norms imply a "huge problem" while the local reflect a "very serious" problem. Relatedly, there is some evidence on both sides of the issue of norms for making the High/Low judgments on which the phase assignments rest. For example, as Chapter VII indicates, both universal and local norms usually generate phase assignments that have regular and robust patterns of covariants. However, on balance, the universal norms tend to isolate the sharper pattern.

There is no need to be exclusive about norms, however. Indeed, various technical but especially practical concerns encourage the view that it may even be useful to represent burnout phases as a range—as best-worst range estimates based on both universal as well as local norms.

Conceptually, also, keeping the issue of norms open no doubt has most obvious appeal in the case of cross-national or cross-cultural research, and two additional but less-recognized reasons also encourage attention to the site-specific features tapped by local norms. Thus, "nation states" and "cultures" often will encompass much intra-category variability. The point also applies to "organizations," which are seldom the monoliths portrayed in much of the literature (e.g., Peters & Waterman, 1982).

Where do these considerations leave us? There is no theoretical or practical reason why local norms as well as universal cannot be included in future analyses. Indeed, prudence encourages this approach, at least for the immediate future. But *if* we authors had to choose, the universal norms would get the nod from us.

G/M SEQUENCING OF SUB-DOMAINS SEEMS WORKABLE

The sequence proposed by the phase model—Depersonalization —> Personal Accomplishment —> Emotional Exhaustion—seems workable, to judge from the replications reviewed above. Indeed, although the point is hardly settled, the G/M Model shows to general advantage when compared to alternatives like the M Model. See Chapter VII.

These comparisons of the patterns isolated by alternative sequencings of the three MBI sub-domains within the phase model seem to be conservative, in addition. The rationale is direct. To begin, whatever the sequencing of those three sub-domains, Is will always be Is, and VIIIs always will be VIIIs—given the same norms for High/Low assignments on the three MBI sub-domains. Relatedly, distributions of the phases often will be bimodal, which means that a large proportion of population usually will be assigned to the two extreme phases. Altogether, this effect often will moderate any differences between alternative ways of sequencing the three MBI sub-domains.

At the same time, now is definitely not the time to close the books on alternative ways of sequencing. For example, alternatives other than the two tested above—the G/M and the M variants considered in Chapter VII—should be studied. Such work would extend as well as replicate existing research supporting the phase model, some of which is reported above and some of which has been published elsewhere (e.g., Kim, 1990; Golembiewski & Munzenrider, 1991a).

PATTERN OF COVARIATION SUPPORTS PHASE MODEL

Let us make official a strong working conclusion supported by the data at virtually all points above. Research supports the validity and reliability of the phase model, as judged by its ability to isolate expected patterns of covariation on a wide range of variables. In fact, about 400 variables have been tested against the phase model, and very few surprises have been observed.

This working conclusion gains special force from a singular fact. Replications in both North America and global worksettings tend to isolate substantially-similar patterns of covariation, using the original phase model as well as the universal norms.

"ACTIVE" VS. "PASSIVE" MODES OF COPING DESERVE MORE ATTENTION

Research with the phase model has advanced far enough to gain a real but still-limited sense of the usefulness of distinguishing "active" vs. "passive" modes of coping, and we are beginning to accumulate estimates of the proportions of "actives" and "passives" in a range of organizations. But there remains a long way to go. For example, "passive" status can constitute a tactical withdrawal from a work setting after determined efforts have proved unavailing. Or deep socialization or perhaps even heredity may predispose some people to "hopelessness," "helplessness," or non-"robust" ways of coping with their environments. The distributions of these two basic kinds of "passives" seem consequential but, plainly, much remains unknown about them.

Both narrow and broad reasons support further work on this possibly-key difference. Narrowly, for example, "active" copers in the advanced stages seem more open to ameliorative interventions than "passives," with the latter suggesting withdrawal and low-energy levels that imply high probabilities of failed interventions, if not stimulus overload for those being "helped." Possibly, for example, those labeled "passive and VIII" might even be damaged by any but low-stimulus interventions (e.g., Golembiewski & Munzenrider, 1988, pp. 208-213). More broadly, "active" vs. "passive" coping may even be a component of a two-factor model of emotions, with the other component being a pleasant/unpleasant dimension estimated by the phases of burnout (Golembiewski & Munzenrider, 1988, pp. 250-253). See also the section concluding this chapter.

At the same time that conceptual reasons support the active/passive distinction, statistical analyses do *not* accord a high salience to the two modes. The effect is there, but seems to account for modest or small proportions of the variance in several studies (e.g., Golembiewski & Munzenrider, 1988, pp. 236-244). See also Chapter IV.

So what evidentiary base exists for moving toward a fuller understanding of activity/passivity? Again, as usual, the focus is on North American and then on global work settings, both of which suggest that observers can reasonably expect several regularities associated with "actives" vs. "passives" at worksettings. Mode of coping with burnout has been variously measured, but all of the studies in Tables VIII.1 and VIII.2 rely on a simple but

Table VIII.1. "Actives," by Phases, in North American Settings

	Phases of Burnout							
	I	*II*	*III*	*IV*	*V*	*VI*	*VII*	*VIII*
"*Actives,*" *in %*								
Site A	86.9%	84.2	70.8	66.7	80.0	70.6	23.5	22.7
Site B	72.4%	65.4	60.6	41.9	57.9	48.0	33.9	33.4
Site OO	96.7%	96.3	89.5	81.0	81.1	84.6	68.6	67.8
Site PP	85.9%	75.0	80.5	83.3	50.0	62.5	33.3	57.6
Site AAA	93.5%	100.0	76.5	85.3	82.5	93.3	73.1	58.8

apparently-useful estimate: those who score greater than 30 on a standard scale for Job Involvement (White & Ruh, 1973) are considered "active," and others are labeled "passive."

Mode of Coping in North American Settings

The illustrative cases in Table VIII.1 suggest five regularities; and other cases that could have been included have the same thrust. First, the proportion of "actives" varies regularly across the phases. Specifically, an average of almost 85 percent of all paired-comparisons reveal a progressively-decreasing proportion of actives, Phases I —> VIII, in the five North American settings.

Second, in effect, the heights of the five implied curves in Table VIII.1 differ even as their slopes are similar. The proportion of "passive" assignments in Phase VIII falls in the 40-60 percent range, more or less. In contrast, 70 percent or more of those in Phase I are classified as "active."

Third, apparently, organization processes—in selection, training, socialization, and out-placement—effect the active/passive proportions by phases. Thus Sites OO and PP have military or para-military missions; and Site AAA is a comprehensive hospital. Commonly, their VIIIs approximate 60 percent actives. Their pattern has two features: it reflects the common drop in actives I —> VIII; and at the same time the pattern at Sites OO, PP, and AAA has over twice the proportion of actives in Phase VIII as Sites A and B. Perhaps this is because the latter have more or less standard commercial and public missions, respectively, and lack the processes associated with high-urgency settings like the other three worksites in Table VIII.1.

Fourth, most deviant cases in the direction of paired-comparisons involve phases with few assignees—typically less than 10 or so assignees. Hence, some of the few cases not fitting the regular pattern may be artifactual due to one or a few outliers among a handful of assignees.

Fifth, despite the regularity by phases, it is not clear how much of the trend is due to nature and how much can be assigned to nurture. Ongoing work with "helplessness" and "hardiness" may provide some perspective on this issue, which is of great significance if the existing ideation about the phase model is reasonably on-target (e.g., Golembiewski & Munzenrider, 1988, esp. pp. 178-179). It already seems that hardiness and the phases covary directly (see Belarus A, B, C, and D, for example).

Mode of Coping in Global Settings

Table VIII.2 obviously is no more than suggestive, since it exhausts a smaller panel of convenience populations than its North American counterpart selects from. But the suggestions do not surprise in implying both universal as well as culture-specific components.

Five points outline the major suggestions implied by Table VIII.2. First, the shifting proportion of actives/passives in global work settings seems regular, phase by phase, and those distributions are non-random by chi-square test in all cases but Belarus A. Nonetheless, the regularity seems a bit less pronounced than in the North American cases. This tentative conclusion is best reflected in the proportions in the two tables of paired-comparisons in the expected direction—the two averages being over 84 percent for North American studies, but less than 76 percent for the global settings illustrated in Table VIII.2.

In sum, in both Tables VIII.1 and VIII.2, the proportion of actives decreases as the phases progress I —> VIII, but the two sets of data also seem distinguishable. This dual effect seems to reflect a basic generic component, as perhaps modified by culture-specific factors. For example, Ghana A counts almost all of those in Phase I as "active," and retains about two-thirds in that status through Phase VIII. Crudely put, Ghana A begins and ends "higher" than other cases in Table VIII.2, but shares with them a decline in the proportion of "actives," phase by phase.

Second, the curves in Table VIII.2 seem less steep than in Table VIII.1, even including the latter's three high-urgency settings. This may be due to socialization patterns that differ from those underlying North American settings. In any case, the mean "drop" in actives, Phases I vs. VIII, approximates 39 percent in North American settings and 45 percent in worldwide populations.

Third, Table VIII.2 may contain national outliers, but it is not clear whether (for example) Japan B and China B are the outliers, or Japan C. Nor does clarity now exist about whether the differences in Table VIII.2 reflect something in nature, something in nurture, or merely the artifactual. Supporting the last interpretation, Japan C constitutes a smallish

Table VIII.2. "Actives," by Phases, in Global Work Settings

"Actives," in %		Phases of Burnout in %							
		I	II	III	IV	V	VI	VII	VIII
1.	Belarus A	76.1%	65.9	47.5	53.8	100.0	63.2	55.6	55.3
2.	Belarus B	88.9%	60.0	9.2	82.2	100.0	51.9	21.4	24.3
3.	Belarus D	75.0%	77.4	42.8	44.7	87.5	39.4	40.0	42.5
4.	Belarus E	87.5%	80.0	56.3	41.7	33.3	0.0	33.3	38.9
5.	China B	46.5%	45.0	28.5	25.0	44.4	38.0	0.0	18.4
6.	Ghana A	97.1%	100.0	83.3	63.9	95.5	84.4	76.5	66.0
7.	Japan A	92.3%	94.7	72.5	59.6	100.0	82.3	66.4	47.4
8.	Japan B	72.2%	61.9	28.6	17.7	66.7	57.8	25.0	15.3
9.	Japan C	66.7%	80.0	40.0	62.5	83.3	82.8	63.6	39.4
10.	Saudi Arabia A	92.3%	87.5	50.0	88.9	73.0	69.0	52.0	33.3
11.	Taiwan B	82.4%	71.4	59.2	36.8	66.7	66.7	42.2	30.8

population with a very large representation of respondents in the three most-advanced phases. The consequence is several phases with a small number of entries, which may make for unstable estimates.

Conceptually, in any case, the generally-variable proportion of actives/passives in a population seems significant. Thus, a wider range of interventions seem applicable where people remain "active." Relatedly, if active/passive status does *not* derive from basic personality predispositions, periodic testing for phase assignments takes on a great saliency, even an urgency, lest individuals move from active —> passive and hence constitute more difficult targets for ameliorating their burnout. A detailed rationale for such implications of active/passive status is available (Golembiewski & Munzenrider, 1988, esp. pp. 236-253).

Fourth, as in Table VIII.1, paired-comparisons in Table VIII.2 in a contrary direction typically are most numerous in populations having phases with a small number of assignees. Japan A and China B fit this generalization, for example. Hence, sub-sample size may be an issue in the quarter or so of paired-comparisons in Table VIII.2 that fall in a contrary direction.

Fifth, to the same point, statistical analyses fail to isolate a major role for the active/passive distinction, but attention to it continues to be motivated by two conceptual features. On the one hand, the active/passive distinction relates to intervention strategy, as in the key question of whether (let us say) a passive VIII may be vulnerable to overstimulation by interventions in programs of conscious change in ways that are less troublesome for (let us say, again) an active VIII. At the very least, this concern is a central one for the responsible intervenor; and a strong conceptual argument can be made in support of that concern (e.g., Golembiewski, 1990, pp. 158-160).

On the other hand, and perhaps of equal status with the concern about overstimulation, the active/passive distinction may be a relevant issue in understimulation. To review, strain can derive from both over- as well as understimulation, as Chapter II especially suggests. Possibly, for example, a passive I (let us say) may be characterized by a profile of variables: he or she may have a *laissez-faire* supervisor, or may be employed by a low-energy organization, or may be in some protected category such as a person nearing retirement who has been shunted aside. Some evidence suggestive of such networks has been reported, as Chapters VII and this one illustrate at several points.

BURNOUT SEEMS GENERIC *AND* CULTURE-SPECIFIC

Overall, the North American as well as global studies have a strong generic component, but they also provide room for cross-organizational, cross-national, and perhaps cross-cultural differences—with "culture" here referring to organizations as well as broad social systems. To summarize, the panels of studies above clearly reflect cross-national effects, but let us now speculate a bit about probable cross-cultural effects. In sum, the analyses above open the doors for cultural features in at least three senses. Thus, the differing incidences of the phases may be explicable in cultural terms, at least in part, as was attempted with Japanese populations. Moreover, the covariation of marker variables X phases focus on direction and pattern, as it were, and this leaves room for cultural factors to become manifest (e.g.) in differing magnitudes. In addition, the persistence of phases may be influenced by cultural features, and the same may be said of active/passive modes—but how much is not known. Basically, on almost all variables, the phases isolate similar patterns of covariants, with the basic differences involving the percentages of paired-comparisons falling in the expected direction and also achieving $P \leq .05$. Cross-cultural differences—at both organizational and social levels—can help account for the latter differences, of course.

A similar conclusion holds for GHQ II—which seeks to distinguish "cases" from "normals" concerning questionnaire responses that indicate symptomology which implies non-psychotic psychiatric symptoms that—if revealed in clinical interviews—would justify treatment. Tables IV.8 and IV.9 suggest two conclusions for North American vs. global populations: both show a marked tendency for "cases" to increase, phase by phase; and the North American populations seem to have a lower base-rate, overall. Of course, these working conclusions may reflect cross-cultural differences, again within *a* global pattern.

However, several factors limit this potential for explanation by cultural features, with four illustrations sufficing for present purposes. Paramountly, *a* pattern of covariation dominates phases X marker variables, and this despite the full panoply of contingent features that are largely free to operate within a substantial panel of North American as well as worldwide studies. Thus, we know that even counterpart organization units in the same agency, with the same missions and technologies as well as with similarly-trained personnel, can differ in significant ways (e.g., Thompson, 1956; Goodsell, 1994, pp. 50-54). And yet *the* pattern of covariants for the phases persists, except for a very small proportion of the marker variables reported above.

That *the* pattern also persists in the global panel of studies provides powerful reinforcement. We have well-developed rationales for expecting differentiated cross-cultural effects (e.g., Hofstede, 1980) and are ill-prepared to explain them even if we expect similar effects.

As a third factor that may suppress cultural effects, research with the phase model is restricted to organizational settings. It appears that technical similarities—as in air traffic controllership—may dominate the effects of different national loci in which that control is being exercised (e.g., Shouksmith & Burrough, 1988). Much the same may be true of the bureaucratic model, which appears dominant in the vast majority of global worksettings (e.g., Golembiewski, 1995), even when other comparative features differ substantially.

Finally, on this brief catalog of factors limiting the ability of cultural features to explain the phase model findings, it already seems clear that several known factors account for some part of the unexplained variance in *the* pattern of covariations between the phases and the marker variables. That is, many phase studies with a less-robust pattern of covariants involve one or more phases with a few entries, as at Belarus. This opens the possibility that outliers can distort effects. Moreover, these semi-deviant studies also often involve populations with large representations of women—for example, the 70-plus percent in Belarus A, as well as the large female representations in Sites like KK. See also Chapter VII.

These general observations aside, what else can be reasonably said at this stage of inquiry about the impact of cultural factors? Three kinds of evidence contribute to this strong working conclusion: the phase model and burnout seem to have a substantial generic component. What is the supporting evidence? The three MBI sub-domains seem to apply broadly; the universal norms seem generally useful, and often more sensitive, than the local norms; and a consistent pattern of covariation typically is isolated by applications of the phase model. Our results also contain room for culture-specific effects, of both organizational and broadly-social varieties, but speculation about degree must dominate in the general absence of specific measurement.

BURNOUT HAS GENDER-SPECIFIC COMPONENT

Within the largely-consistent pattern of covariants of the phase model, gender differences seem to be more relevant than early research suggested. That is, gender and other demographics seem to account for small portions of the variance in phase assignments, even in that half of the cases, more or less, where significant associations with the phases have been found (e.g., Golembiewski, Munzenrider, & Stevenson, 1986, esp. pp. 132-140).

That early view has changed. The closer one looks at the issue, as in Chapter VII, the greater the apparent salience of gender differences *within* a consistent pattern of burnout covariants.

The key research remains a challenge but, as Chapter VII suggests, two major and possibly-interacting approaches seem viable. Thus, tendencies toward differences may exist in how the genders view work and careers, with consequent differences in perceptions and behaviors due to pervasive historical contexts emphasizing differential treatments and prospects. Alternatively, more fundamental and systemic inter-gender differences, on the general order of the brain architectures recently headlined, may help explain the differences-within-a-pattern isolated by the phase model of burnout. Or it could be some complex amalgam of both contributors, or others.

In yet another arena, then, the nature and nurture argument again appears.

PHASES AWKWARDLY FIT
DOMINANT RESEARCH FASHIONS

At various points, the phase model clearly has points of real—if greater or lesser—incompatibility with comfortable research fashions. The point is clearest in connection with population size, and especially so in populations with larger-than-normal concentrations in the extreme phases. Relatively-large Ns can be necessary in phase research, to shorten a long story. And there is evidence throughout *Global Burnout* that the few deviant cases within an all-but-uniform pattern often are associated with a small N and/ or a distribution of cases that leaves one or more phases with a few entries— for convenience, let us say, less than 10.

This large N required by the phase model, exacerbated by bimodal phase distributions in nature, can be off-putting. But there seems no easy way around it, which runs counter to the prevailing fashion of subjecting smallish populations to exotic analytic approaches. Here, we subject relatively-large populations to simpler and less-opaque methods of analysis. Both approaches seek scientific advances, but only time will tell which will disappoint, if not both.

In the interim, statistical technologies exert a strong attraction, even though the "stuckness" of behavioral research can be more proximately traced to lack of perseverance with issues related to choosing between operational definition (e.g., Golembiewski, 1986b). For example, the phase model's focus on points of operational definition discourages reliance on the popular LISREL routines. This may seem to be too bad for the phase model. At least to the present authors, however, the pay-offs of the concern with operational-definition, despite the need for large Ns, far overbalances the admittedly-substantial conveniences of computational routines that seem data-sparing.

MANAGERIAL FEATURES SEEM CENTRAL

As is consistent with the environmental orientation underlying the phases—see Chapter I, for example—numerous managerial features seem associated with burnout. The inventory remains far from complete, but nonetheless is far from an empty set. And as will become clear, attractions aside, focus on these managerial features constitutes another case of poor-fit with dominant research fashion.

This knowledge of burnout covariants implies strategic leverage for change, of course. For example, knowledge of those managerial features consistently associated with the phases can be put to applied uses. That is, *if* X covaries with the phases, and *if* one knows how to intervene so as to influence X, then that suggests a potential for having an impact on burnout. Fortunately, many of the managerial features of concern here present just such a potential for leverage: they can be targeted by conscious and well-known interventions, and with substantial success rates (e.g., Golembiewski, Proehl, & Sink, 1981, 1982; Nicholas, 1982; Robertson, Roberts, & Porras, 1992).

Four emphases review such managerial features associated with burnout in both North American and global studies. That is, the "managerial features" of interest here include:

- managerial styles and their associated consequences
- policies and procedures
- structure
- purpose or ideology, as via mission or culture statements.

All four classes of managerial features may be considered as "inputs" in a basic environmental model of burnout and hence, overall, as trigger variables in causal linkages. However, feedback effects also will occur. Thus, increases in feature X may increase burnout. Then, in turn, increases in burnout can reinforce or heighten feature X. In any case, brief attention gets directed at each of the four classes of managerially-related features.

MANAGERIAL STYLES AND THEIR CONSEQUENCES

Broadly, and all but unanimously, phases I —> VIII are associated with the presence —> absence of behaviors and attitudes consistent with those values-cum-technology usually labeled Participative Management, or PM. Typically, PM encompasses both managerial styles or approaches associated with a range of consequences among employees that are usually consistent with high performance and especially with high satisfaction (e.g., Miller & Monge, 1986).

The studies reviewed above—both in North American as well as global settings—permit quite confident generalizations about the probable covariants of the phases of burnout (e.g., Golembiewski, Hilles, & Daly, 1987; Golembiewski & Rountree, 1996a). When PM variables are activated, burnout decreases. In no particular order, these PM variables tend to be associated with lower burnout:

- higher Job Involvement
- higher Job Satisfaction
- regenerative interaction (Golembiewski, 1990)
- higher Participation in decision making
- greater sharing of information
- one-to-many vs. one-to-one patterns of supervision
- greater autonomy
- high supervisory supportiveness vs. punitiveness.

See also Chapter VII.

Policies and Procedures

Some evidence supports what seems a truism: for good or ill, managerial policies and procedures have an impact on people and their burnout. Again, policies and procedures consistent with the PM rubric tend to be associated with less-advanced phases of burnout. In contrast, policies and procedures consistent with the bureaucratic model tend to generate advanced phases.

This crucial point gets support—coming and going, as it were. On the one hand, deliberate managerial action to induce and support regenerative interaction, and to reinforce that change via policy innovations, served to reduce burnout levels (e.g., Golembiewski & Rountree, 1996a, 1996b). Moreover, the improvement persisted over an extended interval, which was unusually stressor-filled (e.g., Golembiewski, Hilles, & Daly, 1987). On the other hand, conventional policies and procedures associated with reductions-in-force appear to sharply increase burnout (e.g., Noer, 1994). PM alternatives are available (e.g., Golembiewski, 1990, 1995).

To tell the truth, however, support for the impact on burnout of PM policies and procedures is largely inferential. The web seems compelling, but that does not change its basic character (e.g., Golembiewski, 1995). Consider only a simple way of illustrating the point. Substantial evidence suggests that burnout should be moderated by such policies as those which permit greater personal choice and autonomy concerning when and where to work. Indeed, respectively, flexi-time (e.g., Golembiewski, Hilles, & Kagno, 1974) and flexi-place (e.g., Golembiewski, 1995, pp. 144-151) have generated literatures that powerfully imply an amelioration of burnout. However, the direct demonstrations of linkages with burnout have seldom been made (e.g., Golembiewski & Rountree, 1996a, 1996b), as far as we know.

Post-Bureaucratic Structure

Here, again, the burnout literature has strong presumptive associations with well-known managerial features, (e.g., Golembiewski, 1995a), but explicit research on verifying those associations is in very short supply (e.g., Golembiewski & Rountree, 1996a). The point can be detailed economically in terms of a structural trinity: job rotation, job enrichment, and autonomous team structures. The advantages of job rotation have become increasingly clear, as in today's emphasis on cross-training; and one way of extending the logic of job rotation involves designing enriched jobs. These have the added scope that permits an employee a kind of internal and continuous rotation; and autonomous teams extend the job enrichment idea from the individual to the group level, with task groups responsible for a broad range of activities—including some that are still widely-perceived as the "prerogatives of management." For example, numerous industrial systems are now experiencing accelerated development through the full structural trinity (e.g., Williams, 1994), but substantial kicking-and-screaming occurs because of a resistance to sharing what once were "managerial prerogatives."

Detailed research with the phases relates only partially to this developmental trinity (e.g., Golembiewski & Rountree, 1996a, 1996b). Thus, job rotation is a reasonable approach to moderating burnout on some jobs (e.g., Maslach & Pines, 1977). And some have recommended job enrichment, for a wide range of reasons (e.g., Golembiewski & Munzenrider, 1988, esp. pp. 217-218). However, the usefulness of the phase model in connection with job enrichment will be determined in two ways: job enrichment should reduce burnout, overall; and the phases will be useful indicators of those conditions under which efforts toward job enrichment probably will succeed, and when failure is likely because of the advanced phases of burnout experienced by all or most of those targeted for a program of planned change. Finally, some introductory work on burnout and autonomous teams exists (e.g., Novelli, 1990), but it stops short of testing for the expected reduction in burnout on change-over to this post-bureaucratic structural alternative.

Ideological Commitments

On this fourth and final illustrative class of "managerial features," the association with burnout is both most intriguing as well as least researched. Conceptually, the salience of ideological commitment in lowering burnout is reasonable, and the magnitude of the effects may be great. In one case, for example, women working under apparently-adverse conditions also were rated as very low on burnout (Cherniss & Krants, 1983). The women worked numbingly-long hours in service to the terminally-ill, at a stage in their lives when those busy care-givers would more appropriately be the recipients of care. In sum, the women felt self-validation rather than exhaustion. What explained the apparent paradox between conditions at work and the overall reactions of the women? The women had a strong religious commitment to service, and that ideology transcended the mere facts of their tough condition. Indeed, the worse their condition became, the better, for that validated their ideology for providing care. The more worthy they were, to explain, the greater the demands they would experience as a sign that God loved them. Those women were, after all, "brides of Christ," who had earlier set them a model for full service to humankind.

Much management practice has learned a similar basic lesson concerning normative commitment to an ideology. Bluntly, one who knows *why*, and agrees with it, can deal with almost any *what* (e.g., Golembiewski, 1993, esp. pp. 289-291). Some such rationale implies a dual emphasis in many organizations. As one part of the duality, some organizations are decentralized so that individuals at the action level can experience a sense of autonomy and ownership, while responding to local situations. In this regard, these organizations are "loose." As for the other aspect of the duality, some organizations devote considerable attention to various normative statements—policies, culture statements, mission statements, and so on. Constitutions, separations of powers, and other devices also can provide the substance as well as the sense of this rolling consensus (e.g., O'Toole & Bennis, 1992).

In sum, organizations can be normatively "tight" as well as "loose" in an operational sense. When combined, these dual orientations to collective action that preserve individual initiative are frequently called "loose-tight systems." Exemplars exist in both business and government (e.g., Sayles & Chandler, 1971, 1993), and draw energy from dealing with the paradox captured in their very labeling.

And Fashionable Research

These four sets of considerations related to managerial features cannot win for losing, from one revealing angle. As Chapter II alerts the readers, up-front, the discussion above relates to low-priority research fashions. From the burnout point-of-view, the discussion encourages an organizational and managerial reaching-out not common among most of the burnout researchers. From the point-of-view of organizational and managerial development, in addition, the discussion encourages a reaching-out to individual concerns that are not *au courant* there.

Well, nobody promised readers a rose garden.

MACRO-INSTITUTIONAL FEATURES DEMAND ATTENTION

Perhaps the greatest gaps in the burnout literature relate to possible (even probable) linkages with macro-institutional features—social, economic, and political. Such features seem major inputs in an environmental model of burnout, but the most realistic evaluation for burnout research related to macro-institutional features seems clear enough: suggestive, but preliminary (Golembiewski, 1995b, esp. pp. 282-296).

By way of illustration, consider the state of the literature on family features and burnout. Some of the findings do not surprise, even as they clearly need replication. Thus, burnout seems greater in single-parent households (e.g., Elloy & Anderson, 1991); and, for some of the same reasons, women seem more likely than men to populate advanced phases of burnout (e.g., Golembiewski & Munzenrider, 1988, esp. pp. 132-136). At the same time, the infrequent attempts to link phase assignments directly with family features have produced mixed results (e.g., Golembiewski, Bower, & Kim, 1994a, 1994b). This may be due to methodological issues related to the early stage of measurement of the dimensions of family life, or they may involve more basic issues in family research. For example, most employers are leery about encouraging any penetration into the family lives of their employees, based on the early sad experience of the employer in *loco parentis*, as it were, at such locations as the Hawthorne Works or the Ford Motor Co. In short, work <—> family research designs are hard to implement.

Clearly, in any case, the spotty quality of available research concerning macro-institutional features is not due to ignorance about attractive targets. For example, an existential angst, and hence burnout, may result from such features of economic life as the non-portability of pension rights and other benefits. In principle, the point has not escaped the attention of policymakers in most developed nations; and, in principle, the proposed linkage constitutes a clear-enough target for useful research over time. Practically, however, no easy pieces are promised. Of course, all longitudinal designs pose serious problems.

Relatedly, useful research on macro-institutional features could focus on the burnout dynamics associated with adverse personnel actions. Depending on one's tastes, these may be labelled diversely—cut-back, retrenchment, downsizing, or right-sizing. The conceptual case for such associations seems strong; several pairs of the sites in Table VI.1—for example, Sites X and Y, Z and AA—reflect the burnout consequences of adverse personnel actions; and some relevant research is available, both concerning description (e.g, Kilpatrick, 1986) as well as planned interventions (e.g., Golembiewski, Hilles, & Daly, 1987).

MAJOR CONSEQUENCES OF BURNOUT REQUIRE PRIORITY

The phase model of burnout, in both North American and global worksettings, seems to isolate expected effects for both individuals and the systems employing them. This generalization holds, on balance, but its grip varies in strength, and in places has obvious weaknesses.

At the individual level, the phases covary with expected outcomes, regularly as well as robustly, and the high costs of major outcomes seem substantial, even huge. The situation is perhaps clearest in the cases of emotional and physical health. The findings related to satisfaction with the various facets of work also are quite uniformly unattractive.

In sum, both self-reports and archival (or "objective") data quite uniformly support the view that advanced burnout has serious negative consequences for people, albeit with some important reservations. As Chapter IV shows, the basic generalization was only tentatively extended to blood chemistry, and effects there will require long-term tracking of individuals to determine whether T_1 burnout is a leading and revealing indicator of T_N problems with cardiovascular health.

At the level of the employing organization, the evidence is less comprehensive and convincing, even as it trends in similar directions. Thus, self-rated productivity usually falls as the phases progress I —> VIII; and the early evidence which ties usage of medical insurance to the advancing phases also attracts attention. In addition, performance appraisal data show an inverse relationship with burnout. As expected, appraisals fall as burnout phases advance, but relevant research is both rare and poses interpretive problems.

Relatedly, only occasional research has successfully tied burnout directly to performance or productivity, as measured by archival or "hard" data (e.g., Golembiewski & Rountree, 1996a, 1996b). Chapter IV details the attempt at Site B that still remains the major effort of this kind, but it generates only-suggestive results; and non-conclusive results also characterize a later effort to link burnout and supervisory-related performance (e.g., Golembiewski, Bower, & Kim, 1994). In common, such cases reflect an unknown mix of objective dilemmas such as the requirements for the substantial size of populations in phase research, along with the possibility that relevant relationships in nature are variable or highly contingent. In addition, as Chapter VII reflects, gross differences in the representations of the genders may impact on the strength of the pattern of covariation reported in specific studies.

Whatever the costs of the major outcomes of advanced burnout, they need not be endured. As several chapters indicate, although the demonstration has not been made frequently, planned interventions to reduce burnout seem to work. Thus, planned interventions have resulted in decreased turnover (e.g., Golembiewski, Hilles, & Daly, 1987), intent to turnover (e.g., Golembiewski & Rountree, 1996a, 1996b), as well as a range of attractive "hard" and "soft" indicators in a hospital (Golembiewski & Rountree, 1996a, 1996b).

CHRONIC OR ACUTE ONSET REQUIRE DISTINGUISHING

Knowledge about modes of onset also constitutes a major gap in the literature, and remedying that condition requires clinically-oriented studies of specific individuals over time. Longitudinal studies are rare, and even the rarities usually deal with small populations (e.g., Cherniss, 1989). Indeed, the distinction between kinds of onset is seldom made, and no other measure but the phase model directs attention to this distinction.

At the same time, chronic or acute onset seem to be relevant in burnout, and this urges clinical research designs. The phase model, as noted, contains one prototypic chronic flightpath—I —> II —> IV —> VIII, as well as several possible acute flightpaths.

ENTRANCE TO ADVANCED PHASES,
AND EXIT FROM THEM, NEED DISTINGUISHING

A related limitation of the phase model as well as all burnout research involves the "direction" of burnout. For example, if a person is classified as a V, that is useful information. But we seldom know whether that V is "entering" more advanced phases of burnout or "exiting" from them.

This information about entrance/exit can be consequential, both theoretically and practically. For example, such specificity would permit differentiated attention to chronic vs. acute onset. As matters now stand, a V is a V, with mode of onset being unspecified. That may be seriously wrong as well as inelegant. More basically, in addition, the associated longitudinal research might well inform the central issue of the differential sequencing of the three MBI sub-domains in variants of the phase model. Dispute about this sequencing does exist, but little of it is based on data from longitudinal research designs. See Chapter VII.

The basic learning may seem obvious, but its point nonetheless requires restatement. Longitudinal designs—and especially those with a clinical orientation that track personal life-lines—will be necessary to distinguish both entering/exiting as well as chronic/acute onset. Precisely such research is in shortest supply, however.

Existing research with the phase model and the MBI items also has other features bearing on exit or entrance. For example, estimates of "life events" seem of limited value in differentiating acute from chronic onset (e.g., Golembiewski & Munzenrider, 1988, esp. pp. 143-156), and the underlying reasons do not seem obscure. For example, and if for no other reason, the phase model and the MBI items focus on "experienced stressors," and these may not be highly correlated with "objective stressors." Thus, individuals seem to differ in how they experience even the same stressor, not only between individuals but also at different points in the life of the same individual. Oppositely, at its base, the life events literature is rooted in conceptualizations that emphasize "objective stressors."

LEADING, LAGGING, OR SIMULTANEOUS
RELATIONSHIPS AS NEXT-STEPS

The reviews above make a strong case that the phases will covary with a large catalog of variables—mostly self-reports, but including some objective measures—and this consistency is surprising, even astounding, given that we know that relationships in nature do not always (or even often) take the 1:1 form of the analyses above. This consistency implies the centrality of the phases. Hence, the significance of some next-steps for research with the phase model. For openers, and despite the relative consistency of the evidence above, differences in the phases probably have three kinds of relationships with marker variables. The covariation may be simultaneous or nearly so: hence, variations in the phases lead to changes in marker variables, more or less immediately. Or phase changes may trigger proximate but not simultaneous variations in marker variables, and in this sense the phases may be said to be leading. Or phase differences may anticipate long-delayed effects, and the latter may be seen as lagging.

What does the research record of the phase model of burnout imply about these three kinds of relationships? At the very least, differences in burnout can be said to trigger simultaneous covariations, or nearly simultaneous ones, in many variables. The dominant 1:1 model of most phase research is sensitive to such covariation.

Moreover, reasonable conceptual considerations suggest that the phases play a proximate leading role—as in the phases being the driving force in inducing effects in satisfaction at work, physical symptoms, or whatever, given that feedback linkages do exist. Leading effects for the phases also are suggested by a variety of statistical analyses (e.g., Deckard, Rountree, & Golembiewski, 1988).

More speculative evidence also suggests that lagging effects may exist, as in the studies of blood chemistry reviewed in Chapter IV. This may possibly explain the minor associations at T_1 of the phases X blood chemistry described in Chapter IV. In this view, only T_2, T_3...T_N measures of blood chemistry will be associated more strongly with T_1 phases.

The theoretical and practical implications of such effects seem profound. For example, this possibility of lagging effects heightens the urgency of longitudinal research designs in studies of blood chemistry. Let us spell it out. That is, *if* advanced phases at T_1 constitute an early warning about subsequent problems with blood chemistry—and that is a very big *if*, of course—the theoretical and practical implications reach to the very heart of future life. Such early warnings via the phases would have great relevance.

BURNOUT CAN BE AMELIORATED

Given the evidence in Chapter VI about the incidence and persistence of the phases of burnout, doing something about what seems to exist merits a very high priority. Burnout may well be *the* critical behavioral issue of our age, in fact. The phase model permits estimates whose meaning is rooted in numerous studies in various worldwide settings. And those estimates imply bad news, on very definite balance.

As Chapter VII illustrates, dual responses to this section's theme seem appropriate. In order:

Yes, the existing theory and experience permit us to do some reasonable things about burnout, both remedial and preventative. Interventions deal with structures, policies and procedures, as well as interaction. Optimism is especially appropriate because substantial success rates exist for learning designs that can help deal with burnout in before as well as after conditions, as it were. These designs have been developed in the related fields of praxis labelled OD (for Organization Development) and QWL (or Quality of Working Life). Convenient summaries of this work are available (e.g., Golembiewski, 1990b), and detailed surveys of success rates have been available for some time. These surveys are of long-standing (e.g., Golembiewski, Proehl, & Sink, 1981, 1982; Nicholas, 1982) and have been periodically extended and updated (e.g., Golembiewski, 1991; Golembiewski & Sun, 1990).

But, no, very little attention has been directed at ameliorating burnout—whether fore or aft, as it were, whether in North America or worldwide.

These comments highlight an essential challenge, perhaps the paramount challenge. But *Global Burnout* also puts the challenge in an optimistic context.

BURNOUT PHASES INFORM
THEORY ABOUT CHANGE

This section deals with a critical issue in behavioral research and application: the basic theory of change. We put the essential point in bald terms. The phase model is part of a long line of research inspired by a dysjoint between some results of an intervention that did not square with the conventional notion that change is change (Golembiewski, Billingsley, & Yeager, 1976). In addition, the phase model also seems to serve usefully as a surrogate for estimating different kinds of change (e.g., Golembiewski, 1990b).

A little background is unavoidable here. Basically, an intervention seemed to fail, based on the numbers; but participants reported that matters *had improved* in targeted ways.

So what was going on? The statistical machinations are sometimes formidable, but the bottom-line is quite direct. Going by the numbers—comparing a post-test to several pre-test benchmarks—*implied* that the expected things had not happened, but only given the assumption that the psychological space at pre-test was the same as that at the post-test. But that assumption was naive, even simplistic in the basic sense that the intervention sought to basically change the psychological space at post-test, not only in terms of degree but also in terms of the basic state that existed.

So, success in our intent would show up as failure, *unless* we changed our concept of change along with changing basic conditions at the worksite in which we were intervening. We attempted this demonstration, and successfully so, it appears.

Three Kinds of Change

To put it simply, a trinitarian model of change was isolated by statistical means, and it identifies three kinds of change. This new model of change made these distinctions:

ALPHA CHANGE involves a variation in the level of some existential state, given constantly-calibrated intervals on a measuring instrument related to a constant conceptual domain.

BETA CHANGE involves a variation in the level of some existential state, complicated by the fact that some intervals of the measurement continuum associated with a constant conceptual domain have been recalibrated.

GAMMA CHANGE involves a redefinition or reconceptualization of some domain, a major change in the perspective or frame of reference within which phenomena are perceived and classified, in what is taken to be relevant in some slice of reality.

These conceptual distinctions contribute to a direct point. Explaining the differences between the numbers and participant reactions to the intervention required a transformation. Our minds were stuck on alpha change, while our methods induced gamma change. No wonder the numbers did not come out as expected, or that participants experienced the intervention in more nuanced ways than the data. The radical quality of the conceptual distinctions deserves highlighting. Absent proof that alpha-only occurs, it is impossible to make *any* specific interpretation of any T_2 vs. T_1 "change." This is a very powerful statement.

Given the measurement technology then involved in the test for trinitarian change, gamma made a useful distinction but did not solve all problems. Establishing that gamma change had occurred, to simplify a bit, did make a very important point, but in a way unsatisfying for all practical purposes and for most theoretic ones. As then measured, gamma would indicate change in both the psychological domain as well as in the units for estimating degrees of that domain, which is powerful stuff. As then measured, however, gamma *could not reveal* the direction of that fundamental change. And that is the stuff of which pessimism, even despair, is made.

Many change agents were frustrated by this double-bind. Trinitarian change implied a conceptual step forward in one sense, but was severely limited in not identifying the direction of the induced change. And the latter preoccupies change agents.

The potential for frustration with trinitarian change was only raised by a curious fact. The basic distinctions about change have been accepted without serious or significant challenge by opinion-makers (e.g., Tennis, 1986), but progress with measurement conventions has been limited, even after the expenditure of great effort and imagination (e.g., Armenakis, 1988). This constitutes a very unattractive combination. In effect, trinitarian change can inform intervenors about how far they have gone, but not about in which direction.

Details are beside the present point, but the phase model of burnout can serve as a surrogate for gamma in three basic senses. Obviously, the model implies direction: the movement I —> VIII can be translated as preferred —> undesirable. In addition, the phase model conceptually implies at least one gamma difference—that is, between the point at which little or no burnout exists for an individual, and the point(s) at which burnout becomes substantial enough to impact in qualitatively different ways on individual behaviors, attitudes, and relationships. This conceptual feature, in turn, opens the possibility that the phases may even provide a sense of when individuals or collections of them are primed to "go around the bend," of when the emotional system is so loaded that a person is "ready to snap." The active/passive distinction may be of help here; and early stages of work with hardiness by one of the co-authors also seems promising (e.g., Boudreau, Zhilina, Zhilina, & Faiferman, 1996a).

Some early evidence suggests a far more profound feature of the phases of burnout (e.g., Golembiewski & Munzenrider, 1988a, 1988b). Specifically, statistical analysis suggests that *each* of the phases isolates gamma differences in responses. That is, those classified in the 8 phases respond to the MBI items in ways that statistical analysis demonstrates differ regularly and profoundly—that is, responses to the MBI items are structured by respondents in such fundamental ways as to isolate differences in psychological states, in both degree as well as in state, and *phase by phase* (Golembiewski & Munzenrider, 1989). This analysis first involves separate factor analyses of the MBI responses of all those assigned to each of the 8 phases. All pairs of these structures are then compared for their degree of congruence by a technique for comparing the similarities/differences of factorial structures in terms of both degree and pattern (Ahmavaara, 1954). See also the four sub-sections below.

Even in bare introductory form, this is heavy stuff, if still provisional. Consistently, early evidence also suggests that other variables present no such statistical "jumps" when the clusters of responses of those assigned to each of the 8 phases are compared, pair by pair, and phase by phase, on continuous variables like Job Involvement (Golembiewski & Munzenrider, 1990).

Phases and Trinitarian Change

These conceptual introductions to trinitarian change or differences provide a useful foundation for some testing and more-extensive speculation about burnout. Directly, can the trinitarian model point us in a direction to move beyond the present findings?

Four generalizations sketch how far *Global Burnout* takes us. Perhaps oversimply, the phases—in virtually all worksettings so far studied—are associated with progressively-virulent covariants. This generalization can be taken to the bank. In addition, large proportions of all surveyed populations are classified in "advanced phases"—which we can conveniently, if provisionally, define as Phases VI-VIII. Moreover, although several estimates of "stability" are possible, notable proportions of respondents in organizations seem to have a narrow "shelving level" of one or a few phases in which they are likely to be found when observations of the phases are made at two or more points. These latter two generalizations have to be more qualified than the first one, but they clearly constitute no mere wild guesses. Conceptually and with some empirical backing (e.g., Golembiewski, Hilles, & Daly, 1987), one also can make a reasonable case that "active" or "passive" modes of coping provide useful specificity, and especially for the more advanced phases.

And what about going further, based on trinitarian change? Hope exists, as some details suggest. Associated with, but nonetheless beyond, the four generalizations above lies a major question: Do the phases somehow point the way toward a point or zone where the classified individual is in direct danger of "snapping" or "going around the bend," in the senses introduced in Chapter I, conceptually elaborated in Chapter II, and variously circumscribed in subsequent chapters? Or less specifically but with a greater margin of safety, can collections of individuals be so characterized, on average?

"Snapping" or "Going Around the Bend"? For individuals, there is mixed news about the diagnostic power of the phases. *No*, we have not yet identified such a point or zone. However: *Yes*, we have ample evidence that covariants reflect progressive deterioration, phases I $\longrightarrow$ VIII, as in the apparent consistency that the proportions of mental health "cases" versus "normals" increase as the phases advance. See Chapters IV and V for numerous similar covariants. Relatedly, the active/passive distinction also constitutes a way of searching for such breaking-points, although we presently know only that active $\longrightarrow$ passive movement is associated with phase movement I $\longrightarrow$ VIII.

Usefully, even this suggestive evidence implies helpful guides for practice. For example, as much as possible, develop policies, procedures, and structures to keep as many individuals as possible at the less-advanced stages and, having failed that, seek to reduce the proportion of an organization's cadre falling in advanced stages. In addition, as much as possible, monitor the active —> passive movement so as to schedule interventions while the situation is still relatively favorable.

The more-hopeful news—surprising and perhaps seminal, even if provisional—will take more time and space to detail. Basically, the available evidence implies that the phases *each* seem to tap gamma changes or differences, while the marker variables apparently reflect alpha-only changes or differences. And *Global Burnout* suggests a convenient way to get at "tipping points," which adds collective perspective to the individual costs suggested by "snapping" or "going around the bend."

Phases as Multiple Gamma Changes

Conceptual reasons imply, even require, at least one gamma change as the phases vary I —> VIII, but initial developmental work ups that ante (Golembiewski & Munzenrider, 1990). Many phases, or even all of them, may be said to isolate gamma changes or differences. This was initially surprising to us, but fits conveniently with such findings as the progressively-virulent profile of covariants, phase by phase, as well as with the relatively-stable shelving levels of individuals in phases over time. Such findings also are consistent with the view that movements between the phases require great energy for both worsening and improvement. This constitutes good/bad news, of course.

Table VIII.3. Ahmavaara's Analysis of MBI Factorial Structures of Respondents In Adjacent Phases, Site B

Paired-Comparisons	Intraclass Correlation Coefficients	
	$r =$	$r^2 =$
I vs. III.	44	19.4%
II vs. III	.40	16.0
III vs. IV	.62	38.4
IV vs. V	.49	24.0
V vs. VI.	.67	44.9
VI vs. VII	.64	41.0
VII vs. VIII	.67	44.9
	$\overline{X} = .561$	$\overline{X} = 32.7\%$

Let us now sketch some details of our early tests of phases as gamma changes or differences. Table VIII.3 provides partial evidence, abstracted from a longer treatment (Golembiewski & Munzenrider, 1988, esp. pp. 252-259), that respondents in adjacent phases "see" quite different psychological structures in the MBI items. Conventionally, a coefficient in the mid-.80's suggests the congruency of a pair of factorial structures, with the intraclass correlation coefficients in Table VIII.3 referring to both the pattern as well as the magnitude of the pairs of factorial structures. Those coefficients border on the earliest convention for isolating gamma (Golembiewski, Billingsley, & Yeager, 1976): that is, 50 percent or less of shared variance between pairs of observations indicate gamma.

Note also that the coefficients have a similar pattern for all other paired-comparisons (Golembiewski, 1990, pp. 262). So Table 8.3 does not in any way stack the deck.

These results are consistent with a logical implication of the phase model—that it contains at least one gamma difference—while the results also raise other issues. For example, the MBI items underlying the phase model of burnout help isolate the generally-consistent findings summarized in *Global Burnout*. And yet respondents classified in different phases structure those MBI items in substantially as well as subtly-different ways. That simultaneity at once is consistent with existing research on the phases, but also surprises and delights even as it startles concerning the formidable choice-making powers of our respondents.

In any case, much more remains to be said under this heading, but here we can go no further. If nothing else, the phase model promises a way of estimating gamma change that avoids the *cul-de-sac* associated with earlier estimates (e.g., Golembiewski, 1990, esp. pp. 255 ff). And that promise inspires hope about a future sensitivity in interpreting T_2 - T_1 effects far beyond our present capabilities.

Marker Variables as Alpha-Only

Table VIII.4. Ahmavaara Analysis of Factorial Structures of Worksite Descriptors of Respondents in Variously-Distant Phases, Site B

	"Distances" Between Phases in Paired-Comparisons						
	1	*2*	*3*	*4*	*5*	*6*	*7*
Mean r^2 intraclass correlations, in %	78.8	79.1	79.6	83.3	81.1	82.0	90.3

The evidence above gets general reinforcement from a different finding concerning the marker variables. At the very least, the difference implies the results concerning the phases are not somehow easily artefactual. The point has been made, in general, but deserves a bit of explicit support.

A few details sketch this suggestive but far-from-conclusive evidence. Broadly, when the factor structures to be compared involve responses from Site B to conventional marker variables—Job Involvement (White & Ruh, 1973), Job Tension at Work (Kahn et al., 1964), and Participation in Decisions at Work (White & Ruh, 1973)—alpha-only differences are generated by Ahmavaara's technique. Table VIII.4 illustrates these alpha-only differences for respondents classified in pairs of phases having "gaps" 1 —> 7. Alpha-only it is, with the average shared variance approximating 82 percent, which is substantially above the 50 percent cutting-point taken to indicate alpha-only change.

Some Urgent Caveats

This much having been written, we urge caution even as we encourage more-telling attention. Several caveats dominate. Practically, few data sets permit replication of the analytic approach above. For example, multiple factor analyses require perhaps about 10 times or more cases than the 23 MBI items, which puts the researcher in the position of providing a minimum N of 250 subjects. Given the general biomodality of distributions of the phases, not to mention the distributions skewed to the extreme phases observed in (for example) Japan, even far-larger data sets often can can be necessary.

Rather than force replications under less-than-optimal conditions, we simply note the findings at Site B contained in Tables VIII.3 and VIII.4. And we trust that the evidence summarized in *Global Burnout* will legitimate strategic research designs to test our findings in more-than-convenience populations. Conceptually, moreover, while attention-getting and even arresting, we cannot pretend to a reasonable sense of exactly what is going on in the findings we summarize above. In sum, research with trinitarian change has only fairly started.

MORE ABOUT A TWO-FACTOR THEORY OF AFFECT

An earlier volume on the phase model of burnout (Golembiewski & Munzenrider, 1988, pp. 250-253) proposes in its closing pages that its results are consistent with a two-factor theory of affect, and that constitutes the most extensive reach of this volume as well. The grasp of the phase model remains incomplete, but the research intervening between *Global Burnout* and *Phases of Burnout* only re-emphasizes the reasonableness of the linkages between the phases and the two-factor theory of affect.

Hence, these closing comments re-introduce the two-factor model, as well as re-establish some major linkages with the phase model. Two emphases follow. The first deals with a primer on the basic thought and research underlying the circumplex model. The second concerns some conceptual and applied connections between the two-factor theory and the phase model.

Précis of Two-Factor Theory

All science is alike in a fundamental regard: commonly, the search focuses on the type and number of independent factors required to account for the variations obsrved. That search applies to the phase model, to the two-factor theory, and to quantum physics as well.

As with burnout, zesty dispute exists concerning how to circumscribe self-reported affective states. Some observers require a dozen or more independent and monopolar factors (e.g., Nowlis & Nowlis, 1956), but a persistent as well as growing minority sees affective states as related "in a highly systemic fashion" (Russell, 1980, p. 1161) and hence as permitting parsimonious synthesis. For example, Schlosberg (1952) proposes that a two-dimensional space suffices to map self-reported affective states, and he adds that a circular arrangement is the simplest structure for organizing the several emotions.

Russell (1979, 1980) elaborates on Schlosberg's views while focusing on two basic bipolar dimensions: passive $<->$ active; and unpleasant $<->$ pleasant. These can constitute the axes of a two-dimensional space, and all affective states are defined as "vectors originating from the origin of [that simple] space." Russell concludes (1980, p. 1161) that: "...[eight illustrative] affective concepts fall in a circle in the following order: pleasure ($0°$), excitement ($45°$), arousal ($90°$), distress ($135°$), displeasure ($180°$), depression ($225°$), sleepiness ($270°$), and relaxation ($315°$)." Figure VIII.1 sketches the required two-dimensional space.

A few details provide further context. Russell began his analysis with three bipolar factors (Russell & Mehrabian, 1977), including dominance $<->$ submissiveness along with the two other basic dimensions. His later view is that the third dimension may capture additional variance, but only small amounts of it. Moreover, there seems to be a growing agreement that two bipolar factors are sufficient to satisfactorily express self-reported affective states (e.g., Thayer, 1978). These two required factors can be interpreted variously in different pieces of research, but opinion seems to favor two: degree of arousal, and pleasant $<->$ unpleasant (Russell, 1980, pp. 1171-1172).

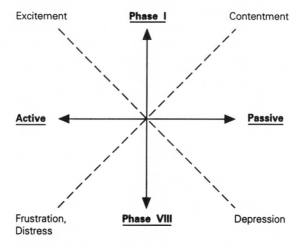

Source: Based on Russell (1980, p. 1164).

Figure VIII.1. Burnout Phases in a Two-Factor Theory of Affect

Phases and the Two-Factor Theory of Affect

It requires no great stretch to visualize some major points of contact between the phases and two-factory theory. In sum, the two-factor theory at once tethers and liberates the phase model of burnout, as can be illustrated in both conceptual and applied senses with the help of Figure VIII.1. Obviously, that figure substitutes the phases of burnout for the pleasant < —> unpleasant dimension of the two-factor theory; and the active/passive distinction provides the surrogate for "degree of arousal."

Overall, the two-factor theory fits with the analyses above. Consider the successful effort to ameliorate burnout at Site T, as abstracted in Table VII.17, which can be conceptualized as having work unit members who initially clustered in the two bottom quadrants in Figure VIII.1. That is, the large majority were in advanced phases of burnout, with one major difference: all were rated "active," excepting only two "passives." Without much forcing, these work unit members can be seen as initially in the bottom two quadrants: the "actives" can be put in the left quadrant, and the "passives" in the right quadrant. It requires only a little more imagination to describe the dominant cluster as initially experiencing "frustration, distress," while the minority cluster may qualify for the label "depression" or a related affective state in the bottom-right quadrant of Figure VIII.1.

Further, the effects of the interventions at Site T were such as to induce general movement toward the upper-left quadrant, where "excitement," or a close analog, seems to describe the resulting emotional tone (Golembiewski, Hilles, & Daly, 1987).

In a related way, the two-factor theory may provide a helpful perspective on the mixed research about "social support." Analysis has demonstrated that social support tends to vary inversely with the phases (e.g., Stevenson, 1988), but Figure VIII.1 urges the needs/to distinguish two possible general effects as well as to differentiate the designs that may induce one effect or the other. Simply, increases in social support may lead either to "excitement" or "contentment." Those outcomes may have significantly-different practical implications, and the two-factor theory thus echoes-by-implication precisely the warning inspired by detailed analysis of social support.

The critical alert implied by the two-factor theory can be encapsulated. Social support may serve as a platform for motivating constructive action to deal with similarly-perceived concerns and goals, or it may only support a kind of "misery loves company" reinforcing the original going-nowhereness. This big difference is suggested by Figure VIII.1.

Far more important, conceptually, the two-factor theory can be seen as integrating the burnout phases into *a general theory of affect.* Burnout need no longer sit uncomfortably among social science concepts, somewhat like a suspect stranger at a family outing: burnout can become central to the analysis of affect.

Practically, moreover, the two-factor theory also liberates in the sense that it implies a pair of useful guides for action. The two-factor theory reinforces the active vs. passive distinction for all phases of burnout, and this not only seems reasonable but also requires different kinds of designs for ameliorating burnout. Hence, the two-factor theory suggests different guides for intervening—when to step on the brakes, as it were, and when to apply the accelerator. In conclusion, the two-factor theory of emotions encourages a useful distinction. Directly, in its earliest formulation, all phases of advanced burnout were interpreted in terms of a critical deficit or deficiency—low *or* negative emotional slack in an individual, which in turn encouraged *an* approach to intervention. In sum, individuals in advanced phases were seen as easily overstimulated, with unattractive consequences. In contrast, the two-factor model suggests greater specificity for interventions. The "active" person in an advanced phase seems to have some emotional slack available, and that critical fact can provide a valuable margin-of-safety for interventions intended to ameliorate burnout. In the revised view, "passives" require more limited interventions. This required heterogeneity can be expressed in terms of specific management roles, policies, procedures, and structures (e.g., Golembiewski, 1990, esp. pp. 143-211).

And this closing-of-loops reflects the essentials of good science.

Two-Factor Theory Recessed?

After its promising start, the two-factor theory seems to have gone into eclipse. Its traces appear now and again (e.g., Darling & Hastings, 1994; Mehrabian, 1992), but it remains unclear whether the obvious eclipse is a waiting-period, a decorous recession, or a full retreat. In any case, the interpretation of phase model findings in terms of two-factor theory constitutes a useful exercise, and one version of how burnout can be integrated into broader theoretical frameworks.

THEORETIC AND PRACTICAL REASONS ENCOURAGE PERSEVERANCE

All in all, to conclude, there seem strong theoretic and practical reasons for accelerating research with the phase model. Perhaps the most compelling motivation derives from Chapter VI, which summarizes startling evidence about the persistence and incidence of the phases, in North American as well as global settings. This working conclusion holds despite the inadequacies in both North American and especially global panels of data about persistence.

Limitations aside, the substantially-consistent findings about virulence, incidence, and persistence of the phase model combine to a conclusion—to us, indeed, an inescapable conclusion. That is, the phases seem to covary in expected ways with most variables that are credibly associated with major relationships at work about which we are relatively certain. Many cases of advanced phase exist, and they have unattractive covariants, and the phases seem to have a substantial persistence. These findings are already threatening, and might well become overwhelming in the absence of well-targeted action.

And What of Tipping Points?

To illustrate one theoretic and practical linkage, consider "tipping points." Broadly, that notion provides a collective counterpart to phase assignments which have clear relevance for individuals even though they do not yet indicate specific points at which people "snap" or "go around the bend."

Can the phases be used to determine the proportions of members in specific advanced phases that will generate major effects in systems? Provisionally, yes. To explain, the concept goes back at least to efforts to understand differences in the incidences of lynchings of Afro-Americans (Matthews & Prothro, 1966, pp. 166-169), and was labelled the "tipping effect" by Schelling (1971, 1978). Nowadays, the notion has attracted such attention in several disciplines (e.g., Crane, 1991; Hutson et al., 1995) that even popular sources are getting into the act (Gladwell, 1966).

What is a "tipping point?" Some doggerel about nonlinearity provides an example. We authors quote loosely, even as we cringe:

> What can said about shaking ketchup in a bottle?
> To begin, none will come, and then a lot'll.

Crane (1991) provides empirical counterpoint in testing this hypothesis: that the percentage of "high status" role models in a community is strongly associated, *after a certain threshold*, with major changes in significant teenage behaviors—drop-out and pregnancy rates. Crane seems to have hit on something. Only minor differences occur as the incidence of such role models varies from 40 to 5 percent or so of the inhabitants of a neighborhood. However, further decreases seem to constitute a tipping point. When the proportion of high status persons drops to about 3 percent, both drop-out and pregnancy rates approximately double.

In sum, systems seem to be able to absorb individual changes, but only up to point beyond which systemic effects suddenly become manifest, and often in surprising force.

The phase model provides a built-in estimate of potential tipping points. What does the evidence suggest? The case for several noteworthy "break ponts" in the phases seems reasonable enough, as the review of gamma change suggests. Morover, numerous studies establish that the phases usually isolate 8 batches which differ significantly in mumerous covariants—physical as well as emotional systems, and so on.

However, this potential is not fully developed. The raw data about the incidence of the advanced phases imply great, even grave, collective problems associated with accumulating burnout. But those aggregate data do not isolate a tipping point for systems even as they urge prompt amelioration for individuals. Fortunately, the phase model provides direct and tested guidance for this amelioration (e.g., Golembiewski, 1990, esp. pp. 155-172), which can remedy personal discomforts before they cascade into systemic disruptions.

AND WHAT OF KELLY, MAURICE, AND MARY?

To conclude, then, what has been learned that can now be of help to people in today's organizations—to those like Kelly, Maurice, and Mary introduced in Chapter I? We authors conclude that much has been learned, even as far more remains to be done. Perhaps paramountly, *Global Burnout* provides useful estimates of the incidence of the phases, and we now have a better sense of their persistence in organizations. Now, moreover, one can hardly doubt the virulence of burnout effects, worldwide. And we have an early orientation toward remedying burnout, as well as inhibiting its initial development. But the key element is the availability of a valid and reliable operational definition of burnout.

Appendix A

North American Worksite Descriptions[1]

Site A is a product-line division of a multinational firm, with respondents representing the broad range of functions from research through audit, as well as all hierarchical levels from porter to president. The response rate approximates 55 percent, N = 296. Numerous details about this business appear elsewhere (e.g., Golembiewski, Munzenrider, & Stevenson, 1986, esp. pp. 9-10). The firm had attractive conditions of employ but was experiencing major market pressures.

Site B is a federal agency whose employees perform a range of jobs that can be emotionally arousing, with clients who can be "difficult." Moreover, the employees constitute a "horizontal slice" of a federal agency at low-to-middle-organization levels involving a range of jobs, nationwide. Specifically, the respondents come basically from the middle ranges of General Schedule (GS) levels, and encompass four classes of employees:

- managers and supervisors, largely GS 11-13, who constitute some 12 percent of the total responding population
- a cadre of employees from one of the established professions, at GS 7-12, or 6 percent
- employees who are in direct contact with clients, at GS levels 5-11, who comprise 70 percent of the respondents
- clerical personnel, generally at GS levels 4-6, who comprise 12 percent of the responding population.

The federal classified service has 18 GS levels, plus the supergrades.

With both management and union support, the national workforce of Site B volunteered responses to a questionnaire. The total population numbered 2,869, located at more than 50 sites across the country, with the field units differing in size but having similar although not identical compositions, missions, and roles. Responses vary for different items and for different purposes, but $N = 1,535$ for the most central usages here.

261

The response rate approximates 54 percent, and comparisons of several conventional demographics—age, sex, race, and so on—suggest that the responding population constitutes an analog of the total population (Stevenson, 1985).

Site C hosted a pilot study, but cannot be considered representative: a basic cohort of 204 constitutes all useful cases from 213 volunteers. Moreover, the 213 are a subset of a population of 600-plus enrollees in the 1989 start-up of the fourth yearly cycle of a well-received corporate wellness program, jauntily named "Be Your Best." In turn, this enrolling population was a subset of the total local employment of some 1,800 who were eligible for the wellness program.

All physiological data were gathered at the time of registration for this fourth wellness cycle. Some of the self-report data were provided at the same time, but an administrative error necessitated a delay of about a month in securing most self-report data. Especially because of the stability of the self-report data demonstrated in other settings (e.g., Golembiewski & Boss, 1991), this delay does not seem critical.

Despite these reservations about representativeness, the 204 research volunteers seem a reasonable analog of both participating and total employees. Several demographics support this general conclusion. Thus, the hierarchical level of respondents closely parallels actual employment:

	$N =$	$\% =$
Executives	12	5.6
Middle Managers	33	15.5
Supervisors	51	23.9
Operators or Workers	116	54.5
No identification	1	0.5
	213	100.0%

Relatedly, gender and age of the volunteers and total employment track reasonably. Respondents were 47.6 percent female, with 21.7 percent being under 30 years of age and an additional 44.1 percent being less than 40. Tl*Site D* participants are a subset of both of two populations: total employment of about 2,400; and a wellness program registration approximating 1,150. Thus, the participation rate in this research can be set at 32.6 percent or 68.1 percent, depending upon the denominator one chooses. $N = 783$.

The research population can be considered a reasonable analog of total employment, as judged by level, age, and gender. Participants are 55.9 percent female; and the largest cohort of participants is in the age group 30-39 (41.4 percent), with about 23 percent each being under 30 and between

40-49, 9.3 percent being 50-60 years of age, about 2.8 percent being over 60, for a mean of 37.3 years. Given 6.9 percent missing cases, respondents come from four levels of organization:

executives	7.3 percent
middle managers	10.9 percent
supervisors	20.6 percent
employees	54.5 percent

Participants come from 7 major departments of the firm, which vary only in random ways on distributions of the 8-phases of burnout assigned to members ($F = .8163, p > .56$).

No doubt, some self-selectivity occurred, both individual and organizational. Thus, about 50 percent of enrollees in the wellness program signed release forms, and some may reasonably argue that these are dominantly individuals who feel good about the program as well as themselves.

Site E is Site A after 1 year, following a comprehensive effort at change involving a shift from "loyalty" to "competence" as the guiding metaphor for corporate culture, policies, and procedures. The response rate approximates 65 percent.

Site F is a collection of Chartered Canadian Accountants who served their several firms in personnel roles and who were attending a specialized training course.

Site G involves a mailed survey to middle-level and senior Canadian managers, $N = 244$ (Cahoon & Rowney, 1984). Respondents were volunteers from firms and public agencies. The stratified sample was cross-matched by sex and hierarchical level.

Site H involves all employees of a hospital in a western Canadian province, excepting only doctors (Boudreau, 1986). Phase assignments totalled 396. The hospital is full-care and comprehensive, and serves a central city of medium size as well as residents of a large surrounding area involved in large-scale agriculture.

Site I refers to police managers from all Canadian levels—federal, provincial, regional, and municipal. $N = 135$. These police were attending a management course at the Canadian Police College.

A slightly-different distribution of phases has been published (Loo, 1994), but various modifications were made here in collaboration with Loo. For example, two of the MBI's original Emotional Exhaustion items were re-scored as Depersonalization, to be consistent with the adaptations discussed in Chapter II.

Site J involves members of a nurses' union in an eastern Canadian province.

Site K involves a corporate chain of life-care retirement communities at 23 locations, and surveys all direct-care employees ($N = 2,123$). Each location has five major organization units: General Administration, Plant Maintenance, Dietary, Housekeeping and Laundry, and Resident Care. The overall response rate approximates 90 percent. No significant differences exist between response rates at the several sites; and virtually all missing cases are part-time help or those who for various reasons were not at work during the hour or so when data were gathered at each local site. The respondents are substantially female, although no specific figure is available.

Site L ($N = 864$) involves employees from the midwestern U.S. region of retirement communities owned by a national corporation (Deckard, 1985). Ten facilities are represented, and 76 percent of all employees participated in the survey. The respondents are largely female (75 percent), with a mean age of 32 and a median age of 30 years. Most of the uncaptured cases involve part-time employees not scheduled for work during periods when the survey administrations took place. A comparison of demographics implies that the responding population adequately represents total employment.

Each of the 10 facilities is structured bureaucratically, with five major departments: General Administration, Plant Maintenance, Dietary, Housekeeping and Laundry, and Resident Care.

Site M involves operating and supervisory employees of a national chain of nursing homes, $N = 2,389$. The chain is generally considered the "Cadillac" of its type (see Rountree, 1982).

Site N includes salespersons and supervisors from a small hardware firm in the mid-west. Response rate is 100 percent.

Site O is the total population of MBA students at a western Canadian university.

Site P includes enrollees at the Police College in Ontario, Canada.

Site Q is an exploration firm in the Canadian oil industry. All employees volunteered responses.

Site R represents the total enrollment of an OB course in a western Canadian university.

Site S constitutes the total enrollment of an undergraduate course in business policy at a western Canadian university.

Site T responses come from corporate HR professional staff of a large firm in the health-care business fielding an effort to ameliorate burnout, which extended over several years. This analysis usually refers to a pre-test and to a short post-test about some 5 months after planned interventions had ended, with both surveys tracking phase assignments and the Work Environment Survey. Data on turnover also were available from corporate records.

Site U involves the executives and middle managers of a city probation office in a western state.

Site V was an educational setting in Canada hosting a program for local police, both male and female.

Site W represents the top three executive and managerial levels of a medical specialties firm. Response rate is 100 percent.

Site X is a clerical section in a municipal government in western Canada.

Site Y is Site X, following a cut-back announcement.

Site Z involves laborers for a local government in western Canada.

Site AA involves the laborers from Site Z after a layoff announcement.

Site BB involves all members of group dental practice A.

Site CC involves all members of group dental practice B.

Site DD is a full-service, non-profit, denominational hospital in the United States, with respondents representing all employees, excluding doctors.

Site EE refers to a full-service, non-profit, denominational hospital, in a western state, with respondents representing all employees, excluding doctors.

Site FF involves all service employees of a midwestern U.S. life-care retirement community, $N = 111$, with a workforce that is 75 percent female (Golembiewski, Deckard, & Rountree, 1989).

Site GG is an *ad hoc* collection of hospital administrators from different locations attending a workshop.

Site HH is post-test at Site FF after 1 year. $N = 89$.

Site II, $N = 196$, involves all employees of a full-care, regional hospital in a Canadian agricultural area, excluding doctors.

Site JJ, $N = 91$, with respondents constituting the entire graduating class of a midwestern state police academy.

Site KK includes 986 Florida teachers from grades K through 6. Details about the population, almost all female, are available in Harrison (1990). She used only 7 of the 8 MBI items regularly used for Hi/Lo assignments on Depersonalization, and the relevant universal norm was adjusted accordingly.

Site LL $N = 622$, is a composite population (Burke & Greenglass, 1989, 1991; Golembiewski & Boss, 1991). Three sub-groups are included:

1. a small division of a consumer goods firm, prior to a planned intervention to reduce stressors. The response rate approximates 55 percent, and $N = 113$
2. a hospital workforce, excluding doctors, with a response rate of 70 percent, and $N = 202$
3. responses from teachers in several public schools in Canada, $N = 307$.

Site MM is an aggregate composed of the first and third sites above about one year apart, and the second set at a two-year interval (Golembiewski & Boss, 1991).

Site NN is a collection of Canadian elementary and secondary school teachers. Response rate approximates 33 percent (Burke & Greenglass, 1989). $N = 746$, with 51 percent males. Many other demographics are specified.

For *Site OO*, the population numbers 1,106, which approximates a response rate of 51.5 percent (Aldinger, 1993).

The responding population mirrors the Air Force closely in some regards, but not all. Thus women constituted 15.1 percent of the respondents, but 27.4 percent of all AF personnel. In contrast, ethnicity of respondents closely parallels AF demographics: 81.3 percent are white, 13.0 percent black, 3.2 were hispanic, and 2.5 are either "other" or unknown. The marital status of respondents also approximate AF-wide figures, with both being in the mid-60 percent range. Enlisted men are overrepresented, but the population includes 114 officers up to the level of colonel.

Site PP includes 213 police from 2 city departments, with a response rate of 48.5 percent. Cities V and C differ in character and in numerous features (Golembiewski, Lloyd, & Scherb, 1992, esp. pp. 427-428).

Site QQ represents a collection of Canadian teachers who responded to a mailed questionnaire, with a 40 percent response rate. Authors report data for only the first wave of respondents who also responded to a survey one year later (Burke & Greenglass, 1991).

Site RR represents matched respondents in a follow-up of respondents described directly above. Responses totalled 362, for a response rate of 43 percent. 307 matches with Site QQ were generated.

Site SS data come from managerial personnel in 172 medical centers of the Veterans' Administration, $N = 352$, with a response rate of over 82 percent. The average respondent is white, 52 years of age, married, with almost 20 years in the VA.

Site TT represents data from blue collar employees at several levels of multiple locations of a firm that is an energy distributor. Respondents are well-paid by community standards, have long tenures, and substantial training. $N = 829$. Recent company actions have stressed the workforce, and the future promises no respite.

Site UU data come from 626 operators and first-line supervisors at two heavy industry worksites. Autonomous teams constitute the basic pattern for structuring (Novelli, Elloy, & Flynn, 1989).

Site VV respondents come from a people-helping southeastern state agency with a rural constituency. $N = 308$, with a response rate of 83.7 percent. Respondents are 45 percent female. The population has over 40 percent of the respondents reporting family incomes greater than $50,000.

Site WW represents physicians in several group practices. $N = 216$ (Deckard, 1992).

Site XX is a convenience collection of MBA students at an eastern U.S. university (Seltzer & Lynn, 1994). A panel of 661 students was contacted as part of a research project on leadership and burnout. Exact response rate is not known, but surpassed 31 percent.

Site YY is a sample matched to those Site XX respondents who, after 2 years, again volunteered responses to a questionnaire. One goal was to assess changes in burnout phases over the interval, but authors provide a strong argument that persons with the most-advanced phases probably were the least-likely respondents to the second wave (Seltzer & Lynn, 1994, esp. p. 246).

Site ZZ, $N = 161$, with most respondents being female (59.6 percent) care-providers at a school for the physically disadvantaged in a southeastern state. The facility was under great and growing financial pressure (Billingsley, 1990).

Site AAA respondents come from a comprehensive hospital in a Middle Atlantic state, excluding doctors. Data were gathered at three points in time: a 1991 pre-test; one year later; and two years later, or 1993. Sub-Ns vary. Munzenrider (1995), reports phase assignments at each of the three time intervals.

For the 1991 data, or T_1, Sub-Ns for marker variables X phases vary from 285-289. In 1992, or T_2, Sub-Ns vary from 292 to 301; and for 1993, or T_3, Sub-Ns vary from 301-310.

Site BBB, $N = 238$, involves respondents from two firms—a manufacturing division and health insurance company. The design is longitudinal and the response rate approximates 60 percent of those who remained in employ during the observational period. Mean age was 36.4 years with a range of 21-64.

Site CCC, $N = 69$, represents an interagency board of federal executives meeting for training as well as business purposes.

Site DDD, aggregates respondents from a firm experiencing a Corporate Wellness Week. $N = 204$, and represents approximately a quarter of the population eligible for the corporate program.

Site EEE, $N = 743$, is a collection of respondents from a firm fielding a Corporate Wellness Week. Respondents come from all corporate levels and units, and approximate one-half of those participating in the Wellness Week.

Site FFF, $N = 79$, is an aggregate of two collections of federal executives assembled for training and development purposes.

Site GGG, $N = 18$, aggregates responses from all first-world or aboriginal students in a management course (Boudreau, 1995).

Site HHH is the full attendance, $N = 78$, of a collection of regional city and county managers attending a training session at a U.S. university.

Site III, $N = 183$, represents a "high technology" firm. Response rate is 31 percent, and all major functions are represented (Polok & Boss, 1994).

Site JJJ, $N = 1064$, which encompasses the field service of a federal agency, which is in the throes of serious transition (Gabris & Ihrke, 1995). The target population approximated 3000, with about 1400 being randomly selected to complete a survey, with the response rate approaching 80 percent.

Site KKK is a composite of several student populations in classes at a midwestern business school. For different worksite descriptors, N varies from 860 to 1,140. The data here deal only with five Job Descriptive Index variables and two other scales—Stressful Life Events and Daily Hassles. Data on several personality variables also were drawn but have not yet been analyzed—Rotter's I/E Scale and eight Myers-Briggs type indicators.

NOTE

1. Sites which get major attention in the text get more extensive coverage than sites referred to largely or exclusively in tables, as in Chapter VI's summaries of the incidence or the persistence of phases.

Appendix B

Global Worksite Descriptions[1]

Belarus A is an aggregate from 7 large organizations in the city of Minsk in Belarus. Some of the parent organizations are huge.

The total usable returns ($N = 312$ of 342 returns) constitute a small fraction of the total population of the 7 organizations, but virtually all of the distributed questionnaires were completed. Personal contacts determined the distribution of questionnaires. The expectation is that only robust covariants of burnout will surface.

Respondents average 41 years of age and tend to be long-term employees, with only about 10 percent having less than 10 years of service with their employing organization and a full 3 percent reporting 40 years or more of employment. Respondents represent 4 hierarchical levels—from executive to operator—but only 57 percent report being rank-and-file and 20 percent say they are supervisors. Respondents are dominantly female—70.7 percent.

Belarus B aggregates respondents from seven worksites—three hospital settings and four involving factory workers, farmers, and teachers. All respondents come from in and around Gomel. Response rates vary widely from setting to setting. $N = 792$, and the collection is 57 percent male.

Belarus C, $N = 200$, is 71.0 percent female.

Belarus D, $N = 474$, is 65.5 percent female.

Belarus E, $N = 93$, with 64.8 percent being female.

Belarus F, $N = 197$, adds 89 cases to Belarus E, and both sub-sets were gathered at the same time from the same convenience population. Communication and postal problems resulted in separation of the two subsets. Belarus E was analyzed approximately 6 months before the additional cases were received in Canada. Belarus F reports on the full data-set.

Canada A, $N = 130$, is a composite collection with many internal differences: for example, 25.2 percent factory workers from a western province and 74.8 percent teachers from an eastern school district; 76.2 percent female; and 89.1 full-time vs. part-time or casual employees (Duplicea & Hubert, 1996).

269

China A is a convenience collection, middle managers and above, assembled from several industrialized settings on mainland China as audiences for a lecture tour. Response rates approximate 100 percent, but respondents represent many worksettings and were highly-selected participants.

China B volunteers came from 10 departments of Beijing's municipal government, with no one unit providing less than 2.7 percent of the population and none providing more than 20.1 percent. The departments include functionally-differentiated units (e.g., audit and personnel), those departmentalized on the basis of area (e.g., western and eastern districts), and also those featuring specific services (e.g., medicine or drugs and preservation of cultural relics). In addition, both "line" and "staff" departments are represented. However, no case can be made for this population as "representative." Beijing's jurisdiction extends to some 13 million inhabitants, with about 75 percent residing in 8 urban districts and the remainder in 5 rural counties. There are about 50 municipal departments.

$N = 259$ for the responding population, whose major aggregate features may be summarized briefly. Respondents are:

- about equally divided in terms of gender (48.3 percent female)
- largely in operating roles (60 percent) but also include over one-quarter first-line supervisors and a bit less than 15 percent who self-identify as middle managers
- a "maturing" workforce with about 11 percent having less than 2 years of tenure and with 40 percent having between 10-25 years of experience.

Ghana A, $N = 287$, come from three urban hospitals. Volunteers from the settings approximate 10 percent of the total employment, $N = 3,710$, including doctors. The respondents who provided demographics are 77.7 percent female, and about one-third of the respondents declined to provide demographics as well as to estimate their productivity (Fiadzo, 1995).

Israel A, 100 nurses, all females, in a composite population.

Italy A, includes all professional employees of a consulting firm in a major city. $N = 10$, and response rate is 100 percent.

Japan A, $N = 981$, involves respondents from 6 health-care locations on Hokkaido. All employees were solicited at worksettings typically in central-city locations. The overall response rate approximates 69 percent, but varies widely between locations.

Japan B, $N = 503$, aggregates respondents from the central islands, who are dominately business employees. Response rates at several locations were high, although no specific record was kept.

Japan C, is a composite population from two northern islands. Respondents ($N = 352$) come from five locations:

- young technical workers in a machinery factory training course, all males, $N = 23$. Ages range from 21-24.
- all Chief Nurses from numerous Hokkaido hospitals at a leadership training seminar, $N = 84$. All are female, average 33.4 years of age, and have a mean of 11.2 years of experience.
- all staff nurses from one public Honshu hospital at a seminar, $N = 46$. All are female, average 30.1 years of age, and have 8.2 years average employment in their specialty.
- 76.5 percent of Chief Nurses and staff nurses from a single Honshu hospital, with $N = 199$ of a total of 260 nurses. The hospital has 408 employees, including medical doctors. All nurses but one are female, average 31 years of age, and have 7.9 years of experience, on average.
- employees of local taxi company, $N = 35$, including 10 of 12 administrators and clerical staff as well as 25 of 120 drivers, randomly selected. Respondents average 32.9 years in age, and include 16 females as well as 19 males. Data about job experience are not available.

Diversity in the sources of subjects was deliberately sought, on the ground that the expected relationships with covariants of burnout should exist, independent of locus. Hence, Japan C constitutes a deliberately-difficult replication of North American results.

Korea A, $N = 61$, represents expatriate students in several graduate programs at a major U.S. state university. The response rate approximates 60 percent.

Poland A, consists of middle-level professionals and managers from several government ministries, $N = 181$. Sampling was casual.

Saudi Arabia A, $N = 264$, represents the professional trainers and support personnel of the Institute of Public Administration, Riyad, Saudi Arabia. The response rate for these middle-level public employees approximates 80 percent (Al-Ebedah, 1995).

Taiwan A, respondents come from 3 municipal police departments in Taiwan, who contributed 623 total usable sets of responses. The response rate approximates 65 percent.

The demographics suggest a close analog of the responding population to all police forces on the island. Respondents are 89.7 percent male, with a median age of 29, and with 71.2 percent having less than 10 years of police service. Seven types of police are represented—administrative, foreign affairs, traffic control, national security, and so on—with about 15.6 percent having "inside" or office jobs. All ranks of police are represented in the following proportions:

	National Rank	%
Non-Commissioned Ranks ...	1 (Lowest)	1.6
	2	77.2
	3	8.7
Officer Ranks	4	4.3
	5	6.1
	6	1.1
	7 (Highest)	1.0

On Taiwan, the lowest-ranked role (1) is identified as "one stripe, one star" and the highest-ranked (7) as "two stripes, three stars."

Taiwan B, involves street-level bureaucrats at 9 of 12 total levels of hierarchical rank, $N = 553$, in the municipal government of Taipei, Taiwan. Response rate was 49 percent. Women outnumbered male respondents by a few cases, although 43 otherwise usable response sheets did not identify gender. Nearly 26 percent of the respondents were older than 51 and nearly 48 percent were younger than 30. Length of service with the agency was correspondingly variable: nearly 32 percent had been employed by the city for 20 years or more, while 18.3 percent had less than 1 year of service. Almost exactly 86 percent fall in the lowest five grade levels. About 75 percent indicated they were married.

Yugoslavia A, $N = 100$, combines data from managerial and supervisory levels at two worksettings, both industrial.

NOTE

1. Sites receiving major attention in the text get more extensive coverage than sites referred to largely or exclusively in tables referring to the incidence or the persistence of phases.

MBI Sub-Domains and General Item Content, Site B, as Adapted[1]

I. Depersonalization (modified)

—uncomfortable about
personal treatment
of co-workers

—more callous

—people seen as
objects

—don't care
about fellow
employees

—strained by working
with people

—stressed by
working with
people

—blamed for
problems of others

II. Personal Accomplishment, Reversed

—understand feelings
of co-workers

—create relaxed
atmosphere at work

—effective in dealing
with problems of co-
workers

—exhilarated

—doing things that
are worthwhile

—influence co-workers
positively

—calmly deal with
emotional
situations

—energetic

III. Emotional Exhaustion (modified)

—emotionally drained
—used up
—fatigued in morning
—burned out

—frustrated
—work too hard
—at end of rope

Note: The full wording appears in Maslach and Jackson (1982). Adaptations here involve changes in
targeting (e.g., co-workers rather than clients) as well as relocations of some items to sub-domains
different from original assignments.

References

Note: * designates a citation in 1990 panel of global studies. ** designates a citation in 1991-1995 panel of global studies.

Adams, J.C. (1978). Improving stress management. In W.W. Burke (Ed.), *The cutting edge* (pp. 246-261).

Adams, J.D. (1981). *Health, stress, and your life style.* Arlington, VA: NTL Institute.

Ahmavaara, Y. (1954). Transformation analysis of factorial data. *Annals of the Academy of Science Fennicae, Series B, 881,* 54-59.

Aldinger, R.T. (1993). *Burnout in the Air Force.* Unpublished doctoral dissertation, University of Georgia, Athens.

Altemeyer, B. (1981). *Right-wing authoritarianism.* Winnipeg, Canada: University of Minnesota Press.

**Al-Ebedah, N. (1995). *A survey of staff burnout and quality of worklife at Institute of Public Administration Saudi Arabia.* Unpublished Master's Thesis, Pennsylvania State University at Harrisburg.

Anderson, C.M. (1982). *Effects of peer support groups on levels of burnout among mental-health professionals.* Unpublished doctoral dissertation, University of Washington, Seattle.

Applebaum, S.H. (1981). *Stress management.* Rockville, MD: Aspen Systems Corporation.

**Appels, A., & Schouten, E. (1991). Burnout as a risk factor for coronary heart disease. *Behavioral Medicine, 17*(1), 53-59.

Armenakis, A. (1988). A review of research on the change typology. In W.A. Pasmore, & R.W. Woodman (Eds.), *Research in organizational change and development* (Volume 2, pp. 163-194).

Armistead, G. (1993). *Burnout in an energy distribution system.* Working paper. Montgomery, AL.

Ashforth, B.E. (1989). The experience of powerlessness in organizations. *Organizational Behavior and Human Decision Processes, 43,* 207-242.

**Aström, S. (1992). Attitudes, empathy and burnout among staff in geriatric and psychogeriatric care. *Scandinavian Journal of Caring Sciences, 6*(3), 160.

**Aström, S., Nilsson, M., Norberg, A., Sandman, P.O., & Winblad, B. (1991). Staff burnout in dementia care. *International Journal of Nursing Studies, 28*(1), 65-75.

*Aström, S., Nilsson, M., Norberg, A., & Winblad, B. (1990). Empathy, experience of burnout and attitudes toward demented patients among nursing staff in geriatric care. *Journal of Advanced Nursing, 15,* 1236-1244.

Heart study: Good news for driven men. (1988, January 14). *Atlanta Constitution,* pp. 1A, 10A.

Bacharach, S.B., Magjuka, R., Torbert, P., & Torres, D. (Eds.). (1991). *Research in the sociology of organizations*. Greenwich, CT: JAI Press.

Barad, C.B. (1979). *Study of burn-out syndrome among Social Security Administration field public-contact employees*. Unpublished Manuscript, Social Security Administration.

Baritz, L. (1960). *The servants of power*. Middletown, CT: Wesleyan University Press.

Barnard, C.I. (1938). *The functions of the executive*. Boston, MA: Harvard University Press.

Bass, B.M. (1990). *Bass and Stogdill's Handbook of Leadership*. New York: The Free Press.

Belcastro, P A., Gold, R.S., & Hays, L.C. (1983). Maslach burnout inventory: Factor structures for samples of teachers. *Psychological Reports, 53*, 364-366.

**Belfiore, M. (1994). The group takes care of itself: Art therapy to prevent burnout. *The Arts in Psychotherapy, 21*(2), 119-126.

**Bennett, L., Kelaher, M., & Ross, M. (1994). Quality of life in health care professionals: Burnout and its associated factors in HIV/AIDS related care. *Psychology and Health, 9*(4), 273-283.

Billingsley, W. (1990). *Preliminary data on burnout phases at a school for the hearing impaired*. Working paper.

Blau, G. (1981). An empirical investigation of job stress, social support, service length, and job strain. *Organizational Behavior and Human Performance, 27*, 279-302.

Boss, R.W. (1979). It doesn't matter if you win or lose, unless you're losing. *Journal of Applied Behavioral Science, 15*, 198-220.

Boss, R.W. (1983). Team building and the problem of regression. *Journal of Applied Behavioral Science, 19*, 279-302.

Boudreau, R.A. (1985). *Transition, revolution and metapsychology: A theoretic proposal for the development of criticism in social psychology*. Unpublished doctoral dissertation, University of Calgary, Alberta, Canada.

*Boudreau, R.A. (1986). *Burnout in a health-care setting*. Unpublished manuscript, University of Lethbridge, Alberta, Canada.

Boudreau, R.A. (1995). *First-world students in a management seminar*. Working Materials.

*Boudreau, R.A., & Golembiewski, R.T. (1989). Burnout and stress in American, Canadian, and Japanese work settings: Nomothetic and ideographic perspectives. *Kaihatsu Ronshu, 44*, 53-77.

*Boudreau, R.A., & Golembiewski, R.T. (1990). Modes of response to advanced burnout: Note on a Japanese urban health-care population. *Kaihatsu Ronshu: Journal of Development Policy Studies, 45*, 37-53.

**Boudreau, R.A., & Golembiewski, R.T. (1995, September 14-16). *Occupational health/burnout profiles of Belarussian, Canadian, and Japanese workers*. Paper presented at Conference on Work Stress and Health '95: Creating Healthier Workplaces. Washington, D.C.

**Boudreau, R.A., Golembiewski, R.T., Stephenson, B. L., & Paulence, R.L. (1996, March 28-30). *The burnout and hardiness of Belarussian workers*. Paper presented at 37th Annual Western Academy of Management. Banff, Alberta, Canada.

**Boudreau, R.A., & Hackson, D.L. (1990). Student stress: Is this snark a boojum? *Journal of Health and Human Resources Administration, 13*, 81-111.

Boudreau, R.A., & Levin, J. (1996a). *Burnout in Belarus, D*. Working Materials. Lethbridge University, Alberta, Canada.

**Boudreau, R. A., & Levin, J. (1996b). *Burnout in Belarus, E*. Working Materials. Lethbridge University, Alberta, Canada.

**Boudreau, R.A., & Levin, J. (1996c). *Working materials on Belarus F*. Lethbridge University, Alberta, Canada.

Boudreau, R.A., Zhilina, I., Zhilina, D., & Faiferman, V. (1996a). *Burnout in Belarus, B*. Working Materials.

**Boudreau, R.A., & Zhilina, I., Zhilina, D., & Faiferman, V. (1996b). *Burnout in Belarus, C.* Working Materials.

Bower, D.W. (1994). *Family circumstances and work performance among Georgia Cooperative Extension agents.* Unpublished doctoral dissertation, University of Georgia, Athens.

Bowers, D.G. (1973). OD techniques and their results in 23 organizations: The Michigan ICL study. *Journal of Applied Behavioral Science, 9,* 21-43.

Bowers, D.G., & Hausser, D.L. (1977). Work group types and intervention effects in organizational development. *Administrative Science Quarterly, 22,* 76-94.

Bray, M. (1913). The overstrain of nurses. *The Canadian Nurse, 9*(3), 153-157.

Bridges, W. (1980). *Transitions.* Reading, MA: Addison-Wesley.

Brown, G.W. (1974). Meaning, measurement, and stress of life events. In B.S. Dohrenwend & B.P. Dohrenwend (Eds.), *Stressful life events* (pp. 217-243).

Brudney, J.L. (1990). *Fostering volunteer programs in the public sector: Planning, initiating, and managing voluntary activities.* San Francisco: Jossey-Bass.

*Burden, R.L. (1988). Stress and the school psychologist. *School Psychology International, 9,* 55-59.

Burke, R.J. (1989). Toward a phase model of burnout. *Group & Organization Studies, 14*(1), 23-32.

Burke, R.J., & Deszca, G. (1986). Correlates of psychological burnout phases among police officers. *Human Relations, 39,* 487-501.

Burke, R. J., & E. R. Greenglass. (1994). Toward an understanding of work satisfactions and emotional well-being of school-based educators. *Stress Medicine, 10*(3), 177-184.

Burke, R.J., & Greenglass, E.R. (1994). Toward an understanding of work satisfactions and emotional well-being of school-based educators. *Stress Medicine, 10*(3), 177-184.

Burke, R.J., & Greenglass, E.R. (1989). Correlates of psychological burnout phases among teachers. *Journal of Health and Human Resources Administration, 12,* 46-62.

Burke, R.J., Greenglass, E.R., & Konarski, R. (1995). *Coping, work demands and psychological burnout among teachers.* Unpublished manuscript.

Burke, R.J., Shearer, J., & Deszca, G. (1984). Burnout among men and women in police work. *Journal of Health and Human Resources Administration, 7,* 162-188.

Burke, W.W. (Ed.). (1978b). *The cutting edge.* La Jolla, CA: University Associates.

Burke, W.W., & Hornstein, H. (Eds.). (1972). *The social technology of organization development.* Washington, DC: NTL Learning Resources.

**Buunk, B.P. (1990). Affiliation and helping interactions within organizations. In W. Stroebe & M. Hewstone (Eds.), *European review of social psychology,* (Vol. 1, pp. 293-322).

Buunk, B.P., & Schaufeli, W.B. (1993). Burnout: A perspective from social comparison theory. In W. Schaufeli, C. Maslach, & T. Marek (Eds.), *Professional Burnout* (pp. 53-73).

**Buunk, B.P., Schaufeli, W.B., & Ybema, J.F. (1990, September 24-27). *Occupational burnout.* Paper presented at ENOP Conference on Professional Burnout, Krakow, Poland.

Cahoon, A., & Rowney, J. (1984). Managerial burnout: A comparison by sex and level of responsibility. *Journal of Health and Human Resources Administration, 7,* 249-263.

Calvert, L.M. (1984, March 1-3). *Proceedings.* Annual Meeting of the Southwestern Division, Academy of Management, San Antonio, TX.

Campbell, A., Converse, P.E., Miller, W.E., & Stokes, D.E. (1960). *The American voter.* New York: Wiley.

Cannon, W.B. (1932). *The wisdom of the body.* Kegan Parl, Trench, Trubner.

*Capel, S.A. (1987). The incidence of and influences on stress and burnout in secondary school teachers. *British Journal of Educational Psychology, 57,* 279-288.

**Capel, S.A. (1991). A longitudinal study of burnout in teachers. *British Journal of Educational Psychology, 61,* 36-45.

Caplan, G. (1974). *Support systems and community mental health.* New York: Behavioral Publications.

Caplan, G., & Killilea, M. (Eds.). (1976). *Support systems and mutual help: Multidisciplinary explorations.* New York: Grune and Stratton.

Caplan, R.D., Cobb, S., French, Jr., J.R.P., Harrison, R.V., & Pinneau, S.R. (1975). *Job demands and worker health.* Washington, DC: U.S. Department of Health, Education, and Welfare, National Institute for Occupational Safety and Health.

Carpini, D.X.M., Siegel, R.S., & Snyder, R. (1983). Does it make any difference how you feel about your job?: An exploratory study of the relationship between job satisfaction and political orientations. *Micropolitics, 3,* 227-251.

Carroll, J.F.X., & White, W.L. (1982). Understanding burnout: Integrating individual and environmental factors within an ecological framework. In W.W. Paine (Ed.), *Job stress and burnout* (pp. 41-60).

**Chan, D.W., & Hui, E.K.P. (1995). Burnout and coping among Chinese secondary school teachers in Hong Kong. *British Journal of Educational Psychology, 65*(1), 15-25.

Chandler, A.D., Jr. (1962). *Strategy and structure.* Cambridge, MA: The MIT Press.

Chapple, E.D., & Sayles, L.R. (1961). *The measurement of management.* New York: Macmillan.

*Chen, W.W., & Lu, L.P. (1993-1994). Assessment of job-related burnout among health education specialists in Taiwan. *International Quarterly of Community Health Education, 14*(2), 207-214.

Cherniss, C. (1980a). *Professional burnout in human services.* Beverly Hills, CA: Sage Publications.

Cherniss, C. (1980b). *Staff burnout: Job stress in human services.* Beverly Hills, CA: Sage Publications.

Cherniss, C. (1989). Burnout in new professionals: A long-term follow-up study. *Journal of Health and Human Resources Administration, 12,* 11-27.

Cherniss, C. (1995). *Beyond burnout.* York and London: Routledge.

Cherniss, C., & Krants, D.L. (1983). The ideological community as an antidote to burnout in the human services. In B.A. Farber (Ed.), *Stress and burnout in the human service professions* (pp. 198-212).

**Cheku, W.H., & Rosen, S. (1994). Validating a "spurning scale" for teachers. *Current Psychology, 13*(3), 241-247.

**Cheku, W.H., Wong, K.W., & Rosen, S. (1994). The effects of spurning and social support on teacher burnout. *Journal of Social Behavior and Personality, 9*(4), 657-664.

Cobb, S. (1976). Social support as a moderator of life stress. *Psychosomatic Medicine, 38*(5), 300-314.

Cochran, R., & Robertson, A. (1973). *Social support and health.* New York: Academic Press.

Coelho, G.V., Hamburg, D.A., & Adams, J.E. (Eds.). (1974). *Coping and adaptation.* New York: Basic Books.

*Cohen, J. (1976). German and American workers: A comparative view of worker distress. *International Journal of Mental Health, 5,* 130-147.

Cohen, S., & Syme, S.L. (Eds). (1985). *Social support and health.* Orlando, FL: Academic Press.

Collins, G.R. (1977). Burn-out: The hazard of professional people-helpers. *Christianity Today,* 12-14.

Cooper, C.L. (Ed.). (1983). *Stress research: Issues for the eighties.* New York: Wiley.

**Cooper, C.L., & Arbose, J. (1984). Executive stress goes global. *International Management, 39,* 42-48.

*Cooper, C.L., & Hensman, R. (1985). A comparative investigation of executive stress: A ten-nation study. *Stress Medicine, 1,* 295-301.

Cooper, C.L., & Payne, R. (Eds.). (1988). *Causes, coping and consequences of stress at work.* New York: John Wiley.

Cooper, C.L., & Robertson, I.T. (Eds.). (1995). *International review of industrial and organizational psychology* (Vol. 10). New York: John Wiley.

Cordes, C.L., & Dougherty, T.W. (1993). A review and integration of research on job burnout. *Academy of Management Review, 18*(4), 621-656.

Cordes, Ç.L., Dougherty, T.W., & Blum, M. (1996). Patterns of burnout among mangers and professionals. *Journal of Occupational Behavior* (in press).

Cousins, N. (1983). *The healing heart: Antidotes to panic and helplessness.* New York: W.W. Norton.

Cox, T., Jr. (1993). *Cultural diversity in organizatons.* San Francisco: Berrett-Koehler.

Cox, T., Kuk, G., & Leiter, M.P. (1993). Burnout, health, work stress, and organizational healthiness. In W. Schaufeli, C. Maslach, & T. Marek (Eds.), *Professional burnout* (pp. 177-193).

Cox, T., Kuk, G., & Schur, H. (1991). *The meaningfulness of work to professional burnout.* Unpublished manuscript, University of Nottingham.

Crane, J. (1991). The epidemic theory of ghetto and neighborhood effects on dropping out and teenage childbearing. *American Journal of Sociology, 96,* 1226-1259.

Cronbach, L.J. (1951). Coefficient alpha and the internal structure of tests. *Psychometrika, 16,* 297-334.

Cross, C. (1973). The worker opinion survey: A measure of shopfloor satisfaction. *Occupational Psychology, 47,* 193-208.

Crowne, D., & Marlowe, D. (1964). *The approval motive.* New York: Wiley.

**Cruikshank, J. (1989). Burnout: An issue among Canadian community development workers. *Community Development Journal, 24*(1), 40-54.

Daft, R.L. (1984). Antecedents of significant and not-so-significant organizational research. In T.S. Bateman & G.R. Ferris (Eds.), *Method and analysis in organizational research* (pp. 3-14). Reston, VA: Reston Publishing Company, Inc.

Daley, M.R. (1979). Preventing worker burnout in child welfare. *Child Welfare, 48,* 443-450.

Darling, M.E., & Hastings, P.A. (1994). An exploration of the affect intensity measure in relation to extraversion and neuroticism. *Psychologie Canadienne, 35*(2a), 145.

Davis, S.M., & Lawrence, P.R. (1977). *Matrix.* Reading, MA: Addison Wesley.

Deal, T.E., & Kennedy, A.A. (1982). *Corporate cultures.* Reading, MA: Addison-Wesley.

Dean, A., & Linn, A. (1977). The stress buffering role of social support: Problems and prospects for systemic investigation. *Journal of Nervous and Mental Disease, 65* 403-417.

Deckard, G.J. (1985). *Work, stress, mood, and ecological dysfunction in health and social services settings.* Unpublished doctoral dissertation, University of Missouri, Columbia.

Deckard, G.J. (1992). *Burnout among selected physicians.* Working Materials.

Deckard, G.J., & Rountree, B.H. (1984). Burnout in dental hygiene. *Dental Hygiene, 58,* 307-313.

Deckard, G.J., Rountree, B.H., & Golembiewski, R.T. (1986). Worksite features and progressive burnout. *Journal of Health and Human Resources Administration, 9,* 38-45.

Deckard, G.J., Rountree, B.H., & Golembiewski, R.T. (1989). Work stressors, burnout, and agitation: A causal path analysis. *Journal of Health and Human Resources Administration, 12,* 95-111.

*DeFrank, R.S., Ivancevich, J.M., & Schweiger, D.M. (1988). Job stress and mental well-being: Similarities and differences among American, Japanese, and Indian managers. *Behavioral Medicine, 14,* 160-170.

**Dell'Erba, G., Venturi, P., Rizzo, F., Porcú, S., & Pancheri, P. (1994). Burnout and health status in Italian air traffic controllers. *Aviation, Space, and Environmental Medicine, 65*(4), 315-322.

Dohrenwend, B.S., & Dohrenwend, B.P. (Eds.). (1974). *Stressful life events: Their nature and effects.* New York: Wiley.

**Dolan, N. (1987). The relationship between burnout and job satisfaction in nurses. *Journal of Advanced Nursing, 12*(3), 3-12.

**Duplicea, L.-A., & Hubert, G. (1996). *Burnout among Canadian employees.* Unpublished Manuscript, University of Lethbridge, Alberta, Canada.

Duquette, A., Sandhu, B.K., & Beaudet, L. (1994). Factors related to nursing burnout: A review of empirical knowledge. *Issues in Mental Health Nursing, 15*(4), 337-358.

Dyer, W.G. (1977). *Team building.* Reading, MA: Addison-Wesley.

Eastwood, M.R. (1975). *The relation between physical and mental illness.* Toronto: University of Toronto Press.

Edelwich, J.H., & Brodsky, A. (1980). *Burnout: Stages of disillusionment in the helping professions.* New York: Human Sciences Press.

Elsdorfer, C., Cohen, D., Kleinman, A., & Maxim, P. (Eds.). (1980). *Theoretical bases for psychopathy.* New York: Spectrum.

Elden, J.M. (1981). Political efficacy at work. *American Political Science Review, 75*, 43-58.

Elloy, D., & Anderson, K.S. (1991). An exploratory analysis of burnout across dual-income and single-income families. *Journal of Health and Human Resources Administration, 13*, 457-469.

Etzion, D., & Pines, A. (1981). *Sex and culture as factors explaining reported coping behaviors of human service professionals.* Working paper No. 696181. Israel Institute of Business Research, Tel Aviv University.

*Etzion, D., & Pines, A. (1986). Sex and culture in burnout and coping among human service professionals. *Journal of Cross-Cultural Psychology 17*, 191-209.

*Etzion, D., Kafry, D., & Pines, A. (1982). Tedium among managers: A cross-cultural American-Israeli comparison. *Journal of Psychology & Judaism, 7*, 30-41.

*Etzion, D., Pines, A., & Kafry, D. (1983). Coping strategies and the experience of tedium: A cross-cultural comparison between Israelis and Americans. *Journal of Psychology & Judaism, 8*, 41-51.

**Evans, B.K., & Fischer, D.G. (1993). The nature of burnout: A study of the three-factor model of burnout in human service and non-human service samples. *Journal of Occupational and Organizational Psychology, 66*, 29-38.

*Evans, G.W., Palsane, M.N., & Carrere, S. (1987). Type A behavior and occupational stress: A cross-cultural study of blue-collar workers. *Journal of Personality & Social Psychology, 52*, 1002-1007.

Farber, B.A. (Ed.). (1983). *Stress and burnout in the human service professions.* New York: Pergamon.

**Fiadzo, E. (1995). *Data on burnout phases and marker variables from three Ghanian hospitals.* Working materials.

**Fiadzo, E., Golembiewski, R.T., Luo, H., Bradbury, M., & Rivera, T.L. (1995). *Burnout in Ghanaian hospitals: Phase model findings in sub-Saharan Africa.* Report prepared for Ghanaian health-care officials.

Fineman, S. (1985). *Social work stress and intervention.* Brookfield, VT: Gower Publishing.

**Firth, H., & Britton, P.G. (1989). Burnout: Absence and turnover amongst British nursing staff. *Journal of Occupational Psychology, 62*, 55-59.

*Firth, H., McIntee, J., & McKeown, P. (1985). Maslach Burnout Inventory: Factor structure and norms for British nursing staff. *Psychological Reports, 57*, 147-150.

*Firth, H., McIntee, J., McKeown, P., & Britton, P.G. (1986a). Burnout and professional depression: Related concepts? *Journal of Advanced Nursing 11*(6), 633-641.

**Firth, H., McIntee, J., McKeown, P., & Britton, P.G. (1986b). Interpersonal support amongst nurses at work. *Journal of Advanced Nursing, 11*(3), 273-282.

Fischer, H.J. (1983). A psychoanalytic view of burnout. In B.A. Farber (Ed.)., *Stress and burnout in the human service professions* (pp. 40-45).

Fox, E.L., & Mathews, D.K. (1981). *The philosophical basis of physical education and athletics.* Toronto: Saunders Publishing.

French, J.R.P., Jr., & Caplan, R.D. (1974). Organizational stress and individual strain. In A.J. Marrow (Ed.), *The failure of success* (pp. 30-60).

Freudenberger, H.J. (1974). Staff burnout. *Journal of Social Issues, 30*(1), 159-165.

Freudenberger, H.J. (1977). Burnout: The organizational menace. *Training and Development Journal, 31*, 26-27.

Freudenberger, H.J. (1980). *Burnout: The high cost of high achievement.* Garden City, NY: Anchor Press.

Fried, K., Rowland, M., & Ferris, G.R. (1984). The physiological measurement of work stress: A critique. *Personal Psychology, 37* 583-616.

Fried, Y. (1988). The future of physiological assessments in work situations. In Cooper, C.L., & Payne, R. (Eds.), *Causes, coping, and consequences of stress at work* (pp. 343-373).

Friedman, M., Rosenman, R.H., & Carroll, V. (1957). Changes in serum cholesterol and blood clotting time of men subject to cyclic variation in occupational stress. *Circulation, 27*, 852-861.

**Friesen, D., & Sarros, J.C. (1989). Sources of burnout among educators. *Journal of Organizational Behavior, 10*(2), 179-188.

Froggatt, K.L., & Cotton, J.L. (1984). Effects of sex and Type A behavior pattern on overload- and underload-induced stress: A laboratory investigation. In J.A. Pearce, & R.B. Robinson (Eds.), *Proceedings*, Annual Meeting of the Academy of Management, pp. 207-211.

Gabris, G.T., & Ihrke, D.M. (1995a, October 20). *Job burnout in a large federal agency: Phase model implications....* Paper prepared for delivery at Annual Meeting, Midwest Public Administration Conference, Grand Rapids, MI.

Gabris, G.T., & Ihrke, D.M. (1995b, December). *The phase model of burnout: Further evidence of expected patterns of behavior in a federal agency.* Working paper.

Ganster, D.C., & Schaubroeck, J. (1991). Work stress and employee health. *Journal of Management, 17*(2), 235-271.

Garber, J., & Seligman, M.E.P. (Eds.). (1980). *Human helplessness: Theory and applications.* New York: Academic Press.

Gardell, B., & Johanson, G. (1981). *Working life.* New York: Wiley.

Garden, A. (1991). Relationship between burnout and performance. *Psychological Reports, 68*, 963-977.

**Garden, A-M. (1987). Depersonalization: A valid dimension of burnout? *Human Relations, 9*, 545-560.

Gergen, K.J., Gulerce, A., & Misra, G. (1996). Pschological science in cultural context. *American Psychologist, 51*(5), 496-503.

Gibson, F., McGrath, A., & Reid, N. (1989). Occupational stress in social work. *British Journal of Social Work, 19*, 1-16.

Gillespie, D.F. (1981). Correlates for active and passive types of burnout. *Journal of Social Science Research, 4*(2), 1-16.

Gladwell, M. (1996, June 3). The tipping point. *The New Yorker*, pp. 32-38.

Glass, D.C., & Carver, C.S. (1980). Helplessness and the coronary-prone personality. In J. Garber & M.E.P. Seligman (Eds.), *Human Helplessness*, (pp. 223-243).

Goldberg, D.P. (1972). *The detection of psychiatric illness by questionnaire.* London: Oxford University Press.

Golembiewski, R.T. (1962). *The small group.* Chicago: University of Chicago Press.

Golembiewski, R.T. (1965). Small groups and large organizations. In J.G. March (Ed.), *Handbook of organizations*, pp. 87-141.

Golembiewski, R. T. (1977). Testing some stereotypes about the sexes in organizations: Differential centrality of work. *Human Resource Management, 16*, 21-24.

Golembiewski, R.T. (1978). *Public administration as a developing discipline* (Vols. 1 and 2). New York: Marcel Dekker.

Golembiewski, R.T. (1979). *Approaches to planned change*, (parts 1 and 2). New York: Marcel Dekker.

Golembiewski, R.T. (1982). Organization development (OD) interventions. In W.S. Paine (Ed.), *Job stress and burn-out* (pp. 229-253).

Golembiewski, R.T. (1983a). Social desirability and change in organizations. *Review of Business and Economic Research, 18*, 9-20.

Golembiewski, R.T. (1983b). The distribution of burnout among work groups. In D.D. Van Fleet (Ed.), *Proceedings* (pp. 158-163).

Golembiewski, R.T. (1984a). The persistence of burnout. In L.M. Calvert (Ed.), *Proceedings* (pp. 300-304).

Golembiewski, R.T. (1984b). Organizational and policy implications of a phase model of burnout. In L.R. Moise (Ed.), *Organizational policy and development* (Vol. 1, pp. 135-147).

Golembiewski, R.T. (1984c). Enriching the theory and practice of team building: Instrumentation for diagnosis and alternatives for design. In D.D. Warrick (Ed.), *Current developments in organization development* (pp. 98-113).

Golembiewski, R.T. (1985). Performance appraisal and burnout. In C.A. Kelley (Ed.), *Proceedings* (pp. 168-172).

Golembiewski, R.T. (1986a) Contours of social change. *Academy of Management Review, 11*, 550-556.

Golembiewski, R.T. (1986b). Organization analysis and praxis: Prominences of progress and stuckness. In C.L. Cooper & I. Robertson (Eds.), *International review of industrial and organizational psychology* (pp. 279-304). New York: Wiley.

Golembiewski, R.T., et al. (1986c). The epidemiology of progressive burnout: A primer. *Journal of Health and Human Resources Administration, 9*, 16-37.

Golembiewski, R.T. (1987). Social support and burnout as covariants of physical symptoms: Where to put marginal dollars. *Organization Development Journal, 5*, 90-98.

Golembiewski, R.T. (1989). A note on Leiter's study: Highlighting two models of burnout. *Group & Organization Studies, 14*(1), 5-13.

Golembiewski, R.T. (1990b). *Ironies in organizational development.* New Brunswick, NJ: Transaction.

Golembiewski, R.T. (1991). OD applications in developmental settings. In S. Bacharach, R. Magjuka, P. Torbert, & D. Torres (Eds.), *Research in the sociology of organizations* (pp. 201-263). Greenwich, CT: JAI Press.

Golembiewski, R.T. (1991). Organization development in the third world: Values, closeness-of-fit, and culture-boundedness. *International Journal of Human Resource Management, 2*, 39-53.

Golembiewski, R.T. (1993). *Handbook of organizational consultation.* New York: Marcel Dekker.

Golembiewski, R.T. (1995a). *Managing diversity in organizations.* University, AL: University of Alabama Press.

Golembiewski, R.T. (1995b). *Practical public management.* New York: Marcel Dekker.

Golembiewski, R.T., Aldinger, R.T., & Luo, H. (1996). Gender and the phase model of burnout: Highlighting an anomaly in a consistent pattern. *Journal of Health and Human Services Administration* (in press).

Golembiewski, R.T., Aldinger, R.T., & Munzenrider, R.F. (1996). Burnout in the U.S. Air Force. *Journal of Health and Human Services Administration* (in press).

Golembiewski, R.T., & Billingsley, K. (1980). Measuring change in OD panel designs: A response to critics. *Academy of Management Review, 5*, 97-104.

Golembiewski, R.T., Billingsley, K., & Yeager, S. (1976). Measuring change and persistence in human affairs: Types of change generated by OD designs. *Journal of Applied Behavioral Science, 12*, 133-157.

Golembiewski, R.T., & Blumberg, A. (1967). Confrontation as a training design in complex organizations: Attitudinal changes in a diversified population of managers. *Journal of Applied Behavioral Science, 3*, 524-547.

Golembiewski, R.T., & Blumberg, A. (1977). Sensitivity training and the laboratory approach. Itasca, IL: F.E. Peacock.

Golembiewski, R.T., & Boss, R.W. (1992). Phases of burnout as central in diagnosis and consultation: Individual level of analysis in organization development and change. In R.W. Woodman & W.A. Pasmore (Eds.), *Research in organizational development and change* (pp. 115-152). Greenwich, CT: JAI Press.

Golembiewski, R.T., & Boudreau, R.A. (1991). *Burnout among nurses.* Unpublished paper.

**Golembiewski, R.T., & Boudreau, R.A. (1992, March 25-28). *Trans-National perspectives on burnout: Is the phase model generic or culturally-bounded in a Japanese replication?* Paper prepared for delivery at the International Conference on Advances in Management, Orlando, FL.

**Golembiewski, R.T., Boudreau, R.A., Deckard, G.J., Goto, K., Munzenrider, R.F., Murai, T., & Scherb, K. (1994). Reports of task force on burnout norms. *Journal of Health and Human Resources Administration, 17*, 4-10.

**Golembiewski R.T., Boudreau, R.A., Goto, K., & Murai, T. (1992). Transnational perspectives on burnout: Is the phase model generic or culturally-bounded in a Japanese replication? *Kaihatsu Ronshu: Journal of Development Policy Studies, 50*, 33-53.

**Golembiewski, R.T., Boudreau, R.A., Goto, K., & Murai, T. (1993). Cultures, norms, and the phase model: Japan as a special case?. *Journal of Health and Human Resources Administration, 17*, 63-75.

Golembiewski, R.T., Boudreau, R.D., Goto, K., & Murai, T. (1993). Transnational perspectives on job burnout. *International Journal of Organizational Analysis, 1*, 7-27.

Golembiewski, R.T., Boudreau, R.A., Kim, B-S, Munzenrider, R.F., & Park, S-J. (1990, September 24-27). *Two aspects of burnout in cross-cultural settings: Are the phase model and its underlying MBI sub-domains generic?* Paper presented at the ENOP Conference on Professional Burnout, Krakw, Poland.

**Golembiewski, R.T., Boudreau, R.A., & Levin, R. (1996). Burnout in Belarus. *Journal of Health and Human Services Administration* (in press).

Golembiewski, R.T., Bower, D.W., & Kim, B-S. (1994a). Family features, performance at work, and phases of burnout. *Journal of Health and Human Resources Administration, 17*, 11-31.

Golembiewski, R.T., Bower, D.W., & Kim, B-S.. (1994b). Performance and phases of burnout. *Journal of Health and Human Resources Administration, 16*, 371-380.

Golembiewski, R.T., & Deckard, G.J. (1994). Physicians as a special case? *Journal of Health and Human Resources Administration, 17*, 63-75.

Golembiewski, R.T., Deckard, G.J., & Rountree, B.H. (1989). *The stability of burnout assignments: Measurement properties of the phase model.* Mimeo.

Golembiewski, R.T., & Hilles, R. (1979). *Toward the responsive organization.* Salt Lake City, UT: Brighton.

Golembiewski, R.T., Hilles, R., & Daly, R. (1987). Some effects of multiple OD interventions on burnout and worksite features. *Journal of Applied Behavioral Science, 23*, 295-314.

Golembiewski, R.T., Hilles, R., & Kagno, M. (1974). A longitudinal study of flexitime effects. *Journal of Applied Behavioral Science, 47*, 503-532.

Golembiewski, R.T., Hilles, R., & Kim, B-S. (1986, May 23-24). *Longitudinal effects of interventions targeted at advanced burnout, active mode.* Paper presented at Fourth Annual Conference on Organization Policy and Development, University of Louisville, KY.

Golembiewski, R.T., & Kiepper, A. (1976). MARTA: Toward an effective open giant. *Public Administration Review, 36,* 46-60.

Golembiewski, R.T., & Kiepper, A. (1983). Organizational transition in a fast-paced public project. *Public Administration Review, 43,* 246-254.

Golembiewski, R.T., & Kim, B-S. (1987). How the city manager sees self. *Dialogue, 9*(4), 59-70.

Golembiewski, R.T., & Kim, B-S. (1989). Self-esteem and phases of burnout. *Organization Development Journal, 7,* 51-58.

Golembiewski, R.T., & Kim, B-S. (1990). Burnout in police work. *The International Review of Police Development, 13*(4), 74-80.

Golembiewski, R.T., Lloyd, M., Scherb, K., & Munzenrider, R.F. (1992). Burnout and mental health among police officers. *Journal of Public Administration and Theory, 2,* 424-439.

**Golembiewski, R.T., & Luo, H. (1996). Burnout in Chinese municipal government. *Journal of Health and Human Services Administration* (in press).

Golembiewski, R.T., & Munzenrider, R.F. (1981). Efficacy of three versions of one burnout measure. *Journal of Health and Human Resources Administration 4,* 228-246.

Golembiewski, R.T., & Munzenrider, R.F. (1983). Testing three phase models of burnout. *Journal of Health and Human Resources Administration, 5,* 374-392.

Golembiewski, R.T., & Munzenrider, R.F. (1984a). Active and passive reactions to psychological burnout: Toward greater specificity in a phase model. *Journal of Health and Human Resources Administration, 7,* 264-289.

Golembiewski, R.T., & Munzenrider, R.F. (1984b). Phases of psychological burnout and organizational covariants: A replication using norms from a large population. *Journal of Health and Human Resources Administration, 6,* 290-323.

Golembiewski, R.T., & Munzenrider, R.F. (1986a). Profiling acute vs. chronic burnout, II: Mappings on a panel of established covariants. *Journal of Health and Human Resources Administration, 9* 296-315.

Golembiewski, R.T., & Munzenrider, R.F. (1986b). Profiling acute vs. chronic burnout, III: Phases and life events impacting on patterns of covariants. *Journal of Health and Human Resources Administration, 9,* 173-184.

Golembiewski, R.T., & Munzenrider, R.F. (1987b, March 30). *Is burnout idiosyncratic or generic? The congruence of factorial studies of the Maslach Burnout Inventory.* Paper prepared for delivery at the Annual Meeting, American Society for Public Administration, Boston.

Golembiewski, R.T., & Munzenrider, R.F. (1987c). Profiling acute vs. chronic burnout, IV: Active vs. passive modes of adaptation. *Journal of Health and Human Resources Administration, 10,* 97-111.

Golembiewski, R.T., & Munzenrider, R.F. (1988a). Burnout as an indicator of gamma change, I: Methodological perspectives on a crucial surrogacy. *Journal of Health and Human Resources Administration, 11,* 218-248.

Golembiewski, R.T., & Munzenrider, R.F. (1988b). Burnout as indicator of gamma change, II: State-like differences between phases. *Journal of Health and Human Resources Administration, 11,* 218-248.

Golembiewski, R.T., & Munzenrider, R.F. (1988c). *Phases of burnout.* New York: Praeger.

Golembiewski, R.T., & Munzenrider, R.F. (1989). Burnout as indicator of gamma change, III. *Journal of Health and Human Resources Administration, 12,* 245-260.

Golembiewski, R.T., & Munzenrider, R.F. (1990). Burnout as an indicator of gamma change, IV: Differences of degree in worksite descriptors. *Journal of Health and Human Resources Administration, 13*, 509-523.

Golembiewski, R.T., & Munzenrider, R.F. (1991a). Alternative combinations of phases of burnout: An illustrative exercise. *Journal of Health and Human Resources Administration, 13*, 489-507.

Golembiewski, R.T., & Munzenrider, R.F. (1991b). Burnout and mental health: A pilot study. *Organization Development Journal, 9*, 51-57.

Golembiewski, R.T., & Munzenrider, R.F. (1991c). Health-related covariants of phases of burnout: A pilot study. *Journal of Health and Human Resources Administration, 14*, 204-225.

Golembiewski, R.T., & Munzenrider, R.F. (1995). Blood chemistry covariants of phases of burnout: A pilot study. *Journal of Health and Human Resources Administration, 18*, 265-283.

Golembiewski, R.T., & Munzenrider, R.F. (1993a). *Blood chemistry and phases of burnout: A replication*. Working paper.

Golembiewski, R.T., & Munzenrider, R.F. (1993b). Health related covariants of phases of burnout: A replication. *Organization Development Journal, 11*, 1-10.

Golembiewski, R.T., Munzenrider, R.F., & Carter, D. (1981, September 27). Progressive phases of burnout and their implications for OD. In *Proceedings*, Organization Development Network, Semi-Annual Meeting, pp. 163-170.

Golembiewski, R.T., Munzenrider, R.F., Scherb, K., & Billingsley, W. (1992). Burnout and psychiatric cases: Early evidence of an association. *Anxiety, Stress, and Coping, 5*, 69-78.

Golembiewski, R.T., Munzenrider, R.F., & Stevenson, J.G. (1988). Centrality of burnout in a federal agency. *Review of Public Personnel Administration, 9*, 28-44.

Golembiewski, R.T., Munzenrider, R.F., & Stevenson, J.G. (1985). Profiling acute vs. chronic burnout: Theoretical issues, a surrogate, and elemental distributions. *Journal of Health and Human Resources Administration, 7*, 107-125.

Golembiewski, R.T., Munzenrider, R.F., & Stevenson, J.G. (1986). *Stress in organizations*. New York: Praeger.

Golembiewski, R.T., & Proehl, C.W. Jr. (1978). A survey of the empirical literature on flexible workhours: Character and consequences of a major innovation. *Academy of Management Review, 3*, 837-853.

Golembiewski, R.T., Proehl, Jr., C.W., & Sink, D. (1981). Success of OD applications in the public sector: Toting-up the score for a decade, more or less. *Public Administration Review, 41*, 679-682.

Golembiewski, R.T., Proehl, Jr., C.W., & Sink, D. (1982). Estimating the success of OD applications. *Training and Development Journal, 72*, 86-95.

Golembiewski, R.T., & Rountree, B.H. (1986). Phases of burnout and properties of work environments. *Organization Development Journal, 9*, 25-30.

Golembiewski, R.T., & Rountree, B.H. (1991). Releasing human potential for collaboration. *Public Administration Quarterly, 15*(1), 32-45.

Golembiewski, R.T., & Rountree, B.H. (1996a). System redesign in nursing, I: Action planning in a medical-surgical unit. *International Journal of Public Administration* (in press).

Golembiewski, R.T., & Rountree, B.H. (1996b). System redesign in nursing, II: Impact of intervention on worksite, stakeholders, and costs. *International Journal of Public Administration* (in press).

Golembiewski, R.T., Scherb, K., & Boudreau, R.A. (1993). Burnout in cross-national settings: Generic and model-specific perspectives. In W.B. Schaufeli, C. Maslach, & T. Marek (Eds.), *Professional burnout* (pp. 217-246).

286 / *Global Burnout*

Golembiewski, R.T., Scherb, K., Lloyd, M., & Munzenrider, R.F. (1992). Burnout and mental health among police officers. *Journal of Public Administration Research and Theory, 2*, 424-439.

Golembiewski, R.T., & Scicchitano, M.. (1983). Some demographics of psychological burnout. *International Journal of Public Administration, 5*, 435-448.

Golembiewski, R.T., Sun, B-C. (1990). Positive-findings bias in QWL studies. *Journal of Management, 16*, 665-674.

**Golembiewski, R.T., Sun, B-C., Lin, C-H., & Boudreau, R.A. (1995). Burnout and covariants among Taiwanese police: A cross-cultural replication of the phase model. In S.B. Prasad (Ed.), *Advances in international comparative management* (Vol. 10, pp. 145-162). Greenwich, CT: JAI Press.

Goodsell, C.T. (1994). *The case for bureaucracy*. Chatham, NJ: Chatham Home Publishers.

Gottlieb, B.H. (Ed.). (1981). *Social networks and social support*. Beverly Hills, CA: Sage Publications.

Gould, R. (1978). *Transformations*. New York: Simon and Schuster.

*Green, D.E., & Walkey, F.H. (1988). A confirmation of the three-factor structure of the Maslach Burnout Inventory. *Educational & Psychological Measurement, 48*, 579-585.

**Green, D.E., Walkey, F.H., & Taylor, A.J.W. (1991). The three-factor structure of the Maslach Burnout Inventory: A multicultural, multinational confirmatory study. *Journal of Social Behavior and Personality, 6*(3), 453-472.

Greenglass, E.R., & Burke, R.J. (1988). Work and family precursors of burnout in teachers: Sex differences. *Sex Roles, 18*(3/4), 215-229.

Greenglass, E.R., Fiksenbaum, L., & Burke, R.J. (1994). The relationship between social support and burnout over time in teachers. *Journal of Social Behavior and Personality, 9*(2), 219-230.

Greer, C.R., & Castro, M.A.D. (1986). The relationship between perceived unit effectiveness and occupational stress. *Journal of Applied Behavioral Science, 22*, 159-176.

Greiner, G.M. (1992). The phase versus traditional approach to burnout diagnosis. *Group & Organization Management, 17*, 370-379.

**Groenestn, E., Buunk, A.P., & Schaufeli, W.B. (1992). Het besmettingegevaar bij burnout (Symptom contagiousness and burnout.) In R.W. Meertens, A.P. Buunk, P.A.M. van Lange, & B. Verplanken (Eds.), *Sociale psychologie en beinvloeding van intermenselijke e gezondheidsproblemen* (pp. 88-103). Den Haag: VUGA.

Gryskiewicz, N., & Buttner, E.H. (1992). Testing the robustness of the progressive phase model for a sample of entrepreneurs. *Educational and Psychological Measurement, 52*, 747-751.

Guilford, J. (1950). *Fundamental statistics in psychology and education*. New York: McGraw-Hill.

Guilford, J. (1954). *Psychometric methods*. New York: McGraw-Hill.

Gurr, T. (1970). *Why men rebel*. Princeton, NJ: Princeton University Press.

Haack, M.R. (1980). *Burnout intervention with nurses*. Unpublished doctoral dissertation, University of Illinois Medical Center.

Hackman, J.R., & Oldham, G.R. (1980). *Work redesign*. Reading, MA: Addison-Wesley.

** Hallberg, I.R. (1994). Systematic clinical supervision in a child psychiatric ward: Satisfaction with nursing care, tedium, burnout, and the nurses' own report on the effects of it. *Archives of Psychiatric Nursing, 8*(1), 44-52.

Harari, H., Jones, C.A., & Sek, H. (1988). Stress syndromes and stress predictors in American and Polish college students. *Journal of Cross-Cultural Psychology, 19*, 243-255.

Harris, R.T., & Porras, J.L. (1978). The consequences of large system change in practice: An empirical assessment. In J.C. Susbauer, *Proceedings '78*, pp. 298-302.

Harrison, E.A. (1990). *An investigation of the relationship between perceived teacher burnout and organizational climate in elementary schools*. Unpublished doctoral dissertation, University of South Florida, Tampa, FL.

Harrison, R. (1972). Role negotiation. In W.W. Burke & H. Hornstein (Eds.), *The social technology of organization development* (pp. 84-96).

Harrison, W.D. (1981). Role strain and burnout in child-protective service workers. *Social Service Review, 54*(1), 31-44.

Harmon, H.H. (1976). *Modern factor analysis.* Chicago: University of Chicago Press.

Harvey, J.B. (1977). Consulting during crisis of agreement. In W.W. Burke (Ed.), *Current issues and strategies in organization development* (pp. 160-186).

Haynes, S.G., & Feinleib, M. (1980). Women, work, and coronary heart disease. *American Journal of Public Health, 70,* 133-141.

Hendrix, W.H., Ovalle, N.K., & Troxler, R.G. (1985). Behavioral and physiological consequences of stress and its antecedent factors. *Journal of Applied Psychology, 70,* 188-201.

**Himle, D.P., Jayaratne, S., & Thyness, P. (1989a). Predictors of job satisfaction, burnout and turnover among social workers in Norway and the USA: A cross-cultural study. *International Social Work, 29,* 323-334.

Himle, D.P., Jayaratne, S., & Thyness, P. (1989b). The effects of emotional support on burnout, work stress and mental health among Norwegian and American social workers. *Journal of Social Service Research, 13*(1), 27-45.

Hochschild, A. (1983). *The managed heart.* Berkeley: University of California Press.

**Hodge, G.M., Jupp, J.J., & Taylor, A.J.W. (1994). Work stress, distress and burnout in music and mathematics teachers. *British Journal of Educational Psychology, 64*(1), 65-76.

Hofstede, G.H. (1984). *Culture's consequences*: International differences in work-related values. Beverly Hills, CA: Sage.

Holmes, T.H., & Rahe, R.H. (1967). The social adjustment rating scale. *Journal of Psychosomatic Research, 11,* 213-218.

House, J.S. (1981). *Work, stress and social support.* Reading, MA: Addison-Wesley.

Howard, G.S., Maxwell, S.E., Wiener, R.L., Boynton, K.S., & Rooney, W.M. (1980). Is a behavioral measure a best estimate of behavioral parameters?: Perhaps not. *Applied Psychological Measurement, 4,* 293-311.

Howard, J.H., Cunningham, D.A., & Rechnitzer, P.A. (1986). Role ambiguity, Type A behavior, and job satisfaction. *Journal of Applied Psychology, 71,* 95-101.

Hutson, H.R., Anglin, D., Kyriacou, D.N., Hart, J., & Spears, K. (1995, October 4). The epidemic of gang-related homicides in Los Angeles county from 1979 through 1994. *Journal of the American Medical Association, 272,* pp. 1031-1036.

Insel, P.M., & Moos, R.H. (1974). *Work environment scale, form R.* Palo Alto, CA: Consulting Psychologists Press.

Ivancevich, J.M., Matteson, M.T., & Preston, C. (1982). Occupational stress, Type-A behavior, and physical well-being. *Academy of Management Journal, 25,* 373-391.

Ivancevich, J.M., Matteson, M.T., & Richards, III, E.P. (1985). Who's liable for stress on the job? *Harvard Business Review, 85,* 60-62, 66, 70, 72.

Iverson, G.R., & Norpoth, H. (1978). *Analysis of variance.* Beverly Hills, CA: Sage.

**Iverson, R.D., Olekans, M., & Erwin, P.J. (1994, August 14-17). *Affectivity, organizational stressors, and absenteeism: A causal model of burnout and its consequences.* Paper presented at 1994 Annual Meeting, Academy of Management, Dallas, TX.

Iwanicki, E.F., & Schwab, R.L. (1981). A cross-validation study of the Maslach Burn-out Inventory. *Educational and Psychological Measurement, 41,* 1167-1174.

**Izraeli, D.N. (1988). Burnout in medicine: A comparison of husbands and wives in dual-career couples. *Journal of Social Behavior and Personality, 3*(4), 329-346.

Jackson, C.N., & Manning, M.R. (1995). Burnout and health care utilization. *Journal of Health and Human Resources Administration, 18,* 31-43.

Jaeger, A.M. (1986). Organization development and national culture: Where's the fit? *Academy of Management Review, 11*, 178-190.

Jaffe, D.T., & Scott, C.S. (1984). *From burnout to balance.* New York: McGraw-Hill.

Janis, I. (1972). *Groupthink.* Boston: Little-Brown.

Janz, T., Dugan, S., & Ross, M.S. (1986). Organizational culture and burnout: Findings at the individual and department levels. *Journal of Health and Human Resources Administration, 9*(1), 78-92.

Jayaratne, S., Tripodi, T., & Chess, W.A. (1983). Perceptions of emotional support. *Social Work Research and Abstracts, 19*(2), 19-27.

Jenkins, C.D., Rosenman, R.H., & Zyzanski, S.J. (1974). Prediction of clinical coronary heart disease by a test for the coronary-prone behavioral pattern. *New England Journal of Medicine, 290*, 1271-1275.

Jenkins, C.D., Zyzanski, S.J., &·Rosenman, R.H. (1979). *Jenkins activity survey.* New York: The Psychological Corporation.

Johnson, K., & Golembiewski, R.T. (1992). National culture in organization development. *International Journal of Human Resource Management, 3*, 269-293.

Jones, J.W. (1981). Dishonesty, burnout, and unauthorized work-break extensions. *Personality and Social Psychology, 7*, 406-409.

Jones, J.W. (Ed.). (1981). *The burnout syndrome.* Park Ridge, IL: London House Press.

Jones, K., & Vischi, T. (1979). Impact of alcohol, drug abuse and mental health treatment on medical care utilization: A review of the research literature. *Medical Care, 17*, Supplement.

Justice, B., Gold, R.S., & Klein, J.P. (1981). Life events and burnout. *Journal of Psychology, 108*(2), 219-226.

Kahill. S. (1988). Symptoms of professional burnout: A review of the empirical evidence. *Canadian Psychology, 29*(3), 284-297.

Kahn, R.L. (1978). Job burnout: Prevention and remedies. *Public Welfare, 16*, 61-63.

Kahn, R.L., Wolfe, D.M., Quinn, R.P., Snoeck, J.D., & Rosenthal, R.A. (1964). *Organizational stress: Studies in role conflict and ambiguity.* New York: Wiley.

**Kandolin, I. (1993). Burnout of female and male nurses in shiftwork. *Ergonomics, 36*, 141-147.

*Karasek, R.A. (1979). Job demands, job decision latitude, and mental strain: Implications for job redesign. *Administrative Science Quarterly, 24*, 285-308.

Karasek, R.A. (1981). Job socialization and job strain. In B. Gardell & G. Johansson, *Working life* (pp. 74-94).

Karasek, R.A., Russeil, R.S., & Theorell, T. (1982). Physiology of stress and regeneration in job-related cardiovascular illness. *Journal of Human Stress, 8*, 29-42.

Kasl, S.V., & Wells, J.A. (1985). Social support and health in the middle years. In S. Cohen & S.L. Syme (Eds.), *Social support and health* (pp. 175-198).

Katz, D., & Kahn, R.L. (1966). *The social psychology of organizations.* New York: John Wiley & Sons.

**Keijsers, G.J., Schaufeli, W.B., LeBlanc, P.M., Zwerts, C., & Miranda, D.R. (1995). Performance and burnout in intensive care units. *Work and Stress, 9*, 513-527.

Keinan, G., & Perlberg, A. (1987). Stress in academe. *Journal of Cross-Cultural Psychology, 18*, 193-207.

**Keinan, G., & Melamed, S. (1987). Personality characteristics and proneness to burnout: A study among internists. *Stress Medicine 3*(4), 307-315.

Kelley, C.A. (Ed.). (1985, March 6-9). *Proceedings.* Annual Meeting, Southwestern Division Academy of Management, New Orleans.

**Kelloway, E.K., & Barling, J. (1991). Job characteristics, role stress and mental health. *Occupational Psychology, 64*, 291-304.

Kerlinger, F.N. (1973). *Foundations of behavioral research.* New York: Holt, Rinehart and Winston.

Kets de Vries, M.F.R., & Miller, D. (1984). *The neurotic organization.* San Francisco, CA: Josey Bass.

Kilpatrick, A.O. (1986). *Burnout: An empirical assessment.* Unpublished doctoral dissertation, University of Georgia, Athens.

Kilpatrick, A.O., Magnetti, S.M., & Mirvis, D.P. (1991). Burnout and job satisfaction among public hospital administrators. *Journal of Health and Human Resources Administration, 13*(4), 470-482.

Kim, B-S. (1990). *Alternative models of burnout phases: Tests of the three MBI sub-dimensions, concurrent validity, and utilities.* Unpublished doctoral dissertation, University of Georgia, Athens.

Klein, K.J., & D'Aunno, T.A. (1986). The psychological sense of community in the workplace. *Journal of Community Psychology, 14,* 365-377.

*Kremer-Hayon, L., & Kurtz, H. (1985). The relation of personal and environmental variables to teacher burnout. *Teaching & Teacher Education, 1*(3), 243-249.

Kubler-Ross, E. (1981). *Living and death and dying.* New York: Macmillan.

Kubler-Ross, E. (1982). *Working it through.* New York: Macmillan.

**Kushnir, T., & Melamed, S. (1992). The Gulf War and its impact on burnout and well-being of working civilians. *Psychological Medicine, 22,* 987-995.

Lakin, M. (Ed.). (1979). What's happened to small group research? *Journal of Applied Behavioral Science, 15*(full issue).

LaRocco, J.M., House, J.S., & French, Jr., J.R.P. (1980). Social support, occupational stress, and health. *Journal of Health and Social Behavior, 21,* 202-218.

Lazaro, C., Shinn, M., & Robinson, P.E. (1984). Burnout, job performance, and job withdrawal behavior. *Journal of Health and Human Resources Administration, 7,* 213-234.

Lazaro, C., Shinn, M., & Robinson, P.E. (1985). Burnout, job performance, and job withdrawal behaviors. *Journal of Health and Human Services Administration, 7,* 213-234.

Lazarus, R.S. (1980). The stress and coping paradigm. In C. Eisdorfer, et al. (Eds.), *Theoretical bases for psychopathology* (pp. 173-209).

Lazarus, R.S., & Folkman, S. (1984). *Stress, appraisal and coping.* New York: Springer.

Lazarus, R.S., & Launier, R. (1978). Stress-related transactions between persons and environment. In L.A. Pervin & M. Lewis (Eds.), *Perspectives in interactional psychology* (pp. 287-327).

Lee, R.T., & Ashforth, B.E. (1991a). Evaluating two models of burnout among supervisors and managers in a public welfare setting. *Journal of Health and Human Resources Administration, 13,* 508-527.

Lee, R.T., & Ashforth, B.E. (1991b). A further examination of managerial burnout: Toward an integrated model. *Journal of Organizational Behavior, 14*(1), 3-20.

Lee, R.T., & Ashforth, B.E. (1993). A longitudinal study of burnout among supervisors and managers: Comparisons between the Leiter and Maslach (1988) and Golembiewski et al. models. (1986). *Organizational Behavior and Human Decision Processes, 54,* 369-398.

Leiter, M.P. (1988). Burnout as a function of communication patterns: A study of a multidisciplinary mental health team. *Group & Organization Studies, 13*(1), 111-128.

Leiter, M.P. (1989). Conceptual implications of two models of burnout: A response to Golembiewski. *Group & Organization Studies, 14,* 15-22.

Leiter, M.P. (1991). Coping patterns as predictors of burnout: The function of control and escapist coping patterns. *Journal of Organizational Behaviour, 12*(2), 123-144.

Leiter, M.P., Clark, D., & Durup, J. (1994). Distinct models of burnout and commitment among men and women in the military. *Journal of Applied Behavioral Science, 30*(1), 63-82.

Leiter, M.P., & Maslach, C. (1988). The impact of interpersonal environment on burnout and organizational commitment. *Journal of Organizational Behaviour, 9,* 297-308.

Leiter, M.P., & Meechan, K.A. (1986). Role structure and burnout in the field of human services. *Journal of Applied Behavioral Science, 22*(1): 47-52.

Lerner, D., & Lasswell, H.D. (Eds.). (1951). *The policy sciences.* Stanford, CA: Stanford University Press.

Lewandowski, L.A., & Kositsky, A.M. (1983). Research priorities for critical care nursing. *Heart & Lung, 7,* 213-234.

Lieberman, M.A., Yalom, I.D., & Miles, M.B. (1973). *Encounter groups.* New York: Basic Books.

Lief, H.I., & Fox, R.C. (1963). Training for "detached concern" in medical students. In H.I. Lief, V.F. Lief, & N.R. Lief (Eds.), *The psychological bases of medical practice* (pp. 12-35). New York: Hoeber Medical Division, Harper & Row.

Lief, H.I., Lief, V.F., & Lief, N.R. (Eds.). (1963). *The psychological basis of medical practice.* New York: Hoeber Medical Division, Harper & Row.

Likert, R. (1967). *The human organization.* New York: McGraw-Hill.

Likert, R. (1977, August 17-19). *Past and future perspectives on system 4.* Paper presented at 1977 Annual Meeting, Academy of Management, Kissimmee, FL.

Lin, N., Dean, A., & Ensel, W.M. (1981). Social support scales: A methodological note. *Schizophrenia Bulletin, 7*(1), 73-89.

**Lin, Y-M., Sun, B-C., & Golembiewski, R.T. (1996). Burnout of street-level bureaucrats in twelve administrative districts of Taipei municipal government. *Journal of Health and Human Services Administration* (in press).

Longenecker, C.O., Gioia, D.A., & Sims, Jr., H.P. (1987). Behind the mask: The politics of employee appraisal. *Executive, 1,* 183-194.

Loo, R. (1994). Burnout among Canadian police managers. *International Journal of Organizational Analysis, 2*(4), 406-417.

Lubin, B., & Zuckerman, M. (1969). Levels of emotional arousal in laboratory training. *Journal of Applied Behavioral Science, 5,* 483-490.

Lundberg, V., & Devine, B. (1975). Negative similarities. *Education and Psychological Measurement, 27,* 797-807.

MacIntyre, A. (Ed.). (1971). *Against the self-images of the age.* London: Duckworth and Co.

Maier, S.F., & Seligman, M.E.P. (1976). Learned helplessness: Theory and evidence. *Journal of Experimental Psychology: General, 105,* 3-46.

Mannheim, K. (1936). *Ideology and utopia.* New York: Harcourt, Brace and World.

Manning, M.R., & Jackson, C.N. (1996). An examination of methodological issues in burnout phase research. *Journal of Health and Human Services Administration* (in press).

Manning, M.R., Jackson, C.N., & Fusilier, M.R. (1996). Occupational stress and health care utilization. *Journal of Health and Organizational Psychology* (in press).

Manring, S.L. (1979). *Career patterns of technically-trained professionals: A person-environment interaction model.* Unpublished doctoral dissertation, Case Western Reserve University, Cleveland, OH.

*Manso-Pinto, J.F. (1989). Occupational stress factors as perceived by Chilean school teachers. *Journal of Social Psychology, 129,* 127-129.

March, J.G. (1965). *Handbook of organizations.* Chicago: Rand McNally.

Marrow, A.J. (Ed.). (1972). *The failure of success.* New York: AMACOM.

Maslach, C. (1976). Burnout. *Human behavior, 5,* 16-22.

Maslach, C. (1978a). How people cope. *Public Welfare, 16,* 56-58.

Maslach, C. (1978b). The client role in staff burnout. *Journal of Social Issues, 34,* 111-124.

Maslach, C. (1982a). *Burnout: The cost of caring.* Englewood Cliffs, NJ: Prentice-Hall.

Maslach, C. (1982b). Understanding burn-out: Definitional issues in analyzing a complex phenomenon. In W.S. Paine (Ed.), *Job stress and burnout: Research, theory and intervention perspectives* (pp. 29-40).

Maslach, C., & Jackson, S.E. (1978). Lawyer burnout. *Barrister, 8*, 52-54.

Maslach, C., & Jackson, S.E. (1979). Burned-out cops and their families. *Psychology Today, 12*(12), 59-62.

Maslach, C., & Jackson, S.E. (1981). The measurement of experienced burnout. *Journal of Occupational Behaviour, 2*, 99-113.

Maslach, C., & Jackson, S.E. (1982, 1986). *Maslach Burnout Inventory*. Palo Alto, CA: Consulting Psychologists Press.

Maslach, C., & Jackson, S.E. (1984a). Burnout in organizational settings. *Applied Social Psychology Annual, 5*, 133-153.

Maslach, C., & Jackson, S.E. (1984b). Patterns of burnout among a national sample of public contact workers. *Journal of Health and Human Resources Administration, 7*, 189-212.

Maslach, C., & Pines, A. (1977). The burnout syndrome in the day-care setting. *Child Quarterly, 6*, 100-113.

Matthews, D.R., & Prothro, J.W. (1966). *Negroes and the new southern politics*. New York: Harcourt, Brace & World.

*Mayou, R. (1987). Burnout. *British Medical Journal, 295*, 284-285.

*McCormick, I.A., & Cooper, C.L. (1988). Executive stress: Extending the international comparison. *Human Relations, 41*, 65-72.

*McCulloch, A., & O'Brien, L. (1986). The organizational determinants of worker burnout. *Children and Youth Services Review, 8*, 175-190.

McIlroy, G.T., & Travis, M. (1981). *Guide to medical laboratory tests*. Minneapolis, MN: Health Risk Management.

Mechanic, D. (1974a). Discussion of research programs on relations between stressful life events and episodes of physical illness. In B.S. Dohrenwend & B.P. Dohrenwend (Eds.), *Stressful life events* (pp. 87-97).

Mechanic, D. (1974b). Social structure and personal adaptation. In G.V. Coelho, D.A. Hamburg, & J.E. Adams (Eds.), *Coping and adaptation* (pp. 32-44).

Mechanic, D. (1994). *Inescapable decision: The imperatives of health reform*. New Brunswick, NJ: Transaction Publishers.

Mechanic, D., & Angel, R. (1987). Some factors associated with the report and evaluation of back pain. *Journal of Health and Social Behavior, 28*, 131-139.

Mechanic, D., Cleary, P.D., & Greenley, J.R. (1982). Distress syndromes, illness behavior, access to care and medical utilization in a defined population. *Medical Care, 20*, 361-372.

Meddis, R. (1972). Bipolar factors in mood adjective checklists. *British Journal of Social and Clinical Psychology, 11*, 178-184.

Mehrabian, A. (1992). Interrelationships among name desirability, name uniqueness, emotion characteristics connoted by names, and temperament. *Journal of Applied Social Psychology, 22*, 1197-1808.

**Melamed, S., Kushnir, T., & Shirom, A. (1992). Burnout and risk factors for cardiovascular disease. *Behavioral Medicine, 18*(2), 53-60.

Meyer, A. (1919). The life chart and the obligation of specifying positive data in psychopathological diagnosis. In *Contributions to medical and biological research* (Volume 2). New York: Paul B. Hoeber.

Miller, D., & Freisen, P. H. (1984). *Organizations: A Quantum View*. Englewood Cliffs, NJ: Prentice-Hall.

Miller, K. I., & Monge, P. R. (1986). Participation, satisfaction, and productivity. *Academy of Management Journal, 29*, 727-753.

Mitchell, M. (1977). Consultant burnout. In J. Jones & W. Pfeiffer (Eds.), *The 1977 annual handbook for group facilitators*, (pp. 145-146).

Moir, A., & Jessel, D. (1989). *Brain Sex.* London: Joseph.

Moise, L. R. (ed.). (1984). *Organizational Policy and Development.* Louisville, KY: Center for Continuing Studies, University of Louisville.

Moos, R. H., & Insel, P. M. (1982). *Manual for the Work Environment Scale.* Palo Alto, CA: Consulting Psychologists Press.

Mullins, A. C., & Barstow, R. E. (1979). Care for the caretakers. *American Journal of Nursing, 9,* 1425-1427.

Munzenrider, R. F. (1986, May 23-24). Is burnout idiosyncratic or generic? Paper presented at Fourth Annual Conference on Organization Policy and Development, University of Louisville, Louisville, KY, May 23-24.

Munzenrider, R. F. (1995). *Incidence of phases of burnout over two years in a hospital setting.* Unpublished working paper, Pennsylvania State University at Harrisburg.

Munzenrider, R.F., Golembiewski, R.T., & Stevenson, J.G. (1984). Sex and other demographic differences in burnout. In L.R. Moise (Ed.), *Organizational policy and development* (pp. 87-105).

Munzenrider, R.F., Ziegenfuss, J.T., Jr., & Lartin-Drake, J. (1996, June 3). *Burnout over a three-year-time-span: A study of persistence and predictive capacities of the phase model of burnout.* Paper presented at the 1996 annual meeting of the American Society for Public Administration. Atlanta, GA.

Nagel, E. (1961). *The structure of knowledge.* New York: Harcourt, Brace and World.

**Naisberg-Fenning, S., Fenning, S., Keinan, G., & Eliur, A. (1991). Personality characteristics and proneness to burnout: A study among psychiatrists. *Stress Medicine, 7*(4), 201-205.

Newton, T. (1995). *'Managing' stress.* London: Sage.

Nicholas, J.M. (1982). The comparative impact of organization development interventions on hard criteria measures. *Academy of Management Review, 7,* 531-542.

Noer, D. (1994). *Healing the hurt.* San Francisco: Jossey-Bass.

Novak, M., & Chappell, N.L. (1994). Nursing assistant burnout and the cognitively impaired elderly. *International Journal on Aging and Human Development, 39*(2), 105-120.

Novelli, L., Jr. (1990). *Two autonomous team locations.* Working Materials.

Novelli, L., Jr., Elloy, D., & Flynn, W.R. (1989). Autonomous work teams and burnout. *Journal of Health and Human Resources Administration, 12,* 202-225.

Nowlis, V., & Nowlis, H.H. (1956). The description and analysis of mood. *Annals of the New York Academy of Sciences, 65,* 345-355.

**Noworol, C., Zarczynski, Z., Zafrowicz, M., & Marek, T. (1993). Impact of professional burnout on creativity and innovation. In W.B. Schaufeli, C. Maslach, & T. Marek (Eds.), *Professional burnout* (pp. 163-175).

**O'Driscoll, M.P., & Schubert, T. (1988). Organizational climate and burnout in a New Zealand social service agency. *Work and Stress, 2*(3), 199-204.

**Ogus, E.D. (1992). Burnout and coping strategies: A comparative study of ward nurses. *Journal of Social Behavior and Personality, 7*(1), 111-124.

*Orth-Gomer, K. (1979). Ischemic heart disease and psychological stress in Stockholm and New York. *Journal of Psychosomatic Research, 23,* 165-173.

Oskamp, S. (Ed.). (1984). *Applied social psychology annual* (Volume 5). Beverly Hills, CA: Sage Publications.

O'Toole, J., & Bennis, W.G. (1992). Our federalist future. *California Management Review, 35*(2), 73-90.

Paine, W.S. (Ed.). (1982). *Job stress and burnout.* Beverly Hills, CA: Sage Publications.

Pasmore, W.A., & Woodman, R.W. (Eds.). (1988). *Research in organizational change and development* (Volume 2). Greenwich, CT: JAI Press.

Patchen, M. (1965). *Some questionnaire measures of employee motivation and morale.* Monograph No. 41. Ann Arbor, MI: Survey Research Center.

Paykel, E.S., Prusoff, B.A., & Uhlenhuth, E.H. (1971). Scale of life events. *Archives of General Psychiatry, 25,* 340-347.

Pearce, J.A., & Robinson, R.B. (Eds.). (1984, August 12-15). *Proceedings,* Annual Meeting of the Academy of Management, Boston, August 12-15.

Perlin, L.I., & Schooler, C. (1978). The structure of coping. *Journal of Health and Social Behavior, 19,* 2-21.

Pedhazur, E.J. (1982). *Multiple regression in behavioral research.* New York: Holt, Rinehart, and Winston.

**Pedrabissi, L., Rolland, J.P., & Santinello, M. (1993). Stress and burnout among teachers in Italy and France. *The Journal of Psychology, 127*(5), 529-535.

Perlman, B., & Hartman, E.A. (1982). Burnout: Summary and future research. *Human Relations, 35*(2), 283-305.

Peters, T.J., & Waterman, Jr., R.H. (1982). *In search of excellence.* New York: Harper and Row.

Pines, A. (1983). On burnout and the buffering effects of social support. In B.A. Farber (Ed.), *Stress and burnout in the human service professions* (pp. 155-174).

**Pines, A. (1993). Burnout: An existential perspective. In W. Schaufeli, C. Maslach, & T. Marek (Eds.), *Professional burnout* (pp. 33-51).

Pines, A. (1994). Burnout in political activism. *Journal of Health and Human Resources Administration, 16,* 381-394.

Pines, A., & Aronson, E. (1980). *Burnout.* Schilla Park, IL: MTI Teleprograms.

Pines, A., & Aronson, E. (1983). Combatting burnout. *Children and youth services review, 5,* 263-275.

*Pines, A., Aronson, E., & Kafry, D. (1981). *Burnout: From tedium to personal growth.* New York: Free Press.

**Pines, A., & Caspi, A. (1992). Causes of burnout in organizational consultation. In R.T. Golembiewski (Ed.), *Handbook of organizational consultation* (pp. 615-619).

**Pines, A., & Golembiewski, R.T. (1996). *Burnout and covariants among Israeli nurses: A replication* Working paper.

**Pines, A.M., & Golembiewski, R.T. (1997). Burnout and covariants among Israeli nurses: Mapping marker variables by Phases. *Journal of Health and Human Services Administration,* in press.

**Pines, A., & Gwende, S. (1995). Exploring the relevance of burnout to Mexican blue-collar women. *Journal of Vocational Behavior, 47,* 1-20.

Pines, A., & Kafry, D. (1981). Coping with burnout. In J. Jones (Ed.), *The burnout syndrome* (pp. 139-150).

*Pines, A., Kafry, D., & Etzion, D. (1980). Job stress from a cross-cultural perspective. In K. Reid (Ed.), *Burnout in the helping professions* (pp. 1-13). Kalamazoo: Western Michigan Press.

Pines, A., & Maslach, C. (1980). Combatting staff burnout in a day care center: A case study. *Child Care Quarterly, 9,* 5-16.

Pinker, S. (1994). *The language instinct.* New York: William Morrow.

Polok, N.A., & Boss, R.W. (1994). The existence of burnout in high technology firms. *Journal of Health and Human Resources Administration, 16,* 304-331.

Plutchik, R. (1962). *The emotions.* New York: Random House.

Pollert, A. (1981). *Girls, wives, factory lives.* London: Macmillan.

Porras, J., & Wilkins, A. (1980). Organization development in a large system: An empirical assessment. *Journal of Applied Behavioral Science, 16,* 506-534.

Prasad, S.B. (Ed.). (1995). *Advances in international comparative management* (Vol. 10). Greenwich, CT.: JAI Press.

**Pretty, G.M.H., McCarthy, M.E., & Catano, V.M. (1992). Psychological environments and burnout: Gender considerations within the corporation. *Journal of Organizational Behavior, 13*, 701-711.

Price, L., & Spence, S.H. (1994). Burnout symptoms amongst drug and alcohol service employees: Gender differences in the interaction between work and home stressors. *Anxiety, Stress, and Coping, 7*, 67-84.

Quinn, R.P., & Shepard, L.J. (1974). *The 1972-73 quality of employment survey.* Ann Arbor: Survey Research Center, University of Michigan.

Quinn, R.P., & Staines, G.L. (1979). *The 1977 quality of employment survey.* Ann Arbor: Survey Research Center, University of Michigan.

Rabkin, J.G., & Struening, E.L. (1976). Life events, stress, and illness. *Science, 194*, 1013-1020.

Ragland, D.R., & Brand, R.J. (1988). Type A behavior and mortality from coronary heart disease. *The New England Journal of Medicine, 318*, 65-69.

Rahe, R.H., & Lind, E. (1968). Psychosocial factors and sudden cardiac death: A pilot study. *Journal of Psychosomatic Research, 15*, 19-24.

Rahim, M.A., Golembiewski, R.T., & Munzenrider, R.F. (1996). *Burnout phases and worksite decriptors in a student population.* Working paper.

Ramsey, J.M. (1982). *Basic pathophysiology.* Reading, MA: Addison-Wesley.

**Randall, M., & Scott, W.A. (1988). Burnout, job satisfaction, and job performance. *Australian Psychologist, 23*, 335-347.

**Rees, R.L.D., & Francis, L.J. (1991). Clergy response rates to work-related questionnaires: A relationship between age, work load and burnout? *Social Behavior and Personality, 19*(1), 45-51.

Reid, K. (1980). *Burnout in the helping professions.* Kalamazoo: Western Michigan Press.

Reynolds, H.T. (1977). *Analysis of national data.* Beverly Hills, CA: Sage.

Roberts, K.H., & O'Reilly, III, C.A. (1974). Failures in upward communication in organizations: Three possible culprits. *Academy of Management Journal, 17*, 205-215.

Robertson, P.J., Roberts, D.R., & Porras, Jr., P.I. (1992). A meta-analytic review of the impact of planned organizational change interventions. In J.L. Wall & L.R. Jauch, (Eds.), *Best paper proceedings 1992* (pp. 201-205).

Roelens, A. (1983). *Job stress and burnout among staff nurses in acute care hospitals.* Unpublished doctoral dissertation, New York University.

*Romo, M., Siltanen, P., Theorell, T., & Rahe, R.H. (1974). Work behavior, time urgency and life dissatisfactions in subjects with myocardial infarction: A cross-cultural study. *Journal of Psychosomatic Research, 18*, 1-8.

Rosato, D. (1995, August 4). On-the-job deaths: Homicide no. 2 cause. *USA Today*, p. 1.

Rosenberg, M. (1965a). *The self-esteem scale.* Princeton, NJ: Princeton University Press.

Rosenberg, M. (1965b). *Society and the adolescent self-image.* Princeton, NJ: Princeton University Press.

Rosenman, R.H., Friedman, M., Strauss, R., Wurm, M., Kositchek, R., Hahn, W., & Wertessen, N.T. (1964). A predictive study of coronary heart disease. *Journal of American Medical Association, 189*, 15-22.

Ross, C.E., & Mirowsky, J. (1979). A comparison of life-event weighting schemes: Change, desirability, and effect-proportional indices. *Journal of Health and Social Behavior, 20*, 166-177.

Rountree, B.H. (1982). *Psychological states in health settings.* Unpublished doctoral dissertation, University of Georgia, Athens, GA.

Rountree, B.H. (1984). Psychological burnout in task groups. *Journal of Health and Human Resources Administration, 7*, 235-248.

Rountree, B.H., & Deckard, G.J. (1982). *Quality of work life study.* Mimeo.

*Rowney, J., & Cahoon, A.R. (1987). *Burnout in a management development cohort.* Working paper.

*Rowney, J., & Cahoon, A.R. (1990). Cross-cultural characteristics of burnout. In *Proceedings* of the International Management Conference, X'ian, China.

Rummel, R.J. (1970). *Applied factor analysis.* Evanston, IL: Northwestern University Press.

Russell, J.A. (1978). Evidence of convergent validity on the dimensions of affect. *Journal of Personality and Social Psychology, 36,* 1152-1168.

Russell, J.A. (1979). Affective space is bipolar. *Journal of Personality and Social Psychology, 37,* 345-356.

Russell, J.A. (1980). A circumplex model of affect. *Journal of Personality and Social Psychology, 39,* 1161-1178.

Russell, J.A., & Mehrabian, A. (1977). Evidence of three-factor theory of emotions. *Journal of Research in Personality, 11,* 273-294.

Ryan, W. (1971). *Blaming the victim.* New York: Pantheon.

Ryerson, D.M., & Marks, N. (nd). *Career burnout in the human services: Strategies for intervention.* Mimeo.

Sarason, I.G., Johnson, J.H., & Siegel, J.M. (1979). Development of life experiences survey. In I.G. Sarason & C.D. Spielberger (Eds.), *Stress and anxiety* (pp. 131-149).

Sarason, I.G., & Spielberger, C.D. (Eds.). (1979). *Stress and anxiety.* Washington, DC: Hemisphere Publishing Corp.

Sauter, S.L. & Murphy, R. (Eds.). (1995). *Organizational risk factors for job stress.* Washington, DC: APA.

Sayles, L.R., & Chandler, M. (1971, 1993). *Managing large systems.* (Early edition). New York: Harper & Row; (Reprinted edition). New Brunswick, NJ: Transaction Publishers.

Schaefer, C. (1982). Shoring up the "buffer" of social support. *Journal of Health and Social Behavior, 23*(1), 96-101.

Schaefer, E.S., & Plutchik, R. (1966). Interrelationships of emotions, traits, and diagnostic constructs. *Psychological Reports, 18,* 399-419.

**Schaufeli, W.B. (1996). The evaluation of a burnout workshop for community nurses. *Journal of Health and Human Services Administration* (in press).

**Schaufeli, W.B., Daamen, J., & Van Mierlo, H. (1994). Burnout among Dutch teachers: An MBI-validity study. *Educational and Psychological Measurement, 54*(3), 803-812.

**Schaufeli, W.B., & Janczur, B. (1994). Burnout among nurses: A Polish-Dutch comparison. *Journal of Cross-Cultural Psychology 25*(1), 95-113.

**Schaufeli, W.B., Leiter, M.P., & Kalimo, R. (1995, September 14-16). *The general burnout questionnaire: Cross-national development and validation.* Paper presented at APA/NIOSH Congress on Work, Stress, and Health. Washington, DC.

**Schaufeli, W.B., Keijsers, G.J., & Miranda, D.R. (1995). Burnout, technology use, and ICU performance. In Sauter & Murphy (Eds.), *Organizational risk factors for job stress* (pp. 259-271).

**Schaufeli, W.B, Maslach, C., & Marek, T. (1993). *Professional burnout.* Washington, DC: Taylor & Francis.

**Schaufeli, W.B., & Van Dierendonck, D. (1991). *The construct validity of two burnout measures.* Unpublished manuscript, University of Nimegen, The Netherlands.

**Schaufeli, W.B., & Van Dierendonck, D. (1993). The construct validity of two burnout measures. *Journal of Organizational Behavior, 14,* 631-647.

**Schaufeli, W.B., & Van Dierendonck, D.. (1995). A cautionary note about the cross-national and clinical validity of cut-off points for the Maslach Burnout Inventory. *Psychological Reports, 76,* 1083-1089.

Schelling, T.C. (1971). Dynamic models of segregation, *Journal of Mathematical Sociology*, *1*, 143-186.

Schelling, T.C. (1978). *Micromotives and macrobehavior. New York: Norton.*

Schlosberg, H. (1952). *The description of facial expressions in terms of two dimensions. Journal of Experimental Psychology*, *44*, 229-237.

Schlosberg, H. (1954). Three dimensions of emotion. *Psychological Review*, *61*, 81-88.

Schneider, B. (1985). Organizational behavior. *Annual Review of Psychology*, *36*, 573-611.

Schwartz, M.S., & Will, G.T. (1953). Low morale and mutual withdrawal on a mental hospital ward. *Psychiatry*, *16*, 337-353.

Scully, R. (1983). The work-setting support group: A means of preventing burnout. In B.A. Farber (Ed.), *Stress and burnout in the human service professions* (pp. 188-197).

Seers, A., McGee, G.W., Serey, T.T., & Garen, G.G. (1983). The interaction of job stress and social support: A strong inference investigation. *Academy of Management Journal*, *26*(2), 273-284.

**Sek-yum, S.N. (1993). Occupational stress and burnout among outreaching social workers in Hong Kong. *International Social Work*, *36*(2), 101-117.

Seligman, M.E.P. (1975). *Helplessness: On depression, development and death.* San Francisco: W.H. Freeman.

Seltzer, J., & Miller, L.E. (1994). Recovery from burnout. *Journal of Health and Human Resources Administration*, *16*,, 244-251.

Selye, H. (1946). The general adaptation syndrome and the diseases of adaptation. *Journal of Clinical Endocrinology*, *6*, 117-230.

Selye, H. (1956). *The stress of life.* New York: McGraw-Hill.

Selye, H. (1976). *Stress in health and disease.* Boston, MA: Butterworth.

Selye, H. (1983). The stress concept. In C.L. Cooper (Ed.), *Stress research.* New York: Wiley.

Selznick, P. (1949). *TVA and the grass roots.* Berkeley: University of California Press.

Shaywitz, B.A., Shaywitz, S.E., Puh, K.R., Fletcher, J.M., Shankweller, D.P., Katz, L., & Gore, J.C. (1995). Sex differences in the functional organization of the brain for language. *Nature*, *373*, 607-609.

Shils, E.A. (1951). The study of the primary group. In D. Lerner & H.D. Lasswell, *The policy sciences* (pp. 44-69).

Shils, E.A., & Janowitz, M. (1948). Cohesion and disintegration of the Wehrmacht in World War II. *Public Opinion Quarterly*, *12*, 280-315.

Shinn, M. (1979). *Longitudinal study of burnout in delinquency workers.* Unpublished research proposal, New York University.

Shinn, M., & Mφrch, H. (1983). A tripartite model of coping with burnout. In B.A. Farber (Ed.), *Stress and burnout in the human service professions* (pp. 227-240).

*Shouksmith, G., & Burrough, S. (1988). Job stress factors for New Zealand and Canadian air traffic controllers. *Applied Psychology: An International Review*, *37*, 263-270.

Sinha, J. (1984). Toward partnership for relevant research to the third world. *Indian Journal of Psychology*, *19*, 169-178.

Sipprelle, R.C., Gilbert, F.S., & Ascough, J.A. (1976). *The affect rating scale: Unipolar, semantic space components of affective state.* Unpublished manuscript, Purdue University.

*Slutsky, B.W. (1981). Two approaches to treating burnout. *Dissertation Abstracts International*, *42*(5), 2086b.

Smith, B.L.R. (Ed.). (1984). *The higher civil service in Europe and Canada.* Washington, DC: The Brookings Institution.

Smith, F.J. (1976). Index of organizational reactions. *JASS catalog of selected documents in psychology*, *6*(1), 54, No. 1265.

Smith, F.J. (1977). Work attitudes as predictors of attendance on a specific day. *Journal of Applied Psychology*, *62*, 16-19.

Smith, F.J., Roberts, K.H., & Hulin, C. (1976). Ten-year job satisfaction trends in a stable organization. *Academy of Management Journal, 19*, 462-469.

Smith, K.W., McKinlay, S.M., & Thorington, B.D. (1987). The validity of health appraisal instruments for assessing coronary heart disease risk. *American Journal of Public Health, 77*, 419-424.

Smith, P.C., Kendall, L.M., & Blood, C.L. (1969). *The measurement of satisfaction in work and retirement.* Chicago: Rand McNally.

Snibble, J.R., Radcliffe, T., Weisberger, C., Richards, M., & Kelly, J. (1989). Burnout among primary care physicians and mental health care professionals in a managed health care setting. *Psychological Reports, 65*, 775-780.

Special Task Force of the Secretary, U.S. Department of Health, Education, and Welfare. (1973). *Work in America.* Cambridge, MA: MIT Press.

Spicuzza, F.J., & DeVoe, M.W. (1982). Burnout in the helping professions: Mutual-aid groups as self-help. *Personnel and Guidance Journal, 61*(2), 95-101.

Spielberger, C. (1979). *Understanding stress and anxiety.* New York: Harper & Row.

**Stearns, G.M., & Moore, R.J. (1993). The physical and psychological correlates of job burnout in the Royal Canadian Mounted Police. *Canadian Journal of Criminology, 35*(2), 127-148.

Steffy, B.D., & Jones, J.W. (1988). Workplace stress and indicators of coronary-disease risk. *Academy of Management Journal, 31*, 686-698.

Stern, G.G. (1970). *People in context: Measuring person-environment congruence in education and industry.* New York: Wiley.

Stern, G.G., Steinhoff, C.R., & Richman, J. (1975). *The organizational climate index.* Syracuse, NY: Evaluation Research Association.

Stevenson, J.G. (1986). *Personal covariants of psychological burnout in field units of a federal agency.* Unpublished doctoral dissertation, University of Georgia, Athens.

Stewart, S., McKenry, P.C., Rudd, N.M., & Gavazzi, S.M. (1994). Family processes as mediators of depressive symptomatology among rural adolescents. *Family Relations, 43*, 38-45.

Stouffer, S.A., et al. (1949). *The American soldier.* Princeton, NJ: Princeton University Press.

Stroebe, W., & Hewstone, M. (Eds.). (1990). *European review of social psychology* (Volume 1). Chichester, England: John Wiley and Sons.

Susbauer, J C. (1978, August 9-13). *Proceedings '78.* San Francisco: Annual Meeting, Academy of Management.

Tanner, D. (1994). *Talking from 9 to 5.* New York: William Morrow.

Tennis, C.W. (1986, August 13-15). *The alpha, beta, and gamma change technology: The response of an invisible college.* Paper presented at Annual Meeting, Academy of Management, Chicago, IL.

Tessler, R., & Mechanic, D. (1978). Psychological distress and perceived health status. *Journal of Health and Social Behavior, 19*, 254-262.

Thayer, R.E. (1967). Measurement of activation through self-report. *Psychological Reports, 20*, 663-678.

Thayer, R.E. (1978). Toward a psychological theory of multidimensional activation (arousal). *Motivation and Emotion, 2*, 1-34.

Theorell, T., & Rahe, R.H. (1972). Behavior and life satisfaction characteristics of Swedish subjects with myocardial infarction. *Journal of Chronic Diseases, 25*, 139-147.

Thoits, P.A. (1982). Conceptual, methodological, and theoretical problems in studying social support as a buffer against life stress. *Journal of Health and Social Behavior, 23*, 145-159.

Thompson, J.D. (1956). Authority and power in "identical" organizations. *Journal of Sociology, 62*, 290-301.

*Titkow, A. (1993). *Stress i zycie spoteczne (Stress and modern Life)*. Warsaw: Panstivowy Instytut Wydawniczy.

Tokar, E., & Feitler, F.C. (1986). A comparative study of teacher stress in American and British middle schools. *Journal of Early Adolescence 6*, 77-82.

Triandis, H., & Berry, J. (Eds.). (1980). *Handbook of cross-cultural psychology*, (Vols. 1-6). Boston: Allyn & Bacon.

Truch, S. (1980). *Teacher burnout and what-to-do about it*. Novato, CA: Academic Therapy Publications.

Turner, R.J. (1981). Social support as a contingency in psychological well-being. *Journal of Health and Social Behavior, 22*, 357-367.

**Van Der Ploeg, H.M., & Van Leeuwen, J.J. (1990) Burnout among Dutch psychotherapists. *Psychological Reports, 67*, 107-112.

**Van Dierendonck, D., & Schaufeli, W.B. (1994). Burnout among general practitioners: A perspective from equity theory. *Journal of Social and Clinical Psychology, 13*(1), 86-100.

Van Fleet, D.D. (Ed.). (1983, March 13-15). *Proceedings*. Houston, TX: Annual Meeting of the Southwestern Division, Academy of Management, Houston, TX.

Veninga, R.L., & Spradley, J.P. (1981). *The work/stress connection: How to cope with job burnout*. Boston: Little, Brown.

Verba, S., & Almond, G. (1963). *The civic culture*. Princeton, NJ: Princeton University Press.

Wall, J.L., & Jauch, L.R. (Eds.). (1992, August 9-12). *Best papers proceedings 1992*. Annual Meeting, Academy of Management, Las Vegas, NV.

Walton, R. (1969). *Third-party consultation*. Reading, MA: Addison-Wesley.

Warrick, D.D. (1981). Managing the stress of organization development. *Training and Development Journal, 35*(4), 36-41.

Warrick, D.D. (Ed.). (1984). *Current developments in organization development*. Glenview, IL: Scott, Foresman.

Weber, M. (1956). *Wirtschoft und gesellschaft*. Tbingen: J.C.B. Mohe.

Weisbord, M. (1978). The wizard of OD: Or, what have magic slippers to do with burnout, evaluation, resistance, planned change, and action research? *The OD Practitioner, 10*, 1-14.

White, J.K., & Ruh, R.A. (1973). Effects of personal values on the relationships between participation and job attitudes. *Administrative Science Quarterly, 18*, 506-514.

Williams, A.W., Ware, J.E., & Donald, C.A. (1981). A model of mental health, life events, and social supports applicable to general populations. *Journal of Health and Social Behavior, 22*, 324-336.

Williams, M. (1994, October 12). Some plants tear out long assembly lines, switch to craft work. *Wall Street Journal*, pp. 11-12.

Wills, T.A. (1978). Perceptions of clients by professional helpers. *Psychological Bulletin, 85* 968-1000.

**Wilson, D., & Chiwakata, L. (1989). Locus of control and burnout among nurses in Zimbabwe. *Psychological Reports, 65*, 426.

*Winnubst, J.A.M., Marcelissen, F.H.G., & Klieber, R.J. (1982). Effects of social support in the stressor-strain relationship: A Dutch sample. *Social Science & Medicine, 16*, 473-482.

Wolferen, K.V. (1990). *The enigma of Japanese power, people, and politics*. New York: Vintage Books.

Wolpin, J., Burke, R.J., & Greenglass, E.R. (1990). Golembiewski's phase model of psychological burnout: Some issues. *Psychological Reports, 66*, 451-457.

Wolpin, J., Burke, R.J., & Greenglass, E.R. (1994). A longitudinal study of psychological burnout and the effect on psychosomatic symptoms. *Journal of Health and Human Resources Administration, 16*, 286-303.

Wyler, A.R., Masuda, M., & Holmes, T.H. (1971). Magnitudes of life events and seriousness of illness. *Psychosomatic Medicine, 33*, 115-122.

**Xie, J-L., & Jamal, M. (1989). *Type A behavior and employee attitudes and behaviors: A study of managers in mainland China.* Paper presented at the Annual Meeting, Human Relations Management and Organization Behavior, Boston.

Yamamoto, K.J., & Kinney, O.K. (1976). Pregnant women's ratings of different factors influencing psychological stress during pregnancy. *Psychological Reports, 39*, 203-214.

Zuckerman, M., & Lubin, B. (1965). *Manual for the multiple affect adjective check list.* San Diego, CA: Educational and Industrial Testing Service.

Zuckerman, M., Lubin, B., & Rinck, C. (1984). *Construction of new scales for the Multiple Affect Adjective Checklist.* Unpublished Msanuscript.

AUTHOR INDEX

SUBJECT INDEX

Affect, two factor theory of
  and active/passive modes of
    coping, 232-236, 256-257
  and phases of burnout,
    256-258
  properties of, 254-256
  and social support, 257
American Cancer Society, 110

Beijing municipal government,
  270
Blood chemistry and phases of
  burnout, 117-126
Burnout
  amelioration of, 233-228
    in global worksettings,
      226-228
    in North American work-
      settings, 223-226
  case studies of, 1-4
  challenges to research about,
    31-38
  and commitment at work, 10-11
  covariants of, 19-20,
    63-82, 84-151,
    199-209
  and culture, 23-25
  and "distances" between phases
    of, 211-215

and entrance to/exit from, 175,
  246-247
environmental model of,
  57-58, 152-154, 239-243
and gender, 190-196,
  210-211
general model of, 33-36
global research on, 14-30,
  78-82, 141-149
  168-173, 176-182,
  185-189, 207-209
and "going around the bend,"
  2-4, 251-252
and group properties, 215-219
and health, 17-18, 83-128
and health insurance, 146-151
in hospitals, 141-143
and ideology, 242-243
incidence of, 4-5, 28-29,
  155-173, 189-190
in Intensive Care Units, 141-143
lack of amelioration of, 29-30
managerial features in, 239-243
and mental health, 95-108
motivations for study of, 5-7
and Maslach Burnout Inventory,
  26-28, 42-56, 229
at multiple levels of analysis,
  215-222